Beyond Regimes

Harvard Contemporary China Series 19

Beyond Regimes

China and India Compared

Edited by

Prasenjit Duara and Elizabeth J. Perry

Published by the Harvard University Asia Center
Distributed by Harvard University Press
Cambridge (Massachusetts) and London 2018

The Harvard Contemporary China Series is designed to present new research that deals with present-day issues against the background of Chinese history and society. The focus is on interdisciplinary research intended to convey the significance of the rapidly changing Chinese scene.

The Harvard University Asia Center publishes several monograph series and, in coordination with the Fairbank Center for Chinese Studies, the Korea Institute, the Reischauer Institute of Japanese Studies, and other faculties and institutes, administers research projects designed to further scholarly understanding of China, Japan, Vietnam, Korea, and other Asian countries. The Center also sponsors projects addressing multidisciplinary and regional issues in Asia.

Library of Congress Cataloging-in-Publication Data

Names: Duara, Prasenjit, editor. | Perry, Elizabeth J., editor.
Title: Beyond regimes : China and India compared / edited by Prasenjit Duara
    and Elizabeth J. Perry.
Other titles: Harvard contemporary China series ; 19.
Description: Cambridge, Massachusetts : Published by the Harvard University Asia Center,
    2018. | Series: Harvard contemporary China series ; 19 | Includes bibliographical references
    and index.
Identifiers: LCCN 2017060568 | ISBN 9780674987104 (pbk. : alk. paper)
Subjects: LCSH: Comparative government. | China—Politics and government. | India—Politics
    and government. | China—Economic conditions. | India—Economic conditions. |
    Transnationalism. | Industrial relations—China. | Industrial relations—India. | Civil
    rights—China. | Civil rights—India. | Comparative industrial relations.
Classification: LCC JF51 .B49 2018 | DDC 320.951—dc23 LC record available at
    https://lccn.loc.gov/2017060568

♾ Printed on acid-free paper

Last figure below indicates year of this printing
27 26 25 24 23 22 21 20 19 18

Contents

Tables and Figures

Tables

Acknowledgments

Beyond Regimes: China and India Compared is the result of a conference titled "The Changing Asian State," held in Singapore in the fall of 2013 and cosponsored by the Harvard-Yenching Institute and the Asia Research Institute of the National University of Singapore. More than 15 papers were presented at the conference, of which the co-organizers of the conference (Prasenjit Duara and Elizabeth Perry) selected six and commissioned two additional contributions to make up the current volume of eight substantive chapters plus an introduction. All chapters were significantly revised in response to the editors' suggestions.

The chapters share a common perspective in arguing that distinctions in regime type ("democracy" versus "dictatorship") alone offer little insight into critical differences and similarities between the Asian giants in terms of either policies or performance. The authors approach China and India via a strategy of "convergent comparison," in which we investigate parallels both temporally and spatially—at various critical junctures and at various levels of the political system, outside and inside the territorial confines of the nation-state. For the past 150 years at least, China and India have been powerfully shaped by trans- and subnational circulatory forces. This volume explores these local and global influences as they play out in the contemporary era through a focus on four intersecting topics: labor relations; legal reform and rights protest; public goods provision; and transnational migration and investment. The intensified globalization of recent decades only heightens the need to view state initiatives against a wider canvas than that afforded by regime type alone. Whereas the precise roles that India and China will play in meeting global challenges ranging from climate change to demographic displacements remain to be seen, it seems clear that their responses are not predictable on the basis of "democratic" versus "authoritarian" regime types. A wide variety of subnational and transnational actors, from municipal governments to international organizations, and from local NGO activists to a far-flung diaspora, have been and will continue to be decisive.

Prasenjit Duara would like to thank the wonderfully efficient staff at the Asia Research Institute and, particularly, research associate Saharah Abubakar for her help with the manuscript. Elizabeth Perry would like to thank the Harvard-Yenching Institute for financial and logistical support for the Harvard workshop and NUS conference that led to the volume, Rush Doshi for compiling the India-China timeline at the back of the book, and Lindsay Strogatz for general research assistance.

Mark Frazier wishes to acknowledge the helpful comments provided by fellow participants at the Asia Research Institute—Harvard-Yenching Institute workshop. He also thanks the India China Institute at the New School for providing research travel support for his project on contentious politics in 20th-century Shanghai and Bombay.

Sanjay Ruparelia wishes to thank Prasenjit Duara and Elizabeth Perry for their probing questions and helpful suggestions on earlier drafts of his chapter, and the Inter-Asia Program of the Social Science Research Council and India China Institute of the New School for supporting fieldwork in India and China.

T. G. Suresh wishes to express his gratitude to Prasenjit Duara for helpful comments on an earlier draft. The chapter evolved from a larger comparative study of construction labor in India and China. Suresh thanks the Asia Research Institute, National University of Singapore, for a one year visiting scholar fellowship in 2012 that helped him to develop and complete a substantial portion of the early research.

An earlier version of chapter 7 appeared as "Cosmopolitan Capitalism: Local State-Society Relations in China and India," *Journal of Asian Studies* 75.2 (May 2016): 335–61. Its author, Kellee S. Tsai, gratefully acknowledges copyright permission from Cambridge University Press. Research for this chapter was supported by the Hong Kong Research Grants Council under General Research Fund grant #16401414. Tsai also thanks Joel Andreas, Erin Chung, Prasenjit Duara, Mark Frazier, Mary Gallagher, Akhil Gupta, Victoria Hattam, Roger Haydon, Devesh Kapur, David Ludden, Elizabeth Perry, Benjamin Van Rooj, Sanjay Ruparelia, Mark Selden, Jack Snyder, Barbara Stallings, Danielle Stockman, Fubing Su, Eric Thun, David Zweig, and audiences at the New School for Social Research's India-China Institute, National University of Singapore, Peking University, and University of Michigan for comments on earlier versions of the paper that became this chapter. Pankaj Chandra, Ying Deng, Carine Foyan, Sasidaran Gopalan, Renqing Li, Xiaoxiao Shen, Xiaoyi Wang, and Kwan To Wong provided valuable assistance in the research process for it. They are of course absolved from its inadequacies.

Min Ye would like to thank the organizers and commentators of three workshops at which earlier versions of chapter 8 were presented: the Fairbank Center at Harvard University, the East Asia Institute at the National University of Singapore, and the India China Institute at The New School. She particularly acknowledges suggestions by Thomas Christensen, Mark Frazier, Stephen Haggard, Iain Johnston, Devesh Kapur, Tarun Khanna, Atul Kohli, Elizabeth Perry, Edward Steinfeld, Ezra Vogel, Lynn White, and Yongnian Zheng.

Contributors

Nara Dillon is Lecturer on East Asian Languages and Civilizations at Harvard University.

Prasenjit Duara is the Oscar Tang Chair of East Asian Studies at Duke University.

Mark W. Frazier is Professor of Politics and Co-Academic Director of the India China Institute at The New School for Social Research.

Devesh Kapur is Professor of Political Science at the University of Pennsylvania, and holds the Madan Lal Sobti Chair for the Study of Contemporary India.

Elizabeth J. Perry is Henry Rosovsky Professor of Government at Harvard University and Director of the Harvard-Yenching Institute.

Manjusha Nair is Assistant Professor in the Department of Sociology and Anthropology at George Mason University.

Sanjay Ruparelia is Associate Professor of Politics at The New School for Social Research.

T. G. Suresh is Associate Professor in the Centre for Political Studies, School of Social Sciences, Jawaharlal Nehru University, New Delhi.

Kellee S. Tsai is Dean of Humanities and Social Science and Chair Professor of Social Science at Hong Kong University of Science and Technology and Research Professor at Johns Hopkins University.

Min Ye is Director of Undergraduate Studies and Associate Professor of International Relations at the Pardee School of Global Studies at Boston University and a joint professor at China's Academy of Western Development.

Abbreviations

ACFTU	All-China Federation of Trade Unions
AIU	Association of Indian Universities
ALL	Administrative Litigation Law (China)
ASSOCHAM	Associated Chambers of Commerce and Industry of India
BIDA	Bombay Industrial Disputes Act (1938)
BIRA	Bombay Industrial Relations Act (1946)
BJP	Bharatiya Janata Party (India)
BKD	Bharatiya Kranti Dal (Indian Revolutionary Party)
BKU	Bharatiya Kisan Union (India)
BMOA	Bombay Mill-Owners Association
CAS	Chinese Academy of Sciences
CASS	Chinese Academy of Social Sciences
CCP	Chinese Communist Party
CDP	China Democratic Party
CDP	Community Development Programme (India)
CII	Confederation of Indian Industry
CMS	New Cooperative Medical System (China)
CPM	Communist Party of India

CPPCC	Chinese People's Political Consultative Conference
CPWD	Central Public Work Department (India)
CSC	China Scholarship Council
ENGO	environmental nongovernmental organization
EPI	export-promoting industrialization
FCRA	Foreign Contribution Regulation Act (India)
FDI	foreign direct investment
FICCI	Federation of Indian Chambers of Commerce and Industry
FIE	foreign-invested enterprise
FRA	Scheduled Tribes and Other Traditional Forest Dwellers (Recognition of Forest Rights) Act (India)
FY	fiscal year
GATS	General Agreement on Trade in Services
GATT	General Agreement on Tariffs and Trade
GDP	gross domestic product
ICCPR	International Covenant for Civil and Political Rights
ICESCR	International Covenant for Economic, Social and Cultural Rights
ICT	information and communications technology
IFI	international financial institution
IIM	Indian Institute of Management
IIT	Indian Institute of Technology
ILO	International Labour Organization
IMF	International Monetary Fund
INC	Indian National Congress
ISC	Indian Supreme Court
ISI	import substitution industrialization
KMT	Guomindang
KRRS	Karnataka Rajya Raitha Sangha (India)

LARRA	Land Acquisition and the Right to Resettlement and Rehabilitation Act (India)
MKSS	Mazdoor Kisan Shakti Sanghathan (India)
MNC	multinational corporation
NCPRI	National Campaign for the People's Right to Information (India)
NGO	nongovernmental organization
NIMZ	national investment and manufacturing zone (India)
NJAC	National Judicial Appointments Commission Act (India)
NPC	National People's Congress (China)
NRDC	National Development and Reform Commission (China)
NREGA	National Rural Employment Guarantee Act (India)
NRHM	National Rural Health Mission (India)
NRI	nonresident Indian
NTC	National Textile Corporation (India)
OBC	"other backward classes"
OGI Regulations	Regulations of the People's Republic of China Open Government Information
PDS	Public Distribution System (India)
PHFI	Public Health Foundation of India
PIL	public interest litigation
PIO	persons of Indian origin
PRC	People's Republic of China
PUCL	People's Union for Civil Liberties (India)
PUDR	People's Union for Democratic Rights (India)
RFCTLARR	Right to Fair Compensation and Transparency in Land Acquisition, Rehabilitation and Resettlement Act (India)
RMMS	Rashtriya Mill Mazdoor Sangh
RSC	Reemployment Service Center (China)

RTE	Right of Children to Free and Compulsory Education Act (India)
RTI	Right to Information Act (India)
SARS	severe acute respiratory syndrome
SEZ	special economic zone (India)
SOE	state-owned enterprise
SPC	Supreme People's Court (China)
STIB	Shanghai Textile Industrial Bureau
STP	Software Technology Park
STSC	Shanghai Textile Shareholding Corporation
TVE	Township and Village Enterprise
UPA	United Progressive Alliance (India)
WSF	World Social Forum
WTO	World Trade Organization

Beyond Regimes

An Introduction

Prasenjit Duara and Elizabeth J. Perry

This volume compares state-society relations in the two most populous countries of Asia—China and India. Our interest lies primarily in the contemporary period, but we ground our comparative understanding in a historical perspective that we believe affords valuable insight into the current problems and future prospects of 40 percent of the world's population. Illuminating as we believe this historical-comparative approach to be, it is fraught with methodological challenges that must be acknowledged and addressed at the outset.

China and India not only have vastly different political systems; their social systems are also markedly divergent. As is well known, India is a parliamentary democracy, whereas China is ruled by a communist party-state. Social divisions in India are deep and myriad, including caste, language, and religion, among others, whereas in China the principal social cleavages are economic (along class lines), political (in relation to state power), and regional (especially urban versus rural but also coastal versus interior). These various disparities obviously have major implications for all the topics considered in this volume: economic development, labor relations, social welfare, higher education, internal and external migration, entrepreneurship, foreign investment, legal reform, and popular protest. The extent to which the Chinese and Indian states are able to address these issues is a function not only of the familiar "democracy versus autocracy" paradigm but also of the distinctive social contexts in which they operate. When viewed from a historical perspective, the divergent foundational events of the two states—a massive social and political revolution in China and a more gradual transition from colonialism in India, along with the very different political institutions to which these events gave rise—have generated strikingly different trajectories over the last 65 years. In light of these glaring distinctions, how can historically-based comparative studies be made meaningful?

The approach we adopt may be called *convergent comparison*. The authors in the volume seek to move away from "methodological nationalism," which privileges national territoriality—the institutional processes, including the type of regime, of the nation-state—as the sole carrier and container of change within the nation. Methodological nationalism views histories as principally those of the sovereign nation. The alternative view by no means denies the role of national institutions and regimes as a major frame of reference; rather, it urges us to appreciate that particular developments within nations are conditioned as much by circulatory global forces *and* subnational currents as by purely national or internal processes. For example, several of the essays in this volume compare particular cities in the two countries in which subnational and global processes interact. Many of the essays reveal global ideas, principles, and practices that were institutionalized in decolonizing Asia during the post–World War II period through a variety of channels (including the organizations of the United Nations); all chapters point to precepts of neoliberalism that were adopted to varying degrees by Asian states in the period after the Cold War. These circulatory forces, which demand local responses, form the zone of convergence; the various subnational and national responses, in turn, form the basis of convergent comparison.

Circulatory history not only forms during critical junctures such as the end of World War II or the end of the Cold War; it is continuous. The varieties of adaptation and innovation recommended by dominant development paradigms, ranging from recipes for economic growth to cultural norms, emanate and circulate from different points in the system or region. Moreover, certain root ideas—such as citizenship—that were planted in the constitutions of many decolonizing nations came to fruition in these societies only decades later, and often by means of a bandwagon or domino effect, as was the case, for instance, in the overthrow of Cold War authoritarian regimes by rights-based movements from Korea to Indonesia. Convergent comparison implies that a cause or a condition for a certain response may not always be immediately visible to contemporaries operating in the thick of events. In a recent work (2014), George Steinmetz, employing the theory of critical realism, argues that comparative histories can illuminate deeper connections at the level of generative causal mechanisms or a conjunction of multiple causal mechanisms that are not necessarily expressed at the surface level. Examining various local, national, and regional patterns allows us to assess the degree to which they converge or diverge in response to the same causal mechanisms.

Despite significant differences in the historical trajectories of China and India, alluded to above, postcolonial nations in Asia shared not only a common historical baseline of radical transformation, but also long-term connections before and during the colonial period within common economic and cultural spaces that are remarkably resurgent today. Patterns of migration and economic and cultural transmission formed along older pathways offer a basis of continuity and comparability. In her chapter in this volume Kellee S. Tsai considers the contemporary economic and political salience of centuries-old migratory networks that spread from parts of India and China across much of Asia.

The contributors to this volume explore a range of activities and processes that are not always bound to formal or national institutions, but are nonetheless part of the generative causal mechanisms in these societies. Sanjay Ruparelia and Manjusha Nair find striking commonalities in the ways in which ordinary citizens deploy a language of "rights" in both China and India. Rural and urban groups in the two societies often appeal to the national government, using the state's own rhetoric against local power-holders. Mark W. Frazier and T. G. Suresh discover that both formal and informal labor regimes undergo change—albeit not necessarily in the same ways (though sometimes with similar effects)—around the same time in both India and China. Convergent responses to similar developments can also produce new kinds of comparable results. Nara Dillon observes this phenomenon with respect to the influence of the World Bank in generating a new consensus on welfare policy. Devesh Kapur and Elizabeth J. Perry, by contrast, highlight the distinctly different ways in which higher education in India and China has responded to common international pressures to "globalize." Similarly, Min Ye stresses the marked divergence in patterns of foreign direct investment in the two countries. In other words, neoliberal economic policies gave rise to parallel dilemmas and discontent, even when the content of particular responses varied substantially.

China and India: Comparative Historical Background

Before launching into a convergent comparison of the two societies, a word about historical studies of India-China connections is in order. Since the 1960s, a blinding impediment in the exploration of China-India relations has been the China-India war of 1962, which cast all other connections between the two countries into the dark shadows of obscurity. As a result, India-China studies of the modern period have been largely confined either to the study of ancient civilizational exchanges or to contemporary realpolitik competition (Duara 2010). Happily, however, a new generation of historians is now breaking out of these ruts to explore a wide range of connections and influences, direct and mediated, between the two societies, not only in the premodern but in the modern period as well. The Tang historian Tansen Sen has extended his study to the contemporary period, looking not merely at Buddhist exchanges but a host of economic, political, cultural ties, cooperative and competitive—which took place under the Muslim and British rulers of India—that extended deep into the 20th century (Sen 2017). Others include Matthew Mosca, whose book (2013) on Qing conceptions and responses to British India in the 19th century influenced the historian-writer Amitav Ghosh, who in turn has studied the impact of opium production and trade for the China market upon India's economy, society, and culture (Ghosh 2009; 2012; 2016). Brian Tsui has generated a wealth of information in his study of Guomindang ties with Indian nationalists in the preindependence period (2013), and Arunabh Ghosh takes us up to the 1950s when there were extensive connections and exchanges between China and India in unexplored fields such as science, demography, industrial technology, culture and much else (Ghosh 2017). These works not only reveal myriad connections beyond the binary of civilizational exchanges and realpolitik, but also reveal how the two societies responded to similar challenges of the time.

Thus, although the histories of China and India had long been intertwined by circulatory forces—inter-Asian overland and maritime trade,

Buddhism, Islam, the introduction of New World silver and gold into Asia, and not least the opium-for-tea trade—it was in the mid-19th century that we begin to see convergent developments in the two societies. The disruptions caused by an aggressive capitalist imperialism spearheaded by the British led in both cases to climactic uprisings: the 1857 Rebellion in colonial India and the Taiping Rebellion (1850–64) and other uprisings in late Qing China. In quelling these rebellions, which evidenced a mélange of familiar and foreign patterns, states in both societies were obliged to undertake institutional reforms (new schools, courts, police, public health regimens, and so on) that led in turn to the gradual expansion of modernizing groups and practices—concentrated in China's treaty ports and India's larger cities.

The ascendancy of indigenous modernizing groups in the newly formed "public sphere" in the late 19th century, achieved through modern educational institutions, law, and the press, as well as modern business practices, was evident in the urban sectors of both countries by the early years of the 20th century. Attendant parallels in the political sphere were quite remarkable. In India the reformist Moderates who urged the "British to be more British in India" were matched by the early generation of reformists in China whose movement culminated in the Hundred Days Reform, conducted under the auspices of an enlightened young emperor who was expected to transition into a constitutional monarch on the model of Meiji Japan. The weakness of these moderate reformists produced a more radical generation of nationalists—the 1911 revolutionaries in China and the "extremists" in India—around the same time in the first two decades of the 20th century.

Mass movements of political mobilization also began in both societies at the same time—shortly after the end of World War I and the Russian Revolution (a period of great global ferment), and continued unabated until mid-century. To be sure, there were significant differences—not least in the leadership's attitude toward violence—between Mao's Communist Party and Gandhi's Congress Party. But the general framework of a mass movement—its goals, rhetoric, visual or representational techniques and results—allows for far richer comparability than has been assumed or attempted to date. Although these movements were certainly cognizant of one another, the question of formal exchanges or conscious imitation of practices is more difficult to ascertain. Nonetheless these parallel movements are highly suggestive of the homogenizing effects of global developments during this period.

The Republic of India (established in 1947) and the People's Republic of China (1949) were founded on fundamentally different political principles, as we have noted. But after riding a crest of mass movements, leaders in both societies faced comparable imperatives of nation and state building. China, following the Soviet Union, explicitly constructed its command economy upon anticapitalist foundations, while the onset of the Cold War gave other new nations such as India the ideas and space for autarkic development with strong socialist characteristics. Although capitalist economics may have encouraged the advent of a competitive market society, the alternative progressive vision of history that promised endless growth and welfare meant that even socialist societies premised upon the rejection of capitalism would have to engage in competition (for resources and technology), both internally and externally. Growth entailed expansionism that was not only territorial and economic, but political and psychological as well.[1]

How did the structure of a competitive nation-state system constrain the ideological choices of decolonizing anti-imperialist leaders? What were their alternative visions? For the People's Republic of China (PRC), the anti-imperialist movement was intended to produce revolutionary socialist societies among the decolonizing nations. For India, the goal was to realize the Nehru-Gandhian ideals of peace, nonalignment, and constitutionalism. From an outcome-blind 1950s perspective, India's subsequent development of a nuclear program was almost as unexpected as China's turn to market capitalism. Both had initially believed that their recent political achievements as well as their older historical greatness entitled them to lead the new nations of the world along alternative paths.

The Republic of India and the People's Republic of China

Both states inherited societies where over 80 percent of the population was rural, agricultural, and largely illiterate. In China, because of the *hukou* household registration system, which discouraged mobility, the share of the rural population remained at 80 percent until the end of the 1970s, whereas in India it fell gradually to 70 percent by the end of the century (Fan, Chan-Kang, and Mukherjee 2005, 7–8). In 2010, 45 percent of the Chinese labor force remained in agriculture, contributing 12 percent of gross domestic product (GDP); in India, 55 percent remained in agriculture and contributed 18 percent of GDP (Bardhan 2010, 43). Inasmuch as the two states sought similar goals for their rural populations, their different institutional systems invite comparative assessments of the variant paths they pursued.

The most important institutional changes in China were introduced in the early to mid-1950s during the period of land reform and collectivization. As is well known, these revolutionary transformations not only produced a radically egalitarian system of rights to land ownership and use; they also significantly improved basic levels of education, health care, and rural infrastructural development. In India, such radical transformations remained out of reach in large part because powerful *rentier* landlords dominated the political structure of the local and state governments. Nor did India have a mobilization apparatus like the Chinese Communist Party (CCP) capable of implementing deep structural reforms in the villages.

Nonetheless, during the First Five Year Plan of the Republic of India (FY 1951–55), the government did invest an impressive 31 percent of its budget in agriculture. Additionally, through a set of land laws, it succeeded in enlarging the base of landownership. Because of these measures, some 40 percent of the land came to be owned by direct producers, while over 12 million tenant farmers acquired secure rights to arable land. The agricultural scene, by and large, was classified into three categories of landholders: those with inheritable and transferable rights; those with permanent occupancy rights (who gradually merged with the first category); and those with obligation to pay rent to the first two groups (Srivastava, Saxena, and Thorat 2007, 75–77). These policies are said to have transferred rights to almost 10 million hectares of land, or more than all the land distributed in land reforms in Japan, Korea, and Taiwan combined (although of course it was much smaller relative to the size of available arable land). Tenant holdings gradually declined until the 1990s, but 33 percent (or roughly 70 million) of the agricultural workforce of 242 million were still classified as casual wage laborers in the same period (Deiniger, Jin, and Nagarajan 2008; Hetzman and Worden 1995).

While tenancy reform and abolition of intermediaries succeeded in reducing poverty in India to some degree, the ability of large landlords to avoid imposition of land ceilings militated against a more radical transformation (Besley and Burgess 2000). And the extensive land reform legislation undertaken in some states had tapered off by the 1980s. At the same time, the discourse of development also began to shift. Many economists, concerned about the optimal size of operational holdings, argued for removal of legislation limiting rents and rights of eviction that allegedly restricted the market in land-use rights in favor of labor-rich, land-poor families. Indeed, they now charged that "the share of Indian households participating in rental markets decreased from 26 percent in 1971 to 11 percent in 2001—a development that is in marked contrast to other countries such as China and Vietnam where rental market activity has increased considerably and was found to significantly increase productivity" (Deininger, Jin, and Nagarajan 2008, 893–94).[2] Concern for market efficiency had replaced the issue of redistribution in the quest for poverty reduction.

With respect to farmers and rural society, we find a parallel shift in recent years in the goals of the two regimes, from redistributive notions of social justice to market efficiency models of economic growth. But historical legacies from the founding period of the Chinese and Indian states remain important for understanding a range of contemporary issues. Both China and India inherited decolonizing ideals that contributed to a fundamental tension with regard to rural society. On the one hand, Maoist and Gandhian thought were built on a deeply romantic if not spiritual notion of agricultural society. On the other hand, the Chinese Communist Party and the Congress Party in India were both fully committed to industrial modernization. Agriculture would have to play a contributory role to that project even if it meant the exploitation of rural society. This contradiction was especially glaring in the Chinese instance.

China's leaders were initially impressed with the Soviet development path which had involved capital accumulation for industrialization by implementing terms of trade (through price controls) that were extremely unfavorable to agriculture. The CCP was also mindful of the "kulak resistance" to Stalinist policies in the early 1930s, convincing the PRC of the advisability of a gentler transition to collective agriculture than had been the case in the Soviet Union. Despite numerous problems in terms of both implementation and outcome, China's collectivization drive proceeded comparatively smoothly prior to the Great Leap Forward), when the PRC elected to depart from the Soviet path in favor of rapid communization. Collectivization brought a number of benefits for the Chinese state. It solved the centuries-long problem of tax evasion by individual landowners and leakages along the path of resource transfer. Moreover, at no point during the 1950s did state investment in agriculture exceed a modest 8 percent of total economic investment. Agriculture basically had to fend for itself, with the rural sector forced to make major sacrifices (including the *hukou* household registration system's blockage of exit options) for the sake of national modernization. These extreme demands were moderated only after the crisis of the Great Leap Forward and the terrible famine that ensued in its wake (Duara 1974).

The pressures on the agricultural population in India were somewhat different. As one author described it, the Congress Party had "a socialist head and a conservative body," with the power of the traditional landed classes in the government preventing significant change. Interestingly, numerous delegations of Indian legislators and planners visited China in the 1950s and were impressed by the economic achievements that China had secured with minimal diversion of available capital to agriculture (Gupta 1998, 49–50). Although by no means only because of the Chinese influence, from the Second Five Year Plan, India turned toward a heavy industrialization model and the share of investment in agriculture dropped to under 20–25 percent of investment from that time on. Meanwhile, the relative neglect of agriculture contributed to food shortages; prices and industrial wages, however, were kept down by the importation of American food aid, known throughout the developing world as PL 480.

The origins of American food aid have been traced to the large surpluses created by New Deal incentives, which subsequently became tied to U.S. foreign policy. Foreign assistance, which early on targeted the Marshall Plan countries of Europe, was responsible for a ninefold increase in U.S. wheat exports between 1945 and 1949. Third World imports of grain grew from 19 percent of world share to 50 percent from the late 1950s

to the late 1960s. Subsidized grain enabled some of the recipient countries, including India, to maintain low labor costs and invest more in the
industrial sector. But as the political nature of this aid became clearer, by
the late 1960s India had determined to achieve self-sufficiency in food and
was able to do so with the introduction and rapid dissemination of the
Green Revolution (ibid. 46, 61–63).

The advance of the Green Revolution (which included early-ripening
varieties of rice seeds) also required greater capital outlays for irrigation
works, electricity for water pumps, and fertilizer use, as well as minimum
price supports and provision of credit. Beginning in this period, and intensifying during the Emergency under Indira Gandhi in the mid-1970s,
the government became committed to providing heavy subsidies for these
inputs. The subsidies, which soon become entangled with electoral politics, were not well targeted and over time benefited large, albeit entrepreneurial, landowners and fertilizer companies at the expense of investment
in rural infrastructure, health and education. By 1991, input subsidies had
increased from 4.4 percent of agricultural GDP to 7.2 percent in 10 years,
comprising 2 percent of total GDP. In one state, only 5 percent of the
electricity subsidy reached small farmers cultivating fewer than two hectares of land. Meanwhile, public investment in agriculture languished
(Fan, Chan-Kang, and Mukherjee 2005, 33–34; Bardhan 2010, 45).

Thus in the first half of the period under consideration, heavy industrial growth in China was enabled by transferring resources from
agriculture (via compulsory grain sales and the "price scissors") while
encouraging agricultural production through organization and mobilization techniques, rather than by means of state financial investment. In
India, foreign aid and the Green Revolution also allowed the state to
focus its resources on industrial development.

In the first few decades of the postwar period, India and China both
followed a state-led import substitution strategy of industrialization. In
this respect, the two giants differed from the East Asian newly industrialized countries, which by the 1960s had adopted an export-led strategy
of industrialization. While the Chinese state was highly centralized under
the dominance of the Communist Party, in time the influence of the Soviet model of state-led centralized planning also became increasingly
significant in India. India not only opted for state control over key
industries—such as chemicals, electric power, steel, coal, transport, and

textiles, but under Prime Minister Indira Gandhi in the mid-1970s, it nationalized private banks, increased restrictions on trade and foreign investment, and imposed price controls over a wide range of commodities. This was the climax of what came to be known in popular parlance as the "License Raj," which privileged a few private firms and state sector behemoths and contributed to considerable inefficiencies in the industrial economy. Per capita GDP grew slowly, at roughly 1.47 percent per annum from the late 1940s until about 1980. Other indices of health and literacy were also very weak, with illiteracy declining just 11 percent from 1960 to 1977, and life expectancy rising only from 43 to 52 years during roughly the same period. Meanwhile, population shot up in both countries between 1951 and 1981: by 78 percent in China and 89 percent in India.

In China, the economic development engineered by the communist party-state through its centralized planning system built on legacies from the Guomindang (KMT) period such as the National Resources Commission. And despite the impressive marketization and privatization that has taken place in the post-Mao era, central planning continues to play a key role in the economy. Moreover, unlike Indira Gandhi's India, Mao's China periodically banned markets and the private sector altogether. Under full-fledged planning, apart from the period of economic disaster attendant upon the Great Leap Forward, China's industrial sector was the fastest growing segment of the economy, contributing 50 percent of all growth until the 1980s and diverting resources from agriculture, services, and transport. While the party-state privileged industrial and state managerial interests over other economic groups, the radical land reform and high mobilizational capacity of the party-state produced superior results in education and health care compared to both rural and urban India.

Reform: Open Door and Liberalization

The introduction of major economic reforms in both countries was separated by over a decade, with China's "opening and reform" (*gaige kaifang*) launched in 1978 and India's "liberalization" in 1991, although Indian reforms had been incrementally undertaken from the mid-1980s. While the immediate circumstances and causes were different (leadership succession in China and depletion of foreign reserves in India), both sets of reformers sought to dismantle the inefficient use of resources by a bloated state sector and highly controlled economy and to release entrepreneurial energies among the population.

The patterns of reform were in some respects mirror images. In China, the reforms were initiated in and by the agricultural sector. The combined effect of cash cropping, market prices, and family farming under the household responsibility system was a dramatic improvement in peasant incomes. Rural industrialization, in the form of Township and Village Enterprises (TVEs), further contributed to village prosperity. The great success of these early rural reforms prompted macroeconomic reforms that led to China's entrance into the World Trade Organization (WTO) and its emergence as a global economic leader. In India, a macroeconomic crisis, particularly in the balance of payments sphere, led to a relaxation of external and internal trade barriers and the so-called License Raj in the industrial sector.

Although growth was much faster in China, per capita GDP increased substantially in both countries: in China by 9 percent per annum from 1995 to 2013, and in India by 4.6 percent per annum from 1995 to 2004 and about 6.7 percent from 2005 to 2014 (World Bank Open Data). Of course, different institutional strengths and weaknesses in the two societies shaped these achievements. India possessed a mature legal and financial infrastructure through which to implement the reforms. It also had a developed tradition of local entrepreneurship in many regions, which flourished during the reform period, leading to increasing differentiation between economically advanced regions or states and less developed ones. This occurred in China, too, once entrepreneurial energies were unleashed. China enjoyed the further advantage of a state with high capacity for social mobilization. However, private entrepreneurs in China were handicapped by the privileged status of state-owned enterprises. The diasporas of both societies were crucially important for the economic achievements of the reform era, although again in different ways. In China, massive Overseas Chinese investment, particularly in export-oriented manufacturing, catalyzed growth and employment. In India, the technical and professional diaspora, particularly in the information technology sector, contributed to success in service sector exports.

China and India started their reforms with similar goals and different systems. Yet while the different systems revealed significantly dissimilar strengths and weaknesses, recent decades have seen considerable convergence in results. As figure I.1 illustrates, the two countries show parallel growth trajectories since the mid-1990s, and especially in the first decade of the 21st century, with India lagging China until 2013 by about 3 percent. Since 2013, GDP growth rates in both countries have been around 6–7 percent.[3]

The achievements of the two countries in poverty reduction have been considerable. The World Bank Global Monitoring Report for 2014 shows that about 7.6 percent of China's population lived under the poverty line, whereas about 17 percent of the Indian population continued to do so. Between 2008 and 2011, China and India together succeeded in lifting some 232 million people out of poverty (with India accounting for 140 million) (World Bank Group 2015, 19–20, 24). As both states moved from a redistributive model of justice and development to a market-oriented one, they engaged in targeted interventions intended to provide safety nets for the poor.

Despite important strides in reducing poverty, income inequality in both countries is rising sharply. For instance, urban-rural inequality (due largely to the *hukou* system) climbed in China from 12 percent in 1990 to 30 percent in 2004. Inequality is considerably higher in India, where maldistribution of land and education also makes for significant inequalities of opportunity (Bardhan 2010, 98, 100). Equally disturbing is the damage that breakneck development has perpetrated on the natural environment. According to the World Bank, the costs of environmental degradation measured in economic terms represent over 9 percent of GDP equivalent in China (World Bank Group 2015, 125). A 2013 report estimated the cost in India at 5.7 percent.[4] These costs threaten to erase much of the economic gains made by both countries. While environmental pollution affects everybody, it afflicts the poor disproportionately. For example, water scarcity in both countries—where several rivers no longer discharge into the sea and the water table has declined precipitously—affects agriculture and food prices, which in turn cause particular hardship to the poor, who spend a much greater portion of their budget on food items. How China and India attempt to overcome these effects of the kind of development they have pursued will depend not only on state

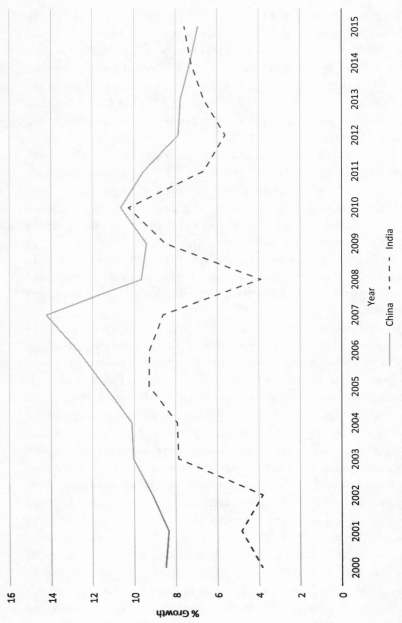

Figure I.1 GDP growth (annual %) in China and India, 2000–2015

Source: World Bank national accounts data and OECD National Accounts data files.
http://data.worldbank.org/indicator/NY.GDP.MKTP.KD.ZG?locations=CN
http://data.worldbank.org/indicator/NY.GDP.MKTP.KD.ZG?locations=IN
Accessed March 8. 2017.

policies, but also on the vigor of social and political institutions capable of moderating and redirecting the trajectory of development.

State and Society: Three Temporalities

Given the substantive and chronological parallels in the postwar development of China and India, we propose demarcating their historical trajectories into three "temporalities." A temporality may be understood as a complex of related topics or problems associated with the dominant governing principle of a period of time—say import substitution or state building in new nations. The start of each temporality is signaled by the acceleration of a significant global process that begins to demand responses from national and/or local systems. While the temporal complex is associated with a given period, it is also separable from it in that a temporality may reveal its aspects or effects in another period. These surviving effects are typically compounded into the problematique of the new temporality.

In each temporality, dominant circulatory forces interact with local or internal institutional processes to produce a distinctive though comparable situation. The tripartite division allows us to observe the extent to which problems of an earlier period may continue, merge, complicate, or dissolve in subsequent periods. Finally, while we believe that the threefold temporal division may be applicable to other decolonizing Asian societies, the elements we select by no means exhaust the stock of historical trends and practices even in China and India; they are meant simply as illuminating examples. Schematically, they may be represented as

- Temporality I: struggles of state- and nation-building
- Temporality II: logic of citizenship and rights
- Temporality III: responses to globalization and neoliberalism

TEMPORALITY I

All post–World War II decolonizing Asian states faced the challenge of transforming often powerful inherited historical structures that were deemed incompatible with or obstacles to their vision of a strong,

centralizing nation-state able to lay the foundations for sustained economic development. In China, many of these structures had been eliminated during the Civil War between the CCP and the KMT (1945–49);
but the new communist regime was still saddled with inherited attitudes
and behavior as well as with the daunting task of territorial integration.
Indian elites were more rooted in landed wealth, caste, and linguistic
and religious institutions that would have to be gradually transformed,
or at least appeased, before they could be overcome. These tasks were
understood within the global paradigm of modernization of traditional
societies.

By virtue of the revolution, the Chinese Communist Party after 1949
faced fewer obstacles to its state and nation building goals, but the task
it set for itself—to root out older attitudes and generate a radically new
sense of identity and belonging—was also more ambitious. The collectivization of land and an extractive approach to agriculture sought to
break peasant attachments to land ownership, marketing communities
and festivals, and kinship and religious loyalties as well as age-old strategies of upward mobility. The PRC would repeatedly encounter passive
(and occasionally active) resistance to its rural mobilization projects until
the late 1970s when the post-Mao regime finally acceded to peasant de-
sires for control (if not legal ownership) of land and market production
of cash crops through the household responsibility system. Even then, rural
opposition to state extraction persisted until the historic abolition of the
agricultural tax in 2006. In more recent years, rural protests have been
triggered primarily by conflicts over land sales and concerns about environmental pollution.

Despite such contestation, socialist developmentalism, which was an
integral part of the Chinese nation-building project, bequeathed an
important positive legacy with regard to the right of farmers to a safety
net of land use derived from the Mao-era collectives. During the foundational period of nation and state building, the newly established Chinese government encountered problems in consolidating its sovereignty
claims with regard to Tibet, and in the 1960s fought territorial conflicts
with its various neighbors including its erstwhile ally, the Soviet Union.
As recently as 1979, Chinese troops invaded fellow communist Vietnam.
These conflicts have been mostly addressed, but some old ones such as

Taiwan and the Indian border issues, together with other new tensions regarding maritime sovereignty in the South China Sea, fester and could well emerge as flash points in the near future.

India faced an equally vexed set of external challenges, emerging from the divisions of the British Empire, particularly with regard to Kashmir and the Himalayan borders, which have yet to be satisfactorily resolved. Internally, the government policy of reorganizing administrative states along linguistic lines limited the fissiparous effects much anticipated at the time; but to this day, the Indian nation-state faces demands for statehood (or provincial status) from myriad groups, prolonging the ongoing task of nation- and state-building of Temporality I.

In addition, the early period in independent India promoted the problem of democratic clientelism. In essence, democratic clientelism reflected a compromise between the continued power of landed and business elites and the representational politics of a democracy that was adopted at a time when the population was largely illiterate and the middle class was very thin. Politicians mobilized along identity lines—of caste, religion, language, and the like—to broker deals with elites for mutual benefit while neglecting pressing development tasks. As we will see, there is a structural mutuality between democratic clientelism and identity rights that continued into the present, although there are signs that it is being questioned at the polls and in new political movements.

TEMPORALITY II

While the logic of citizenship rights was of course embedded in the nation-state model from the start, the dominant form of group identity politics—of *class* identity in the case of China—tended to obscure the potential of (individual) rights-based citizenship and civil society of the sort usually associated with the modern nation-state. The Civil Rights Movement in America and subsequent social and political movements of educated youth across the Western hemisphere and Japan into the late 1960s (inspired to varying degrees by China's Cultural Revolution) also signaled the beginnings of new forms of civil protest. By the late 1970s, as educated middle classes grew across Asia, civil society movements began to call for the replacement of military authoritarian regimes in South

Korea, the Philippines, Taiwan, Indonesia, and elsewhere. In India, civil society received a fillip from opposition to the suppression of freedoms during and after the Emergency imposed by Indira Gandhi (1975–77), when the press, elite intellectuals, political mass movements, and not least, a shamed judiciary, launched a range of rights-based movements and judgments. In several ways, however, the rights movement in India converged with the group identity movements of Temporality I. For instance, the Dalit or former untouchable community and "other backward castes" (OBC) succeeded in instituting affirmative action legislation for their communities by working simultaneously through legal mechanisms and the representative politics of democratic clientelism.

In China, while the institutional guarantees and social space for civil rights and rights activism are heavily dependent upon the dictates of the party-state, the Constitution of 1982 declared the goal of introducing "rule by law" and the need to enhance "citizens' right to legal justice." Laws that were instituted in the aftermath of this constitutional guarantee evoked an enthusiastic response from many groups in society. Nonetheless, the twin legacies of a strong, authoritarian state and socialist ideals continue to shape Chinese society. The New Socialist Countryside Campaign, launched by the PRC in 2005 under Hu Jintao and Wen Jiabao, was an indication of this situation (Perry 2011, 30–61). The current Precision Poverty-Alleviation Campaign, directed by Xi Jinping, is a more recent illustration. While the CCP imposes severe limits on political freedoms, the socialist promises of the regime impel it also to focus on collective social and economic needs/rights, including consumer rights and socioeconomic entitlements such as the aforementioned land use rights. As a result, popular protests in rural China, particularly those directed against environmental pollution and land grabs by local cadres and developers, which were rampant over the last decade, reveal a rhetoric of justice that mixes Maoist ideals and the idea of a paternalistic central government together with rights discourse.

TEMPORALITY III

The third temporality references contemporary globalization, a period that came into being with the end of the Cold War, the collapse of Soviet-style socialism and the declaration of the Washington Consensus. Often characterized as a period of "neoliberalism," many of its core ideas have circulated within Asia over the last 20 years, albeit with significant modifications. By and large, neoliberalism involves a trend toward privatization of public services and the commons (such as water and forests), engagement of public-private partnerships, and, more fundamentally, a model and mentality of market efficiency that is viewed as the organizing principle for state and society alike.

While they seldom adopt the new model wholesale, many Asian states have introduced some version or other of its component principles—for instance, by privatizing some industries and services or by creating special economic zones or spheres of trade and technology where the market functions more freely than elsewhere. All the essays in this volume touch upon the conditions and challenges attendant upon the influence of neoliberalism, whether from the perspective of labor relations, migration, welfare, protest, legal reform, higher education, or foreign investment. Yet, as the authors explain, reactions to contemporary pressures of globalization are also highly dependent upon earlier patterns of state building and citizenship.

Asian states have experimented with new models of economic citizenship that differ considerably from older welfare models of subsidies and grants-in-aid. Examples include grassroots micro-credit and microfinance projects that seek to engage rural people as entrepreneurs and new medical insurance schemes in rural China where families are required to make copayments for services that were once free. Local cadres in China are encouraged to develop income-generating schemes to enrich rural communities (and, at least before the recent anticorruption campaign, also themselves). The government of India has launched a program to give every needy household a bank account to deposit previous in-kind subsidies as cash payments. Whether or not this financialization of society proves beneficial, the idea of the citizen is changing fundamentally in the process. The liberal idea of a "rational actor" free to pursue her interests in the market place is being replaced by the neoliberal idea of a citizen in whom "human capital" must be invested in order to develop her full potential (Akçali, Yanik, and Hung 2015).

How have neoliberal tendencies and processes interacted with other persistent temporalities? In India, the Temporality II growth of rights- and issue-based civil society organizations and nongovernmental organizations

(NGOs) (e.g., environment and anticorruption efforts) has been accelerating and has accompanied the ascendancy of the neoliberal regime in various capacities, as watchdogs against corruption and environmental devastation or as partners in various public-private schemes of development. Although this general trend of citizen consciousness appears to have made some inroads into the historical relationship between identity politics and democratic clientelism, reflected in the election of issue- and development-based political leaders and parties, the structural mutuality remains in place. China is seeking to push through the privatization and marketization of large segments of its empire of state enterprises, most significantly the banking sector. At the same time, under Xi Jinping China has revived Maoist rhetoric and nationalist ideology to clamp down on political freedom. Nonetheless, the expansion of civil society rights and groups—particularly the so-called environmental NGOs (ENGOs)—which were a product of Temporality II—has continued. For instance, the number of officially sanctioned ENGOs rose from 2,768 in 2008 to 8,000 in 2013. A new law intended to limit foreign support for NGOs has yet to make a major dent in this trend. Whether these civil society groups will manage to adapt to the tightening political climate, let alone work to loosen it, remains to be seen.

A Preview of the Volume

The chapters to follow compare state-society relations in India and China over time through a focus on four intersecting topics: labor relations, legal reform and rights protest, public goods provision, and transnational migration and investment. In each case, changing state policies, motivated in large part by international patterns and pressures that reflect shifting temporalities, have generated uneven—and often unexpected—responses at various levels of the political and social system.

Chapters 1 and 2 concern labor, a central issue for all developing societies, but particularly so for those with large populations only recently uprooted from the countryside like India and China. Temporality I saw in both countries concerted attempts to incorporate their massive emerging labor sectors into new conceptions of state and nation. Mark W. Frazier, through a fine-grained comparison of the textile industries of Mumbai and Shanghai, demonstrates the long-term effects of sharply contrasting forms of state strategy and capacity in the two Asian giants. Beginning in the 1950s, the Chinese state mobilized its newly created labor force through intensive political campaigns, whereas the Indian state adopted a legal/bureaucratic framework. This divergence in approach not only shaped the first generation of state-labor relations; it affected the subsequent implementation of industrial policy as well. When both countries moved to dismantle their textile sectors in the 1990s, the continuing influence of these longstanding differences remained visible in Shanghai's resort to state-managed campaigns versus Mumbai's reliance on legal arbitration. T. G. Suresh's examination of construction workers in India and China offers a poignant contrast to Frazier's study. Unlike the textile industry studied by Frazier, where in both societies the state presence was highly visible, unorganized construction workers have suffered from what Suresh calls "state absenteeism." In the 1950s, construction workers in India were excluded from the legal rights that the Indian state bestowed upon workers in the formal sector. And although in Mao's China even informal labor was to some extent incorporated under state control, the post-Mao era has seen a retreat of the state and the reemergence of older forms of labor relations in the Chinese construction sector. As in the precommunist period, native-place networks of labor recruitment create divisions and conflicts among the informal work force. Suresh concludes that, differences in political regime and social relations notwithstanding, construction workers in both societies are subject to a similarly distressing degree of abuse and exploitation.

Chapters 3 and 4 focus on legal reform and rights protest. Temporality II, marked by the specification of rights to political citizenship, would seem to offer the greatest room for divergence between "democratic" India and "authoritarian" China. Yet even here we find surprising similarities that defy distinctions based on regime type alone. Sanjay Ruparelia traces in both societies since the 1980s a parallel process of enhancing citizens' rights to legal justice. In the case of China, this has involved the promulgation of numerous new laws. In the case of India, it has been manifested in greater judicial intervention. In both countries, the result has been a notable increase in rights-based activism aimed especially against the growth of corruption and inequality that has accompanied a rise in economic prosperity. While growing grassroots legal activism initially offered hope to those searching for the seeds of a vibrant civil society, Ruparelia cautions that the recent emergence of strongmen leaders—Xi in China and Modi in India—raises disturbing questions about the future of legal reform and citizen rights in both countries. Focusing on the rural countryside, Manjusha Nair observes a similar phenomenon of rights-based protest in both countries. She attributes the resemblance to the common pressures of a world capitalist economy that, Nair argues, since the 1950s have given rise in China and India alike to "state-embedded villages." Such equivalences in state-society relations induce disgruntled villagers in both countries to cite laws and rights accorded by the central state in local efforts to combat grassroots corruption and injustice.

Chapters 5 and 6 assess the situation of two critical public goods—social welfare and higher education—the salience and shape of which have been significantly transformed by the imperatives of post–Cold War globalization. Temporality III has brought appreciation of the positive connection between investment in such public goods and national economic development, generating newfound state interest in the quality and impact of these kinds of social services. Nara Dillon traces the long-term impact of India and China's economic constraints on the development of their welfare states and social citizenship. More recently, neoliberal welfare reforms have helped close the gap between goals and reality, rather than leading to welfare retrenchment. This long history of parallel welfare state development has been shaped by shared international influences and economic development strategies. Rather than democratic electoral politics or communist class struggle, courts and campaigns have had a bigger impact on the differences that have emerged between the Chinese and Indian welfare states. Devesh Kapur and Elizabeth J. Perry observe a similar convergence in the goals of recent higher education reforms in the two Asian giants, as China and India seek to create "world-class universities" capable of promoting scientific innovation and thereby propelling national growth in the globally competitive "knowledge economy" of the 21st century. Despite a parallel process of "massification," however, the outcomes have been quite different in the two countries. "Socialist" China has actually been more willing to sacrifice egalitarian ideals in pursuit of rising in the academic rankings of "world-class universities."

Political differences explain the divergence, according to Kapur and Perry, but in ways that challenge conventional accounts of the influence of regime type on education policy.

Chapters 7 and 8 examine changing patterns of transnational labor and capital mobility under the increasingly integrated and interdependent global economic system characteristic of Temporality III. Kellee S. Tsai explores state-society relations among transnational traders, high-tech entrepreneurs, and coastal cosmopolitans in three paired locales in China and India. She demonstrates the advantage of a "dual-definitional stretch," expanding her analysis both downward (by disaggregating levels of the state) and outward (by deterritorializing society to include transnational migrants) in order to explain recent economic strides. Local governments and internationally mobile actors, she shows, have been decisive drivers of the developmental success story in both countries. Min Ye examines a key difference in the Chinese and Indian economic reforms: the significance and sources of foreign direct investment (FDI). China's far greater reliance on FDI reflects the outsized contributions of its diaspora. Thanks to the combined advantages of a huge diaspora and fiscal decentralization, both of which are products of much earlier times, local governments in contemporary China have succeeded in attracting an impressive infusion of capital from Overseas Chinese funders. By contrast, local governments in India—despite India's system of political federalism—have proven far less entrepreneurial in this regard.

These essays show that distinctions in regime type alone offer little insight into critical differences and similarities between the Asian giants in policies and performance. A strategy of convergent comparison, in which we investigate parallels both temporally and spatially (at various critical junctures and at various levels of the political system, outside as well as inside the territorial confines of the nation-state) serves us far better. In addition to the topics treated in this volume—labor relations, legal reforms and rights protests, public goods provision, and transnational labor and capital mobility—a number of other key issues affecting both China and India are amenable to analysis by this comparative method.

One such issue, of abiding concern to both societies, is the continuing effort to combat political corruption. In the 1950s, India adopted a legal/institutional approach whereas China turned to mass campaigns to curb endemic corruption among officials in their newly established governments. In 2011, anticorruption demonstrations erupted across India; marked by civil disobedience and hunger strikes reminiscent of Mahatma Gandhi's struggle for independence, the contemporary movement showed the lasting influence of earlier modes of popular protest. The following year, Xi Jinping's anticorruption campaign was announced in China; complete with discipline inspection teams, self-criticisms, and public denunciations, the current initiative (which has already led to the investigation of some 2 million officials) displays the unmistakable imprint of earlier Maoist anticorruption campaigns. Despite their different historical pedigrees, the contemporary movements address similar problems of bribery, embezzlement, and fraud, stoked largely by the lucrative opportunities made available to government officials under liberalizing market reforms.

Anticorruption movements are not the only other phenomena that might benefit from a convergent comparison of international, regional, and local circulatory processes that have taken shape over successive temporalities. The strikingly similar brands of popular nationalism and strongman leadership that we find in rather disturbing form in both China and India today are yet another. That larger (and smaller) circulatory forces, rather than simply national or regime-level tendencies, are at work in this unhappy convergence is suggested by the fact that a number of other states (whether democracies such as the United States and Japan or autocracies such as Russia and Turkey) have also embraced muscular nationalist agendas under the leadership of populist strongmen.

At least over the last 150 years, states and societies have been powerfully shaped by trans- and subnational circulatory forces. The intensified globalization of recent decades only heightens the need to view state initiatives against a wider background in order to evaluate their impact on epochal issues ranging from climate change and environmental degradation to worldwide pandemics and demographic displacements. While the precise roles that India and China will play in meeting such challenges to global governance remains to be seen, it seems clear that their responses will not be predictable on the basis of "democratic" versus "authoritarian" regime types. Nor will they be a simple product of national state preferences. Rather, a wide variety of subnational and transnational actors—from municipal governments to the World Bank and from local

NGO enthusiasts to a far-flung diaspora—will also have a decisive voice. This is sure to be the case even if future history should show that we may currently be standing on the threshold of a Temporality IV, a xenophobic retreat from globalization, in which democracies and dictatorships alike reassert the primacy of the nation-state.

Notes

1. Ironically, it was socialist China that was more bent on competitive success in the world than capitalist India; see for instance the rhetoric of the Great Leap Forward in China (1958–60), which strived to overtake British steel production in 15 years. India seems to have been caught between a Nehruvian ideal of socialism and a de facto "License Raj," which practically dampened competitiveness.

2. See also Saxena 2013; Saxena, a former secretary in the Planning Commission wrote, "The fears about big land owners forcibly taking over the land of small owners, because of restoration of tenancy as a legal institution, are unrealistic and unwarranted. . . . However, it is not the intention to legalise reverse tenancies. Only agricultural labour, marginal and small farmers are being proposed to be permitted leasing-in of land from both small and big farmers, as the basic purpose of legislation is to improve their control over land."

3. See World Bank IBRD-IDA databank for China and India http://data.worldbank.org/indicator/NY.GDP.MKTP.KD.ZG?locations=CN; http://data.worldbank.org/indicator/NY.GDP.MKTP.KD.ZG?locations=IN.

4. http://www.worldbank.org/en/news/press-release/2013/07/17/india-green-growth-necessary-and-affordable-for-india-says-new-world-bank-report.

References

Akçali, Emel, Lerna K. Yanik, and Ho-Fung Hung, eds. 2015. "Inter-Asian (Post-) Neo-liberalism? Adoption, Disjuncture and Transgression." *Asian Journal of Social Science* 43: 5–21.

Bardhan, Pranab. 2010. *Awakening Giants, Feet of Clay: Assessing the Economic Rise of China and India.* Princeton: Princeton University Press.

Besley, Timothy, and Robin Burgess. 2000. "Land Reform, Poverty Reduction, and Growth: Evidence from India." *Quarterly Journal of Economics* (May): 389–425.

Deininger, Klaus, Songqing Jin, and Hari K. Nagarajan. 2008. "Efficiency and Equity Impacts of Rural Land Rental Restrictions: Evidence from India." *European Economic Review* 52.5: 892–918.

Duara, Prasenjit. 1974. "The Great Leap Forward in China: An Analysis of the Nature of Socialist Transformation." Special issue of *Economic and Political Weekly* (Bombay) 9.32–34: 1365–90.

———. 2010. "Shaping Transnational Asian Studies New Directions in China–India Research." Guest editor's introduction. *China Report* 46.4: 327–32.

Fan, Shenggen, Connie Chan-Kang, and Anit Mukherjee. 2005. *Rural and Urban Dynamics and Poverty: Evidence from China and India.* DSG discussion paper 23. Washington, DC: International Food Policy Research Institute. Available at https://ideas.repec.org/p/fpr/fcnddp/196.html.

Ghosh, Amitav, 2009. *Sea of Poppies: A Novel.* Vol. 1 of *The Ibis Trilogy.* London: John Murray.

———. 2011. *River of Smoke.* Vol. 2 of *The Ibis Trilogy.* London: John Murray.

———. 2016. *Flood of Fire.* Vol. 3 of *The Ibis Trilogy.* London: John Murray.

Ghosh, Arunabh. 2017. "Before 1962: The Case for 1950s China-India History." *Journal of Asian Studies* 76.3: 697–727. doi:10.1017/S0021911817000456.

Gupta, Akhil. 1998. *Postcolonial Developments: Agriculture in the Making of Modern India.* Durham, NC: Duke University Press.

Heitzman, James, and Robert L. Worden, eds. 1995. "Agriculture." In *India: A Country Study.* Washington, DC: U.S. Government Publishing Office for the Library of Congress. http://countrystudies.us/india/102.htm.

Mosca, Matthew V. 2013. *From Frontier Policy to Foreign Policy: The Question of India and the Transformation of Geopolitics in Qing China.* Redwood City, CA: Stanford University Press.

Perry, Elizabeth J. 2011. "From Mass Campaigns to Managed Campaigns: 'Constructing a New Socialist Countryside.'" In *Mao's Invisible Hand: The Political Foundations of Adaptive Governance in China,* edited by Sebastian Heilmann and Elizabeth J. Perry, 30-61. Cambridge, MA: Harvard University Press.

Saxena, N. C. 2013. "Tenancy Reforms vs. Open Market Leasing—What Would Serve the Poor Better?" Discussion paper. New Delhi: Planning Commission, Government of India. http://planningcommission.nic.in/reports/articles/ncsxna/index.php?repts=leasing.htm.

Sen, Tansen. 2017. *India, China, and the World: A Connected History.* Lanham, MD: Rowman and Littlefield.

Srivastava, Ravi, N. C. Saxena, and Sukhadeo K. Thorat. 2007. "Land Institutions, Policy, and Reforms in India." In *The Dragon and the Elephant: Agriculture and Rural Reforms in China and India,* edited by Ashok Gulati and Shenggan Fan, 71–96. Baltimore, MD: Johns Hopkins University Press for the International Food Policy Research Institute.

Steinmetz, George. 2014. "Comparative History and Its Critics: A Genealogy and a Solution." In *A Companion to Global Historical Thought,* edited by Prasenjit Duara, Viren Murthy, and Andrew Sartori, 412–36. Chichester, UK: Wiley-Blackwell.

Tsui, Brian Kai Hin. 2013. "China's Forgotten Revolution: Radical Conservatism in Action, 1927–1949." Ph.D. diss., Columbia University, New York. https://academiccommons.columbia.edu/ . . . /ac . . . /Tsui_columbia_0054D_11085.pdf.

World Bank. Open Data. http://data.worldbank.org/indicator/NY.GDP.PCAP.KD.ZG; http://data.worldbank.org/indicator/NY.GDP.MKTP.KD.ZG?locations=CN; http://data.worldbank.org/indicator/NY.GDP.MKTP.KD.ZG?locations=IN; http://www .worldbank.org/en/news/press-release/2013/07/17/india-green-growth-necessary-and -affordable-for-india-says-new-world-bank-report.

World Bank Group and International Monetary Fund. 2015. *Global Monitoring Report 2014/2015: Ending Poverty and Sharing Prosperity.* Washington, DC: World Bank. doi:10.1596/978-1-4648-0336-9. https://openknowledge.worldbank.org/handle/10986 /20330.

PART I

Labor Relations

CHAPTER I

The Origins of State Capacity

Workers and Officials in Mid-20th-Century Shanghai and Bombay

MARK W. FRAZIER

Asian states in the 20th century maintained an antagonistic, if not repressive, relationship with industrial workers. Scholars have characterized these states as asserting a high degree of autonomy from social forces, especially industrial labor. In part as a result of this autonomy, the classic East Asian developmental states were able to pursue growth, investment, and low consumption without having to make concessions in the form of wage increases and public welfare expenditures (Johnson 1987; Koo 1987; Deyo 1989). More recent analyses have argued that a state's ability to pursue rapid growth and strategic industrial goals is better understood in terms of how closely a state is aligned with domestic capitalists. Atul Kohli (2004) contrasts the "cohesive-capitalist" South Korean state in the latter half of the 20th century with the "fragmented-multiclass" post-1947 Indian state. Under Kohli's framework, states can be aligned along what he terms a "political effectiveness continuum." At one end are states that remain distinct from powerful social forces as they pursue capitalist development (i.e., South Korea), while at the other extreme can be found states with officials who rule through patrimonial means as mere extensions of elite social groups (ibid. 10).[1]

This chapter shifts the discussion of the Asian state and its connections with social forces to the initial phases of postcolonial, postrevolution state building, and from relations with capitalists and business owners to industrial labor. I also move the level of analysis from the national to the municipal or local state. This perspective helps to illuminate the origins and variation in state capacity without reference to regime type, and shows that different forms of state capacity produce different outcomes in state-labor relations. Through a paired comparison of the critical decade of the 1950s in the cities of Shanghai and Bombay/Mumbai,[2] the discussion covers attempts by the new regimes to regulate labor markets and to neutralize unions. When viewed from the municipal level, state capacity varies in form, and less so in degree (low capacity versus high capacity). Different *types* of state capacity facilitated some forms of labor institutions, while constraining others. Some forms of state capacity also created opportunities for mobilization (or demobilization) by particular segments of the labor force.

However, as the discussion shows, a particular form of state capacity is not a product of strategic design by state officials with specific goals. State capacities are in part inherited from past regimes, and in part the product of contestation among officials and social forces. State officials, especially in the postcolonial context, drew upon preexisting or holdover institutions, and at the same time, brought state capacities into being through their actions, policy styles, and rhetoric. During their engagements with various categories of social groups ("peasants," "workers," "capitalists"), states revealed and invited connections with their moving parts—their institutions, policies, and agents. From this process, state capacities emerged from the mutual engagements among those positioned on both sides of the constructed and contested boundary between state and society.[3] As Timothy Mitchell (1991) notes, one of the defining traits of political life within the modern state is the production and reproduction of "state effects"—practices that bring the state into view as an organization, that invoke state authority, and that delineate a rough boundary between states and nonstate spaces. This is not to say that states are merely discursive. Rather, state power and forms of capacity are enacted through mutual engagements between those who lay claim to the institutions and practices that constitute the state and its authority.

During the 1950s, new ruling parties in China and India sought to expand state authority and to transform social relations. In these projects, the Chinese and Indian states attempted to impose fixed categories and orders on complex societies. In the realm of labor relations, both states sought to standardize and rationalize highly complex practices related to pay and other forms of compensation in the industrial workforce. Each also sought to impose hegemonic union structures, allegedly to represent the interests of workers, but also to demobilize labor protest and prevent labor disputes from disrupting production goals. To a large extent, both regimes succeeded in these goals, and in so doing deployed different forms of state capacity. I label these as "political-mobilizational" in Shanghai and "legal-bureaucratic" in Bombay.

While it may seem intuitive to some readers why Bombay and Shanghai would make for an insightful comparison, the analytical rationale needs clarification. Both cities before 1947 and 1949 had been hotbeds of labor unrest, and labor organizers, including nationalists and communists, went to great lengths to gain the support of workers and unions in the cotton textile sector. The new states in the 1950s faced the trade-off between elevating the status of the working class while also demobilizing their political power. Bombay and Shanghai in the 1950s were thus crucial testing grounds for new ruling parties to enact their respective visions of the new nation by transforming social relations within these urban bastions of imperialism and global capitalism. Each city's industrial workforce was a vital constituency for both the Chinese Communist Party (CCP) and the Indian National Congress (INC), not so much for their power in numbers as for the imperative that each party faced to demonstrate that it enjoyed support from and acted in the interests of an urban, modern working class. In Shanghai factories, party, government, and mass organizations sought to mobilize (and to demobilize) workers through political movements or campaigns. In Bombay, the INC developed a complex legal and bureaucratic apparatus with specialized industrial courts, labor officers, and legislation that mandated mediation and arbitration in labor disputes. The effect was to intervene with detailed rulings on pay, hiring, bonuses, and other matters that factory owners and unions had previously settled within the workplace through the disruptive tactics of strikes and lockouts.

In both cities, ruling parties undertook labor policies intended to stabilize employment for leading sectors such as textiles, to standardize pay rates within these sectors, and to neutralize union organizations as independent sources of power. The means to achieve these policy ends differed substantially. In Bombay, the INC deployed industrial and labor courts that it had inherited from the early stages of local INC rule in the 1930s. In Shanghai, the CCP paired mass mobilization with industrial planning.

While efforts to demobilize labor, to neutralize unions, and to standardize pay and benefits practices though the industrial sector largely
succeeded, in both cities the emergence of contrasting forms of state capacities carried long-term implications. The process of forming state
capacities in Shanghai and Bombay in the 1950s was one of state exposure as well as state expansion. Industrial workers, key constituents in
the new regime because of their impressive past records of popular protest in both cities, became familiar with state agencies, policies, rhetoric,
and actors. In Shanghai, some industrial workers acquired both "literacy"
of the state and the facility to engage the state during moments of state-
led political mobilization. In Bombay, the state made itself legible through
the production of numerous texts, produced in specialized labor tribunals, in corporatist agreements on issues such as wages and bonuses, and
in actual laws and policies. Workers in both cities who were marginalized
by the new set of labor policies would mobilize in subsequent decades to
make demands of state officials. By the 1960s, the effort to standardize
wage practices and to demobilize labor showed signs of erosion. Clientelism within the workplace and political mobilization of disaffected casual workers outside the workplace were prevalent in both cities in the
1960s and 1970s.

The investigation of state capacity in the 1950s also raises the question
of variation across time. In the last section of this chapter, I consider the
long-term effects of these early forms of state capacity on the dismantling of the textile sector in Bombay and Shanghai during the 1990s. The
policies of state-led liberalization, as direct reactions against state-socialist
or corporatist planning of the 1950s, suggest a convergence of temporalities
as identified by Prasenjit Duara and Elizabeth Perry in the introduction
to this volume. As Duara and Perry note, a "temporal complex is associated with a given period, [but] it is also separable from it in that a temporality may reveal its aspects or effects in another period." In the realm of
state-labor relations, the forms of state capacity that enhanced state-
building efforts in the 1950s (defined as Temporality I) in Shanghai and
in Bombay were of central importance in the introduction and implementation of policies that cast aside each city's large and influential textile
workforce through the broader frame of globalization, market competition, and land commodification (Temporality III).

Shanghai: The Legibility of the Socialist State

At first glance, the CCP's transformations of Shanghai in the early 1950s represent a case of overwhelming state power successfully deployed against a city of capitalists, crime syndicates, Nationalist Party holdovers, and other potential sources of resistance to CCP rule. The far more complicated story of postrevolutionary Shanghai—discussed in part here through the lens of the city's textile workforce but found in numerous studies of Shanghai in the 1950s[4]—raises problems for accounts that take the perspective of a dominant revolutionary state acting on a pliable urban society to transform the latter.[5] As state officials sought to impose new categories to govern the complex world of work through political mobilization, they brought the state into view. Policies and officials became targets for both grievances and mobilization.

The CCP tried to claim a deep connection with the Shanghai textile workforce, dating back to the historic strike waves of the mid-1920s, but its underground organization was thin at best among most segments of the mill workforce. After taking control of the city in May 1949, the CCP soon faced spiking unemployment and labor unrest. By official estimates, a total of 3,939 labor disputes occurred between June 1949 and May 1950.[6] During the 12 months of 1950, union officials recorded 9,480 labor disputes involving 819,072 workers, with the leading causes being disputes over reemployment and subsidies for workers who lost jobs when factory owners shut down their plants (SMA, C1-2-232). During these disputes, workers attacked bosses, demanded higher wages, and surrounded factory owners in some cases. Some party cadres proved to be overenthusiastic in this atmosphere and would later come in for criticism for mobilizing workers against their capitalist bosses in the atmosphere of Shanghai's "liberation."

China's entrance into the Korean War in fall 1950 proved another occasion for CCP cadres to mobilize Shanghai workers, in this case through production drives and other contributions to the war effort. In less than a year, the CCP further honed its techniques in party-led mobilization. These campaigns were centered within the workplace, and targeted sectarian groups and patron-client networks headed by labor bosses, as well as former Nationalist Party labor organizers. Throughout the course of these movements—known as the Suppression of Counterrevolutionaries, and the Five Antis—grassroots party cadres encouraged mill workers to speak out against former bosses, managers, and others who had repressed workers in the past. Certain campaigns, including the Suppression of Counterrevolutionaries in 1951, drew upon workers' pickets to root out and turn over targeted individuals (including ex–Nationalist Party labor activists) to public security departments (Perry 2006).

The Five Antis campaign of 1951–52 triggered antagonism by Shanghai workers against business owners and factory managers in ways that the CCP never anticipated. Military and civilian authorities issued strict orders for business owners not to close factories, workshops, and service sector establishments during the campaign, but when they defied these orders, wage payments as well as food distribution came to a halt. With unemployment spiking and food shortages breaking out, workers took action against owners of Shanghai businesses and factories. While the most violent reactions against capitalists proved to be those in small and medium enterprises and retail shops, several larger factories (including textiles) are mentioned in internal reports on the excesses of the campaign. Drawing from the repertoires used two years earlier in the 1949–50 labor unrest, workers in the Five Antis campaign surrounded business owners for extended periods or organized struggle sessions against them. A study based on union reports from the Shanghai Municipal Archives revealed that 73 capitalists committed suicide in February 1952, when the campaign reached its peak (Yang 2006, 10).

How did campaigns make the state more legible to industrial workers? The campaigns gave workers both a window of opportunity and the language with which to make demands against their employers. In many factories, especially during the Five Antis, workers endeavored to calculate what was owed them from past oppression under capitalists. Some created "exploitation accounts" (*boxue zhang*) and presented them to factory management with the demand that "we've been exploited by capitalists for 30 years, and now we're emancipated [*fanshen*]" (ibid. 8). Furthermore, the campaigns imparted the practice of workplace mobilization as a temporally defined, site-specific frame for making grievances and anchoring claims within the context of the campaign. In this process of mobilization, as state officials publicized new policies, they also engaged themselves with the workforce in ways that gave the latter opportunities to "read the state."

Such mutual legibility also took place as party authorities in Shanghai attempted to impose some degree of order on a highly complex set of practices by which managers in both state and private factories compensated their workforce. The attempt to gain administrative controls over pay meant in many cases the elimination of "irrational" wage practices such as bonus payments that amounted to one or more months of basic pay, as well as various subsidies that factories had introduced during the episodes of hyperinflation in the late 1940s. In taking over the regulation of wages, state officials made themselves the target of criticisms and demands from workers. State policy was to reduce or eliminate bonuses, subsidies, and other nonwage forms of income in order to link pay with productivity. The complexities of pay and the contention over wage reforms were acute within the private sector. When textile mills were nationalized in 1954–56 along with the rest of the private sector, workers suffered cuts in real income. After state officials had brought "irrational wage practices" under control, by abolishing year-end bonuses that equaled two months of wages, and by terminating a bonus for regular attendance, many workers suffered a substantial decrease in income, according to a 1956 report by the Shanghai committee of the China Textile Union (SMA, C16-2-99). Such declines in income were acutely felt after the conversion of private firms to state ownership in 1956. Workers in these mills had far lower rates of pay and benefits than workers in older state-owned factories.

Shanghai trade unions, classified as "mass organizations" but also under the control of the CCP, were in an inherently ambiguous position. Simply put, they tried to straddle both sides of a state-society boundary that was never very clearly delineated. As a mass organization, the All-China Federation of Trade Unions (ACFTU) was to serve the traditional Leninist "transmission belt" function of bringing mass opinions to the party leadership. For a brief period, it looked as though the ACFTU would exercise a more autonomous role, and it was given branch offices across sectors and districts in Shanghai, to aggregate worker interests beyond the enterprise level. Yet this proved to be too threatening to party authorities in the city. It soon became readily apparent that local branches of the ACFTU were subordinated to party committees and management within the factory. Union cadres were criticized for having "leftist thought" and for stirring up workers in private firms to struggle against capitalists. Cotton weaving was mentioned in one report as a sector in which union cadres supported workers and encouraged them to physically surround capitalists and demand wage increases (SMA, C16–2-1). The city-wide labor federation had to organize a rectification campaign in fall 1950 involving nearly 1,900 cadres from all 19 sector-based unions. Meetings organized to understand the mass line would often turn into situations in which the masses "rectified party members and union leadership" (ibid.). From the episodes of labor protest in the early 1950s and the subsequent campaigns to rectify the union, it is clear that labor union officials accused of "economism" or "overly leftist behavior" had been mobilizing workers against factory management.

During the early 1950s, conflict raged between trade unionists in the ACFTU and party officials over the union's role in representing workers. Li Lisan, the ACFTU leader and founder of the CCP labor movement dating from the early 1920s, was removed from his position in 1952 for his attempt to make the union more autonomous from the CCP. He had also been accused of economism for condoning strikes in Shanghai and other cities at a time when the CCP center wished to prioritize stability and production over mobilization (Perry 2007, 68–69). Whether the officially sanctioned labor union with a monopoly on representing worker interests could in fact exercise that function remained a heated subject of debate, even in the pages of official newspapers such as *Worker's Daily* (*Gongren Ribao*) during the 1950s (Harper 1969). Local officials, none more so than the Shanghai party secretary Ke Qingshi, ignored pleas from the ACFTU center in Beijing to grant some autonomy to district-level and industrial union branches of the ACFTU (ibid. 106). The CCP carried out a second round of purges within the ranks of the ACFTU after labor protests in 1956–57. Li's replacement as ACFTU head in 1952 would also be removed, in 1958, for pursuing an independent line and condoning strikes as a legitimate form of political action, or a "contradiction among the people." Yet in the aftermath of nationalization in 1956, a labor protest against management was no longer targeted at capitalists. Demands for wages and benefits and other workplace grievances were by definition directed against "administration," or state and party cadres who had assumed full responsibility for workplace issues. From the perspective of state legibility, Shanghai workers in the former private sector mills and other factories now saw and read the state at a much closer distance than before. Union branches within these mills faced a narrowing boundary between state and society. Union officials who refused to position themselves as state officials were moved aside in favor of party appointees who would.

The 1950s was also a decade of standardization and simplification of a complex socioeconomic ecology of workplaces in a city with innumerable small factories, shops, and other workplaces. Labor and industry officials imposed uniform standards and categories within factories as well as smaller establishments, including occupational categories, each with its own skill standards and wages. Enterprises from the smallest to largest were also placed in a matrix of administrative relationships with various state and party agencies. The act of imposing such groups and boundaries was messy, and within factories, workers as well as managers evaded or resisted these measures. When it came to determining wage grades and corresponding levels of basic income, factory officials found themselves with a litany of complaints from those whose skills were judged as lacking. If they took the path of least resistance and simply awarded a skill assessment that gave everyone favorable skill grades, they faced criticism from the city's industrial and financial bureaus that demanded a skill-based hierarchy in pay (Frazier 2002, 148–55).

These displays of state power also had the consequence of revealing the specific agents and policies of the state to the ranks of Shanghai's contentious workforce. Shanghai workers, drawing on a repertoire of protests dating back to the 1920s, used moments of political mobilization to make demands for specific issues such as wage increases and bonuses. In the 1950s, while welcoming an elevated status in political rhetoric and the construction of new housing complexes for workers in the city, they continued to deploy official language and policies to highlight the unfairness and inequities of how state support was distributed. As Feng Chen (2014) argues in an article that draws on internal reports from Shanghai and other cities, the state "presented itself" to workers as a liberating force. But the actual practice of state administration revealed a vast disconnect with the state's rhetoric. This disjuncture between political rhetoric and practice was perhaps most obvious in the statements about workers as "masters of the state," while state policies at the same time enacted sharp barriers between workers according to their place of employment.

In stabilizing employment, standardizing wages, and demobilizing unions, Shanghai authorities also sowed the seeds for labor protests in subsequent years. State labor policies first and foremost marginalized a large segment of workers who were accorded lower wages and fewer benefits than counterparts in state-owned enterprises (SOEs). In Shanghai's large private sector mills and factories, the transition from private to state ownership brought about actual reductions in pay and benefits in many cases. Employees in small-scale workshops, many of which were formed into collective enterprises, were in an even less desirable position than erstwhile private sector employees. The political-mobilizational forms of state capacity that had been brought to bear within core industrial sectors of Shanghai also were deployed during the rapid changes in ownership and collectivization of smaller production units and their employees.

Shanghai workers who had been marginalized by state socialist policies brought their longstanding criticisms of wage and employment stratification out in the open. The Hundred Flowers movement (1956–57) offered a signal from the leadership to engage in protests against the bureaucratic norms and habits that Mao Zedong and others feared would undermine the party's relations with the masses. Workers with grievances against the wage and employment policies took to the streets to contest claims of socialist welfare and inclusion.

The Shanghai strike wave of 1957 and labor protests in other cities taking place in the spring of that year were in large part motivated by the outsiders of the emerging socialist labor force to gain access to its privileges (Perry 1994; Chen 2014). Strikes were common in private sector firms that had recently been brought under state ownership. The extension of apprenticeship training programs was a proximate cause for the timing of the strikes, according to a Textile Union report from Shanghai (SMA, C16–2–178). But the broader source lay in the fact that so many nationalized firms, especially in the textile sector, had lower wages and benefits after 1956. By one estimate, 88 percent of the disputes arose from the replacement of an "old, irrational wage system" (that gave workers higher pay levels) with a new standardized pay system established by state ministries (ibid.).

Other reports written on the strikes identified as an important source of tension the emerging clientelism that had seeped into what were supposed to be bureaucratic (impersonal) and democratic (consultative) practices of management. Resistance to such clientelism, a Shanghai Textile Union report observed, took place using a tactic once deployed against capitalist owners and managers in private enterprises. Now, in the newly nationalized mills and factories, workers would detain state-appointed factory cadres by surrounding them for extended periods. These state officials were accused of behaving in an undemocratic fashion, of taking arbitrary actions to reduce wages, and of abusing the new labor allocation system of recruiting workers. A personnel department head at the No. 2 Woolen Mill during one hiring allotment had put new hires to work for his personal use—as an auto mechanic, a shoe polisher, a housekeeper, and a tea pourer (ibid.).

In subsequent years, Shanghai workers would hold the state to its declarations and demand that the state live up to its policies whenever the political opportunity structure presented itself. Campaigns were double-edged swords for the CCP. They were boundary-drawing episodes that pushed state officials into new realms of workers' lives, but they also brought officials under scrutiny by making them vulnerable to periodic calls from the top to counter corruption and bureaucratism. Over the ensuing decades, outsiders of state socialism—such as apprentices, temporary workers, or anyone without full-time employment and benefits in SOEs—launched attacks on the local party and representatives of the state within the factory. When the Central Cultural Revolution Group in late 1966 issued its "Ten Points on Industry," it granted workers permission to form their own revolutionary groups, as university and middle school students had, provided they continued to engage in production (MacFarquhar and Schoenhals 2007, 143–44). Rebel workers in Shanghai and others cities would quickly defy that condition. Labor politics in the Cultural Revolution was far too complex to be reduced to a simple pursuit of grievances by part-time workers on the margins of the state socialist system. But the latter figured prominently in Shanghai groups such as the Revolutionary Rebel Headquarters and in episodes such as the "wind of economism" in late 1966–early 1967, when they made demands to abolish apprenticeships, temporary employment, and other unpopular and exclusionary labor policies (Lee 1978; Perry and Xun 1997, 97–117).

In short, by the late 1950s, a highly fragmented labor force was engaged directly and actively with the grassroots state (in the form of

enterprise party committees and their factory cadres). A macro-level social policy to steer subsidies and benefits to the urban sector (including
investment capital, jobs, and consumer goods) took shape as a micro-
level project to provide lifetime employment, factory housing, schools,
and much else delivered by and within the factory. What is usually
viewed as a period of rapid state penetration and domination of social
relations and of society more generally was also one in which the constitution of state power made its officials and policies more accessible and
visible to industrial workers. In this context, as Neil Diamant noted in
his study of mobilization around and resistance to the PRC Marriage
Law of 1950, "In China, societal resilience in the face of state policy is, or
should be, as much a part of the story of post-1949 politics and history as
the narrative of growing state power over society" (Diamant 2001, 475).
One of the bases of such resilience can be found in how campaigns to
promote state policies illuminated points of entry to specific parts of the
state and state officials.

The evidence from labor relations in Bombay in the 1950s highlights
a contrast in the form, rather than the degree, of state capacity. State corporatist polices to concentrate representation within the ruling party's
union were codified in law. Political mobilization took the form of would-
be labor leaders tapping resentment among textile workers who carried
grievances against state policies on labor disputes and representation.

Bombay: Buttressing Legal-Bureaucratic Legibility

In the realm of labor relations, the transition from the colonial regime in
Bombay took place well in advance of formal independence in 1947. After
its electoral victories in local elections in 1937 in the Bombay Presidency,
the Indian National Congress moved quickly to gain control over urban
administration, including labor relations. In 1938, the INC imposed draconian labor measures in Bombay that would lay the groundwork for
labor relations in subsequent decades. In Bombay, like Shanghai, labor
organizers had successfully led numerous sector-wide and city-wide general strikes in the 1920s and 1930s. In response to the perceived threat of
growing Communist Party support in the city, INC politicians and Brit-

ish authorities created a system of compulsory arbitration under the Bombay Industrial Disputes Act (BIDA) of 1938. The law made all strikes illegal unless they took place at the end of a lengthy arbitration process. The city's labor leaders fiercely resisted the proposed legislation, and when it passed, they organized a strike among textile workers in November 1938. The strike and processions opposing the BIDA turned violent and led to the deaths of dozens of protestors.

Thus, nearly a decade before formal independence, the Indian state had imposed a legal-bureaucratic apparatus to administer labor relations. After 1947, the labor arbitration regime expanded into fields of wage determination, bonus settlements, and even classification of jobs within Bombay's textile mills and other large enterprises. Officials ranging from the labor officer, the director of labor welfare, the minister of labor, the Labor and Housing Department, as well as a wide array of judicial officials in the Industrial Court and the Labor Appellate Tribunal, issued rulings on disputes and infractions that would in most other contexts have remained the purview of management (and usually of shop floor bosses) to dismiss an individual worker.[7] The main target of this project was the workforce of approximately 250,000 textile employees in Bombay's 60 private- and state-owned mills. The 1948 Factories Act also established the position of chief inspector of factories in Bombay, as well as medical inspector of factories, who was responsible for examining cases of workplace illnesses arising from chemical dyes and other agents used in textile production.

In attempting to render the Bombay mill workforce more legible, through the standardization of pay and employment practices, among much else, the state also became a more visible entity toward which workers and labor organizers could make claims and express grievances. Usually these claims followed legal channels called for in arbitration laws, and occasionally they did not. Despite the best intentions of the BIDA authors, the act never eliminated strikes. However, the intent of the BIDA to undermine communist labor leaders generally succeeded. By the early 1950s, the popularity of the Communist and Socialist Party unions had declined precipitously following a number of unsuccessful strikes led by the two parties and their unions. Over the 1950s and ensuing decades, repressive labor legislation became a lightning rod around which would-be union organizers attempted to rally the mill workforce. But the BIDA and successor legislation continued to constrain the legal authority and power of most unions.

The 1946 Bombay Industrial Relations Act (BIRA) expanded the BIDA by setting strict rules on the ability of unions to represent workers in bargaining with employers. The terms of the BIRA put into effect a monopoly in labor representation of textile workers by the INC-controlled Rashtriya Mill Mazdoor Sangh (RMMS). In 1947, the RMMS could demonstrate membership of just over the required threshold of 15 percent of the textile workforce, but the communist-affiliated unions could claim a much larger share. In December 1947, the Communist Party's union and the newly formed Socialist Party's union led a strike that brought 209,000 workers, nearly the entire mill workforce, off the job for one day (Morris 1955, 300). Yet under the BIRA, the membership records of the RMMS reflected that only it possessed legal authority to represent textile workers in the city.

The BIRA also strengthened the powers of the Industrial Court. The latter, staffed by labor ministry officials, laid down rules and standards for pay and hiring in the Bombay textile mills in no less a detailed fashion than what the industrial planners did for Shanghai's mills in the 1950s. In May 1947, the Industrial Court issued a decision that standardized wage rates across the entire Mumbai textile industry. "For the first time in history, every cotton mill in Bombay was required to pay according to a standardized schedule from which no deviation was permitted" (ibid. 299).

The Industrial Court continued its active involvement in the determination of bonuses after independence. Disputes over year-end bonuses became a major point of contention, as mill owners linked bonuses to the size of annual profits (the smaller the profits, the smaller the bonuses). Unions argued that bonuses were a legally mandated form of deferred payment. In August 1950, another industry-wide strike took place that shut down all but three of the city's mills for over two months. The eventual breaking of this strike weakened support for the two unions under Socialist and Communist Party affiliation. After 1950, the INC-led RMMS exerted its dominance over labor relations, and received generous support from state coffers (ibid. 302).

Labor dispute records dating from the late 1940s indicate an early frustration on the part of textile workers with the RMMS dominance, for its unwillingness to support workers in disputes. As a group of weavers from the India United Mills No. 1 wrote in 1949 in a letter to the Labor Department director of Bombay, "We beg to submit that this Union [RMMS] does not enjoy our confidence. It did not take troubles to hold a meeting of weavers concerned in this dispute and neither did it try to explain what the dispute is about. It has acted in its own arbitrary way." It requested the Labor Department head to personally and directly investigate their grievance and to refer the dispute (over the dismissal of 301 weavers) to the Wage Board (MSA, File 816/16, II).

The labor courts in Bombay intervened, in the person of the Chief Conciliator under the Labor Office, to resolve a 1948 dispute at United Mills over the allocation of four looms to each weaver, instead of the usual two-loom allocation (ibid.). Beginning in late 1951, the Srinivas Mill was involved in an extended dispute over the wage setting of various classes of employees. Groups of employees who recorded numbers on various mechanical instruments and looms sought to be classified as clerks, on the grounds that their jobs involved some "writing work" (MSA, File 2035/46, M-41). The dispute dragged on through 1953 and was brought before the Labor Appellate Tribunal, which eventually issued specific rulings applicable to all mills on which jobs and tasks could be regarded as clerical, and subject to higher pay levels.

The entrance of the state into labor relations, which relegated unions to a supplemental role in assisting state goals, met with opposition not only from workers and rival unions but also from some labor officials. In the early 1950s, the minister of labor, V. V. Giri, tried to reverse compulsory arbitration and promote collective bargaining between unions and employers. He opposed the involvement of "any courts at all" in the labor relations process, and expressed his concern over the long-term effects of the state's "spoon-feeding" unions—and by implication, the hegemonic RMSS (Morris 1955, 307). Because of his maverick views, the INC government dismissed Giri in 1954. As an observer in the mid-1950s accurately noted, "Since [the BIDA enactment in 1937], every arrangement for keeping step with the rising cost of living—every significant wage increase, every annual bonus, every major standardization of workplace relations—has been granted through the agency of the state and as a result of the intervention of the state" (ibid. 306).

In a parallel with Shanghai, labor policies in Bombay divided the mill workforce into employment categories of full-time permanent and part-time temporary. The De-casualization Scheme introduced in 1949 in the Bombay mills codified separate realms of work status. The plan, as its name implies, was to rid the mills of their dependence on the "curb market" of jobless mill hands hired informally and for short periods. Instead, idle workers were to register with individual mills as *badlis* or temporary workers, who could then be called upon when work orders picked up. The De-casualization Scheme enrolled an average of 2,500 workers during the mid-1950s (James 1959, 549–50). The program had the effect of "producing non-competing groups within the industrial workforce: those who have a full-time job with no danger of losing it and those who persist on partial employment and have little prospect of obtaining better" (ibid. 556). The Bombay Mill Owners Association (BMOA) declared by 1954 that the scheme had the effect of "eliminating bribery, corruption, and favoritism in the recruitment of textile workers" (MSA, File DCS-1458). Developments in subsequent years would show this to be a considerable exaggeration.

In the roughly two-decade period spanning formal independence, labor relations in Bombay had seen the dramatic expansion of state authority, down to individual decisions on job classifications and bonuses that were once the purview of employers and workers' representatives. The demobilization of the mill workers, and the establishment of exclusive job protections to mill workers, laid the groundwork for a populist reaction in the 1960s with the rise of a movement first directed at the lack of jobs for "native sons" of Bombay. The Shiv Sena would evolve into much else, but it began over jobs for Marathi-speaking residents who made up just under half of the city's population but were largely underrepresented outside the manufacturing sector and in public sector jobs. In mill districts, Marathi *badli* workers and unemployed surplus workers served as the rank and file in the Shiv Sena protests (Shaikh 2005, 1898–99). While full-time workers cohered around communist unions, within the mills, the Shiv Sena was successful in mobilizing the outer margins of the mill workforce by deploying cultural resources, neighborhood associations, and other networks within the living quarters and public spaces outside the mills.

If Bombay mill workers encountered the state through legal-bureaucratic modes, their resistance took two forms: one by way of challenging management decisions through the arbitration regime, and the other through occasional wide-scale mobilization against the very laws and institutions that comprised the arbitration regime. Union politics and mobilization from the 1960s to the 1990s was aimed at ousting the RMMS from its perch as the beneficiary of state support and patronage. No clearer example of the latter can be seen than in the massive 1981–82 mill strike. The strike failed in terms of its demands, and led to mass layoffs in the textile sector, but it succeeded in dismantling the monopoly that the RMMS had held over wage agreements at the plant level.

The strike began in October 1981, initially as a protest by workers at a few mills against an industry-wide bonus agreement between the mill owners' association and the RMMS. It quickly expanded into an industry-wide strike led by Datta Samant, who announced the formation of a new independent union (unaffiliated with any political party), called for basic wages to increase from the monthly rate of 250 rupees to 400 rupees (depending on length of service), and demanded permanent job status for the 100,000 temporary workers in the industry. Samant was a relative newcomer to labor organizing, but because of the opposition to the RMMS, he was able to attract 150,000 workers to his newly formed union during the strike. In many respects, the strike was also an attempt to dismantle the industrial relations regime and the exclusive bargaining rights given to the RMMS for the preceding four decades. Reports on the strike reflect the antagonism with which workers viewed "state-controlled unionism" and viewed the RMMS as part of a "state-supported monopoly" (Union Research Group 1982, 63). The RMMS was accused of making agreements with individual level departments, leading to vast differences in how the same jobs across the mills were paid. RMMS cadres commonly collected wages from management and distributed them, with the usual deductions, directly to workers (Bhattacherjee 1989, M-71). This practice had been the source of over half of the textile sectors' strikes by the early 1970s (ibid. M-73). Such "state-controlled unionism" was also condemned for ignoring seniority and for making pay differentials based on personalistic ties (Union Research Group 1982, 64; Bhattacherjee 1989, M-73). In its place, strikers sought to move bargaining to the enterprise level, to pursue plant-specific agreements between unions and workers.

The BIRA also came in for direct attack, and as the strike lengthened, demands rose to abolish the decades-old labor law. "This is the first occasion since the promulgation of the BIR Act that its very existence has been challenged," a sympathetic report noted ("Storming the Citadel" 1982, 59). "We're fighting for money, but much more important than that, we are fighting to get the RMMS and the BIR Act out. . . . RMMS and BIR must go at any cost," a group of Crown Mills workers told a journalist (Anand 1982, 6). In August 1982, Bombay police went on strike as well, and the ensuing riots led to the declaration of martial law in the city—not before striking mill workers had ransacked the homes of two RMMS leaders (ibid. 29–30).

The strike lasted for 18 months and brought a resounding defeat for Samant and Bombay's textile workers. A full-time workforce of 139,000 had declined to 60,000 by the end of the strike, with most workers returning to their home villages outside Bombay (Bhattacherjee 1989, M-73). But the strike also undermined the decades-old corporatist structure in which the RMMS and the BMOA exercised a monopoly over the representation of textile workers and mill owners. In the wake of the strike, a form of union practice emerged that became the exception to the more general rule nationwide in India in which unions were closely tied to political parties. In Bombay it became commonplace by the 1980s for independent unions at the factory level to bargain with management. In this context, the RMMS still played an influential role in working out individual agreements with mill ownership—including those that would authorize the shutdown of mills in the 1990s—but it was no longer the sole agent representing workers.

State capacities of contrasting forms and content emerged through the mutual engagement between workers and officials during the 1950s in Shanghai and Bombay. In Shanghai, this engagement took the form of campaigns in which party cadres sought with mixed success to mobilize and demobilize industrial workers. In Bombay, a legal-bureaucratic apparatus had the effect of both stabilizing labor relations and provoking strikes by frustrated workers and unions excluded from the monopolistic representation and arbitration system.

If different forms of state capacity took shape during the crucial decade of the 1950s, how did subsequent transformations within the political economies of Shanghai and Bombay interact with these older forms of state capacity? One might hypothesize that the late-20th-century economic reforms in China and India generated new forms of state capacity, through new modes of state legibility and mutual engagements (and possibly disengagements) between state officials and social forces. How these contrasting forms of state capacity from the 1950s changed over time is an important question that can be treated here with only partial evidence drawn from the textile sectors of Shanghai and Bombay and their respective fates in the 1990s. The evidence suggests that both states, in pushing for the dismantling of the textile sectors in the two cities, drew on preexisting styles of governance and forms of state capacity in pursuing neoliberal policies.

State Capacities under State-Led Liberalization and Globalization

The dominant narrative of late-20th-century neoliberal reforms posits a "retreat of the state" and the expansion of markets, as well as the outsourcing of state functions to private or nonstate entities. Yet when states are viewed in a sharper and more disaggregated context, as agencies and officials making and manipulating markets, it is clear that the organization referred to as "the state" expanded in any dimension one chooses: in the number of officials, in the ability of these officials to enrich themselves and their agencies, and in terms of their authority over local decisions. Not every agency and level of administration benefited from market reforms, and some clearly lost power. But there is little question that the idea of a "retreating state" is entirely inconsistent with the practices of state officials and agencies in the marketized economies.

These dynamics were on vivid display in the textile sectors of Shanghai and Bombay. In both cities, local officials promoted or condoned— and in most instances benefited from—the restructuring and phasing out of the textile sector with its mass bankruptcies and job losses. The commodification of urban land made mill districts highly prized assets. The physical sites of mills became zones of contention, over who held claims to the land, and over the disposition of mill compounds and worker housing. The respective forms of state capacities developed in the 1950s weighed heavily on the process of textile restructuring in each city. In the introduction of a socialist-legalist project in Shanghai, the CCP deployed certain political-mobilizational capacities to move ahead rapidly with the layoffs of textile workers. In Bombay, legal-bureaucratic capacities influenced patterns of debate and conflict over the dismantling of the textile sector. Yet in both cities, the period also represented a significant erosion of existing state capacities: the labor law regime introduced in Shanghai was politically demobilizing in its effects, as workers became legal subjects encouraged to file individual legal claims against employers. In Bombay, the erosion of legal-bureaucratic state capacity opened up multiple avenues for transactions and extralegal coercive measures to take place even as labor laws remained on the books.

Under state-led liberalization, state officials introduced market-based measures such as labor productivity and profits as new lenses for reading and interpreting the industrial sector. By these metrics, the textile sector was viewed as bloated, inefficient, and unproductive. Mass closures and layoffs took place in textiles, usually through collaboration between local officials and enterprise managers or owners. Urban land prices in Shanghai and Bombay made the grounds on which the textile mills stood far more valuable than any other asset. Thus both land and labor were interpreted through an accounting exercise in valuation, assets to be consolidated and repurposed—through severance or pension deals for labor, and high-end commercial real estate ventures for land.

In Shanghai, the city authorities administered the closure of roughly half of the city's textile mills in a five-year period between 1993 and 1997. This reduced employment from 550,000 to 280,000, with further reductions bringing employment to 195,300 by year-end 2000 (Shanghai Municipal Statistics Bureau 2002, 150). The mass layoffs were accomplished with remarkably few episodes of collective resistance from laid-off workers, in contrast to numerous incidents of protest among laid-off workers from the state-owned enterprises in other cities during the same period. While it is true that Shanghai municipal authorities possessed the fiscal resources to provide some support for displaced textile workers, the payouts did not keep pace with the rise in the cost of living for a city like Shanghai. The relatively stable layoff process in Shanghai's textile sector was closely monitored under the auspices of the Communist Party's propaganda department and mass organizations. Textile restructuring might be likened to a "managed campaign," carried out through the coordination of the Municipal Party Committee and deploying personnel from propaganda, the ACFTU, women's federation, and even the creation of a specialized "leadership small group" for textile restructuring (Perry 2011).

Far from withdrawing from labor relations, as both proponents and critics of neoliberal state policies might claim, the local state and party in Shanghai managed the restructuring process throughout. The Shanghai Textile Industrial Bureau (STIB) became a state corporation, the Shanghai Textile Shareholding Corporation (STSC) in 1995. The new entity would be positioned as the regulator (and beneficiary) of lucrative sales of mill land that transpired during the mid-1990s. As early as 1991, the STIB began converting the land (partial or complete) from the city's mills into commercial housing units, and by late 1994 at least 41 of the city's mills had some or all of their land converted into housing units.[8] The first experiment in the city's bankruptcy filings for state-owned enterprises took place in the Shanghai No. 2 Weaving Mill in late 1994. In January 1998, the Municipal Party Committee organized a "small leadership group" to carry out the further reduction of the textile sector under state administration ("Shanghai Annals" n.d.). Such restructuring kept mill ownership firmly in state control. By 2000, the domestic private sector made up less than 3 percent of industrial output in the sector (Zhang 2003, 1567).

In keeping with the capacities and governance traditions of the CCP to mobilize workers when propagating new policies, the Shanghai CCP, its union, and labor bureau cadres coordinated publicity campaigns to popularize the reemployment of laid-off workers and to promote the new legal regime of labor relations. Shanghai authorities opened the first of the generally successful Reemployment Service Centers (RSC) in 1996, for laid-off workers in textiles and electronics. Party and union cadres were told by the head of the STSC to propagate the importance of labor relations work under the conditions of a market economy (and to refrain from complaining about the irrelevance of union cadres under liberalization).

The STSC convened "Earnest Forums" (恳谈会) with municipal government and party leaders, in which the STSC reminded the city leadership of the long-term contributions of Shanghai's textile workers and the crucial importance of providing resources for the retraining and reemployment project (Huang 2006). Under the reemployment program, enterprises wishing to dismiss workers had to apply to an RSC and provide a rationale for the cuts in personnel, such as documentation on restructuring, mergers, or bankruptcies. By the late 1990s, the reemployment centers of these two sectors had processed a reported 116,500 workers through reemployment channels (Lee and Warner 2004, 178–79). Shanghai was also an experimental site beginning in 1992 for the introduction of conversion of state-owned enterprises to shareholding companies, and in the sale and bankruptcy filings of those enterprises. At the same time, Shanghai mill workers, like those elsewhere in state enterprises, took part in the privatization of enterprise housing by being able to purchase their dwellings at significantly reduced prices (Zhu 2000).

As studies of state-owned enterprises in Shanghai have shown, the development of institutionalized channels for mediation and arbitration under the 1995 Labor Law was particularly strong in Shanghai's state enterprises (Gallagher 2005; Guthrie 2001). A textile worker fired when her mill was privatized noted how legal aid centers provided her and fellow plaintiffs with the "ability to talk," and as Mary Gallagher put it, "helped her form the words needed to appear in court" (Gallagher 2006, 807). At the same time, a project to create social insurance based on individual fee-paying participants succeeded in rapidly expanding health and pension benefits for the retirees of Shanghai's mills and other defunct state enterprises. Labor disputes in Shanghai filed through arbitration and litigation rose rapidly after the enactment of the 1995 Labor Law. Arbitration cases in Shanghai between 1995 and 2000 rose from 2,554 to 11,046, and court cases exceeded 5,100 by 2000 (Chen 2004, 33–35). Legal claims involving labor relations were, for the most part, individual cases attempting to redress violations by employers. Workers who took their grievances to court learned that the new labor laws and regulations fell well short of what was promised by the state (Gallagher 2006).

As in the 1950s, the role of union personnel remained ambiguous, with officials caught in a dilemma between representing workers' interests and facing retribution from the party, versus acting at the behest of

CCP overlords and continuing to lack credibility with workers. ACFTU branches assisted individual legal cases and made broader calls for enforcement of existing laws (Chen 2004, 29). In the latter, as well as in the promotion of new laws, the union exerted a certain degree of authority. Chen concluded in a study over a decade ago of Shanghai labor relations, "It is the unions' status as a state agency under the current political system, rather than as the representative of organized labor, that enables them to mount effective efforts in the legal arena in the area of labor relations" (ibid. 43).

The dismantling and reemployment of the Shanghai textile workforce in the 1990s thus illustrates a convergence of marketization and related reform policies with older styles of political-mobilizational governance— or as noted above, a convergence of an older temporality of state-building with a new temporality of globalization and neoliberalism. Some obvious contradictions were inherent in the propagation of a rationalized legal order for labor relations using the techniques of cadre mobilization at grassroots levels to carry out the mass layoffs and reemployment project. But the generally stable textile sector restructuring in Shanghai can be explained in part by the political controls that the local party utilized in its handling of mass layoffs within the textile workforce.

In Bombay, the restructuring process in the 1990s bore the imprints of its legal-bureaucratic state capacities and modes of engagement from the 1950s. Bombay's mill owners and their powerful association exerted considerably greater influence in the 1990s. In the aftermath of the 1982 strike, the decline of the corporatist bargaining structure created multiple channels for plant-level agreements between individual owners and plant-level union representatives (from the RMMS or from the so-called independent unions) (Sherlock 1996, L36–L37). The pattern of engagements among officials, unions, owners, workers, and their representatives, while decentralized, remained within the channels of the existing legal and bureaucratic infrastructure from the 1950s. The Bombay Industrial Relations Act, while the subject of much criticism from all sides, remained firmly in place. While workers continued to pay only lip service to the no-strike provisions of the BIRA, the legislation propped up the RMMS and positioned it as a vital node in the high-stakes encounters over the sale of mill lands.

The RMMS retained exclusive representation rights within the textile sector, and as such its approval was needed to authorize plans from

mill owners to retrench or close mills. RMMS support was also necessary to reach individual agreements with owners on productivity and layoffs (ibid.). This made RMMS officials especially susceptible to bribes
and other forms of influence, no more so than in the scramble for the
disposition of mill lands in Bombay.

In the most notorious of what came to be known as the "mill murders" of the 1990s, Sunit Khatau, the owner of the Byculla mill and a leading industrialist in Bombay, collaborated with the leaders of a major
organized crime group to manipulate elections for leadership positions
in the RMMS. This was after Khatau's plan had gained approval from
the state government and from a restructuring commission for industry,
but was denied by the RMMS president on the grounds that it lacked a
plan to provide sufficient resources to workers who would lose their
jobs. Khatau collaborated with the Gawli gang to replace the RMMS
president in union elections, and the winning candidate had close ties to
the Gawlis. Khatau's strategy drew him into a dangerous alliance, and
members of a rival organized crime group murdered him in May 1994.[9]
Two other high-profile "mill murders" took place in the mid-1990s. One
victim was the leader of the 1982 strike, Datta Samant, and the other
the owner of the Raghuvanshi Mills. Laid-off millworkers and their sons
were often easy targets of gang recruitment.[10]

The infiltration of organized crime into textile unions and ownership
reveals how mill owners sought out extralegal and coercive means to get
around the legal and administrative channels in place for the disposition
of mill lands and workers. The procedures are indeed complex, and closely
tied to the legacies of the 1950s. Mill land had to gain approval from the
state government as well as the Bureau of Industrial and Financial Restructuring, and then approval from the RMMS, which was to ensure
that some share of land sale revenues were used for compensation of laid-
off workers. The process applied to both private and public mills under
the National Textile Corporation (NTC). In the case of the latter, additional layers of approval were needed. This led to a practice in which privately owned mills made incremental sales that skirted the law or evaded
it, while the sale of land by publicly owned mills faced greater scrutiny
and more forceful opposition. "While the NTC mills have been frozen
in time, the owners of the private mills have surreptitiously been parcel-
ing out chunks of land for redevelopment, either by themselves or by sale

or lease to builders" (D'Monte 2002, 206). By 2000, one-quarter of the estimated 40,000 workers remaining in the textile sector were not receiving pay on time, with several mills suspending pay for more than a year (Swami 2001). Most textile firms used provisions of the national Industrial Disputes Act of 1947, which prohibited layoffs in firms of greater than 100 employees without state approval, to bring about the same result as a workforce reduction. They sought and gained approval for Voluntary Retirement Schemes that were often anything but voluntary from the perspective of the workers.

In short, Bombay mill owners, unions, local governments, and workers followed the provisions of the existing legal-bureaucratic framework to subvert the intentions of long-standing laws and policies related to labor relations. It was a process consistent with what Rob Jenkins (1999), in a national level study, has labeled as "reform by stealth." While it is tempting to conclude that Shanghai's more orderly (and less violent) transfer of textile mill lands and layoffs of mill workers reflects a relatively "higher" level of state capacity to effect a smooth restructuring of a pillar industry and its contentious workers, such a view would be incomplete. When viewed from the broader historical perspective that incorporates the origins and forms of respective state capacities, the different outcomes of textile restructuring can be explained as legacies of prior eras of engagement between state agents and social forces, with differences in how states presented themselves in policies, rhetoric, and political style.

Conclusion

In the late 20th and early 21st centuries, the connection between autonomy from social forces and state capacity was nowhere more prominent than in the contrasts that scholars and pundits drew between China and India. The Chinese state produced the Shanghai "miracle" and its showcase Pudong New Area in the 1990s, while the Indian state had struggled since the 1970s to enact its vision of Navi (New) Mumbai across Thane Creek opposite the Island City. The Indian prime minister in 2004 said that Mumbai should emulate the urban planning example of Shanghai, and calls went up from urban developers for Mumbai to become the

next Shanghai by emulating infrastructure projects and the forcible eviction and relocation measures to achieve them (Chattaraj 2012). Contrasts
between airports, highways, and skyscrapers deepened the association between infrastructure provision and the respective capacities of the two
states.

There are merits to the contrasts that some draw between the municipal governance, infrastructure, and bureaucratic personnel in the two
states. But to reason that successful outcomes in urban planning, public
goods provision, and overall development are a result of high levels of state
capacity is something of a tautology. To say that states with high capacity can deploy their capabilities to achieve development goals elides the
question of where capacities come from, how they change over time, and
how global-historical temporalities influence state goals at different times.
For example, in his study of the Indian state (2003), Vivek Chibber notes
how the demobilization of labor in the 1950s had the effect of strength-
ening and emboldening India's business sector against state attempts to
create a planning regime in which capital could be disciplined, regulated,
and directed for national goals. In losing labor as a potential bargaining
ally vis-à-vis capitalists, the Indian state undermined its own developmental aspirations. Chibber's claim illustrates how the production of state
capacity depends in part on the state's engagement with social forces (and
the relative balance of power among them).

State capacity and state building, rather than conceptualized in terms
of capabilities, such as taxation, conscription, mobilization, and public
goods provision, can be fruitfully explored as relational processes. As state
officials undertake the difficult task of making societies legible, with the
introduction of new agencies, rules, and policies, and new categories and
standards for complex social relations and groups, the state becomes an
entity that itself can be read and acted upon by these reorganized social
forces. As we saw in the cases of labor relations in Shanghai and Bombay, ruling parties in the 1950s made use of specific governing techniques
to mark the boundaries between state and society. The differences between
the political-mobilizational capacity seen in Shanghai and the legal-
bureaucratic capacity on display in Mumbai should not imply that one
state was more or less successful relative to the other, or that one enjoyed
greater autonomy to pursue its goals. Through mutual engagements with
social forces, different state capacities emerged over time. Workers, par-

ticularly those who had been marginalized by new labor policies, found it possible at times to engage state officials and institutions using the rhetoric and ideologies implicit in these different forms of state capacity. In the 1990s, when the two states deployed market forces that dismantled industrial workplaces and their job protections, they did so in part by deploying repertoires of state capacity from the 1950s, even as the neoliberal project produced new forms of state capacity and forms of engagement between states and social forces. As T. G. Suresh demonstrates in chapter 2 in this volume, "state absenteeism"—a seemingly purposive withdrawal by the state from labor relations in the construction sector—reflects how states may choose to stay out of labor relations in one sector while promoting and displaying new capacities in another, such as urban planning and development. An absentee state in one sector might be highly present and powerful in another.

If the comparison offered here between Shanghai and Bombay provides useful insights into variation in state capacity at the city level, by extension one could fruitfully examine the production of state capacity in other cities. As the discussion showed, state capacity in China and India was drawn in part from national-level political institutions and the norms and practices of political leaders who came to dominate those institutions in the mid-20th century. If state capacity is also formed from the engagements between state and social forces within the urban context, then one might hypothesize that to the extent that the configuration of social forces varies across cities—in terms of factory workers, informal labor, capital, merchants, and so on, then the capacities of the state would also vary, within the broader parameters of national institutions. While no other cities in China and India in the early 1950s had attained the same levels of industrial development approaching those of Bombay and Shanghai, cities such as Calcutta and Guangzhou, also part of the 18th-and 19th-century imperialist political economy, might make for useful comparisons in observing the development and trajectories of state capacity.

How and why initial forms of capacity change over time remains an important question. In the discussion of the 1950s versus the 1990s, we saw that the legacies of state capacity from earlier decades partially influenced the forms that state capacity took during processes of deindustrialization. This suggests a possible institutional trajectory in which forms of state capacity in one era can be deployed for very different purposes in a subsequent era. The state capacities in Shanghai and Bombay that were used in the 1950s to demobilize textile workers (a form of labor) were subsequently deployed in the 1990s to deindustrialize and then financialize urban land (a form of capital). But new state capacities can also be created at identifiable junctures. If new forms of state capacity emerged when local states in Bombay and Shanghai in the 1950s sought connections with each city's urban industrial workforce, further evidence could reveal a similar process under way during the late 20th and early 21st century. During this period, local states actively developed ties with and support from the business sector and urban professionals. One could say that the "fragmented-multiclass" Indian state began to shift from a broad and shallow commitment to multiple sectors toward a narrower and deeper commitment to private capital. At the same time, the Chinese state abandoned its commitment to workers and sought alignments with capitalists and intellectuals. The long-term effects of these political realignments on respective forms of state capacity will go a long way in defining the character of these states in the 21st century.

Notes

1. Kohli's polar opposite of the cohesive Korean state is the neopatrimonial case of Nigeria.

2. This chapter, which focuses largely on the 1950s, uses "Bombay" since the name change to Mumbai occurred in 1995.

3. Joel Migdal places emphasis on "mutual transformations" that take place during periods of state engagement with society, a process in which the "preferences and bases for action" (2001, 254) originally held by social forces and states are transformed. I prefer the term *mutual engagement* to avoid the assumption that engagements between state and society necessarily transform preferences and actions. See also Migdal, Kohli, and Shue 1994. Three of the contributions in the Migdal et al. volume (those of Atul Kohli, Vivienne Shue, and Elizabeth Perry) address state-society engagements in China and India.

4. A very short and only partial list would include Diamant 2000; U 2007; and several urban- and Shanghai-focused contributions in Brown and Pickowicz 2007.

5. Such accounts are generally found in older studies of regime consolidation in the PRC, but a more recent study emphasizing the tactics of terror and paternalist rule in the early PRC can be found in Strauss 2002.

6. Shanghai Municipal Archives (hereafter SMA), C1–2–232.

7. Maharashtra State Archives (hereafter MSA), File 2035/46.

8. See Perry 2011, and "Shanghai Textile Industry Gazetteer" n.d.

9. The presumption was that the Byculla land deal would give the Gawlis excessive power and wealth, so rival gangs exercised their own veto of sorts. The sale of the mill continued on for several years in contestation among the owner's widow, state agencies, unions, and the courts.

10. For details, see D'Monte 2002, 154–72.

References

Anand, Javed. 1982. "The Tenth Month: A Chronology of Events." In *The 10th Month: Bombay's Historic Textile Strike*, 1–41. Bombay: Factsheet Collective.

Bhattacherjee, Debashish. 1989. "Evolution of Unionism and Labor Market Structure: Case of Bombay Textile Mills, 1947–1985." *Economic and Political Weekly* 24.21 (May 27): M67–M76.

Brown, Jeremy, and Paul G. Pickowicz, eds. 2007. *Dilemmas of Victory: The Early Years of the People's Republic of China*. Cambridge, MA: Harvard University Press.

Chattaraj, Shahana. 2012. "Shanghai Dreams: Urban Restructuring in Globalizing Mumbai." Ph.D. diss., Princeton University.

Chen, Feng. 2004. "Legal Mobilization by Trade Unions: The Case of Shanghai." *China Journal* 52 (July): 27–45.

———. 2014. "Against the State: Labor Protests in China in the 1950s." *Modern China* 40.5: 488–518.

Chibber, Vivek. 2003. *Locked in Place: State-Building and Late Industrialization in India*. Princeton: Princeton University Press.

Deyo, Frederic C. 1989. *Beneath the Miracle: Labor Subordination in the New Asian Industrialism*. Berkeley: University of California Press.

Diamant, Neil J. 2000. *Revolutionizing the Family: Politics, Love, and Divorce in Urban and Rural China, 1949–1968*. Berkeley: University of California Press.

———. 2001. "Making Love 'Legible' in China: Politics and Society during the Enforcement of Civil Marriage Registration, 1950–66." *Politics and Society* 29.3: 447–80.

D'Monte, Darryl. 2002. *Ripping the Fabric: The Decline of Mumbai and Its Mills*. New York: Oxford University Press.

Frazier, Mark W. 2002. *The Making of the Chinese Industrial Workplace: State, Revolution, and Labor Management*. New York: Cambridge University Press.

Gallagher, Mary Elizabeth. 2005. *Contagious Capitalism*. Princeton: Princeton University Press.

———. 2006. "Mobilizing the Law in China: 'Informed Disenchantment' and the Development of Legal Consciousness." *Law and Society Review* 40.4: 783–816.

Guthrie, Doug. 2001. *Dragon in a Three-Piece Suit: The Emergence of Capitalism in China*. Princeton: Princeton University Press.

Harper, Paul. 1969. "The Party and Unions in Communist China." *China Quarterly* 37: 84–119.

Huang, Jinping. 2006. "Jiaqi zaijiuye xiwang de jinqiao" (Framing and launching the golden bridge of reemployment hope). *Shanghai dangshi yu dangjian* (Shanghai party history and party building) (December): 27–30.

James, Ralph C. 1959. "Labor Mobility, Unemployment, and Economic Change: An Indian Case." *Journal of Political Economy* 67.6 (December): 545–59.

Jenkins, Rob. 1999. *Democratic Politics and Economic Reform in India*. New York: Cambridge University Press.

Johnson, Chalmers. 1987. "Political Institutions and Economic Performance: The Government-Business Relationship in Japan, South Korea, and Taiwan." In *The Political Economy of East Asian Industrialism*, edited by Frederic C. Deyo, 136–64. Ithaca: Cornell University Press.

Kohli, Atul. 2004. *State-Directed Development: Political Power and Industrialization in the Global Periphery*. New York: Cambridge University Press.

Koo, Hagen.1987. "The Interplay of State, Social Class, and World System in East Asian Development: The Cases of South Korea and Taiwan." In *Political Economy of East Asian Industrialism*, edited by Frederic C. Deyo, 165–81. Ithaca: Cornell University Press.

Lee, Grace O. M., and Malcolm Warner. 2004. "The Shanghai Re-Employment Model: From Local Experiment to Nation-Wide Labour Market." *China Quarterly* 177 (March): 174–89.

Lee, Hong Yung. 1978. *The Politics of the Chinese Cultural Revolution: A Case Study*. Berkeley: University of California Press.

MacFarquhar, Roderick, and Michael Schoenhals. 2007. *Mao's Last Revolution*. Cambridge, MA: Belknap Press of Harvard University Press.

Migdal, Joel S. 2001. *State in Society: Studying How States and Societies Transform and Constitute One Another*. New York: Cambridge University Press.

Migdal, Joel S., Atul Kohli, and Vivienne Shue, eds. 1994. *State Power and Social Forces: Domination and Transformation in the Third World*. New York: Cambridge University Press.

Mitchell, Timothy. 1991. "The Limits of the State: Beyond Statist Approaches and Their Critics." *American Political Science Review* 85.1: 77–96.

Morris, David. 1955. "Labor Discipline, Trade-Unions, and the State in India." *Journal of Political Economy* 63.4 (August): 293–308.

Perry, Elizabeth J. 1994. "Shanghai's Strike Wave of 1957." *China Quarterly* 137 (March): 1–27.

———. 2006. *Patrolling the Revolution: Worker Militias, Citizenship, and the Modern Chinese State*. Lanham, MD: Rowman and Littlefield.

———. 2007. "Masters of the Country: Shanghai Workers in the Early People's Republic." In *Dilemmas of Victory: The Early Years of the People's Republic of China*, edited by Jeremy Brown and Paul G. Pickowicz, 59–79. Cambridge, MA: Harvard University Press.

———. 2011. "From Mass Campaigns to Managed Campaigns: 'Constructing a New Socialist Countryside.'" In *Mao's Invisible Hand: The Political Foundations of Adap-*

tive Governance in China, edited by Sebastian Heilmann and Elizabeth J. Perry, 30–61. Cambridge, MA: Harvard University Press.

Perry, Elizabeth J., and Li Xun. 1997. *Proletarian Power: Shanghai in the Cultural Revolution*. Boulder, CO: Westview Press, 1997.

Shaikh, Juned. 2005. "Worker Politics, Trade Unions, and the Shiv Sena's Rise in Central Bombay." *Economic and Political Weekly* 40.18 (April 30): 1893–900.

"Shanghai Annals, Chronology" (in Chinese). N.d. Office of Shanghai Annals. Shanghai Municipal Government. http://www.shtong.gov.cn/node2/node2247/node81547/userobject1ai101970.html. Accessed March 1, 2014.

Shanghai Municipal Statistics Bureau. 2002. *Shanghai Tongji Nianjian 2001* (Shanghai statistical yearbook, 2001]. Beijing: Zhongguo tongji chubanshe.

"Shanghai Textile Industry Gazetteer" (in Chinese). N.d. Office of Shanghai Chronicles. Shanghai Municipal Government. http://www.shtong.gov.cn/node2/node2245/node4483/node56675/index.html. Accessed March 1, 2014.

Sherlock, Stephen. 1996. "Class Re-Formation in Mumbai: Has Organized Labor Risen to the Challenge?" *Economic and Political Weekly* 31.52 (December 28): L34–L38.

"Storming the Citadel: The Bombay Industrial Relations Act." 1982. In *The 10th Month: Bombay's Historic Textile Strike*, 51–59. Bombay: Factsheet Collective.

Strauss, Julia C. 2002. "Paternalist Terror: The Campaign to Suppress Counterrevolutionaries and Regime Consolidation in the People's Republic of China, 1950–1953." *Comparative Studies in Society and History* 44.1: 80–105.

Swami, Praveen. 2001. "A Raw Deal and Desperation." *Frontline* 18.8 (April 14). http://www.frontline.in/static/html/fl1808/18081030.htm. Accessed March 15, 2014.

U, Eddy. 2007. *Disorganizing China: Counter-Bureaucracy and the Decline of Socialism*. Stanford: Stanford University Press.

Union Research Group. 1982. "Wages of Wrath: The Need for a New Union Policy." In *The 10th Month: Bombay's Historic Textile Strike*, 60–81. Bombay: Factsheet Collective.

Yang, Kuisong. 2006. "1952nian Shanghai Wufan shiwei" (The complete story of the 1952 Shanghai Five Antis). *Shehui Kexue* (Social science) 4: 5–30.

Zhang, Le-Yin. 2003. "Economic Development in Shanghai and the Role of the State." *Urban Studies* 40.8: 1549–72.

Zhu, Jieming. 2000. "The Changing Mode of Housing Provision in Transitional China." *Urban Affairs Review* 35.4 (March): 502–19.

CHAPTER 2

Labor and State Absenteeism

The Intersecting Social Experience of Construction Workers in India and China

T. G. Suresh

In the mainstream narratives, India and China represent two contrasting models of state; the former is presented as a resilient constitutional democracy but suffering from governance deficit; thinly spread institutions that have conceded authority to competing nonstate interests stemming from religion, language, and caste; limited infrastructural capacity to secure social compliance; and modest fiscal resources to meet social sector spending. This catalog of state scarcities could well be much longer. In contrast, China, by most accounts, is a state corporatist regime that commands effective infrastructural capabilities geared to achieve social compliance; its governance institutions are densely spread from provincial to prefectural and down to the village level. Barring a few instances, it faces minimal resistance from nonstate interests of any kind; nor is it inclined to tolerate such interests. The Chinese state also controls substantial fiscal resources that it mobilizes and uses as it chooses to. These models are often compared for their sharply varying transformative roles in their respective societies, as well as for the developmental outcomes they have produced.

Any inferences we make from these available narratives may lead us to conclude that the experiences of the social actors in each case are vastly different because they are embedded in vastly different state models that shape their lives. Therefore, historical variance has always been a key analytical reference in comparative studies on India and China. But the insertion of India and China into global economic flows and the new set of economic rationalities have changed the story of divergence outlined above. In the postreform period (which the editors of this volume identify, in their introduction, as Temporality III), many of the structural processes in economic relations in India and China are converging and showing similar patterns. This chapter aims to show that the social experience of labor and the structures that fashion it are closely comparable. I propose that in Temporality III the micro-level processes involving the tripartite exchange among labor, capital, and the state are closely parallel. Despite their variance in institutional capability, the state in both the cases has either conceded or deliberately created nonjuridical spaces from which its own norms and instrumentalities are withdrawn or made to be passive, where, in other words, the state is absent. I will elaborate on this state absenteeism in India and China and the debilitating social consequences it has produced on construction labor in the postreform period.

This chapter is divided into four sections. It begins with a brief discussion outlining the crucial differences between the state in postcolonial India and the socialist state in China in their approaches to the labor question. The second section examines structural factors that relate to the cycles of construction from a comparative historical perspective, to trace the changes in the social forms of construction labor. The intersecting social forms of construction labor in the postreform era are explained in the third section. How state absenteeism produces intersecting social experiences for construction workers is discussed in the fourth section. In the conclusion I outline some key preliminary findings of my study.

The State and Labor Question in India and China

The "labor question" was a main focus of debate and activity in a critical arena of state practices in India during the planning era and in China under socialism. In India, the years between 1948 and 1979 can be called the era of labor regulations, as it was in this period that the Indian Parliament enacted a series of labor laws that sought to provide stability in employment and wages, recognized workers' union rights, and granted certain welfare entitlements. The labor regulatory regime that the planning era state created can be understood as having three aspects. One is a complex legal discursive field that sought to clarify how employment is defined, how economic compensation is measured, what the eligibilities for welfare entitlements are, what the scope is of union rights, and so on. The second is a labor bureaucracy that mediated between the legal normative field and the real world of work.[1] The third relates to trade unions, as the embodiment of the collective agency of secularized labor in India that negotiated and, at times, was in contention with the capital and state.

This regulatory regime, although it survived into the reform era, left the world of industrial labor in India largely unchanged. The traces of its transformative impact are confined to what is often referred to as formal sector employment. Given this limited effectiveness, it is pertinent to ask why the regulatory instrumentalities of the postcolonial state remain inconsequential for 90 percent of workers in India, those in the informal sector. The main reason is the self-limiting scope of the regime's applicability. The laws define employment with reference to activity that draws on a specified amount of industrial input, such as electricity, and involves a minimum of 20 workers. This definition is the origin of "dualism" in Indian labor, or the bifurcation of employment into a formal sector that fulfills the norms set out in laws and an informal sector that is sui generis and not covered by the regulations.[2] In the labor literature, as well as in the narrative of the state, this bifurcation is also expressed in the different descriptive categories the two sectors are assigned to: the organized sector, which is included in the legal regime, and the unorganized sector, which is excluded from it. The social context of state regulation constituted a protective envelope around workers in the factories, mills, plants, and offices run by the state, and those run by private enterprise. The regulations functioned well in places where big capital, the state, and big unions were concentrated and less well as the density of those three factors declined.

A peculiar characteristic of the state in India has been that its norms and instrumentalities have never entered the social world of unorganized labor. What has been referred to as labor in the unorganized sector comprises wage seekers of rural origins, who till recently had very limited interface with the modern industrial sectors. A multitude of workers from rural communities, from village artisans to skilled masons, were compelled to follow a peculiar mode of wage seeking that converted them into temporary sojourners in nearby towns or distant cities for regular intervals for work (Breman 1996). They routinely encountered economic actors such as petty traders, brick kiln owners, construction contractors, and the like, who either by habit or by economic compulsion had created a regime of exchange far outside the formal norms of the state. Under this rather ingenious system, labor power was controlled by (for example) a brick kiln owner or a construction contractor, but the wage-labor exchange was externalized to the labor intermediaries. This exchange regime through its practices posed open resistance to the formal norms of the state as well as to its labor rhetoric. The long absence of the state from the social world of the unorganized sector workers brought about both normative and historical consequences.

The normative field of modern secular conceptions of labor is largely the creation of the postcolonial state in India. During the planning era it produced a complex legal as well as rhetorical archive that conferred on labor modern secular rights and entitlements. While the urban organized sector workers were able to draw upon this archive and often borrowed the vocabularies of the state to frame their economic demands, the unorganized sector workers were historically excluded from developing any interface with the state and its secular rhetoric on labor. The exchange regime that controlled their labor was dominated by cultural conceptions based on parochial and ascriptive values, where the scope for assuming modern labor rights was nonexistent. The vernacular expressions of the labor anxieties of migrant construction workers are therefore largely devoid of the categories of legal rights. Second, the long absence of the state has left unorganized sector workers to turn to locally viable survival options. It is a fact that the rural communities in many provinces have barely any social relations with the state. In fact, they have been well socialized into a life that draws no resources from the state.

In marked contrast, since the founding of the People's Republic, the social world of the rural labor in China had been thoroughly reorganized by the postrevolutionary state. The state permeated rural society through novel ideational categories as well as through institutional models that brought all forms of labor exchange under a formal regulatory system. Labor was conferred a privileged political status in the communist discursive schemes.[3] The transformative impacts of the state had been far-reaching. At one level, many of these entail a general secularization of labor that freed them from preexisting cultural conceptions. The state-labor interface made available to the rural workers a modern language of rights. As in India, labor historians have documented the active presence in prerevolutionary China of labor intermediaries in the form of labor contractors, traditional guilds, and brotherhood networks (Chesneaux 1993; Perry 1993). The Chinese socialist state effectively ended labor intermediation and also the labor contracting system. Although some form of contract system continued, it was a formal arrangement, where production teams from the rural communes worked in urban collectives. But in the postreform period, this situation changed. State absenteeism paved the way for the return of older forms of social labor such as the intermediation and contract labor, most conspicuously in the construction sector.

State, Building Cycles, and Construction Labor

The main aim of this chapter is to show how the social experiences of construction workers in India and China are shaped by parallel regimes of accumulation that formed during those countries' respective postreform periods. I posit that the social experiences of the migrant construction workers in both the cases are very similar, despite their stations in two different economies. In broad terms this convergence has its origins in the capitalist economic rationalities characteristic of Temporality III, as defined by the editors of this volume in their introduction. The large-scale labor mobilization of the migrant construction workers and their prolonged presence in the cities is closely associated with and contingent upon the building cycles that began in China during the early 1990s and in India roughly a decade later.

Literature on construction labor usually avoids discussions of the production system into which construction workers are inserted. In this chapter, I hope to address this methodological lapse by locating them well within the building production system to explain the ways in which construction workers are excluded from the redistributional scheme. At another level the chapter's focus on building cycles and building-production networks will illuminate the regime of accumulation that came in Temporality III. I use the term "building cycle" to refer to the range of distinctive phases of building and architectural production in a city. This study concentrates mainly on Delhi and Shanghai, the two cities where building cycles are comparable in scale and duration. In this section I give a brief historical outline of building cycles and the actors who impelled them, in order to define their distinctive characteristics; I identify three building cycles in all. Both Delhi and Shanghai became sites of modern city building as a direct result of interventions by the British Empire. In the case of Delhi, the first cycle was initiated by the British colonial government's decision to shift the capital from Calcutta to Delhi in 1911.[4] The large-scale construction of the imperial city in the wilderness of the Aravali hill range west of the river Yamuna started around early 1916 and lasted for about 20 years. The cycle mainly entailed the architectural production of iconic imperial buildings. The "empire in stone," as Delhi was rhetorically christened by one of its architects, Herbert Baker, was essentially a political project that aimed to embody the sovereignty of the British Empire in the Subcontinent. The two key architects, Baker and Edward Lutyn, despite their difference over the choices of design had shared a common view that, for the imperial city, traditional Indian architectural style offered very few stylistic choices—although some design aspects of it, such as the *chajja* (wide-projecting cornice), *chhattri* (free-standing canopied turret), and *jaali* (pierced-stone lattice screen), were accommodated (Metcalf 1989). The crucial point here is that with the rejection of traditional Indian architecture, the projects excluded the large building craft communities, in particular those from today's Rajasthan region. Thomas Metcalf (2002) has provided an excellent account of the debate that surrounded the question of architectural choices for the new imperial capital. The course of the cycle was marked by building iconic structures under the supervision of British engineers with local contractors managing labor.[5] This period is important in the artisanal history of construction trade because it saw the beginning of the disintegration of northern India's craft communities.

The second cycle began in the immediate postindependence years. Conceived by India's democratic government through planning bureaucracies, the construction focused mainly on the modern functional spaces such as apartment complexes for government employees, government office buildings, and other public buildings. This cycle integrated rural artisans as well as unskilled labor from neighboring provinces such as Rajasthan, Uttar Pradesh, and Punjab into the construction sector in

Delhi. The second cycle lasted for about 30 years, from the late 1950s to the 1980s. Johri and Pandey's (1972) pioneering study of construction workers in Delhi during this period show through extensive field surveys that indebtedness compelled rural labor into the reserve army of *jamadars* or contract labor bosses for a prolonged period (ibid.). The construction labor in this phase was mainly composed of migrant workers routed through the two key intermediaries, the *thekedars* (petty contractors of building works) and *jamadars*.

The third building cycle, which is presently running its course and which has produced large-scale assemblages of construction workers, began toward the end of the 1990s. This phase has concentrated more on the outlying peripheries of New Delhi. Four new agglomerations, Dwaraka and Gurgaon in southwest, and Noida and Ghaziabad in the east, trace its trajectory. If the two preceding cycles were driven by the state as responsible for planning and as the main source of investment capital, the present cycle is stimulated by radically new economic factors such as private real estate firms. It heralds the arrival of mass production technologies as the decisive technical apparatus that leads to the standardization of building skills.

The use of building cycles to identify periods of large-scale production of built spaces may not help us as much in charting the history of construction in Shanghai. There was continuous building there from the later part of the 19th century through the 20th century. Since the 1870s, when the *li long* (lane/courtyard houses) neighborhoods were built, and in the early decades of the 20th century—when the riverside Bund (*waitan*) was transformed into one of the world's most alluring architectural landscapes though the construction of workers' quarters after 1949— up until recent years, with the development of the financial district of Lujiazui in Pudong, Shanghai's physical transformation has been continuous.

The period under socialism, 1949–89, has been treated as a "dark age" in the Shanghai's urban history. Urban studies scholars and historian have denounced this period as the city's half-century of suppression. Not a single new building was constructed in the French concession or in the former international settlement in this period. The city was frozen in an urban morphology that it had inherited from the settlement era. Denison and Guang (2006) depicted Shanghai's encounter with its communist destiny as an antidesign era. Bergere (2004) traced the metamorphosis of the city from a metropolis into an unloved city during 1949–79, when the CPC leadership reduced the city to a shadow of its former preeminence. The reason for the city's long affliction was attributed not so much to socialism itself, as to the deep antiurban bias that Mao had against it.

But this now conventional requiem for communist Shanghai needs to be looked at from a different perspective as well. Chinese urban studies scholars have provided an alternative representation of this period by focusing on the spatial restructuring of the city for collective welfare. Yan Zhongmin and Tan Jianzhong have documented empirical evidence for the large-scale construction of residential blocks for industrial workers, which replaced the more than 300 slum settlements Shanghai had inherited from the earlier era (Yan and Tan 1990). The new apartments built since the 1950s removed the slum zones of Fangualong. The image of a frozen morphology implicated in many studies may be a useful critique of Maoist socialism, but most often it is proffered without adequate empirical grounding. Since the 1950s Chen Yi's communist administration focused on reducing population density in the inner city and the construction of suburban industrial districts in places beyond the Zhongshan road circle. Yan and Tan (ibid.) note that the area of newly built-up periphery is much greater than that of the city before the liberation. Shanghai's built-up area is now 278 square km, more than three times the city's area before 1949. Some of the new housing quarters were built near the city core, as at Caoyang and Kongjiang, in the biggest industrial zones of the Yangpu and Putuo districts.

The third building cycle in Shanghai began in 1991, when the National People's Congress approved the master development plan for the city. Since then, architectural and building production has become the dominant spatial practice of the city. It can be understood as an uninterrupted and coordinated intervention conceived and implemented from above by the Shanghai Municipal Government. This process has created a vast mass of vertical structures concentrated in the Pudong, Huangpu, and Luwan districts.[6] In 2010 the municipality reported 4,000 buildings above 20 stories high (Shanghai Municipal Statistical Bureau 2011). Pudong was incorporated into a Central Business District that extended the traditional city core of the Huangpu waterfront, the Bund. The rise of the Lujiazui financial district in Pudong made it the core site for global flows of capital, which had a cascading effect on other businesses, and a mass production of standardized building structures followed quickly.

It appears that the present building cycle is the most sustained one, as it has run an unbroken linear course, accelerating and surpassing the production of preceding years. The magnitude of engineering, logistics of production, and institutional coordination involved in this cycle will likely have no parallel in urban history. Why is Shanghai experiencing such a high-density building cycle over such a long stretch of time? There are four explanations that may provide a broader understanding of what is driving this long cycle. The first is Shanghai's return to the global economic circuit. After an interval of nearly half a century, the city developed linkages with the global capitalist economy from which it had been separated under the communist central planning. Second is the promotion of the city by the municipal government (Wu 2000). Notable among these promotions was the decision to hold a global architectural design competition for Pudong's Lujiazui Financial Centre project (Chen 2007). It prodded international architects, construction firms, and land developers to think of Shanghai as the next big urban design idea. Third is the city's model of generating land rent by the local state. Fourth is the corporatist institutional capacity of the municipal government to coalesce different societal interests for larger urbanization objectives.

A notable feature of the large-scale production of built spaces in both Delhi and Shanghai is that they reveal the logic of standardized mass production. The hallmark of this process was the production of large-scale built spaces driven by public demand for housing, by the need for an infrastructure to reduce travel time, by the shifting of retail from street to integrated arcades, and by the physical location of businesses. Since collective consumption requires standardization, the urban built spaces express uniformity. They operate as the propelling logics of the urban habitat. The city needed a multitude of large-scale, functionally similar built spaces that articulate as well as synchronize the urban economy. Uniformity becomes such a pervasive feature of the urban built spaces that the city looks as if it was assembled by standardized mass production. The form of new urban built spaces converge into standardized, replicable, mass modules, which fundamentally transformed the way building production had been organized until then. It now required greater coordination of works in terms of centralization, synchronization, and sequencing. But crucial to these changes was the question of how to organize the labor-time required for realizing a quantitative leap in building production?

CONSTRUCTION LABOR IN INDIA AND CHINA:
INTERSECTING SOCIAL FORMS

As I indicated at the start of the chapter, comparative accounts of India and China are often about contrasting models of economic rationalities, political regimes, and institutional capacities. Since the two societies are embedded in vastly different sets of economic relationships and are governed by mutually exclusive political ideas, the social outcome they produce will be correspondingly varying, or so the argument goes. But the limits of these narratives of divergence will become clear when we look beyond macro-level generalizations. The social history of construction labor in postreform India and China is one such site that defies the familiar comparative reasoning. The social form in which the construction labor is mobilized, the mode through which workers are incorporated into the building production networks, the economic exploitation they are subjected to, and above all the dehumanization they experience are all very similar in both cases. The point to be noted here is that the nature of the state makes no difference. Whether it is the Chinese corporatist regime with its formidable fiscal resources, or the Indian constitutional democracy with its predilection for popular political rhetoric, construction workers in both places are subjected to nearly equal scales of expropriation. I aim, in this section, to demonstrate the intersecting social histories of construction labor in both Delhi and Shanghai.

My comparative analysis is based on three sets of sources: the narrative data collected from construction sites in the southwest district of Delhi since 2011, personal observations of sites in Chengdu and Shanghai during 2008 and other shorter visits to Guangzhou, and academic writings and statistical accounts and advocacy literature available on China. Although migrant construction workers are very visible in the cities of India and China, there is very limited academic study of this sociological category. The Indian case is particularly confounding as there is scarcely any academic literature on the subject. What is available are a few labor market studies and advocacy literature produced by nongovernmental organizations as well as the concerned citizen groups. These sources offer limited scope for analysis, as all they present is quantitative survey data.

This incongruity between the compelling social presence of construction workers and their near absence in academic representation is common to India and China. Migrant construction workers have been more widely visible in Chinese cities and for a longer period than in India. But still, very few Chinese sociologists or labor ethnographers have investigated construction sites. Moreover, what research there is on Chinese labor is subsumed under the vast migration literature, and specific details on construction labor are unavailable. Even narratives of the floating migrant population barely reveal why peasant construction work took particular social forms as the workers traveled from the rural areas to the cities, not to mention providing details about their employment. However, Chinese labor economic scholars have taken up the issue of endemic wage arrears in the construction sector and have forcefully argued for new policies to address the issue.[7]

Despite this lack of information, we can identify a convergence in the specific social forms in which migrant construction labor is mobilized in India and China. They share three common social characteristics. First, labor in the construction sector has become a function of migration and is composed primarily of circulating peasant communities. Breman, in his study of the nomadic workforce in Gujarat (2010),[8] has argued persuasively that labor migration is actually labor circulation. Chan (1994) has indicated a closely parallel circulatory trend in Chinese migration since the early 1980s. This floating population is by its nature "elusive and seasonal," and a portion of it is made up of seasonal circulators (ibid.). Second, mediated labor has become an institutional norm in the sense that the construction labor market is a function of intermediaries. Third, a new form of work-residence system or "residential bounding" has corraled workers into a system akin to social quarantine.

When did construction labor become a labor market exclusively for migrant rural communities? Until about two decades ago, the construction labor market in India was largely formed along regional lines, and local labor had some degree of presence. Van der Loop's accounts (1996) of construction labor in Tamil Nadu demonstrate the regional and local domination of the construction labor market in the period of his study. In the Travancore region, traditional building skills such as carpentry were restricted by caste (Harilal 1989). Since caste was closely tied to the native traditions, these communities were resistant to distant migration. Delhi was an exception to the regional trends of the time because the workers were gathered and brought to the city by *jamadar* intermediaries from the nearby provinces of Rajasthan and Uttar Pradesh (Johri and Pandey 1972). In Delhi, rural migrants dominated construction labor even during the building of the imperial capital, and that historical trend has continued.

The onset of the latest building cycle in India has deeply altered the regional bound-labor circulation. There have been significant changes in the social composition of construction labor since late 1990s, when the predominant social form of construction labor underwent a structural shift, from that of migrant labor to circulatory labor. Until the late 1990s the social stratum that dominated the labor market was migrant workers. This was the case with marginal urban labor in general, as it was composed of rural migrants mainly from the provinces of Uttar Pradesh, Bihar, Rajasthan, and Haryana (Banerjee 1986). During the decades before the new cycle, when such construction was still in the planning phase, they formed a well-entrenched marginal labor category with strong ties to the city, in the sense that most of them become residents of the Jhuggi and Jopri districts (squatter settlements).This enabled them, over a period, to become local labor.

But the urban process driven by the current building cycle has completely changed this situation. Those earlier rural migrants were replaced by the new circulating peasants who constituted the new social labor. My field work in south Delhi construction sites and labor quarters clearly establishes this point. Nearly all production-level workers in construction, such as *beldars*,[9] masons, brick layers, and *saria* workers,[10] are transient rural laborers and peasants brought to the city specifically for jobs in construction. People from local Jhuggi settlements are completely excluded. As social labor, the circulating workers are different from the earlier migrant workers, who settled in the city. The peasants move back and forth between Delhi and their native places depending on the demand for their labor. The transitory nature of their movements insulates them from other segments of the urban marginal workforce. This insulation prevents them from developing any linkages with the local labor strata and allows them no possibility of getting residence in the slum squatter settlements in the city.

Second, during the last decade, the regional origins of peasant construction workers have diversified considerably. In the early 1990s, the majority of workers came from specific districts in four provinces, Madhya Pradesh (the areas of Chattarpur, Mahua, Tikamgarh, and Jhansi), Rajasthan (Sawai-Madhopur, Sikar, and Dosa), Bihar (mainly Samsatipur), and Uttar Pradesh (Sultanpur and Azamgarh) (Sewa Bharat 2006). But during 2010–11 in the south Delhi construction sites, a much wider range of native-place origins were observed (my field notes). A number of new district names appeared as native places of young workers; most conspicuous was the significant presence of workers from distant regions such as Orissa (Kalahand-Bolangir districts) and West Bengal (Malda district).[11]

The changes in the social composition of building workers in Delhi cannot be treated as mere labor market changes; they point toward a structural shift. Social labor is now composed of circulating rural workers that have replaced the earlier migrants. The distinction between the two is that the new construction workers have a high degree of spatial mobility as transients between the construction sites in Delhi and their native places. Their mobility is determined by the intermediaries tied to construction firms and demands on their labor-time. These factors are linked to the industrial dynamics of urban production processes. The earlier migrants became building workers only after their arrival in the city through kinship or native-place networks and were able to develop more stable spatial relations with the city, where they eventually joined the slum settlements. In a way, the migrants retained a certain agency in relation to employment as well as habitat.

In China a major change in the social composition of construction labor broadly intersects with the onset of the latest building phase, which, during the early 1990s, was concentrated in "growth pole" cities in eastern China such as Shanghai, Shenzhen, and Dongguan before it spread to other areas. By the opening decade of the 21st century, construction labor came to be dominated by rural migrants (Sha and Jiang 2003). A number of sources, including surveys and statistical reports, migration literature, and labor market studies, have established this shift. In comparison to India, where the earlier construction labor migration into cities helped rural wage seekers develop ties with the local economy and eventually find residence in the cities, the Chinese migration flows that began in the early 1990s have always been circulatory. As has been well

documented, what makes the Chinese migration circulatory is the institution of *hukou*, which prevents rural migrants from developing spatial
ties with formal labor markets and forecloses any possibilities of their
gaining local residence status. Therefore rural migrant workers become
"floaters" in the cities for some duration, typically a year, and then return
to their home villages before they again return to the cities.

The origins of population mobility that eventually reconstituted social labor in Shanghai can be traced back to the late 1980s and early 1990s,
when rural workers from suburban areas and coastal provinces migrated
into the city in search of wage labor. These migratory streams, in the context of easing the household registration system and market reforms,
began to alter the demographic structure of Shanghai. The gradual shift
in the demographic composition of the city is captured in the three rounds
of population surveys conducted by the Shanghai Municipal Government: the Shanghai Floating Population Surveys of 1993 and 1995, and
the Shanghai Residents and Floating Population Survey of 1996. The survey data provide clear indications about how urban social labor was
changing in line with a new set of demographic, economic, and institutional dynamics. I draw from three studies based on these surveys to sub-
stantiate my larger proposition, that construction labor and migration
are intersecting in Shanghai. The surveys show that the rural labor migrants in Shanghai concentrate in manual laboring, petty trading, artisanal work, and home services. Roberts (2002) has enumerated the main
occupations of labor migrants in Shanghai:

> Manual labor (40 percent) which included jobs in factories, construction
> (27 percent), commerce (18 percent) which included entrepreneurs making
> and selling products, street vendors and service personals, handicrafts
> (9 percent) which encompassed low- technology production process such
> as weaving and repairs, farming in Shanghai counties (4 percent), and
> domestic service (2 percent).

In the mid-1980s, about one-fifth of Shanghai's rural migrants were
estimated to be in the construction sector and in the control of more than
400 construction teams. Until the late 1980s, workers from the municipality constituted a significant portion of the building labor. *Labor News*
reported that half of the construction teams working in Shanghai were

from the city itself. It was during the late 1980s to early 1990s that rural migrants come to dominate the construction labor market in Shanghai. The period between 1986 and 1990 was considered the "construction phase" of the migration, when roughly two-thirds of the city's registered migrants were male workers of construction teams (*jianzhu dui*) (White 1998). The 346 registered Shanghai local teams at the start of 1989 employed 358,000 workers, and the 300 teams from outside used 370,000 contract workers (ibid.). In 1995 Shanghai had around 100,000 rural inhabitants from suburbs, counties, and other provinces working in construction sites. Typically the rural workers were employed in labor-intensive activities such as site clearance, soil excavation, and bricklaying (Zhang 2000).

The second social characteristic common to construction labor in both India and China is intermediation. The basic model of intermediation is that the labor market formation is an exclusive function of intermediaries. They exert almost monopoly control over recruitment, tenure, and terms of work, and are responsible for wages. Intermediation creates social conditions at multiple levels of labor processes that make rural migrants heavily dependent on the intermediaries. But we cannot understand intermediation entirely in terms of an economic exchange. What makes it a coherent social relationship is its underlying cultural energy, deriving from the native-place affinities shared by the rural migrants and the labor intermediaries.

In the present temporality, the forms of labor intermediations in India and China have close parallels. But their origins can be traced to distinctive historical contexts. In India labor historians have vividly documented the active presence of labor intermediaries since colonial times: the intermediary represented a complex blend of roles from labor contractor, foreman, and headman, among others (Roy 2008). The institution of the labor contractor continued to survive in the postcolonial period, with all the peculiar characteristics it had inherited from the past. Building construction during the planning era before the latest building cycle was carried out mainly by *jamadars*, who worked as labor contractors for construction firms and supervised the work through their *mistrs* (skilled masons) and *munshis* (clerks, accountants) (Vaid and Singh 1966). Intermediation has become so well entrenched that its historical continuity has never been broken. In my field explorations in south Delhi I encountered two kinds of labor intermediaries, the *thekedar* (work contractor) and the *jamadar*. No worker enters a construction site or a labor barrack unless he or she is recruited by a *thekedar* or a *jamadar*. They play a complex yet decisive role in the labor-capital exchanges in urban constructions and form the crucial link between the urban capital and the rural labor.

A construction firm relies on a *thekedar* or *jamadar* for much of the labor it requires, for the simple reason that there is no labor market in the urban economy that it can mobilize and incorporate into its production system. At the same time, a firm does not want any direct interface with the rural labor. The logic of the present regime of accumulation requires a firm to separate itself from the social agency of labor and the liabilities arising from it. What it wants to control is the labor power embodied in specific tasks such as masonry, manual labor, bar bending, and so on. Such a separation of labor power from social agency is possible when you have an external institutional agent to supply the former by managing the latter. A *thekedar* does precisely this. On the other side, the rural worker anxious to escape a chronic livelihood crisis seeks admission into the networks of a *thekedar* for opportunities to work for wages in the urban sector. Intermediation also has regional variations. In Bangalore, for instance, the main conduit between the construction firms and rural labor is the *mistri*, who mobilizes and recruits workers (Shivakumar, Yap, and Weber 1996).

In India the social agency of labor intermediaries has shown extraordinary resilience. They have survived two grand historical temporalities: the colonial and the modern postcolonial planning era committed to secular rationalities. A new century is well under way, recasting India with radically new economic ideas. But ironically, in the rural areas as well as in the urban sectors we still come across—perhaps more frequently than ever before—the old and most familiar labor intermediaries. Their unbroken passage from the age of colonialism and well into the first decades of the 21st century only suggest the limits of the state in India.

In contrast to the long continuities in India, the social history of labor intermediaries in China is marked by fundamental ruptures during the socialist period and their potent revival in the postreform era. Historical accounts of Shanghai labor, for instance, have documented how rural itinerants are routed to the urban sectors by the labor contractors. The

postrevolutionary state raised effective ideational and institutional critique of the role of labor intermediaries and was able to practically eradicate their social agency. Under Mao-era socialism, as Kang Chao has
reported, construction workers were directly recruited by state-owned
companies or urban collectives, and their terms of employment and wages
were regulated by the norms of the state (Kang 1968). However, when
the postreform state embraced completely different economic rationalities
from that of the socialist period, it introduced universal contract-based
employment models and opened social and economic possibilities for
intermediation. We may note here that the return of mediation is to be
understood in terms of a general norm that extended to all forms of economic exchanges including international projects.

Since the late 1990s employment in the construction industry in
China has become a function of mediation. All kinds of sources, from
official reports, surveys, academic publications, to reportage literature
have established the endemic nature of labor intermediation. Origins of
this system can be traced back to the reintroduction of the labor contract
system. Shanghai instituted the contract system in construction as early
as 1983.[12] The Chinese use of intermediation can be understood with respect to two modes of mediated employment. In the first mode, rural
peasant migrants are recruited by a labor contractor (*baogongtou*) from
the village using his native-place ties and affinities and it is he who brings
them into the cities to work in construction sites. His role is crucial as he
facilitates this rural-to-urban sector labor migration by securing the mandatory local government approvals, paying license and management
fees, providing dormitory accommodation in the construction site, and
disbursing allowances for day-to-day expenses. But these services come
with a serious rider; the peasant migrants must agree to work in the construction site for eleven consecutive months without wages and may return home only during the spring festival in January. Swider (2011) has
provided an illustrative account of this mediated employment, where the
contract arrangements have inbuilt barriers that foreclose migrants' integration into the cities and weakens their social connection with their
families and hometowns, a social experience that she calls "permanent
temporariness."

The second mode is the migrant workers' recruitment into the rural
construction contract teams (*baogong dui*). These teams can be of varying

size and industrial capability. A basic model of the team can be defined as a small-scale construction enterprise controlling building tradesmen and unskilled labor. Each team is divided into smaller labor gangs, which work in separate areas of building construction, such as cement masonry, plastering, carpentry, shuttering and casting, bar bending, and electrical fitting and installations. The main resource of the team is the building labor it has organized under a single authority, who is typically a work contractor. Yuan and Xin (1992) call them mobile peasants with establishments. At the lower end of this contracting hierarchy are the teams where the workers are collected and steered by an experienced team leader. The labor contract team from Wei Wei county of Anhui province, illustrated by Yuan, Wang, and Zhang (1997), is an example of this form.

Residential Bounding and Social Quarantine

In the construction sector the site of production has become at the same time the site of residence. The majority of rural migrants live on the construction site during the entire tenure of their work. Lines of shack tenements that resemble a mini slum have become a common sight in the construction sites of Delhi. A different physical installation, a dormitory made of fabricated sheets held together with metal clamps, is an indispensable visual marker in the construction sites in China. While they differ in their appearance, functionally in both the societies, the social body of the construction workers is placed into a formation where the traditional division between worksite and residence has tended to disappear. This form of residential bounding can be seen as an institutional innovation of capitalism that seeks control over the social body of the migrant workers, and it raises questions about the spatial dimension of production.[13]

The standard layout of construction sites expresses a spatial logic that integrates labor lodging into the building production. Both are located within the work site, making residence and production process inseparable from each other. Integrated workers' quarters had become a common feature of the construction sites in Delhi by the early 2000s. The rural workers brought to the city through *jamadar* or *thekedar* intermediaries are given temporary shelter in slum-like tenements made of corrugated steel, tin sheets, bricks, wooden poles, plastic, and tarpaulin sheets. The scarce infrastructural condition provides no protection from Delhi's frigid winter chill and during summer the corrugated steel huts transform the labor quarters into furnace-like chambers where living is almost beyond human endurance. These quarters or *basti*, in migrant parlance, are governed by an allocation system based on work sequence. Specific quotas of the quarters are allocated to *thekedars* for different work orders or labor supplies.

As construction work progresses, a composite multicultural society quietly forms in the *basti*. The Bengali-speaking Muslim *beldari* workers from Malda may be neighbors to Hindi-speaking *saria* workers from the Siwan district of Bihar, shuttering and casting workers from Gorakhpur, cement-pouring workers from Chattisgarh, and so on. On average most workers spend about 14 hours in the worksite, where they will be under continuous pressure to perform, and the shelters are used mainly for cooking and sleeping, that is, for the reproduction of labor power. But even in these extremities of banality, sometimes life spring up with all its hope, sound, and colors, especially during festival nights, days off, or pay days when one can hear the bands of folksingers or *bhajan*s accompanied by the *dholak* rhythms.

The social world in the *basti* is largely self-governed. The construction companies usually post watchmen in the settlements, mainly to register their authority amid the rural migrants and also partly to see general compliance with the work schedule. If there is no watchman, the *thekedar* sometimes assigns a *munshi* to oversee how much of the work quota has been completed by each laborer. But none of these arrangements constitutes a quasi-state in the labor camps, which can shape everyday life in a particular way. In fact the construction companies in India are least interested in social engineering of any kind, as long as they maintain control over the social body of the working class. What allows the rural migrants to adapt to the social world in labor camps is in part a function of culture, as they are largely composed of social modules based on affinities of native place, kinship, and identities.

A novice in the construction site will already have group membership in the networks of native place affinities, kinship, or identity-based communities. He will be part of a well-knit social unit sharing common bond, transplanted from villages of Chattisgarh, Uttar Pradesh, Bihar, or West Bengal to the urban sectors of Delhi. In the labor camp as well as in work sites, he will have his fellow villagers or relatives to work with, as well as to share the tin barracks in the labor *basti*. I would argue that the migrant construction workers in Delhi largely avoid the corrosive effect of estrangement in their everyday life because the social module they are part of draws on affinities of common native place, language, or kinship, which provide them the framework of a community. Their socialization is bounded up in these identities and therefore defines the "circumference of their sympathy."[14]

At the same time, a salient feature of life in the labor camp is its permanent state of fluidity. The residence of rural migrants in a particular labor camp is decided by the length of the labor time required. The construction schedule in different stages, such as drilling and ground excavation, pillar work, shuttering and casting, insulation, electrical fitting, tiling and carpentry, makes each category of labor redundant at the end of its stage, which therefore needs to be retired and replaced at once. This turnover is accomplished through labor intermediaries who transfer the groups of workers to other construction sites where they are required. The rural workers who fill the worksite *basti* are periodically replaced by new arrivals from faraway villages. Working in construction can corrode the stationary foundations of life as it involves constant shifting from one site to another.

The labor camp in China has better infrastructure conditions than those found in the Delhi region. A specially built space often referred to as "the dormitory" is a fabricated, mass housing facility of modules made of synthetic planks, metal clamps, and tin sheets. Everywhere, they are painted white and blue and are easily identifiable against the dull, ashy tones that dominate the construction site. In terms of design, physical form, and functionality, the dormitories possess and express certain industrial elements and purpose. Most of them consist of two to three blocks, with facilities for sanitation, water supply, and electricity. In general, they are located within the construction site, thus making residence and the production process inseparable from each other. There are manufacturers of prefabricated dormitories in China, a fact that indicates how much the dormitory system has become part of the industrial logic in the construction sector. The spread of dormitory lodging for migrant peasant builders in China occurred in the 1990s, a period that saw the beginning of the most recent building phase.

Although the kinds of infrastructure available for peasant builders in the dormitories of China and the shack tenements in Delhi region are different, the social world that forms in both places is similar in many respects. In both cases the temporary occupants are drawn from rural populations and are attached to their labor intermediaries. Their most salient sociological trait is a shared affinity based on native places, whether by province or by region. The rural construction teams of China (*baogong dui*) often have workers from same villages, which create sharp identity markers in the dormitories. Place names such Sichuan, Zhejiang, and Anhui become cultural and identity categories into which social labor in the dormitories are fragmented. Anxieties relating to labor processes often generate group conflicts along these lines. Swider (2008) has reported group clashes between Chinese workers belonging to different provinces. In contrast to dormitories in China, the labor camps in Delhi are socially more acquiescent.

What are the larger social consequences of this residential bounding? Work-residence separation is largely absent in the ethnographic narratives of the construction workers in Delhi. The workers often invoke the Hindi term *majburi*—helplessness—to rationalize their enforced quarantine in the labor camp. The need to find wage-paying work leaves them with no choice but to accept the harsh conditions. But another reason for their acquiescence is that they are periodically freed from its confinement, to attend seasonal farming needs in their *khetibadi*, to celebrate a festival, perform a *puja*, or attend a relative's wedding. The rural migrants often return to their villages.

The large-scale residential bounding in which social labor is incorporated into the production processes can be seen as one of the novel instrumentalities of capitalism. In China this form of work-residence, which Pun and Smith (2007) call the dormitory labor regime, has been spreading since the late 1980s. In their analysis of the spatial politics of production in two garment factories in Dongguan, Pun and Smith presented some of its larger social consequences. Through the dormitory system, capital gets continuous access to the labor reserve from the countryside, depresses the demand for better wages, and weakens collective organization of workers. Although infrastructure and conditions in the dormitories in the construction sites of China and the *basti* of the Delhi region are different from those in the Dongguan garment factories, their larger social consequences have close parallels.

STATE ABSENTEEISM AND THE INTERSECTING SOCIAL EXPERIENCES OF CONSTRUCTION WORKERS

Construction workers in India and China are subjected to multiple levels of informality. No institutional actors ever try to mediate the processes of wage-labor exchanges between the rural migrant workers and capitalist builders. In both cases there exists a complete absence of norms we usually associate with a modern state. The differences between the two countries is that while in India these kinds of informalities have been historically familiar characteristics of wage seeking for the rural poor, in China they have been introduced with postreform economic rationalities.

Rural construction workers in Delhi do not possess any records of formal relevance.[15] Their existence on the construction site as well as in the city has no legal status. There are no formal records of any kind that register their names, domicile, employment status, the wages they receive, their employer, and so on. The only register where their names are entered is a workbook maintained by the *thekedar* or his *munshi*. Typically, a workbook is a personal diary of a *thekedar*, where he enters the wages earned for a day's work. The entire process of wage-labor exchanges are based on oral agreements between a rural migrant and his *thekedar* or *jamadar* intermediary and the personal trust between the two. The normative conceptions that govern these exchanges are very much cultural and therefore fall outside the realm of modern law. But when we explore the question of how this informality finds social expression in urban economic sectors such as Delhi, we see that much of it is in fact a product of the structural milieu in which the local state is an important actor. It can be seen as an example of how the state causes its own norms to be sidelined in the wage-labor exchanges.

The passivity of the state is deliberate. The state simply does not apply juridical norms to the social world of labor. In formal terms, the social world on the construction site ought to be governed by a normative field created by the government in Delhi and at the federal level. And there are a number of rules and norms in existence. But these formal norms find no reference in the narrative of the rural migrants.

Specifically, the Building and Other Construction Workers Welfare Board that Delhi constituted under a state rule requires that construction firms maintain a muster roll, a wage register, overtime register, and similar,[16] and that construction workers registered with the welfare board must receive a photo identity card. The Building and Other Construction Workers (Regulation of Employment and Conditions of Service) Act of 1996, issued by the Government of the National Capital Territory of Delhi, lays out detailed rules stipulating the registration of workers, fixation of wages, sanitary facilities, accommodation, crèches, and so on.[17] Detailed technical guidelines regarding concrete work, demolition, excavation, scaffold construction, piling, and the like, are provided in the Delhi building and construction workers rules formulated in 2002.[18] The regulatory framework for labor recruitment through subcontractors such as *khatedars*, *sardars*, *jamadars*, and agents, and the entitlements of rural migrants, are provided for in the Interstate Migrant Workmen (Regulation of Employment and Conditions of Service) Act of 1979. Above all, there is a federal law, the Contract Labour (Regulation and Abolition) Act of 1970 that has as its objective the abolition of contract labor. In addition to these, there are laws such as the Minimum Wages Act that are applicable to construction workers. But these juridical norms of the state do not enter the social world of construction workers, nor do they influence the wage-labor exchange. It has been a peculiar institutional practice of the Indian state to address a social question through legislation and then absolve itself from enforcing it. Hence the norms of the state often collapse into inconsequential legal discourse.

Interestingly Chinese institutional practices in postreform years have tilted markedly toward this Indian practice of norm making through legislation and then vacating the very institutional spaces where these norms are to be applied. Although selective state absenteeism in China is an increasingly noticeable institutional trend, perhaps the most glaring examples of this are the pervasive and entrenched labor informalities in the construction sector. Like the wage seekers in India's unorganized sector, the majority of migrant construction workers in China have no formal employment relations with the construction firms. This produces a series of adverse outcomes for the workers, including extreme forms of wage flexibility, precarious employment tenure, denial of social insurance, and above all the transforming of the workers into a social multitude without any rights.

The extent to which the labor informalities have pervaded the construction sector has now been well documented. A field survey conducted by Chinese Academy of Social Sciences (CASS) in July 2007 revealed that 53 percent of China's construction workers did not have labor contracts and that 41 percent of those who had signed contracts were not in possession of a copy of the document.[19] An investigation by the advocacy group Human Rights Watch (Asia) revealed the different ways in which construction companies and China's labor bureaucracy create conditions that erode the formal regimes of employment. In Beijing, migrants usually start work on the basis of verbal agreements with building site supervisors; some have signed contracts that are then confiscated for "safekeeping" by their employers.[20] The experience of more than 40 workers when they approached the Beijing Daxing District Labor Supervision Unit Office seeking assistance to recover wages in arrear points to another informality: the workers discovered that the labor contract documents they had received from their employers were not in conformity with the required legal standard.

State absenteeism has decimated the economic rights of the construction workers in the Delhi region. Wage settlements usually involve a peculiar social exchange external to a formal economic regime. Conventional wage rate discussions are of very limited scope in understanding why wages in construction have been held down for so long and have not risen in response to factors such as inflation. There are three reasons why this is so. In the first place, the gap between the mandated wage rate and what workers actually receive as wages is very wide. The Central Public Work Department (CPWD) has detailed guidelines for calculating wage rates based on skill levels and category of worker: for example, for *beldari* work, masonry, and bar bending.[21] The government of Delhi periodically revises the minimum wages applicable in the city and, by law, paying wages below that rate is an offence. But in the construction sector these formal regulatory prescriptions have no meaning. Construction workers are given subsistence-level wages well below the minimum wage. Second, neither skill nor category of work is considered in the wage calculations of contractors. They do not recognize differences in specialization such as that between brick laying and shuttering, or that between tiling and electrical fitting. What contractors do, instead, is to divide the workers into two flat categories of labor, the *mistri* (skilled workers) and the rest (unskilled). The *mistri* earns a slightly higher wage, and the rest are paid a standard lower rate. In masonry, carpentry, *saria* work, tiling and flooring, and some others, there are few *mistris* who earn more than the "unskilled" workers. Third, the reason why the agency of the workers or factors such as inflation or formal regulation do not come into play in the calculation of wages is that these wage rates have been decided and agreed upon between the rural migrants and their labor intermediaries in the villages. If there is a problem, the only recourse for the worker is to appeal to the verbal agreement made in the village.

Wages are also closely tied to different kinds of social exchange. Even before coming to the cities many rural peasants receive a few months' wages in advance from the *thekedar*. The practice of wage advance is a familiar one in labor mobilization, and has been reported by labor historians. In the case of workers from the Malda district of west Bengal, however, a different mode of wage negotiation exists. These are mostly *beldari* workers brought to the construction sites by a *thekedar* for a two-month period. They are paid 55 days of wages as advance in their villages; the remaining five days of wages go to the *thekedar* as deduction for his commission and expenses for their travel, and so on.

In India. the social consequences of all the informalities produced through state absenteeism are twofold: first, workers are obliged to accept extremely low, survival-level wages that do not rise with inflation and that are held down for unusually long periods; second, because wages are agreed upon between the peasants and the *thekedar* in their home villages, there can be no kind of negotiation that invokes formal wage regulations.

In comparison to India, where state inaction is common throughout all state institutions, in China state inaction is selective and purposeful. The institutional capacity of the Chinese state is well documented and does not require any further elaboration here. But what has not been recognized in the literature is the rise of exchange domains largely freed from the purview of the state regulatory regime. Labor informalities in the construction sector are a direct outcome of this state absenteeism. The freeing of wages from the regulative overview of the state, which thus allow wages to be determined by the vagaries of construction capital, seems to be deliberate, and the consequences on labor have been devastating.

Wage setting in the construction sector is an extreme form of labor expropriation, scantily recorded in China's modern history. It is rooted in the specific forms of Chinese labor intermediation, in the construction contracting system, and in state absenteeism. Since the late 1990s various sources have reported that a large proportion of Chinese migrant construction workers do not receive the wages they should have accumulated in one year. Typically, a rural migrant recruited by a labor contractor (*baogongtou*) enters into a verbal agreement that he will work for 11 consecutive months and return to his home village only during the January-February spring festival. The total wage for the year of work is crucial in the migrants' economic calculus. They are motivated to toil for long months with the assumption that at the end they will receive a lump sum which can then be used at home to pay debts, or fees for their children's education, and so on. Most workers will meticulously record their labor time—the days they have worked, their overtime—to calculate their total pay. But all their hard labor, the frugal life of the dormitories, and their perseverance can end up counting for little. The only record most workers possess is a receipt showing their names and the amount owed to them. In China's construction sites, there are abundant personal testimonies that wage shortfalls are the common fate of many migrant workers (Pun, Lu, and Zhang 2010).[22]

When the labor contractor is not able to pay, he violates not only the verbal agreement but also the personal trust that workers have placed on him. Sometimes shared native-place affinities play an important role in cementing such personal trust. Therefore for many workers, unpaid wages leave them also with a deep sense of being betrayed. There are even instances when labor contractors abscond with workers' wages. Narratives about labor contractors who are interested only in personal enrichment and who care little for the workers are reported in the Chinese media, creating a public perception that the labor contractors are the main reason for nonpayment of wages in construction (wage arrears). As Pun, Lu, and Zhang (2010) have argued, the root cause of wage arrears is a structural problem at multiple levels of the subcontracting system. It exists because it increases productivity in construction by deliberately inducing flexibilities in the regulatory system. Hewu (2007) traces the wage disparities to three systemic problems: the absence of relevant legislation, local government regulation, and general disorder in the labor contract system. Hence to attribute the endemic wage arrears to the irresponsible behavior of some labor contractors is to reduce a structural problem to a more superficial one about personalities. The response of the Chinese state seems to imply an attempt to transfer responsibility to the contractors. In August 2005 the Ministry of Construction stipulated that the labor-contracting companies should be established, and that henceforth migrant workers should only be recruited through these labor service companies. A provision for formal labor-servicing entities was also incorporated in the 2008 labor law. Such state regulations aimed at correcting the behavior of labor contractors may give the appearance of regulations to ameliorate the problems of wage earners, but they do not in fact bring about any improvement in the economic rights of the construction workers. For labor contractors, the new regulations were translated into labor brokerages with new nomenclatures such as labor service companies, labor dispatch companies, and labor placement companies (Zhang 2008).

The labor problem in China is partly due to Chinese exceptionalism. Unlike the Indian state, the Chinese state is deeply implicated in the construction sector. The state dominates the construction sector through its ownership of land, something inherited from the socialist era, and through the state-owned construction companies that are usually assigned the construction projects. Provincial and local governments often use construction as a means both to what they claim as development and to collect "opportunity rent" from the capitalist financing the construction. The state meanwhile collects opportunity rent from the rural construction contract teams (*baogong dui*) that participate in the building work in the cities.

The construction teams are a basic organizational unit of Chinese labor. A team that seeks entry into building work in a city is required to obtain formal approvals, licenses, and permits from a number of administrative departments in the township of their origin as well as in the municipality where they work. This licensing regime comprises labyrinthine bureaucratic departments, including the township labor bureau, a resident committee, a public security bureau, and a transport and construction commission, and involves payment of taxes or management fees. The extraction of opportunity rent is well entrenched in the Chinese local and state practices that cause additional economic burdens on labor. How the system impinges on labor is illustrated by a migrant worker with the Zhejiang Construction Team from Shaoxing county working in Shanghai. In 1989, the team's payments to different bureaucracies amounted to 30–50 percent of its workers' total wages, according to this worker: "Besides paying taxes according to regulations in Zhejiang, we must pay management fees to the province, county, the township, the company, and the construction team, altogether five mother-in-laws. We separately pay other fees to the Shanghai project quality supervision office and the construction worksite management. This amounts to 30–50 per cent of our wages" (quoted in Solinger 1998).

Conclusion

The notion we see in the literature that state and social processes in India and China can be studied by using different methodological templates because they are constituted by different institutional configuration needs some reappraisal. India and China are no longer static regime types producing distinctive social outcomes. At the level of political economy in both countries, many of the norms, institutional practices, and therefore the social experiences they produce intersect. In this chapter I hope to have shown how the economic and social outcomes for construction workers, specifically, intersect in this way. I have outlined some of the larger comparable processes in both cases.

The persistence of an unorganized labor sector is one of the historical features of the Indian economy. Working in the unorganized sector has been, therefore, a familiar mode of survival for the rural poor in India. During the long socialist central planning era, China on the other hand, was able to effectively bring the rural poor under the formal institutional regime, thus largely avoiding an unorganized labor sector from shaping rural people's lives. But the exhaustion of the "household responsibility" system in the 1990s and the social phenomenon of wage seeking that ensued created something akin to India's unorganized sector in China. Along with its rise, the institutional norms that had mediated

labor processes earlier have gradually disappeared. The space vacated by
the state is now occupied by structural factors, the offspring of the new
temporality. This is the historical setting where the social outcomes for
rural wage seekers in both countries are converging.

In both India and China, building cycles function as a structural
factor shaping the large-scale social outcome for construction labor. Building cycles are set off by urbanization processes. Under capitalism, the
labor time required for the large-scale production of built spaces is produced by shaping the social body of rural migrants. For the rural migrants, the building cycles open new avenues for wage seeking. By the
early 1990s in China and a decade later in India, the stage was set for a
large-scale interaction between building capitalism and rural wage seekers. In my account, I show how the norms and instrumentalities of the
state have been made inactive in these interactions, and campare the harsh
implications for construction labor in each country.

India and China are similar in the social form in which labor is organized in construction. First, the labor market in each case is composed
almost exclusively of rural migrants who possess either land *khetibadi* in
India or rural *hukou* entitlements in China. Second, employment has become a function of intermediation, in the sense that labor is recruited
from rural districts, transferred en masse to the cities, and brought to the
construction site by labor intermediaries, labor contractors, and rural construction contract teams in China and *thekedars* and *jamadars* in India.
Labor intermediation creates institutional separation between labor and
capital, thus inhibiting any possibilities of an interface between the workers and construction firms. Third, the social body of the migrant worker
is inserted into the spatial system of production, a form of residential
bounding akin to social quarantine.

State passivity is marked throughout the wage-labor exchange in both
cases. In India, the labor question in construction is regarded as a problem of the unorganized sector and therefore warranting at least limited
state action. The state has accordingly created a dense, normative archive
of legislation that is supposed to regulate the labor processes. But these
modern norms have no actual effect on the economic rights of the construction workers. The norms become an inconsequential discursive field
because the state has vacated its own institutional space in the construction sector. The social exchange between migrant workers, labor inter-

mediaries, and construction site supervisors are, instead, often bounded by cultural norms familiar to them.

In China state passivity is double-edged. As in India, the Chinese state has also vacated institutional space in the construction wage-labor exchange, leaving rural migrants to the vagaries of construction capitalism. But there exists a crucial difference. The Chinese state is deeply implicated in the construction sector. The central government, as well as the local managerial elite, uses the construction sector for what they claim to be development and also for collecting opportunity rent from building capitalists. The state also subjects the rural construction teams to a licensing regime and extracts opportunity rent from them. State absenteeism in the Chinese construction industry is selective, in that it is restricted to the wage-labor exchange. The persistence of severe wage shortfalls in China and the comparatively lesser degree of shortfalls in India provoke questions about the very different economic calculus shared by the rural migrants in the two cases. Wage flexibilities in the form of short-term delayed payments have been reported from Delhi region, but they have never developed into an endemic industrial trend as in China. A plausible explanation may be found in the different economic calculuses that shape labor migration in the two cases. At the same time, variance in regime models, state capacities, and economic resources between India and China is not very salient in the social experience of construction workers.

Notes

1. For Frazier, this "legal bureaucratic apparatus" makes the state a more legible entity. See Frazier's chapter in this volume.

2. The Factories Act of 1948 defines a factory as "any premise where ten or more workers are working . . . and in any part of which a manufacturing process is carried on with the aid of power . . . or where twenty or more workers are working without the aid of power."

3. For instance, the Trade Union Law of 1950 explicitly assigns to trade unions the responsibility of workers' political education and the protection of their class interests. See State Council 1961.

4. As the commercial capital of Punjab, Delhi was prosperous before the British moved the imperial capital. But population increase and urban expansion gained momentum with its new political status (Gupta 2002).

5. In Khushwant Singh's memoir about his father, Sobha Singh, who was a building contractor in colonial Delhi, provides anecdotes about the migrant construction workers from Rajasthan during the construction work of the imperial city of Delhi. See Singh 2010, 2–14.

6. During the early 1990s, private companies supported by the local government had an active role in the building construction in the Pudong new district. The building programs developed through such public-private partnership are locally known as *shengbu lou*: "The so-called *shengbu lou* policy granted preferential treatment on land price and taxation to those Chinese companies that had direct or indirect link with ministries or provincial or local government at the beginning of the Pudong development" (Chen 2007, 110).

7. Wage had fallen seriously in arrears throughout China's construction industry. In Shanghai, a survey conducted by Beijing University scholars in 2011 revealed that only 6 percent of the construction workers had their salaries paid at the end of every month. "Construction Workers," *Shanghai Daily*, December 14, 2011.

8. In south Gujarat, people seeking wage-paying work are recruited on a temporary and casual basis and are treated as transients who remain outsiders in the area. When their labor power is no longer required, they return to their villages. Breman (2010) observes that the mobility of the rural poor in search of wage-earning opportunities is generally restricted to different rural areas and usually lasts only for a season.

9. *Beldar* is a Hindi term for the male unskilled workers who constitute a significant numerical group in a construction site. Women workers of the same category is referred to as *coolies*. Since *beldari* or *coolie* work does not require any skill, it provides rural migrants an early break into wage-earning opportunities in construction sector. A *beldar* is assigned a range of auxiliary work on a construction site, from transportation, cement mixing, and cleaning and clearing.

10. In the construction site parlance, *saria* refers to a whole range of tasks involving the bending of iron bars for frames for columns and shuttering panels. Usually *saria* workers form a group under a *thekedar* (petty contractor).

11. Workers from the Malda district of Bengal constitute a distinct presence in the construction sites of Delhi. Brought to Delhi by labor contractors and typically assigned *beladri* work, they are engaged for short periods. A Malda worker usually receive 25 days of monthly wages as advance payment in their villages before they travel to Delhi. The labor contract will collect five days wages as his commission.

12. The contract system referred here is a work contract where specific tasks of construction are subcontracted to firms outside the principal contractor. "Shanghai Institutes Contracting System at All Levels of Priority Projects," *Xinhua General News Service*, July 9, 1983.

13. The idea of residential bounding is suggested by Prasenjit Duara. I have found it a useful concept in the analysis of labor process in construction sites.

14. I have borrowed this phrase from Kohn 1939.

15. The official statistical reporting does not capture the presence of rural migrants in the construction sector or in any industrial activities in Delhi. For example the Directorate of Economic and Statistics uses two broad employment categories: main workers and marginal workers. See *Delhi Statistical Handbook* 2008. Similarly, the Na-

tional Sample Survey uses three categories: self-employed, casual workers, and workers. None of these categories identifies the rural migrants in construction. See *Employment and Unemployment Situation in Delhi*, NSS 61st Round, July 2004–June 2005.

16. See The Building and Other Construction Workers Welfare Cess Act, 1996 (Delhi: Commercial Law Publishers, 2010).

17. See The Building and Other Construction Workers (Regulation of Employment and Conditions of Services Act, 1996) (Delhi: Commercial Law Publishers, 2010).

18. See The Delhi Building and Other Construction Workers (Regulation of Employment and Conditions of Service) Rules, 2002 (Delhi: Universal Law Publishing, 2010).

19. Cited in "Construction Workers Alienated," *China Daily* (Beijing), July 9, 2007.

20. "One Year of My Blood" 2008.

21. Construction contractors are expected to follow the labor rates guidelines of the CPWD. The CPWD lists about 20 work descriptions, including skilled labor categories such as blacksmith, carpenter, mason, stone chiseler, painter, rock excavator, with slightly varying wage rates. Director General of CPWD, *Delhi Scheduled Rates 2014* (New Delhi, 2014).

22. I thank Biao Xiang for introducing me to this work at an early stage of research.

References

Banerjee, Biswajit. 1986. *Rural to Urban Migration and the Urban Labor Market: A Case Study of Delhi*. Delhi: Himalaya Publishing House.

Bergere, Marie-Claire. 2004. "Shanghai's Urban Development: A Remake?" In *Shanghai: Architecture and Urbanism in Modern China*, edited by Seng Kuan and Peter G. Rowe, 36–53. New York: Prestel.

———. 2009. *Shanghai: China's Gateway to Modernity*. Translated by Janet Lloyd. Stanford: Stanford University Press.

Breman, Jan. 1996. *Footloose Labor: Working in India's Informal Economy*. Cambridge: Cambridge University Press.

———. 2010. *Outcast Labour in Asia: Circulation and Informalization of the Workforce at the Bottom of the Economy*. Delhi: Oxford University Press.

Chan, Kam Win. 1994. "Urbanization and Rural Urban Migration in China since 1982." *Modern China* 20.3 (July): 243–81.

Chen, Yawei. 2007. *Shanghai Pudong: Urban Development in an Era of Global-Local Interaction*, Amsterdam: Delft University Press,.

Chesneaux, Jean. 1993. *The Chinese Labor Movement, 1919–1927*. Stanford: Stanford University Press.

Denison, Edward, and Guang Yu Ren. 2006. *Building Shanghai: The Story of China's Gateway*. Chichester, UK: John Wiley and Sons.

Gupta, Narayani. 2002. *Delhi between Two Empires, 1803–1931: Society, Government and Urban Growth*. Delhi: Oxford University Press.

Harilal, K. N. 1989. "Deskilling and Wage Differentials in Construction Industry." *Economic and Political Weekly* 24.24 (June 17): 1347–52.

Hewu, Qingying. 2007. "Tracing the Causes of Owed Wages in the Construction Industry." Translated from Chinese. *China Labor News*, September 4.

Johri, C. K, and S. M. Pandey. 1972. *Employment Relationships in the Building Industry: A Study in Delhi*. New Delhi: Shri Ram Centre for Industrial Relations and Human Resources.

Kang, Chao. 1968. *The Construction Industry in Communist China*. Edinburgh: Edinburgh University Press.

Kohn, Hans. 1939. " The Nature of Nationalism." *American Political Science Review* 33.6 (December): 1001–21.

Metcalf, Thomas R. 2002. *An Imperial Vision: Indian Architecture and Britain's Raj*. Delhi: Oxford University Press.

"'One Year of My Blood': Exploitation of Migrant Construction Workers in Beijing." 2008. *Human Rights Watch* 20.3C (March).

Perry, Elizabeth. 1993. *Shanghai on Strike: The Politics of Chinese Labor*. Stanford: Stanford University Press.

Pun, Ngai, and Chris Smith. 2007. "Putting Transnational Labor Processes in Place: The Dormitory Labor Regime in Post-Socialist China." *Work, Employment and Society* 21.1: 27–45

Pun, Ngai, Huilin Lu, and Huipeng Zhang. 2010. *Big Construction Site: Living Conditions of Migrant Construction Workers* (大工地：建筑业农民工的生 存 图景). Beijing: Peking University Press

Roberts, Kenneth D. 2002. "Rural Migrants in Urban China: Willing Workers, Invisible Residents." *Asia Pacific Business Review* 8.4: 141–58

Roy, Thirthankar. 2008. "Sardars, Jobbers, Kanganies: The Labor Contractor and Indian Economic History." *Modern Asian Studies* 42.5: 971–98

Sewa Bharat. 2006. *Socio-Economic Status of Construction Workers in Delhi—A Study*. Delhi: Sewa Bharat.

Sha, Kaixun, and Zhenjian Jiang. 2003. "Improving the Rural Laborer's Status in China's Construction Industry." *Building Research and Information* 31.6: 464–73.

Shanghai Municipal Statistical Bureau. 2011. *Shanghai Statistical Yearbook*. Beijing: China Statistical Press.

Shivakumar, M. S., Sheng Yap Kioe, and Karl E. Weber. 1996. "Recruitment and Employment Practices in Construction Industry: A Case Study of Bangalore." *Economic and Political Weekly* 26.8: M27–M40.

Singh, Khushwant. 2010. "My Father the Builder." In *Celebrating Delhi*, edited by Mala Dayal, 1–14. Delhi: Penguin Books India

Solinger, Dorothy. 1998. "Job Categories and Employment Channels among the 'Floating Population.'" In *Adjusting to Capitalism: Chinese Workers and the State*, edited by Greg O'Leary, 33–47. Armonk, NY: M. E. Sharpe.

State Council, Legislative Affairs Office. 1921. *Important Labor Laws of the People's Republic of China*. Peking: Foreign Languages Press.

Swider, Sarah. 2008. "Behind Great Walls: Mode of Employment among Migrant Construction Workers in China's Internal Labor Market." Ph.D. diss., University of Wisconsin-Madison.

————. 2011. "Permanent Temporariness in the Chinese Construction Industry." In *From Iron Rice Bowl to Informalization: Markets, Workers and the State in a Changing China*, edited by Sarosh Kuruvilla, Ching Kwan Lee, and Mary E. Gallagher, 138–54. New York: Cornell University Press.

Vaid. K. N., and Gurdial Singh. 1966. "Contract Labor in the Construction Industry: A Study in Rajasthan." *Indian Journal of Industrial Relations* 1.3: 306–37.

Van der Loop, Theo. 1996. *Industrial Dynamics and Fragmented Labor Markets: Construction Firms and Labor in India*. New Delhi: Sage Publication.

White, Lynn. 1998. *Unstately Power*. Vol. 1, *Local Causes of China's Economic Reforms*. Armonk, NY: M. E. Sharpe.

Wu, Fulong. 1990. "Place Promotion in Shanghai, PRC." *Cities* 17.5: 349–61.

Yan, Zhongmin, and Jianzhong Tan. 1990. "Areal Expansion of Urban Shanghai." *Geo-Journal* 21.1–2: 57–64.

Yuan, Victor, and Wong Xin. 1999. "Migrant Construction Teams in Beijing." In *Internal and International Migration: Chinese Perspectives*, edited by Frank N. Pieke and Hein Mallee, 103–18. Richmond, UK: Curzon Press.

Yuan Yue, Wang Xin, and Zhang Shaoli. 1997. "The Construction from Outside Beijing: A Case Study of Labor Contract Teams." *China Academic Journal Electronic Publishing House*. http://www.cnki.net 04/04/2014 (in Chinese).

Zhang, Rong Fang. 2008. "Analysis of the Labor Placement System in China." *Canadian Social Sciences* 4.2: 29–34.

Zhang, Y. 2000. "Shanghai in Transition: The Construction Industry in Shanghai's Local Economic Transition and Urban Redevelopment in the 1990s." Ph.D. diss., University of the West of England, Bristol, UK.

PART II

Legal Reform and Rights Protest

CHAPTER 3

Contesting the Right to Law

Courts and Constitutionalism in India and China

SANJAY RUPARELIA

Since the 1980s, the People's Republic of China has witnessed a massive concerted effort to introduce *fazhi* (rule by law), as set out in the 1982 Constitution.[1] A significant justification for the shift was the need to enhance "citizens' right to legal justice" (*gongmin de hefaquanyi*) (Lee 2010b, 50, 57). The Chinese Communist Party proceeded to unveil a series of legislation through the 1990s that proclaimed various rights of citizens, encompassing new procedures for civil affairs as well as laws to protect consumer rights. Indeed, by the end of the decade, the PRC had signed the International Covenant for Civil and Political Rights (ICCPR) and the International Covenant for Economic, Social and Cultural Rights (ICESCR), ratifying the latter several years later. Interestingly, the passage of these various laws coincided with a growing tide of social activism (*shehui huodongjia*) demanding civic rights and basic entitlements, ranging from subsistence and labor to property, work, and land, codified in the new legal regime (Lee and Hsing 2010, 2). A variety of actors, from "barefoot lawyers" in the countryside and public attorneys in the cities to "rights defense" (*weiquan*) activists, mobilized the law to press various claims (Alford 1995; Fu and Cullen 2008; Xing 2004). The meaning and ramifications of these laws, and aim and character of the campaigns and movements associated with their emergence, inspire much debate. Some observers perceive incipient demands for greater civil liberty and political freedom, heralding a demand for liberal capitalist democracy (Gilley 2004; Goldman 2005; Liu 2006; He 2012).

Others argue that rights claims frequently invoke traditional socioeconomic entitlements to livelihood vis-à-vis corrupt local administrations, manifesting a form of "rules consciousness," which buttresses the legitimacy of central political authorities and the regime as a whole (Pei 2006; Perry 2008; Ching 2008). In between lie observers that foresee how "rights talk" might unwittingly encourage a spiral of claims and new movement repertoires, unleashing counterhegemonic struggles (Zweig 2010; Gallagher 2005; O'Brien and Li 2006). Nevertheless, most scholars of China agree that the emergence of substantive legal reforms and rights-based struggles is a significant historical development.

Intriguingly, India has witnessed analogous developments since the 1980s, inaugurating a new era of greater judicial intervention and rights-based campaigns. Public-spirited lawyers, new civic organizations, and grassroots social movements began to invoke the law and the 1950 Constitution, pressing the courts to uphold civil liberties, address economic deprivations, and combat social exclusion (Kothari 1984; Katzenstein, Kothari, and Mehta 2001; Baviskar 2010). As in China, rights-based legal activism generates scholarly debate in India. Many celebrate social activists and activist judges for seeking to represent the interests of deprived social groups and to expand the status of socioeconomic rights (Baxi 1985; Mehta 2007; Sibal 2010). Others worry that such rights-based struggles, given the inconsistent jurisprudence and limited capacities of the apex judiciary since the 1990s, demand far too much effort and time for relatively meager results (Rajagopal 2007; Joshi 2009). And some fear that judicializing political life undermines the separation of powers and reduces the possibility of flexible democratic governance. Yet three decades of sociolegal activism has clearly expanded the legitimacy, character, and scope of rights-based claims in India.

What explains the growth of rights-based activism, particularly through appeals to the courts, law, and constitutionalism, in India and China over the last three decades? How are these various rights justified, conceptualized, and pursued by state actors and social forces in terms of their moral imaginaries, political strategies, and social repertoires? Why have many prominent rights-based struggles in India and China simultaneously demanded greater transparency, responsiveness, and accountability from the state? What are their successes and failures to date?

Finally, do these developments constitute a fundamental transformation in the meaning and practice of citizenship in India and China in a globalized neoliberal era, or does the trajectory of rights-based legal activism in each country reveal their lineages of state formation, economic modernization, and nation building?

This chapter addresses these questions. In broad strokes it analyzes how the repertoire of rights, constitutionalism, and the law—as a technique and site of contestation—have been used to secure as well as limit civic, political, and socioeconomic entitlements in India and China since the late 1970s. Many scholars have explored the striking nexus between prosperity, corruption, and inequality in both countries since the 1980s, which inaugurated an era of high economic growth. Rapid capital accumulation simultaneously lessened absolute material poverty and exacerbated social, sectoral, and spatial inequalities, albeit in varying degrees. To be sure, the pattern and dynamics of growth entrenched many forms of corruption, generating widespread attention to the relationship between legal rights, social welfare, and political accountability. Yet few studies compare the causes, character, and consequences of rights-based struggles to demand legal recognition, political change, and institutional reform in India and China over the last three decades.[2] The surprising contemporaneous timing of these developments warrants greater scrutiny.

Suffice to say, such a comparison may seem fanciful, even bizarre. The Republic of India is a federal parliamentary democracy, which selects its rulers through relatively free and fair elections based on universal suffrage. The 1950 Constitution entrenches a separation of powers and checks and balances between the legislature, executive, and judiciary. It recognizes political liberties and civic freedoms—of speech and expression, assembly, movement and association, and the right to hold property—as fundamental rights in Part III, relegating the social and economic rights enumerated under the Directive Principles of State Policy—covering livelihood, pay, work, education, and health—to the nonjusticiable and nonenforceable provisions codified in Part IV. Last, the Constitution empowers the Supreme Court of India to adjudicate general appeals between directive principles and fundamental rights, and to resolve interjurisdictional conflicts, disputes of interpretation, and civil law through

a variety of provisions. The Court has consistently exercised its prerogative, compelling parliament to introduce many amendments to circum-
vent its rulings since Independence.

In contrast, the PRC is a communist regime, where a hegemonic
party monopolizes formal power on the basis of democratic centralism,
limiting judicial independence and political enfranchisement. In principle, the National People's Congress (NPC) is the supreme organ of state
power. Formally, the Standing Committee of the NPC enjoys the authority to interpret, revise, and supervise the implementation of the Constitution, yet it reportedly never has (Kellogg 2009, 16–20). Moreover, the
Constitution contains no independent mechanism to redress rights violations or review lower-level legal documents, while the civil legal system
lacks the principle of precedence.[3] Indeed, the CCP does not envisage the
Constitution as having direct legal application. And the Supreme People's
Court (SPC) has historically renounced the power to review and apply
the basic law. Hence many scholars argue that legal rights in China represent the programmatic goals of the state apparatus, rather than limitations upon its power (Nathan 1986). Comparing the origins, trajectory
and consequences of rights-based legal activism in such different political-
constitutional regimes may well be a misguided endeavor.

These dissimilarities are plainly significant. Nonetheless, analyzing
rights-based legal activism in India and China offers a fascinating lens to
grasp the changing nature of citizenship and state-society relations in both
countries amid the progression of market-oriented reforms since the 1980s.
In particular, the evolution of rights, law, and constitutionalism in each
country over these years confirms *and* challenges the conventionally
assumed significance of macro-level regime differences as well as the capacities of their respective states. On the one hand, a convergent comparative approach illustrates the limits of analyzing India and China in
standard terms. First, the 1980s witnessed a massive proliferation of state-
level parties in Indian democracy, greatly expanding the electoral choices
available to its citizens. In contrast, post-Maoist China remained a one-
party authoritarian state, compelling its citizens to stake their demands
and redress their grievances either through traditional social institutions
or the evolving legal system, quashing every attempt to challenge the
supremacy of the CCP. Yet rights-based activism grew in both countries,
indeed far more in India, despite their contrasting political regimes.

Domestic factors played a role in each case. The relative unresponsiveness of electoral politics to the basic material needs of many subaltern groups, given the ascendance of demands for recognition and representation based on identities of caste, language, and religion, drove social activists to the courts in the world's largest democracy. Conversely, the desire for greater political contestation encouraged their counterparts in China to demand greater democratic reform. Yet generative causal mechanisms and global circulatory forces also shaped each trajectory. The common historical experience of arbitrary state power, albeit significantly different in scope, scale, and severity, compelled domestic actors in each country to reclaim the law in both countries beginning in the 1980s. And the rise of rights activism and judicial review, and of social mobilization and civil society, reflected the "new constitutionalism" (Gardbaum 2001; Hirschl 2004; Tushnet 2008) and "third wave" of democratization (O'Donnell and Schmitter 1986; Huntington 1991; Linz and Stepan 1996) that characterized the larger historical conjuncture of the late 1970s.

Second, notwithstanding its tremendous constitutional authority and growing institutional autonomy in the 1990s, the magisterial pronouncements and landmark rulings of the Indian Supreme Court (ISC) often had little immediate effect. The self-restraining character of much high jurisprudence, the decreasing organizational capacity of the Court to handle an ever growing backlog of cases, and the inconsistency of its rulings, reflecting the size, fluctuating composition and protocols of its collegium, exposed the limitations of rights-based legal activism in India. Put differently, the indirect symbolic effects of Supreme Court rulings frequently outweighed their direct material impact in many domains. Hence many rights activists in India progressively utilized the Court to dramatize public concerns, mobilize social coalitions, and put political pressure upon the legislature and executive to introduce administrative reform and policy change—a strategy pursued, ironically, by their counterparts in China.

On the other hand, however, the increasingly divergent impact and fate of rights-based activism in India and China since the turn of the century reaffirms the significance of their respective political regimes and state forms. Strikingly, new ruling dispensations emerged in each country in 2004, pledging to tackle mounting political corruption and socioeconomic inequalities. In India, the Congress Party–led United Progressive

Alliance (UPA) legislated a variety of landmark welfare acts and gover-nance reforms, pledging to uplift the *aam aadmi* (common man) through "inclusive growth." Significantly, many rights activists who had pressed the apex judiciary to secure basic socioeconomic entitlements since the 1980s played a major role in drafting these bills. In China, the new ad-ministration of Hu Jintao and Wen Jiabo similarly promised to create a "harmonious society" through a "scientific view of development" (see UNDP 2005). Yet the introduction of major welfare reforms during its tenure coincided with declining judicial autonomy, major constitutional reversals and intensifying political repression of many rights activists in the name of regime stability and social harmony. Significant counter-currents exist in both countries, admittedly. The Indian state has invoked draconian powers, sanctioned by the Constitution itself, to crush the re-surgent Naxalite movement in the so-called red corridor of the country over the last decade. The apex judiciary has intervened, to some extent, to curtail these excesses. Nonetheless the anti-Maoist campaign has under-scored the vulnerabilities of India's liberal democratic regime. Conversely, some rights-based struggles have won important victories in China over the last decade, helping to shape new procedures, regulations, and laws. Moreover, the coming to power of Narendra Modi and Xi Jinping since 2014, two avowed strongmen, has considerably narrowed the space of rights-based activism and political dissent in civil society and the judicial system in both countries. Yet the scale, scope, and severity of repression that has occurred under Xi in China is far greater than comparable trends in India thus far, given the constitutional authority of its apex judiciary and myriad opposition parties and successive electoral trials Modi has to face. These differences underscore why political regimes and state forms still matter.

Reclaiming the Constitution and Law since the Late 1970s

The CCP introduced significant legal reforms starting in the late 1970s. Indeed, few states have so rapidly transformed their apparatus of law (Liebman 2011, 167). Scholars typically date the beginning of reform to a speech given by Deng Xiaoping in 1978, which emphasized the need to establish a civil code and criminal code, regulations for procedure, and laws governing enterprises, labor, and foreign investment (Pei 2006, 66). In 1982, the party revised the Constitution, recognizing several new civic rights: to personal dignity, against false accusations, and to the sanctity of the home. It placed limits upon these new personal freedoms, stating that such "rights may not fringe upon the interests of the state, of society, of the collective, or upon the lawful freedoms and rights of others." Nonetheless, the new Constitution represented an attempt to routinize "socialist legality" (Baum 2011, 46–48), presaging broader changes. The same year the NPC introduced legislation stating that mediation, previously understood as the "primary method" for resolving disputes, should henceforth only be "emphasized" (Minzner 2011, 941). In 1986, the national legislature passed the General Principles of Civil Law, seeking to regulate economic transactions by stipulating clear relations between persons and property (Tong 1989). And in 1989, it approved the Administrative Litigation Law (ALL), allowing citizens to file private suits against state organs regarding "specific administrative acts" (*juti xingzheng xingwei*). Significantly, the new legislation exempted laws (*falu*), regulations (*fagui*), rules (*guizhang*), normative documents (*guifanxing wenjian*), and "reasonableness" (*heli xing*) of action from its jurisdiction. The statute also failed to specify substantive standards to assess administrative action (Mahboubi 2014, 142). Nonetheless, its passage capped a series of important legal reforms in state-society relations, which the regime publicized through mass education campaigns (Selden and Perry 2010, 8).

Three factors encouraged the CCP to legalize its claim to rule. First, many scholars argue that its top leadership, especially Deng Xiaoping, sought to prevent the arbitrary exercise of state power that had reached its zenith during the Cultural Revolution. According to some, Deng believed four major flaws beset the PRC: bureaucratization, unlimited tenure, extensive official privileges, and the overcentralization of power. Hence he believed that crafting a system of collective political leadership with a younger generation, and holding officials accountable through stiffer protocols and constitutional reform would strengthen party discipline and regime stability. In the mid-1980s, the CCP established a high-level task force led by Zhao Ziyang, charged to examine the value of administrative decentralization, legal reform, and greater inner-party democracy. It produced few specific measures. Moreover, although endorsed by the 13th party congress, divisions emerged. In particular, Deng resisted the proposal of creating greater checks and balances within the regime, preferring to improve state functioning through greater administrative streamlining (Pei 2006, 47–57). Nonetheless, these high-level debates revealed a growing consensus that formal political authority required a stronger legal foundation.

Second, the strategic incremental liberalization of the economy necessitated a framework "holding law in one hand and reforms in the other" (Ocko and Gilmartin 2009, 93). The reform process gradually dismantled traditional mechanisms of resource allocation and social exchange, notably the brigades and communes during the decollectivization of agriculture. Private investment required greater regulatory clarity. The weakening of work units and neighborhood associations and the issuance of temporary residence permits in the mid-1980s induced urban migration, creating the need for laws to handle disputes among relative strangers (Alford 1993, 58; Minzner 2011, 942).

Last, many figures in the central party apparatus saw legal reform as a political instrument to impose greater control, particularly in the far-flung peripheries. Liberal figures in the NPC supported the ALL on grounds that it would encourage greater political contestation. But conservatives in the State Council backed the law in order to secure greater local accountability (Nathan 1986; Mahboubi 2014, 142). Local political leaders often cracked down on popular resistance. Yet some authorities also periodically encouraged disgruntled segments to express their grievances concerning unpaid wages, land disputes, birth control policies, and other sources of contention. New legal channels simultaneously provided a safety valve for local social discontent and prevented a vertical "bifurcation" in the party apparatus (Selden and Perry 2010, 15).

That said, the introduction of new procedures, regulations, and laws encouraged many quarters of society to press for change too. Social activism (*shehui huodong*) had grown tremendously (Lee and Hsing 2010, 2). Some groups demanded sweeping political reforms. Radical elements of the short-lived Democracy Wall movement from 1978 to 1980, inspiring the student-led mobilizations that swept major cities in 1986–87, arguably sought wholesale regime change. The labor strike wave in 1980, in contrast, articulated class demands in classical Maoist terms (Perry 2010,

22). Others sought to utilize the evolving legal apparatus directly. Individual lawsuits, the vast majority seeking to resolve "historical" grievances involving personal injuries sustained during the late Maoist era, quickly soared (Minzner 2013, 2). In between lay incipient efforts to promote the "judicialization of the Constitution" (*xianfa sifahua*) (Kellogg 2009, 224–27). In 1985, the inaugural meeting of the China Law Society established a Constitutional Law Research Committee, which recommended setting up a "constitutional supervision committee" under the Supreme People's Court and a "constitutional litigation system" (ibid. 223). Several landmark interventions suggested its possible ramifications. In 1988, the Shanghai Intermediate People's Court protected the "right to reputation" of a claimant after her husband committed her to a psychiatric hospital on false grounds in the so-called *Democracy and Law* case (ibid. 228). The same year, the Supreme People's Court ruled against the constitutionality of a private labor contract, which sought to exempt an employer, Zhang Xuezhen, from responsibility for fatal injuries suffered by her employee, Zhang Guosheng. Significantly, the Court never specified *how* the contract violated either the law or the constitution (ibid. 229). Nonetheless, these early interventions captured the attention of many legal observers in China and abroad. Indeed, the import of the law and the courts arguably lay elsewhere. Following the suppression of the Tiananmen movement in 1989, many individuals filed suits against state institutions and the CCP, including prominent figures such as Wang Meng, Dai Qing, and Guo Luoji. Significantly, all of them invoked the Constitution or the recently drafted Civil Law to seek injunctions, compensation, and apologies for defamation, seizure of constitutionally protected information, and abuses of power. Reportedly, few of them expected to win their cases. Rather, they invoked the law to juxtapose the gap between ideals and reality marred by systemic political corruption, to rally sympathetic officials by evoking "notions of justice that ran deeply through the course of Chinese history" (Alford 1993, 46), and to proselytize issues among a wider public (ibid. 57–60). Put differently, the courts provided a "singular platform to broadcast a message" for these initial rights cases, shaping legal, political, and moral vocabularies of contestation (ibid. 62).

The catalyst, scope, and pace of high constitutional reform and rights-based legal mobilization took a very different form in India in the 1980s.[4]

Unlike in China, the Supreme Court and the proliferation of new social organizations and political formations that had emerged following the Emergency (1975–77) comprised its key agents. On the one hand, the Court began to draw an intimate link between the fundamental civil liberties and political rights in Part III of the Constitution vis-à-vis the nonenforceable social and economic goals in Part IV. Beginning with *Maneka Gandhi v. Union of India* in 1978, it started to reinterpret the meaning and ambit of Article 21, which recognized the "right to life" (Thiruvengadam 2012, 348). The apex judiciary also democratized the basis and potential of public interest litigation (PIL) by relaxing *locus standi*, appointing fact-finding and monitoring commissions, and issuing *continuing mandamus* to track cases through the lower courts, and performing administrative tasks in many instances. On the other, an upsurge of new social formations, ranging from civil rights activists and women's organizations to environmental groups, used public interest litigation to push the Indian Supreme Court in a progressive direction. Arguably, the two most important comprised the People's Union of Civil Liberties (PUCL) and People's Union for Democratic Rights (PUDR), whose ranks encompassed many eminent citizens from law, journalism, and academia such as V. M. Tarkunde, Arun Shourie, and Rajni Kothari. The emergence of these innovative nonparty organizations created new political coalitions and social alliances that served as "midwives to judicial activism" (Baxi 2006, 48). The first wave of public interest litigation involved civil liberties, such as the fundamental right to bail and legal aid in *Madhav Hayawadanrao Hoskot v. Maharashtra* (1978). The second phase emphasized basic socioeconomic entitlements of severely marginalized citizens, such as *P.U.D.R. v. Union of India* (1982), which sought to protect unorganized labor from exploitation. The third phase of progressive jurisprudence highlighted environmental concerns, such as the Supreme Court injunction in 1992 against construction to protect the Taj Mahal. Governance matters comprised a central dimension of high judicial activism and sociolegal rights mobilizations in India from the start, however, when judges asserted they had a "right to information" in the so-called first Judges case (1983) and when environmental activists claimed the same in the wake of the Bhopal disaster.[5]

Suffice to say, the ability of judges in India to challenge the executive and legislature on constitutional grounds was unimaginable in China. The scope and range of claims brought to the apex judiciary, moreover, was far more extensive in these years. Indeed, the Indian Supreme Court even began to *make* law under the authority of Article 141, issuing new rules for the adoption of children by foreigners in *Laxmi Kant Pandey v. Union of India & Anr.* (1986). Despite these obvious differences, however, the general motivation for engaging the courts and promoting the importance of constitutionalism was similar in both countries in the 1980s. The turn toward the law in India was a moment of "catharsis," seeking to grant the Court a "new historical basis of legitimation," following its abdication of responsibility during Emergency rule in the mid-1970s (Sathe 2002, 107). Although the violations of civil liberties and political rights during the Emergency were far smaller in scale and intensity than anything experienced during the Cultural Revolution, Indira Gandhi had justified authoritarian rule on grounds of radical social change. By pursuing coercive "developmental" measures, most notoriously slum clearance projects and compulsory sterilization programs, she unwittingly highlighted the significance of basic civil liberties and political rights for social well-being. Hence public interest litigation in India in the early 1980s focused on violations of fundamental civil liberties and perceived socioeconomic rights, and the intimate nexus between them. Authoritarian state practices encouraged a progressive legal turn.

Popularizing Rights, Law, and Constitutionalism Post-1991

The CCP renewed efforts to establish its political supremacy, the parameters of law, and the superiority of socialism over liberal bourgeois values in the aftermath of the Tiananmen incident. In 1991, the State Council released the First White Paper on Human Rights, which reiterated the priority of social and economic rights and privileged the "right to subsistence" (*shengcun quan*) (Trevaskes and Nesossi 2012). Nevertheless, the CCP pursued legal reform, empowering new social actors to press various claims against the state. In 1991, the NPC ratified the Civil Procedure Law, making court mediation voluntary and requiring courts to issue decisions in the absence of an agreement (Minzner 2011, 941). The state established some 270,000 arbitration committees at the enterprise level to channel labor disputes and demobilize worker discontent (Lee 2010a, 62). And the passage of the Consumer Protection Law in 1993 encouraged a boom in public interest litigation. Initially, the latter mostly catered to the concerns of the urban middle classes, suing companies for excessive telephone charges, fake goods, or poor safety measures for food products. Workers and peasants often took their everyday grievances to the streets, fomenting direct protests, which quadrupled in number over the decade.[6] But the possibilities of the Consumer Protection Law soon encouraged various advocates, such as Guo Jianmei, Zhou Litai, and Tong Lihua, to take advantage of public interest litigation on behalf of the rights of women, labor, and children, respectively (Fu and Cullen 2011, 1–6, 19–20). The rhetoric of equality inherent in the law, the relative accessibility, transparency, and predictability of the courts, and the lack of genuine alternative venues spurred these suits (ibid. 3–4). The passage of the Lawyers Law in 1996, which recognized attorneys as independent "legal practitioners providing legal services," and the expansion of legal-aid institutions, encouraged further recourse to the courts (Liebman 2011, 181). If anything, the CCP continued to emphasize the significance of law in matters of governance. The NPC had passed 255 laws and 84 pieces of legislation between 1979 and 2000 (Pei 2010, 46). In 1999, the NPC incorporated a provision, "Ruling the country *by* law" (*yifa zhiguo*), into Article 5 of the Constitution (Lee 2010b, 50).

The growing legalization of rule manifested itself in a variety of ways. The overall percentage of cases resolved by mediation fell substantially, from approximately 70 percent in the 1980s to 30 percent by the end of the 1990s (Minzner 2011, 943), while litigation skyrocketed (Pei 2010, 46). Suits filed under the ALL increased from less than 2000 in 1989 and roughly 35,000 in 1994 to greater than 90,000 by the end of the decade. A growing percentage of cases concerned claims against urban demolition and rural dispossession (Mahboubi 2014, 144–45). The shift toward public interest litigation seemed to reflect a deeper change among political dissidents too. Many began to champion workers' rights, the need to battle political corruption and environmental concerns on behalf of ordinary citizens during the 1990s.

Yet championing rights claims through the law had clear limits. Attempts to push the scope of change too far provoked a backlash. This was plain in the formal political realm. In 1997, a number of well-known dissidents who had been previously jailed, perceived a gradual political thaw.[7] The death of Deng Xiaoping, the signing of the ICCPR as well as the ICESCR by the PRC, and planned visits by U.S. president Bill Clinton and the UN high commissioner for human rights, Mary Robinson, intimated an opening. Hence they established a number of groups—such as Corruption Watch, Religion Watch, Peasant Watch, Labor Watch, and Law Relief Hotline—signaling their concerns. Invoking the rights and duties of citizenship and justice, they signaled their intention to establish a China Democratic Party (CDP) in 1998, calling for free multiparty elections and a separation of powers. Significantly, the leading members of the incipient party sought to register the latter with the authorities, underscoring the moderate aims and legal methods that characterized the dissident movement generally. But the 1982 Constitution, which enunciated a right to form parties, had no legal procedures for doing so. Moreover, many provincial authorities created new regulations that made it harder, such as requiring proof of funds and details of members and disallowing former political detainees from leading such organizations. Frustrated, more radical elements established party branches, which invited a harsh political crackdown, divided its leadership, and crushed the movement. The lesson was twofold. On the one hand, the formation of various "watch" groups signaled the increasing perceived nexus between corruption and inequality among important sections of Chinese society in the late 1990s, and the importance of legality and everyday civic surveillance to combat it. On the other, though, the extremely brief existence of the CDP underscored how the state could use the law in conjunction with brute coercive power to prevent the emergence of organized political opposition.

Ordinary citizens seeking to use the law to defend everyday interests also encountered a more constrained environment. Litigation had limits, as the trajectory and performance of the ALL revealed (Mahboubi 2014, 143–45). Public authorities issued new ancillary laws through the 1990s providing for greater state compensation, as well as administrative reconsideration, licensing and punishment. The remit of the ALL also expanded, by "not applying" (*bu shiyong*) norms at the level of rules and below that conflicted with higher law, and by deploying the general "abuse of authority" standard to assess "reasonableness." Indeed, the Supreme

People's Court discarded the "positive listing" of justiciable cases in 2000, maintaining only the "negative" list, enabling citizens to scrutinize where the law was silent. However, the number of suits filed under the ALL, of which approximately 20 percent earned a favorable ruling, leveled after 1998. Indeed, the percentage of suits withdrawn by litigants increased over time, from 30 to 60 percent. Local party officials intervened with greater frequency, making it difficult to secure legal representation, while courts increasingly refused to accept cases or enforce rulings. The trajectory of suits under the ALL mirrored the decline in litigation generally by the turn of the century, and a growing progovernment bias in judgments and settlements. Indeed, some observers claimed that many citizens increasingly saw the judiciary as corrupt (Pei 2006, 68, 71), in marked contrast to the relatively high public esteem of the Indian Supreme Court in the 1990s.

Still, a significant number of activists and lawyers in China retained faith in the law to catalyze political change. The passage of the Legislation Law in 2000, which stated that laws should conform to the Constitution, created the possibility that various subnational laws and regulations could be unconstitutional and thus subject to revision or nullification (Kellogg 2009, 220). The promise of constitutionalism became tantalizingly real with the *Qi Yuling* case in 2001, when the Supreme People's Court ruled that the claimant had had her right to education violated by the defendant, Chen Xiaoqi, who had stolen her school test scores to gain admission into a local business school in Shandong province a decade earlier. Significantly, the Court failed to pass any judgment on the law, claiming that it merely sought to fill a legal gap (ibid. 231–34). Nonetheless, the ruling encouraged many others to appeal to the courts. Perhaps the most successful was Sincerity/Yirenpeng (*gandan xiangzao*), a self-help group that brought a series of antidiscrimination suits on behalf of individuals who had lost their jobs and access to schooling because they had contracted hepatitis B, violating the right to equality codified in the Constitution. National media attention grew in 2003 with the *Zhang Xianzhu* case, brought by Professor Zhou Wei, who reportedly accepted it to establish the legitimacy of judicial review. Again, the Wuhu court refrained from passing judgment on the constitutionality of the relevant laws. But it pronounced that local authorities had failed to apply standards properly. The case galvanized social pressure, provoking a wave of suits, leading state authorities to revise government regulations in the matter (ibid. 237–46). But perhaps the most striking evidence of popular constitutional mobilization was the case of Sun Zhigang, a college student wrongfully apprehended and beaten to death in police custody under a law permitting the detention of rural migrants. His death caused an outcry, leading three young legal scholars, Yu Jiang, Teng Biao, and Xu Zhiyong, to issue a letter to the Standing Committee of the NPC requesting it to review the constitutionality of the so-called Custody and Repatriation measure:

> To the Standing Committee of the National People's Congress, As citizens of the People's Republic of China, we believe that the Measures for the Internment and Deportation of Urban Vagrants and Beggars which was enacted by the State Council on May 12, 1982 and has been since in force to this day goes against the Constitution and relevant laws. We hereby propose to you that the Standing Committee of the National People's Congress re-examine the Measures for the Internment and Deportation of Urban Vagrants and Beggars.[8]

The proposal drew immediate support from eminent legal scholars, including Jiang Ping, He Weifang, Sheng Hong, Shen Kui, Xiao Han, and He Haibo, who collectively issued another letter requesting a special investigation procedure. Shortly thereafter, the State Council released a new decree, Measures on Aid and Management for Urban Vagrants and Beggars, abolishing the 1982 regulation. Again, the NPC failed to issue a public opinion that clarified the rationale behind the pronouncement (Pils 2006, 1233–35), limiting the scope of genuine constitutional reasoning. Nonetheless, the "constitutionality review system letters" written by these intellectual activists set a rare precedent.

Indeed, the timing of their appeal converged with a broader social upsurge in 2003, which some commentators christened the "Year of Citizenship Rights." Workers claimed the "right to labor and subsistence," pensioners the "sacred right not to have to labor," migrants the right to form unions (Li 2010, 47). The passage of the 2003 Rural Land Contracting Law, which empowered contract holders as property owners and established a market for land use rights, triggered "protracted court battles" and social mobilization (Lee 2010b, 60). The commanding heights of the party seemed to recognize the legitimacy of these various struggles, ratifying the ICESCR. The failure of the PRC to endorse the ICCPR signaled its persistent deep suspicion of classic bourgeois rights. Yet the emergent trends of the late 1990s, which saw greater participation by unskilled workers in social protests and allowed various activists to mobilize public opinion across a far larger scale with greater speed through new media technologies, expanded the repertoire of social protest (Wright 2002, 919–21). The onset of the SARS epidemic, provoking widespread calls for the "right to be informed" in a manner that recalled similar demands by the environmental movement in India in the 1980s, and expectations that the impending administration of Hu Jintao and Wen Jiabao would be progressive, led many observers to hail the potential of constitutionalism (Pils 2006, 1226–29).

Developments in law and politics in India in the 1990s, once again, diverged in significant ways from China. If anything, the Supreme Court greatly enhanced its relative institutional autonomy, arguably becoming the most independent in the world. In 1993, in *Supreme Court Advocates on Record Association v. India,* the apex judiciary arrogated the final power of appointment and promotion regarding its own collegium as well as high courts unto itself, claiming that judicial independence was necessary to protect the rule of law and fundamental rights. It also declared in *S. R. Bommai v. India* that a state legislative assembly could not be dissolved without parliamentary assent, constraining the power of the executive branch. Yet the shifting composition and strategic abdication of the ruling political establishment in New Delhi, in government as well as parliament, also served to enhance the clout of the Court. The increasing electoral participation of historically subordinate groups, encouraging the proliferation of new state-based parties, engendered high electoral volatility and greater parliamentary fragmentation. Minority governments, often ruled by diverse multiparty coalitions, became the norm. Elected politicians, keen to "legitimize unpopular decisions that they did not have the courage to take and to avoid taking decisions that were likely to incur unpopularity," began to refer many sensitive questions to the Court (Sathe 2004, 247, 263, 272). Hence the latter sought to "force other institutions of governance to do what they are supposed to do by using new and powerful methods of investigation and monitoring . . . for illegality, unreasonableness and procedural lapses" (Dhavan 2000, 326, 333).

Despite the growing political clout of the Supreme Court, however, rights-based activism in India confronted various setbacks in the 1990s. First, public interest litigation was self-limiting. Perhaps most importantly, the Court accepted less than 2 percent of all writ petitions filed in the 1990s.[9] Constitutionally, it was perhaps the most accessible apex judiciary in the world. But rights activists had a hard time getting their cases heard. Moreover, in many cases regarding basic socioeconomic rights, the Supreme Court essentially highlighted the failure of the executive to meet its self-declared obligations to specific citizens who had suffered harm. Put differently, the Court enunciated a notion of "conditional social rights," limiting their scope (Khosla 2010, 739–56). Many of its interventions failed to address the real concerns of most disadvantaged citizens. The apex judiciary played a "limited" and "indirect" role in ensuring the most basic elements of public health and primary education, for instance, especially in rural areas and poorer regions.[10] Indeed, some observers claimed that many of its widely hailed rulings expressed a "jurisprudence of exasperation." The imprecise case law and a case-by-case approach of the Supreme Court often failed to define the content of the right being claimed, leaving much discretion and unpredictability (Rajamani and Sengupta 2010, 90; Shankar and Mehta 2008, 178).

Second, the apex judiciary failed to adopt a consistent orientation toward many socioeconomic rights claims. On the one hand, the Supreme Court issued its most assertive judgment ever in 1992, stipulating that "every child of this country has the right to free education until he completes the age of 14 years. . . . [T]he state cannot deprive the citizen of his right to education except in accordance with the procedure prescribed by law."[11] Yet the Supreme Court generally took a less progressive stance toward the provision of education and health after economic liberalization began (Shankar 2012, 166). A number of judgments effectively weakened the thrust of the 73rd and 74th amendments, which sought to empower local elected representatives over state bureaucrats (Mehta 2007, 80). Similarly, the Court issued several rulings curtailing the rights of labor, tenants and students (Sathe 2002, viii–ix). And by the late 1990s it had taken a series of controversial environmental decisions, which had enjoyed progressive jurisprudence. In 2000, the apex judiciary ruled against the Narmada Bachao Andolan, a grassroots anti-dam movement that sought to protect local tribal communities from being evicted along the

Narmada river, arguing: "The displacement of these people [local tribal communities] would undoubtedly disconnect them from their past, culture, custom and traditions, but then it becomes necessary to harvest a river for the larger good . . . [displacement] would not per se result in the violations of their fundamental or other rights."[12]

Finally, the increasing tendency to turn to the courts to resolve political disputes and social problems created a massive predicament. The staggering case overload facing the judiciary—20,000 in the Supreme Court and 3.2 million in the high courts by 2001—made routine justice extraordinarily hard (Shankar and Mehta 2008, 154 n. 32). "Due process," many lamented, "*is* the punishment" (Mehta 2007, 72). In short, the direct material effects of high judicial activism in India, especially with regard to basic socioeconomic provisions, often failed to live up to its vaunted rhetoric.

That said, social activists and activist judges in India began to express growing concern over a state "riddled with corruption . . . on a disturbingly excessive scale" (Dhavan 2000, 333), echoing public sentiments in China. On the one hand, the Supreme Court pressed the Central Bureau of Investigation to pursue officials suspected of illegal financial activities, including many senior politicians implicated in the *hawala* (informal money transfer) scandal in the mid-1990s (Rudolph and Rudolph 2001, 134–35). The Court also tried to reduce political interference in high criminal investigations concerning political officials, seeking to strengthen the autonomy of the CBI in *Vineet Narain v. Union of India* and conferring statutory power to the Central Vigilance Commissioner in the late 1990s, even issuing orders regarding processes of selection, transfer, and tenure regarding the latter (Rajamani and Sengupta 2010, 88). And in 2002 the Court declared, in *Union of India v. Association for Democratic Reforms,* that citizens had the right to know whether candidates standing for election had been implicated in past or pending criminal offences, what the assets and liabilities of their family and dependents were, and their educational qualifications (Sathe 2002, ix–xii).

On the other hand, many activist campaigns and grassroots organizations began to highlight the scourge of corruption too. The most notable was the Mazdoor Kisan Shakti Sanghathan (MKSS) from Rajasthan. The MKSS demanded access to local government records to see whether poor rural laborers had been paid their minimum wages in food relief projects as mandated by the state. Critically, its key slogan, *Hum janenge, hum jiyenge* ("If I know, I shall live"), evoked landmark Supreme Court rulings of the 1980s. The MKSS eventually collaborated with other civic organizations and grassroots movements to spearhead the National Campaign for the People's Right to Information (NCPRI). More broadly, sociolegal activists popularized the idiom of constitutionalism in their fight against the everyday corruption of the local state in order to secure the welfare of the poor. Their struggles ultimately led to a breakthrough. In 2001, the PUCL filed a writ petition, *P.U.C.L. v. India & Ors.,* detailing the widespread incidence of malnutrition and hunger in the country despite excess food stocks rotting away in public granaries. Acknowledging that the health of school-age children impinged directly upon the right to education, and recognizing the problem of unequal resource entitlements, the Court instructed every state government to introduce cooked midday meals in all government-related primary schools within six months (Chandhoke 2005, 10). The landmark decision helped to galvanize many activists to mobilize for change, catalyzing the Right to Food and Work Campaign, Campaign for Dignity and Survival, and several others. Although relatively few in number, these landmark rulings galvanized important sections of civil society in the 1990s, whose rights-based discourse slowly penetrated the wider political arena.

Reexamining the Nexus between Rights, Welfare, and Accountability in India since 2004

The formation of the United Progressive Alliance (UPA) in 2004, a large multiparty coalition led by the Congress, crystallized a new phase in India. Seeking inputs from leading rights activists during the campaign, its electoral manifesto pledged to legislate a "right to information" and "right to work" as well as other welfare measures. Upon capturing office, the dynastic leader of the party, Sonia Gandhi, established the National Advisory Council, inviting a distinguished group of intellectuals, activists, and former government servants to devise the promised welfare legislation. The UPA passed a series of landmark acts, seeking to enhance the civic rights, social opportunities, and economic security of its most disadvantaged citizens during its two consecutive terms in office (2004–9 and 2009–14). It introduced three flagship initiatives in 2005. The Right to Information Act (RTI) mandated all government agencies to release information regarding their activities to individual citizens upon request in a timely manner. The National Rural Employment Guarantee Act (NREGA) granted adult members of every rural household the right to demand 100 days of unskilled work at stipulated minimum wages from the state. And the National Rural Health Mission (NRHM) sought to expand basic services in the rural sector by amplifying public spending and encouraging social participation and governance reform in local institutions. The Scheduled Tribes and Other Traditional Forest Dwellers (Recognition of Forest Rights) Act (FRA), passed in 2006, empowered these communities the right to own traditionally cultivated land and to protect forests. In 2008, the government passed the Unorganized Workers' Social Security Act to cover informal labor (see chapter 5 by Dillon in this volume for greater analysis). And at the end of its first term, the UPA introduced the Right of Children to Free and Compulsory Education Act (RTE), which made the enrollment, attendance, and completion of schooling of every child between the age of six and 14 the obligation of the state. The second avatar of the UPA exposed substantive policy differences among its leadership, engendering considerable paralysis. The Right of Citizens for Time Bound Delivery of Goods and Services and Redressal of Their Grievances Bill, introduced in 2011, required all public authorities to publish citizens' charters detailing specific benefits and timelines regarding their delivery. The bill lapsed due to inadequate parliamentary support. A similar fate befell the LokPal Bill, 2011, which established a national public ombudsman with the power to investigate and prosecute cases of corruption implicating all public servants, including the executive. Nevertheless, the governing coalition eventually legislated further welfare reforms. In 2013, the UPA passed the National Food Security Bill, which entitled 50 and 75 percent of the urban and rural population respectively to highly subsidized food grain per month, as well as the Right to Fair Compensation and Transparency in Land Acquisition, Rehabilitation, and Resettlement Act (LARRA). The latter required the state to gain the consent of local communities whose land it sought to designate for compulsory acquisition, compensate landowners between two to four times extant market valuations, and provide for rehabilitation and resettlement to all persons whose livelihoods depend on designated land.

Three features distinguished the new welfare architecture erected by the UPA. First, much of it was enacted by Parliament, making these new entitlements legally enforceable rights. Second, many of them cited prior landmark rulings of the Supreme Court. The RTI Act, 2005, acknowledged several judicial precedents, beginning with *S. P. Gupta v. Union of India* in 1982 and culminating with *Association for Democratic Reforms v. Union of India* 20 years later. NREGA cited the 2001 writ petition filed by the PUCL. And the RTE Act invoked the famous 1992 ruling by the Court. The fact that it took almost two decades to enact the bill underscored the limits of high judicial activism. Nonetheless, its passage reflected the historic role played by the Court. Finally, perhaps the most distinctive feature of the new welfare regime was its effort to enhance political transparency, responsiveness and accountability. This was the overt purpose of the RTI. Yet a number of ostensibly "social" acts sought to achieve similar goals. The NREGA devolved the responsibility of planning, implementing, and monitoring work projects to the *gram sabha* (village assembly), enjoined the latter to disclose information proactively through wall writing, public boards, and new information systems, and authorized villagers to hold and participate in social audits of local public officials. Similarly, the LARRA obliged local state officials to consult affected village assemblies of their intent to acquire land, conduct a social impact assessment involving village assembly representatives and nongovernmental experts, and minimally gain the consent of 70 percent of project affected persons in order to proceed. Indeed, amongst other provisions, it also enjoined state governments to create a Land Acquisition, Rehabilitation, and Resettlement Authority, headed by High Court judges with the power to call witnesses, summon records and impose a schedule of penalties. Whether the preceding accountability mechanisms in these bills could sever the "structural mutuality between democratic clientelism and identity politics" (see the introduction by Duara and Perry to this volume) that in practice marred such welfare schemes preoccupied their architects and critics alike. Nonetheless, India's new welfare regime symbolized the cumulative struggles of three decades of rights-based legal activism.[13]

In China, similar moves took place. The new political dispensation under Hu Jintao and Wen Jiabao, which espoused the "primacy of social

justice" (Lee and Hsing 2010, 1), also unveiled a series of reforms to ameliorate the myriad socioeconomic inequalities that had grown rapidly since
the 1990s. The new policy framework had begun in 2002 with the establishment of the urban minimum income guarantee program. However,
like the UPA in India, the Hu-Wen administration focused its attention
toward the countryside. In 2003, it introduced the Rural Tax and Fee
Reform, abolishing many levies, and established the New Cooperative
Medical System (CMS), seeking to resurrect the provision of rural health
care that had gradually collapsed after agricultural decollectivization. The
Hu-Wen administration subsequently increased rural subsidies and eliminated the agricultural tax, seeking to address growing sectoral imbal-
ances. It also sought to improve social opportunities in the countryside,
launching the New Expense Guarantee System for Rural Education in
2006, Rural Minimum Standard Security Scheme in 2007, New Rural
Pension Scheme in 2009, and Social Insurance Law in 2010 (see chapter 5 by Dillon in this volume for greater analysis). The passage of these
new policies, despite their failure to reverse the terms of trade, had positive
effects. Net per capita rural incomes, even in poorer regions of the southwest, rose substantially. Rural land contracting assured a critical safety
net and enhanced the leverage of small peasants vis-à-vis large agribusi-
nesses. And rural public services for education and health improved, albeit insufficiently (Donaldson 2014).

The contemporaneous introduction and sectoral focus of the new
welfare regimes in India and China seem quite uncanny in retrospect.
The conjunction of distinct causal forces, domestic and international,
explains their macro-level convergence. First, by the late 1990s greater economic liberalization had enhanced socioeconomic disparities within
many regions of the world. The articulation of the Millennium Development Goals, promulgated by the United Nations in 2000, highlighted
the persistence of basic human deprivations in large expanses of the
global South. The formation of the World Social Forum in 2001 expanded the global justice movement, leading to calls for alternative developmental paradigms. And many external institutions that had spearheaded neoliberal policies, most notably the World Bank, began to
advocate more universal welfare measures in light of the negative social
consequences wrought by rapid structural adjustment (see the chapter by

Dillon in this book). Hence many states in Asia, Latin America, and Africa had devised new welfare regimes since the millennium.

Second, despite the different content, sequence, and impact of market-oriented reforms in each country, the specific developmental trajectories of India and China in the 1990s gradually compelled their respective political elites to address the nexus between prosperity, corruption, and inequality. The post-1992 reforms of the PRC transformed China into a global manufacturing powerhouse. Yet severe problems of urban eviction, rural dispossession, and environmental pollution generated fierce social protests. The official number of "mass group incidents"—likely an underestimate—rose tenfold from approximately 8,700 in 1993 to 87,000 in 2005 (Perry 2010, 11). The liberalization of trade and investment stimulated astonishingly high levels of industrial growth and urban migration in the booming coastal regions, but at the cost of escalating class inequalities within most provinces and between the poorer interior regions and the coast. And the increasing political clout of state-owned enterprises (SOEs) and pursuit of unbridled economic growth fostered a system of "crony capitalism," marred by "grand theft and insider looting" (Huang 2009, 285).

The inherently opaque context of corrupt transactions, and their frequently overt politicization, makes it hard to determine exact trends. Nonetheless, purportedly both the number of officials investigated for corruption and amount of money at stake expanded massively in China in the 1990s, reflecting the enormous increase in off-budget revenues gained through coercive land grabs as well as new exit options created by liberalized investment laws, fewer travel restrictions, and greater financial autonomy of state-owned enterprises. The devolution of power to the provinces, which had unleashed industrial growth through greater horizontal competition, produced a "decentralized predatory state" (Pei 2006, 132–56).

Similarly, the material well-being of many citizens in India improved tremendously by the turn of the century, albeit less dramatically and more narrowly than in China. Liberal economic reforms stimulated faster aggregate growth, structural diversification and technological change. The deregulation of trade, industry, and investment expanded the size and diversity of the corporate capitalist class, especially in information technology, biotechnology, and business outsourcing, creating global leaders in these fields (Chatterjee 2011, 23). But chronic human destitution in many regions and widening socioeconomic disparities provoked many counter-reactions. Significantly, the pattern of growth in India showed remarkable parallels with the trajectory in China, broadly conceived. The rate of absolute poverty reduction and wage growth, though still positive, substantially decelerated in the 1990s due to a more pro-urban reorientation (Bardhan 2010, 93–94). In addition, the devolution of power to the regions following economic liberalization unleashed dynamic interstate competition for scarce private investment and foreign capital, encouraging many chief ministers to style themselves as "chief economic officers." Yet the reforms inaugurated by New Delhi in 1991 failed to eradicate many older forms of corruption while generating new opportunities. On the one hand, the deregulation of industry, trade, and foreign exchange reduced the scope for bureaucratic manipulation. On the other, politicians and officials continued to accrue many rents post-liberalization as fixers of local development services, controllers of public sector employment and purveyors of national defense contracts (Jenkins 1999, 86–106).

Indeed, since many state-level governments in India introduced economic policy changes in the 1990s through stealth, ambiguity, and improvisation, new opportunities for graft and theft were fashioned by privatization, dereservation, and subcontracting. High electoral volatility and levels of anti-incumbency shortened political time horizons, which encouraged greater rent seeking. Compulsory land acquisition in India for industry, mining, and infrastructure was lesser in scale than in China. Nonetheless, it still generated considerable social resistance, not least given the historically poor record of compensation, rehabilitation, and resettlement of earlier governments (Bardhan 2010, 139–41). Hence these processes of accumulation by dispossession encouraged "protests of negotiation" in both countries, whose terms, tactics, and trajectories suggest broad developmental parallels despite obvious regime-level differences: of rural inhabitants seeking to claim state entitlements as equal citizens (see chapter 4 by Nair in this volume). Such developments helped to reignite a Maoist insurgency against the extraction of minerals and commodities in the severely neglected parts of the tribal-dominated hinterland, led by the so-called Naxalites, challenging the sovereignty of the state in almost a third of its districts by 2006. In short, the deepening "probusiness tilt" of the state and new economic opportunities in post-liberalization India expanded the scale of corruption in the 1990s (Kohli 2012, 55–56), mirroring the trajectory many perceived in China. The groundswell of demands for greater social equity in each country circa 2004 highlighted a serious failing with their patterns of growth, distribution, and reform.[14]

While the UPA integrated rights-based laws and innovative accountability reforms into the new welfare agenda in India, however, the Hu-Wen administration increasingly tried to sever their linkages in China. Indeed, it discouraged legal adjudication and rights-based activism, reimposing the socialist hierarchy between various rights. In 2004, the CCP advocated a return to "big mediation" (*da tiaojie*) to resolve complex disputes, especially land seizures and mass layoffs. Crucially, it recommended that such mediation should occur without the participation of the nominal parties to the dispute (Minzner 2011, 946). The new resolution aimed, ostensibly, to build "a harmonious society" (*hexie shehui*). Translated into practice, it sought to make sure that "small problems do not leave the village, large problems do not leave the township, and conflicts are not passed up to higher authorities" (ibid. 938). In addition, the CCP revised Article 33 of the Constitution, declaring "the state respects and protects human rights." Yet the same article emphasized the inseparability of rights and duties (*quanli yiwu xiang yizhi*). If anything, the new political order stressed the importance of protecting society, resurrecting a slogan previously touted by Deng: "Stability crushes everything else" (*wending yadao yiqie*). "Stability maintenance" (*weiwen*) and "social management" (*shehui guanli chuangxin*) framed policy henceforth (see Trevaskes and Nesossi 2012). Violent rural protests against punitive levies, invoking legal rights and social citizenship, compelled the state to introduce many of the major welfare reforms noted above. Yet the meaning, sequence, and techniques that characterized these mobilizations revealed the long-standing practice of rural peasants appealing to central authorities to curb predatory local officials, repertoires of protest that defined the revolutionary era and before (Perry 2010, 20).

Accordingly, the official bar association issued new rules in 2006, deterring lawyers from taking on "mass cases" (Minzner 2013, 5). The Supreme People's Court issued an opinion the following year, encouraging lower courts and judges to prefer mediation, especially in cases "involving large numbers of people" and "that are very sensitive, receiving significant social attention" (Minzner 2011, 945–48). Labor-related suits, following the passage of the Labor Contract Law and the global financial crisis in 2008, doubled in number (Lee 2010a, 75). But civil and political rights, and judicial independence, became increasingly scrutinized. In 2008, the CCP appointed a former provincial public security chief, Wang Shengjun, as the president of the Court. Wang proceeded to launch the "Three Supremes" campaign, instructing judges to adjudicate according to party interests, public opinion, and legal rules. Indeed, the Court proceeded to withdraw its landmark interpretation in the *Qi Yuling* case. Underlining the new political dispensation, the State Council charged the Court's vice president, Huang Songyou, who had played a key role in the famous 2001 ruling, with political corruption in Guangdong (Kellogg 2009). By 2010, the CCP had tied the promotion of mediation to the larger goal of creating a "harmonious society": "Mediation has priority, and trials should be fused with mediation" (*tiaojie youxian, tiaojie shenpan jiehe*). The percentage of cases mediated by the Supreme People's Court doubled from 31 percent in 2004 to 62 percent in 2009 (Minzner 2011, 943–44). Consolidating the shift, the NPC passed the Law on People's Mediation in 2010, which revised the previous target responsibility system. Apart from stipulating explicit quotas, the act issued clear sanctions and offered material incentives to judges to force judicial settlements (*qiangzhi tiaojie*) in cases involving labor disputes and domestic violence (ibid., 945, 949–64).

The turn to greater mediation concealed persistent variation in judicial practices. Progressive motivations and practical concerns also mattered. Local courts continued to experiment, fashioning new rules and procedures in ambiguous circumstances and where the law was silent. In some cases, they directly contravened higher existing norms, laws, and procedures (Liebman 2011, 169). More generally, many judges genuinely sought to enhance "justice for the people" (*sifa weimen*) by reducing court fees, emphasizing legal education through *pufa* campaigns, improving the accessibility of judges, and ensuring that problems were solved. Eventually, the surge in disputes, especially regarding labor, began to overwhelm the courts (Liebman 2014, 99). Hence genuine populist motives led the Supreme People's Court to proactively seek out leading experts to understand public opinion and push local courts to publicize filings, hear-ings, and decisions (Liebman 2011, 171, 178–83). Many judges sought to ensure that aggrieved litigants received some compensation, especially in cases involving medical negligence, disputes over labor and land, and corporate bankruptcy, even if no legal basis existed (Liebman 2014, 99–101). Such actions resonated with wider regime-level initiatives. The Second White Paper on Human Rights and the first National Human Rights Action Plan (2009–10), both issued by the State Council, maintained the priority of social and economic rights. In fact, they provided legitimacy to the new social welfare system by placing greater emphasis on redistributive rights, including new entitlements regarding labor, environment, and health (Trevaskes and Nesossi 2012). The leadership of the CCP genuinely believed that its legitimacy, especially in an era of rapid change, required greater emphasis upon political responsiveness rather than procedural litigation. In doing so, they merely invoked powerful legal traditions dating back to the revolutionary era, and even before (Liebman 2014, 103).

In addition, the return to mediation failed to halt litigation. Civil lawsuits almost doubled during the Hu-Wen era (ibid. 102). Public interest advocates continued to deploy the language of rights. The most successful organizations contested discrimination, such as Yirenpeng, mobilizing public support through new media strategies to pressure substantive policy changes. Similarly, public interest advocates with close ties to the state, such as Zhicheng, pursued evidence-based case research in order to convince sympathetic government officials to improve the law.[15] Despite losing the majority of cases, environmental lawyers made important strides through public lawsuits, winning approximately 30 percent according to the estimates of one prominent organization. Indeed, even when judges ruled against them due to insufficient material evidence or pressure from powerful commercial interests, higher political authorities often proceeded to shut down the accused companies and arrest complicit officials.[16] And many labor activists persisted with litigation in order to "showcase" "mistakes and holes" in the law.[17] They demanded collective bargaining rights within the existing union structure. On the one hand, pursuing claims through the courts produced decreasing returns. Lengthy arbitration processes sapped limited organizational resources and failed to alleviate the immediate socioeconomic vulnerabilities of workers. In any event, the lack of precedence in the legal system limited the impact of successful individual cases. On the other, insisting that workers had a right to bargain collectively "sounded more economical," whereas "freedom of association . . . sounded political."[18] And Maoist slogans of antiimperialist class struggle often accompanied such demands, making them harder to ignore. These mixed outcomes demonstrated the indirect responsiveness of state institutions to legitimate social grievances. Yet they underscored the limits of using the courts to politicize sensitive issues, especially regarding matters that had the potential to mobilize large numbers, and the unwillingness of authorities to accept such claims directly.

In India, despite the very real gains made regarding political transparency and social welfare under the UPA, the Indian rights movement confronted very sharp limits in other domains too. Prominent activists risked harassment, arrest, and imprisonment by the state for criticizing the war against the Maoist insurgency in the "red corridor" of the country. Perhaps the best known case involved Binayak Sen, the vice president of the PUCL, who had worked for decades to improve basic health services for poor Adivasi communities in Chhattisgarh. In 2007, the state government charged him with sedition for allegedly helping the Naxalites. Some rights activists managed to sway the apex judiciary to intervene in related matters. Several prominent intellectuals filed a writ petition to the Supreme Court to investigate the failure of the Chhattisgarh state government to implement the land and tribal forest rights of the Adivasis guaranteed by the Constitution and to improve basic public services of education and health. The petition also requested the Court to rule on the legality of the Salwa Judum, a vigilante militia of tribal youth organized by the state to fight the Naxalites. In 2011, the apex judiciary instructed the state government to disband the militia and implement basic constitutional guarantees, reprimanding the latter for engendering "a miasmic environment of dehumanization of youngsters of the deprived sections of the population, in which guns are given to them rather than books, to stand as guards, for the rapine, plunder and loot in our forests . . . [creating] a regime of gross violation of human rights . . . as [have] done Maoist/Naxalite extremists."[19] The ruling set an important precedent. Historically, the Supreme Court often deferred to the executive in national security matters on constitutional grounds. Special provisions enabled the government to legislate preventive detention measures for such purposes. But the practical effect of the ruling was short-lived:

the state government simply changed the name and formation of the militia. The persistence of repressive paramilitary operations against self-declared Naxalites and their alleged sympathizers since 2006 lays bare several illiberal constitutional provisions of the world's largest democracy.

But the scope for dissent in China, as the fate of many "rights defense lawyers" (*weiquan lushi*) over the last decade highlights, was far smaller. One of the most prominent organizations to emerge was the Sunshine Constitutionalism Social Science Research Center, later renamed Gongmeng/Open Constitution Initiative, established by Xu Zhiyong and Teng Biao shortly after their successful appeal against the custody and repatriation of rural migrants in 2003. Gongmeng sought to protect freedom of speech and of belief, and to oppose torture. In 2004, the organization supported a colleague, Gao Zhisheng, after he released an open letter requesting the regime to stop persecuting a Falun Gong adherent named Huang Wei, who had been accused of distributing propaganda and sentenced to reeducation through labor (*laojiaosuo*). The Buddhist-inspired religious movement had developed regional appeal, encompassing many distinct social groups, characteristics that suggested the possibility of an incipient counterhegemonic movement in the eyes of the CCP (Selden and Perry 2010, 23). Gao defended Huang, arguing that his arrest and detention, neither of which had been authorized by the Procuracy or the People's Court, had violated procedure as well as the Constitution.[20] The authorities released Huang on health grounds after six months. Yet they failed to declare his innocence. The Legislation Law and the ALL, under Article 12(2), only permitted "concrete [legal] challenges." Moreover, Article 5 of the Constitution required legal violations to be "investigated" only, not "invalidated." Gao proceeded to initiate a "relay hunger strike" with Zhao Xin and Hu Jia, invoking Mahatma Gandhi and Martin Luther King, to fashion a "congregation of passive fasters in new virtual public sphere" and raise the power of civil society. Their daring act, which challenged the Guiding Opinion of the All China Lawyers Association Regarding Handling Cases of a Mass Nature, instigated further repression.

The appeal of impact litigation, designed to court media support and the wider public in order to pressure state officials, inspired Gongmen to escalate its activities. The organization criticized the household registration system, *hukou*, for denying migrant workers' children equal access to education, and offered pro bono litigation. It demanded through non-violent protests that public officials should disclose their assets, reminiscent of similar transparency demands made by rights activists in India in the 1990s. And its leaders arranged, through online petitions and writing, signature and leaflet campaigns, "same-city dinner gatherings." The immediate focus of these activities was to promote justice in each case. Yet the larger strategic aim was "publicization"—to expose how the law actually operated (Pils 2006, 1242).

Strikingly, a key focus of Gongmen became the new Regulations of the People's Republic of China Open Government Information (OGI Regulations). Promulgated by the State Council, the new regulation sought to "safeguard the public's right to know, the right to participate, and the right to supervise" and to "help curb corruption at its source, largely reducing its occurrence."[21] Like the RTI in India,[22] the OGI allowed citizens to request "information recorded and preserved . . . by administrative agencies in the course of carrying out their duties" and receive it within 30 days, encouraging proactive disclosure by government agencies as well. Unlike the RTI, however, the OGI Regulations attached many restrictive conditions. Public authorities could only disclose information that was "fair," "accurate," "coordinated with other agencies," and which did not threaten "state security, public security, economic security, or social stability," including "important policy decisions on state affairs" and "economic and social development." Indeed, the regulations imposed potential administrative penalties for not establishing mechanisms protecting secrecy as well as criminal sanctions for "disclosing information that should not be disclosed." In short, the right to information encountered stiff obstacles in China, imposing tough penalties for perceived improprieties.

In 2009, local state authorities shut down Gongmeng for tax evasion, citing legal irregularities. The move portended a wider crackdown. The Beijing Number 1 Intermediate Court sentenced Liu Xiaobo, who co-drafted Charter '08, to 11 years in prison for inciting subversion. The members of Gongmeng regrouped, renaming themselves the New Citizens Movement. Yet many potential benefactors, sensing the risks, refrained from supporting their activities.[23] The open call for rule of law and constitutionalism, and for officials to disclose their assets publicly, had crossed a line.

Shortly after becoming general secretary of the CCP in late 2012, on the 30th anniversary of the 1982 Constitution, Xi Jinping publicly affirmed the rule of law. Prominent liberals such as Mao Yushi, He Weifang, and Dai Qing released an open letter, demanding an independent judiciary and democratic reforms. They subsequently appealed, less stridently, for China to ratify the ICCPR. In early 2013, the State Council appointed Zhou Qiang, a known legal reformer, as president of the Supreme People's Court (Minzner 2013, 10). Yet the regime suppressed further calls for constitutionalism, shutting down its liberal party magazine, *Yanhuang Chunqiu*, for publishing the following statement: "If we hold our constitution against our reality, we discover a huge gap between the constitution and the behavior of our government created by the system, the policies and laws currently in force. Our constitution is basically void." The *Southern Weekend*, releasing an editorial that invoked the "dream of constitutionalism," was similarly censored.[24] Shortly thereafter, the Xi administration released an announcement identifying the "Seven Don't Mentions": universal values, freedom of the press, civil society, civic rights, historical mistakes committed by the Communist Party, elite cronyism, and an independent judiciary.[25] Some NGO leaders privately supported the strategy, claiming that many individuals "are not ready for rights. . . . [T]hey don't understand the difference between procedures and outcomes. . . . [R]ule of law takes generations [to build]."[26] But more radical activists expressed scorn: "There is a popular joke: a villager lost his house, so he complained to the official in charge, land seizures are unconstitutional. But the official just laughed. 'The Constitution is not written for you, it is written for us!' In modernity, a dictator cannot say he is a dictator."[27]

At the Third Plenum in late 2013, the Xi administration pledged to strengthen the concept of "rule of law China" (Liebman 2014, 97). Among other measures, it promulgated decisions to abolish reeducation through labor on grounds that it violated the Constitution, to relax the one-child policy for parents with no siblings, and to improve the delivery of justice by instructing courts to abide by the revised Criminal Procedure Law, which prohibited torture. It also vowed to attack the specter of sleaze, theft, and bribery that engulfed the polity, to capture "tigers and flies," inaugurating the most sweeping anticorruption campaign since the revolution. The main instrument in the battle against venality, however, was the

Discipline Inspection Commission of the CCP, whose extensive powers of investigation and detention lacked any judicial oversight (ibid. 105). Conspicuously, prominent legal rights activists had championed each of the preceding measures for years, including the blind "barefoot lawyer" Chen Guangcheng, who captured international attention following his exile to the United States in 2012. But the authority to introduce such reforms, or even to demand them, was the prerogative of ruling political elites. In early 2014, despite being under house arrest, political authorities charged Xu Zhiyong with disturbing public order, sentencing him to four years in prison. His downfall foreshadowed a wider assault on rights activists in the run-up to the 25th anniversary of Tiananmen and beyond.

Concluding Remarks

A convergent comparison of rights-based activism in India and China since the late 1970s offers a number of insights—comparative, theoretical, and historical in nature. Such an approach suggests both the significance and irrelevance of classical political differences for understanding the relationship between the nation-state paradigms, logics of rights and citizenship, and the ramifications of globalization in each country across the three stylized temporalities informing this volume. First, despite manifest differences in their respective political regimes, the trajectory of rights-based activism in India and China underscores the significance of courts, law, and constitutionalism as sites, techniques, and discourses of contestation. Common experiences and convergent patterns played a role in both countries: the experience of arbitrary political excesses of the 1970s, desire of key state organs to recover political legitimacy and institutional stability in the 1980s, and the growing causal nexus between prosperity, corruption, and inequality since the 1990s. The broader shift to the new constitutionalist paradigm that emerged across the world in the 1970s, concomitant with the third wave of democratization, highlights the play of global circulatory forces.

That said, these macro-level convergences reflected the conjuncture of distinct causal factors rather than general underlying mechanisms, which typically produce constant effects and even uniform outcomes. The key state institution in India was the Supreme Court, seeking to restore its credibility after the Emergency. In contrast, the principal state organ in China was the all-powerful CCP, seeking to impose collective discipline and political stability. Political circumstances diverged significantly too. The 1980s witnessed growing electoral participation by historically subaltern groups and the proliferation of new state-based parties in India, undermining Congress dominance and inaugurating the demise of single-party majority governments in New Delhi after 1989. The Democracy Wall movement and growing student mobilizations revealed powerful aspirations for greater political liberalization in China. Yet their suppression, culminating in Tiananmen in 1989 and the dismantling of the CDP a decade later, underscores the difference. Similarly, accelerating market reform and global economic integration provided a major rationale for constitutional revision and legal development in China in the 1980s and 1990s, respectively.[28] In contrast, the distinguishing trait of high constitutionalism in India in the 1980s was progressive social litigation. The reorientation of the Supreme Court in the 1990s, when it began to question rights of labor, indigenous communities, and the environment, indicates some convergence with Chinese developments. Both countries witnessed considerable public interest litigation on behalf of relatively disadvantaged groups in these years, as political corruption, economic insecurity, and social dispossession mounted. Still, the imperatives of liberalization and globalization exerted less influence upon high judicial activism in India. These differences mattered.

Nonetheless, the trajectory of rights-based activism in India and China since 1980 reveals the limitations of using regime-level variables to explain some important developments. Many Chinese dissidents frequently argue that securing civil, political, and socioeconomic rights presumes the existence of representative democratic institutions. Yet the record of democracy in India since the 1980s, despite its deepening, demonstrates the importance of courts, law, and constitutionalism for recognizing, protecting, and expanding such rights.

Second, despite their massively differential powers, rights-based activism in India and China often encouraged their respective apex judiciaries to articulate "political jurisprudence." Again, the specific causes of this macro-level convergence differed significantly: the self-restrained

jurisprudence regarding socioeconomic rights, weak enforcement, and judicial overload of the Indian Supreme Court versus the conflicting internal values of the constitution and strict political limits imposed upon the
Supreme People's Court. Of course, the Indian Supreme Court expanded
its vast constitutional authority over the last 30 years, accumulating extraordinary powers in various domains. Indeed, if every legal question
eventually became political in China (Liebman 2014, 103), every political question in India usually became legal. Nevertheless, rights-based legal
activism produced ironically similar outcomes more often than theoretical explanations based on political regime typologies would suggest. The
use of the law and the courts as a "springboard" encouraged a rich inter-
active dialogue between activists, scholars, and judges in both countries,
helping to form new civic networks, generate media attention, and enhance
social awareness (Fu and Cullen 2011, 3, 15–16, 22–23). The indirect symbolic ramifications of landmark judicial rulings, either to implement the
law or reinterpret constitutional values, outweighed their direct material
impacts. Hence the measure of rights-based activism, its realization, has
often been administrative reform and policy change.

Third, the justification, conceptualization, and pursuit of rights-based
activism in India and China over the last 30 years reveal important
distinctions in terms of their moral imaginaries, political strategies, and
social repertoires. Significantly, the successes and failures of such campaigns reflect the lineage of their different political regimes, logics of
national citizenship and state formation, and patterns of development.
Many scholars argue that contemporary rights mobilizations in China frequently summon Maoist idioms of justice: peasants and workers claim
the "right to rebel" against corrupt local officials (Perry 2008, 45). "Protests of desperation" invoke violated social contracts. Of course, many aggrieved groups join "protests against discrimination," highlighting the
violation of new legal contracts (Lee 2010b). Yet these claims of citizenship and legal justice, skeptics argue, simultaneously bureaucratize and
depoliticize conflicts (Lee and Hsing 2010, 9–10). Suffice to say, the emergence of the *weiquan* movement in China over the last decade challenges
sweeping generalizations, given its explicit political embrace of modern
democratic constitutionalism. Moreover, a number of perspectives inspire
its myriad followers, from neoconservatives like Hayek and liberals such
as Berlin to figures such as Mahatma Gandhi and Martin Luther King.

Such a mélange of influences risks generating incoherence. And the arguments put forward by many rights lawyers sometimes imply that regime change will independently resolve basic class struggles. Still, the increasingly radical demands of the rights defense movement over the last decade clearly represented an attempt to *politicize* the rules of rule, leading to its hard suppression. In the absence of widespread economic crisis, a charismatic oppositional leader with a genuine counterhegemonic ideology and state collapse, however, the majority of rights-based mobilizations in contemporary China likely strengthens the authority of the current political regime (Perry 2010, 28).

In relative contrast, rights activism in India over the last three decades has largely sought to establish an alternative paradigm of social citizenship and democratic governance. The origins, identity, and character of these movements, to be sure, embodied older historic idioms too: *Adivasi* claims, Naxalite discourses, and Gandhian precepts. Nonetheless, the social activists and activist judges who spearheaded these campaigns since the late 1970s largely sought to exploit conceptual tensions in the 1950 Constitution, incorporating socioeconomic entitlements. They subsequently converted these legal victories into parliamentary legislation over the last decade by forging coalitions with sympathetic politicians. Moreover, many of these newly legislated rights deliberately seek to ameliorate socioeconomic inequalities by enhancing the transparency, responsiveness, and accountability of the state. Achieving the former in a neoliberal era, needless to say, demands more than simply ensuring the latter. It requires attacking the growing structural inequalities—which inspired the Maoist insurgency to reemerge in India over the last decade— that afflicts many Asian societies. Nonetheless, the fusion of new welfare entitlements and mechanisms to reduce official corruption tests many existing principles, rules, and methods of rule, *politicizing* the latter. The increasingly divergent impact and fate of rights-based activism in India and China since 2004 reaffirms the importance of regime differences and state forms.

The rise of two self-avowed strongmen in India and China since 2014, part of a wider global phenomenon since the 2008 financial crash, challenges this assessment to some degree. Programmatically, Narendra Modi and Xi Jinping espouse a number of common overarching aims: to lessen political corruption, pursue the next phase of economic modernization, and project national power in the evolving global order. Strategically, both leaders have centralized state power within their parties and offices to a degree unseen in recent decades, surrounding themselves with loyal disciples from their provincial bases in Gujarat and Zhejiang, producing respective cults of personality. Concomitantly, they have sought to narrow the scope for critical reporting, social activism, and political dissent in state and society, eroding the independence of institutions. By framing many of their actions in singular nationalist tropes, Xi and Modi have questioned the legitimacy of rival political views.

Nevertheless, to date the scale, scope, and severity of repression launched by Xi far exceeds analogous developments spearheaded by Modi. Beginning in 2013, the Xi administration began allowing charities and community service organizations to register themselves independently. Yet internal CCP documents claimed that efforts to promote civil society represented "an attempt to dismantle the party's social foundation . . . [and] a serious form of political opposition."[29] Mounting pressures faced by rights lawyers, independent media, and labor unions in the judicial system and public sphere underscored this highly restrictive interpretation of social autonomy. Journalists suspected of "picking quarrels and provoking troubles" online could lose their press cards and face criminal indictment.[30] The harsh crackdown on rights lawyers in the summer of 2015, facing charges ranging from "creating a disturbance" to "inciting subversion of state power," led to many covert detentions and forced public confessions. By early 2016, the central administration declared that media "must speak for the party's will" and "protect the party's authority," and that statements by retired party cadre must be consistent with the views of Xi as "core leader."[31] The subsequent passage in the spring of the Foreign Non-Governmental Organizations Management Law prohibited religious groups, required all projects receiving foreign support to be registered and enabled certain associations to be deemed "unwelcome," including such prominent organizations as the Ford Foundation and Asia Society.[32] By the summer the government began implementing an older regulation that made it illegal to hire reporters or publish content from anonymous sources, muzzling outlets such as Tencent, Sina, and Caijing that "[did] not adhere to correct guidance of public opinion," and introducing similar regulations to prevent lawyers from mobilizing online support for their clients.[33] The judicial system remained active, pushed by the government to address the growing problem of severely indebted companies, compelling judges to impose settlements based on the 2007 bankruptcy law. Yet it disproportionately targeted small and medium enterprises.[34] Indeed, despite the sweeping anticorruption campaign against many party officials, state administrators, and military personnel, which reportedly had ensnared up to 750,000 individuals associated with rival political factions, the vast majority received minor disciplinary warnings. Only roughly 5 percent were prosecuted for the highest penalties by the courts.[35] The high-level campaigns and mobilizational approach of Chinese party-state, which remains distinct from the legal-bureaucratic orientation of its Indian counterpart (see chapter 1 by Frazier in this volume), remains conceptually insightful. The concentration and personalization of power by the Xi administration, which increasingly seeks to delegitimize claims to rights-based constitutionalism and institutional autonomy in the judicial system and civil society, has deepened the fusion of power that formally defines China's underlying political regime.

The general orientation of the Modi government toward rights activists, civil society, and the higher judiciary in India bears a striking resemblance to these developments.[36] Since 2014, it has intensified the drive to control domestic NGOs supported by foreign donors and international NGOs, which had been initiated by the previous UPA administration. Disparaging such organizations as "monkey traders" that "[try] to pull Modi down" (Mody 2015), the Union government has either suspended or revoked the licenses of approximately 10,000 NGOs receiving funds under the Federal Contributions Regulation Act, 2010, roughly one-quarter of the total number active in India.[37] The failure of many social organizations to file annual statements as required by law was a valid concern. Yet labeling NGOs that campaigned against nuclear energy, genetically modified seeds, and extensive mining activities as "antidevelopment," "antinational," and having "subversive links" has stifled the activities of organizations from Greenpeace to the Ford Foundation. These moves intended to delegitimize social criticism and political dissent.

Similarly, the Modi government assailed many of the landmark social acts introduced by the UPA, which granted statutory rights to information, education, forests, employment, and land, for frustrating the pursuit of rapid industrialization. Many of these programs had suffered from relative neglect by their architects in the second UPA administration, sometimes even opposition. The need to generate decent employment and rising wages through greater structural diversification and faster economic growth was a legitimate concern too. By delaying the appointment of key officials overseeing the RTI, weakening prolabor provisions of and restricting funds for the NREGA, and seeking to undermine the social consent safeguards in the Land Acquisition and the Right to Resettlement and Rehabilitation Act (LARRA) through executive ordinance, however, the Modi government has sought to undermine civil liberties, political transparency, and social entitlements in the name of economic modernization.

Finally, pressures on rights activists and apex judges have grown. In the spring of 2015, Modi counseled the chief justices of the higher judiciary not to be swayed by "five-star activists," including prominent critics of the prime minister. He also lamented at the number of tribunals and backlog of cases in the system. Both were serious legal concerns. Yet the Modi government also introduced the 99th amendment, the National Judicial Appointments Commission (NJAC) Act, to wrest greater power over such matters to the executive branch. Again, the power of the Indian Supreme Court to appoint higher justices and its general institutional accountability was a genuine political concern that enjoyed growing support among many legal observers as well as rival parties. Yet the composition of the proposed high-level commission threatened to undermine judicial independence (Mehta 2015). In short, these attempts by the Modi government to curb the autonomy of rights activists, social organizations, and legal actors in the judicial system and civil society exhibit a striking convergence with developments under the Xi administration.

Yet divergences persist. The failure of the Modi government thus far to galvanize sufficient backing in parliament to amend the LARRA through legislation, and the fact that recent state-level elections have enabled opposition parties to damage the aura of the prime minister, underscores the differences. Indeed, the decision of the Supreme Court to strike down the 99th amendment on constitutional grounds and the generally favorable orders given by the courts to NGOs seeking to reinstate their regulatory status under the Foreign Contribution Regulation Act (FCRA) (Bhatnagar 2016), demonstrates the continuing salience of regime-level differences. The backlog in the courts, which the Modi government has exacerbated by blocking recommended judicial appointments (Sharma 2016), is growing worse. But the scope for rights, law, and constitutionalism in India, despite mounting threats, is still far greater than in China.

Notes

1. I wish to thank Prasenjit Duara and Elizabeth Perry for their probing questions and helpful suggestions on an earlier draft of this essay, and the Inter-Asia Program of the Social Science Research Council and India China Institute of the New School, which supported my fieldwork in India and China.

2. For comparative historical analysis, see Ocko and Gilmartin 2009.

3. I thank Arun Thiruvengadam for emphasizing this point to me.

4. I analyze the evolution of high judicial activism in India, and the role of rights-based social activists in PIL, in "A Semi-Progressive Juristocracy: The Unexpected Social Activism of the Indian Supreme Court" (under review). The following discussion of the Court, unless otherwise noted, summarizes the details and arguments of this paper.

5. Interview with leading social activists, Delhi.

6. See table 1.1 in Pei (2010, 37).

7. The following paragraph entirely relies on Wright 2002.

8. See "Sun Zhigang's death and reform of detention system." http://www.humanrights.cn/zt/magazine/20040200482694708.htm.

9. See Nicholas Robinson, "Hard to Reach," *Frontline*, February 12, 2010.

10. For details, see Shankar and Mehta 2008, 152–63.

11. *Miss Mohini Jain v. State of Karnataka & Ors.*, 1992. Quoted in Shankar and Mehta 2008, 151. A larger bench of five justices supported the ruling in a subsequent case, *Unni Krishnan, J. P. & Ors. etc. v. State of Andhra Pradesh & Ors.*, 1993 (1) SCC 645.

12. *Narmada Bachao Andolan v. Union of India and Ors.* (2000) 10 SCC 664. See Rajagopal 2007, 157–86.

13. Suffice to say, the performance of this new welfare regime varies tremendously, both in terms of distinct policy domains and state-level performance. I assess its record in forthcoming work.

14. As far as I know, little evidence suggests that either the Hu-Wen administration or the Sonia Gandhi–Manmohan Singh government had explicitly discussed their new welfare regimes or sought to imitate each other. A number of contacts and exchanges between rights-based organizations in India and China had reportedly occurred through the World Social Forum (WSF). I explore whether these interactions led to exchanges of ideas, strategies and tactics in forthcoming work.

15. Interview with a prominent legal activist, Beijing, June 9, 2014.

16. Interview with a prominent environmental lawyer, Beijing, June 10, 2014.

17. The following insights are based on interviews with prominent labor activists conducted in Hong Kong, January 20 and 23, 2015.

18. Ibid.

19. Quoted in Ramachandra Guha, "The Continuing Tragedy of the Adivasis," *The Hindu*, May 28, 2013.

20. The rest of the paragraph draws explicitly on Pils 2006, 1229–61.

21. The following discussion of the OGI Regulations summarizes Jamie P. Horsley, "China Adopts First Nationwide Open Government Information Regulations," May 9, 2007. http://www.freedominfo.org/2007/05/china-adopts-first-nationwide -open-government-information-regulations/.

22. It may not be a coincidence. Xu Zhiyong studied the RTI in India.

23. Interview with prominent legal activists, Beijing, June 8, 2014.

24. *Financial Times*, January 5–6, 2013.

25. See http://chinadigitaltimes.net/2013/05/sensitive-words-seven-say-nots-and-more/.

26. Interview with a prominent NGO official, Beijing, June 9, 2014.

27. Interview, Hong Kong, June 2, 2014.

28. I thank Liz Perry and Ho-Fung Hung for emphasizing this point to me.

29. *Financial Times*, July 28, 2016.

30. *New York Times*, February 22, 2016.

31. *New York Times*, February 16 and March 19, 2016.

32. *Financial Times*, April 29, 2016.

33. *New York Times*, July 5 and July 26, 2016; *Financial Times*, October 12, 2016.

34. *Financial Times*, June 23, 2016.

35. *Financial Times*, October 10, 2016; *New York Times*, November 20, 2016.

36. Unless noted, the following summary highlights developments I have explored in greater detail in Ruparelia 2015.

37. *Hindustan Times*, June 17, 2016.

References

Alford, William. 1993. "Double-Edged Swords Cut Both Ways: Law and Legitimacy in the People's Republic of China." *Daedalus* 122.2: 45–69.

———. 1995. "Tasseled Loafers to Barefoot Lawyers: Transformation and Tension in the World of Chinese Legal Workers." *China Quarterly* 141: 22–38.

Bardhan, Pranab. 2010. *Awakening Giants, Feet of Clay: Assessing the Economic Rise of China and India*. Princeton: Princeton University Press.

Baum, Richard. 2011. "The Road to Tiananmen: Chinese Politics in the 1980s." In *The Politics of China: Sixty Years of the People's Republic of China*, 3rd ed., edited by Roderick MacFarqhuar, 340–471. Cambridge: Cambridge University Press.

Baviskar, Amita. 2010. "Social Movements." In *The Oxford Companion to Politics in India*, edited by Niraja Gopal Jayal and Pratap Bhanu Mehta, 381–90. New Delhi: Oxford University Press.

Baxi, Upendra. 1985. "Taking Suffering Seriously: Social Action Litigation in the Supreme Court of India." *Third World Legal Studies* 4.6: 107–32.

————. 2006. "The (Im)Possibility of Constitutional Justice: Seismographic Notes on Indian Constitutionalism." In *India's Living Constitution: Ideas, Practices, Controversies*, edited by Zoya Hasan, E. Sridharan, and R. Sudarshan, 31–63. New Delhi: Permanent Black.

Bhatnagar, Gaurav Vivek. 2016. "Modi Regime Using FCRA to Block Aid Flow to Marginalized Communities, Say Activists." *The Wire*, November 6. https://thewire.in/42261/modi-regime-using-fcra-to-block-aid-flow-to-marginalised-communities-say-activists/.

Chandhoke, Neera. 2005. *Democracy and Well-Being in India*. Geneva: UNRISD, 2005.

Chatterjee, Partha. 2011. "Democracy and Economic Transformation in India." In *Understanding India's New Political Economy: A Great Transformation*, edited by Sanjay Ruparelia, Sanjay Reddy, John Harriss, and Stuart Corbridge, 17–34. New York: Routledge.

Ching, Kwan Lee. 2008. "Rights Activism in China." *Contexts* 7.3: 14–19.

Dhavan, Rajeev. 2000. "Judges and Indian Democracy: The Lesser Evil?" In *Transforming India: Social and Political Dynamics of Democracy*, edited by Francine R. Frankel, Zoya Hasan, Rajeev Bhargava, and Balveer Arora, 314–52. New Delhi: Oxford University Press.

Donaldson, John A. 2014. "Agricultural Development, Welfare and Livelihoods in Rural China: Prospects and Probabilities from Hu to Xi." Paper presented at the workshop "Changing Role of State in Asia II: Comparative Perspective," Asia Research Institute, National University of Singapore, May 30–31.

Fu, Hualing, and Cullen, Richard. 2008. "Weiquan (Rights Protection) Lawyering in an Authoritarian State: Building a Culture of Public-Interest Lawyering." *China Journal* 111 (59): 111–27.

————. 2011. "The Development of Public Interest Litigation in China." In *Public Interest Litigation in Asia*, edited by Po Jen Yap and Holning Lau, 9–34. New York: Routledge.

Gallagher, Mary. 2005. *Contagious Capitalism: Globalization and the Politics of Labor in China*. Princeton: Princeton University Press.

Gardbaum, Stephen. 2001. "The New Commonwealth Model of Constitutionalism." *American Journal of Comparative Law* 49.4: 707–60.

Gilley, Bruce. 2004. *China's Democratic Future*. New York: Columbia University Press.

Goldman, Merle. 2005. *From Comrade to Citizen: The Struggle for Political Rights in China*. Cambridge, MA: Harvard University Press.

He, Weifang. 2012. *In the Name of Justice: Striving for the Rule of Law in China*. Washington, DC: Brookings.

Hirschl, Ran. 2004. *Towards Juristocracy: The Origins and Consequences of the New Constitutionalism*. Cambridge, MA: Harvard University Press.

Huang, Yasheng. 2009. *Capitalism with Chinese Characteristics: Entrepreneurship and the State*. New York: Cambridge University Press.

Huntington, Samuel P. 1991. *The Third Wave: Democratization in the Late Twentieth Century*. Norman: University of Oklahoma Press.

Jenkins, Rob. 1999. *Democratic Politics and Economic Reform in India*. Cambridge: Cambridge University Press.

Joshi, Anuradha. 2009. "Do Rights Work? Law, Activism and the Employment Guarantee Scheme." *World Development* 38.4: 620–30.

Katzenstein, Mary, Smitu Kothari, and Uday Mehta. 2001. "Social Movement Politics in India: Institutions, Interests, and Identities." In *The Success of India's Democracy*, edited by Atul Kohli, 242–69. Cambridge: Cambridge University Press.

Kellogg, Thomas E. 2009. "Constitutionalism with Chinese Characteristics? Constitutional Development and Civil Litigation in China." *International Journal of Constitutional Law* 7.2: 215–46.

Khosla, Madhav. 2010. "Making Social Rights Conditional: Lessons from India." *International Journal of Constitutional Law* 8.4: 739–56.

Kohli, Atul. 2012. *Poverty amid Plenty in the New India*. New York: Cambridge University Press.

Kothari, Rajni. 1984. "The Non-Party Political Process." *Economic and Political Weekly* 19.5: 216–24.

Lee, Ching Kwan. 2010a. "Pathways of Labor Activism." In *Chinese Society: Change, Conflict and Resistance*, 3rd ed., edited by Elizabeth J. Perry and Mark Selden, 57–79. New York: Routledge.

———. 2010b. "Workers and the Quest for Citizenship." In *Reclaiming Chinese Society: The New Social Activism*, edited by You-Tien Hsing and Ching Kwan Lee, 42–63. New York: Routledge.

Lee, Ching Kwan, and You-Tien Hsing. 2010. "Social Activism in China: Agency and Possibility." In *Reclaiming Chinese Society: The New Social Activism*, edited by Ching Kwan Lee and You-Tien Hsing, 1–14. New York: Routledge.

Li, Lianjiang. 2010. "Rights Consciousness and Rules Consciousness in Contemporary China." *China Journal* 64: 47–68.

Liebman, Benjamin L. 2011. "A Return to Populist Legality? Historical Legacies and Legal Reform." In *Mao's Invisible Hand: The Political Foundations of Adaptive Governance in China*, edited by Sebastian Heilmann and Elizabeth J. Perry, 165–200. Cambridge, MA: Harvard University Press.

Liebman, Benjamin L. 2014. "Legal Reform: China's Law-Stability Paradox." *Daedalus* 143.2: 96–109.

Linz, Juan J., and Alfred Stepan. 1996. *Problems of Democratic Transition and Consolidation: Southern Europe, South America, and Post-Communist Europe*. Baltimore: Johns Hopkins University Press.

Liu, Xiaobo. 2006. "Reform in China: The Role of Civil Society." *Social Research* 73.1: 121–38.

Mahboubi, Neysun A. 2014. "Suing the Government in China." In *Democratization in China, Korea and Southeast Asia? Local and National Perspectives*, edited by Kate Xiao Zhou, Shelley Rigger and Lynn T. White III, 141–55. New York: Routledge.

Mehta, Pratap Bhanu. 2007. "The Rise of Judicial Sovereignty." *Journal of Democracy* 18.2: 70–83.

———. 2015. "A Lesser Evil." *Indian Express*, October 17.

Minzner, Carl. 2011. "China's Turn against the Law." *American Journal of Comparative Law*, 59.4: 934–84.

————. 2013. "China's Turn against the Law." *Human Rights Watch*. https://www.hrw
.org/news/2013/10/30/chinas-turn-against-law.

Mody, Anjali. 2015. "Why Narendra Modi Shouldn't Be Afraid of NGOs." *Scroll.in*,
February 26, 2016, https://scroll.in/article/804152/why-narendra-modi-shouldnt-be
-afraid-of-ngos.

Nathan, Andrew J. 1986. "Sources of Chinese Rights Thinking." In *Human Rights in
Contemporary China,* edited by R. Randle Edwards, Louis Henkin, and Andrew Nathan, 125–64. New York: Columbia University Press.

O'Brien, Kevin J., and Lianjiang Li. 2006. *Rightful Resistance in Rural China*. New York:
Cambridge University Press.

Ocko, Jonathan K., and David Gilmartin. 2009. "State, Sovereignty and the People: A
Comparison of the 'Rule Of Law' in China and India." *Journal of Asian Studies* 68.1:
55–100.

O'Donnell, Guillermo, and Philippe C. Schmitter. 1986. *Transitions from Authoritarian
Rule: Tentative Conclusions about Uncertain Democracies*. Baltimore: Johns Hopkins
University Press.

Pei, Minxin. 2006. *China's Trapped Transition: The Limits of Developmental Autocracy*.
Cambridge, MA: Harvard University Press.

————. 2010. "Rights and Resistance: The Changing Contexts of the Dissident Movement." In *Chinese Society: Change, Conflict and Resistance*, 3rd ed., edited by Elizabeth J. Perry and Mark Selden, 31–56. New York: Routledge.

Perry, Elizabeth J. 2008. "Chinese Conceptions of 'Rights.'" *Perspectives on Politics* 1:
37–50.

————. 2010. "Popular Protest: Playing by the Rules." In *China Today, China Tomor-
row: Domestic Politics, Economy, and Society*, edited by Joseph Fewsmith, 11–28. New
York: Rowman and Littlefield.

Pils, Eva. 2006. "Asking the Tiger for His Skin: Rights Activism in China." *Fordham
International Law Journal* 30.4: 1209–87.

Rajagopal, Balakrishnan. 2007. "Pro-Human Rights but Anti-Poor? A Critical Evaluation of the Indian Supreme Court from a Social Movement Perspective." *Human
Rights Review* 18.3: 157–86.

Rajamani, Lavanya, and Arghaya Sengupta. 2010. "The Supreme Court." In *The Oxford
Companion to Politics in India*, edited by N. G. Jayal and P. B. Mehta, 80–97. Oxford
University Press.

Rudolph, Lloyd I., and Susanne H. Rudolph. 2001. "Redoing the Constitutional Design: From an Interventionist to a Regulatory State." In *The Success of India's Democracy*, edited by Atul Kohli, 127–62. Cambridge: Cambridge University Press.

Ruparelia, Sanjay. 2015. "'Minimum Government, Maximum Governance': The Restructuring of Power in Modi's India." *South Asia: Journal of South Asian Studies* 38.4: 755–75.

Sathe, S. P. 2004. *Judicial Activism in India: Transgressing Borders and Enforcing Limits*.
2nd ed. New Delhi: Oxford University Press.

Selden, Mark, and Elizabeth J. Perry. 2010. "Introduction: Reform, Conflict and Resistance in Contemporary China." In *Chinese Society: Change, Conflict and Resistance*,
3rd ed., edited by Elizabeth J. Perry and Mark Selden, 1–30. New York: Routledge.

Shankar, Shylashri. 2012. *Scaling Justice: India's Supreme Court, Social Rights, and Civil Liberties*. Oxford: Oxford University Press.

Shankar, Shylashri, and Pratap Bhanu Mehta. 2008. "Courts and Socioeconomic Rights in India." In *Courting Social Justice: Judicial Enforcement of Social and Economic Rights in the Developing World*, edited by Varun Gauri and Daniel M. Brinks, 146–82. New York: Cambridge University Press.

Sharma, Nagendra. 2016. "Modi Government's Signal to Judiciary to Fall in Line Will Only Enhance Credibility of Legal System." *Firstpost*, August 17, http://www.firstpost.com/india/modi-govts-signals-to-judiciary-to-fall-in-line-will-only-enhance-credibility-of-legal-system-2961532.html.

Sibal, Amit. 2010. "From 'niti' to 'nyaya.'" *Seminar* 615: 28–34.

Thiruvengadam, Arun K. 2012. "Revisiting *The Role of the Judiciary in Plural Societies*: A Quarter-Century Retrospective on Public Interest Litigation in India and the Global South." In *Comparative Constitutionalism in South Asia*, edited by Sunil Khilnani, Vikram Raghavan, and Arun K. Thiruvengadam, 341–69. Oxford: Oxford University Press.

Tong, Rou. 1989. "The General Principles of Civil Law of the PRC: Its Birth, Characteristics and Role." Translated by Jonathan K. Ocko. *Law and Contemporary Problems* 52.2: 151–75. http://scholarship.law.duke.edu/cgi/viewcontent.cgi?article=3995&context=lcp.

Trevaskes, Susan, and Elisa Nesossi. 2012. "Human Rights." *The China Story*, August 7.

Tushnet, Mark. 2008. *Weak Courts, Strong Rights: Judicial Review and Social Welfare Rights in Comparative Constitutional Law*. Princeton: Princeton University Press.

United Nations Development Programme (UNDP). 2005. *China Human Development Report*. Beijing: UNDP.

Wright, Theresa. 2002. "The China Democracy Party and the Politics of Protest in the 1980s–1990s." *China Quarterly* 172: 906–26.

Xing, Ying. 2004. "Barefoot Lawyers and Rural Conflicts." In *Reclaiming Chinese Society: The New Social Activism*, edited by Ching Kwan Lee and You-Tien Hsing, 64–82. New York: Routledge.

Zweig, David. 2010. "To the Courts or to the Barricades?: Can New Political Institutions Manage Rural Conflict?" In *Chinese Society: Change, Conflict and Resistance*, 3rd ed., edited by Elizabeth J. Perry and Mark Selden, 123–47. New York: Routledge.

CHAPTER 4

State-Embedded Villages

Rural Protests and Rights Awareness in India and China

MANJUSHA NAIR

In 2006, Kevin O'Brien and Lianjiang Li proposed the term "rightful resistance" for the protests that took place in the Chinese countryside against the malfeasance of local state government authorities, specifically those at township and county levels. These protests were more limited in scope than social movements, and noisier, more public and consequential than everyday forms of resistance. They were "a form of popular contention that operates near the boundary of authorized channels, employs the rhetoric and commitments of the powerful to curb the exercise of power, hinges on locating and exploiting divisions within the state, and relies on mobilizing support from the wider public" (ibid. 2). O'Brien and Li pointed to many examples of such resistance in contemporary rural China: among them, the practices of increasingly citing laws when challenging malpractices of local government bodies, and of withholding tax payments because people had not received the fertilizer or fuel subsidies that the state was obliged to provide. In one of the poorest villages in Henan, a group of villagers, while contesting a fee, cited the state council regulations that had been distributed at the prefectural level, implying that they would take their case up to the prefecture if the county officials refused to abide by the rules (Cheng 1994, 11–12, cited in O'Brien and Li 2006).

Huaiyin Li distinguished "rightful" from "righteous" resistance as emerging from two different cultures of the peasants (2009, 51–52). The "righteous" actions of peasants derived from an ethics based on the necessity of providing for their own survival, which for them superseded all other ethical considerations; this position shaped their responses to authorities such as tax collectors and grain procurers and manifested itself in the underreporting of harvests, hiding of grain, bribing, and demanding food from the government. Notions of injustice and fairness rooted in a moral economy (Arnold 2001; Scott 1976; Thompson 1971) were behind this righteous resistance. In contrast, "rightful" resistance used the language of the official media; it challenged not the official policies but the grassroot public officials that abused their power, and used petitions and other officially sanctioned tactics, resorting to disruption when the occasion demanded it.

In neighboring India, the countryside witnessed protests of a different kind. These involved farmers' groups, independent from political affiliations, which mounted local, regional, and at times national protests against what were portrayed as breaches of promise by the state. To give a few examples, the farmers of Kandela, a small village in Jind district of Haryana, blocked a highway and abducted some policemen on May 29, 2000. The farmers were demanding free electricity and water, as promised by the Haryana state chief minister during the previous assembly elections. A majority of the farmers had not paid electricity bills since the early 1990s and believed that electricity charges were never reflected in the wholesale support prices of the wheat and paddy, the crops that they cultivated.[1] More recently, in February 2015, farmers from different parts of Tanjavur district in Tamil Nadu resisted attempts by primary agricultural cooperative societies to recover loans provided by the state. The farmer-leader claimed that at a time when farmers were seeking waiver of their crop loans following crop loss because of drought, pests, and floods between 2011 and 2014, the loan recovery proceedings against the farmers amounted to an assault on their livelihood. The farmers alleged that those who came to demand repayment of crop loans from the cooperative societies did not seem to be employees of the societies and that they behaved rudely toward women, who were disturbed by their behavior and attitude. The farmers said they wanted the central state to present a separate agricultural budget so that farmers could get a better deal. "We have been insisting on remunerative price for our produce and once that was achieved, we need not lean on other factors," they said.[2]

These two protests have characteristics of both rightful and righteous resistance. The rural inhabitants of Tanjavur district found it unjust to repay loans against crop failures, and resented the mistreatment of women by officials. They and the people of Kandela protested the alleged fixing of crop prices. Both groups had employed a means of resistance aimed at making rightful demands on the state, acting as if the rights granted them by the state had been violated: the state had failed to fulfill the promise of free electricity and water, in the one case, the farmers were pressured to repay loan provided by the state, in the other, and in both cases the state set crop prices to their disadvantage. As such, these protests were a contrast to the peasant revolts of the past, which were based on a moral economy of fairness and justice (Dhanagare 1973; Gough 1974). As Partha Chatterjee (2011, 229) points out, the state in the later cases was blamed for perceived inequalities in the distribution of benefits. As he claimed, the use of violence in these agitations had a far more calculative, almost utilitarian, logic, and a range of tactics was employed to elicit the right responses from officials, political leaders, and especially the media.

In this essay, I focus on a puzzle: in both India and China, residents of rural areas reveal a similar awareness of their state-granted rights through their protests, but they live under vastly different political systems. We see massive differences in state capacity and the level of democracy in the two nations, which would normally elicit a widely different understanding of citizen rights and protest mobilizations. Charles Tilly (2006) characterized India as a low-capacity democratic regime and China as a high-capacity nondemocratic regime; where state capacity is defined as control over the resources, population, and so forth, and democracy, by the existence of political rights and civil liberties. According to Tilly, in high-capacity nondemocratic regimes such as China, instead of organized social movements, protests take the form of less organized disruption against the exercise of arbitrary power. He claims that low-capacity democratic regimes such as India allow for a more organized, extensive repertoire of nonviolent and less disruptive protests. However, rural protests in India and China do not draw on spontaneous or insurgent or organized repertoires exclusively, but combinations of these. Do the protests in both nations perhaps point to an underlying similarity in state-society relations beyond what could be explained by regime types?

I would like to propose that the similarities in popular protests in India and China have emerged from the particular symbiotic state and rural society relations that have been put in place in those countries since the 1950s. These relations are anchored in world-historical processes, where the imperatives of national development in India and China in a world-capitalist economy have interacted with politics, whereby the Indian and Chinese states have sought from the vast body of rural population the legitimacy to govern. These processes have resulted in a governance structure where the nation-state has created village collectives and incorporated them, both as targets of development and sites of economic production. As a result, what has emerged is what we might call the "state-embeddedness" of these villages, in which rural residents depend on the state and view it as their direct protector, bringer of development, and granter of welfare. Rural society in India and China in the post-1950s era was characterized by such "state-embedded" villages. Of course this state-embeddedness differed in the two countries, due to the different will and capacities of these states to negotiate and impose changes in existing social organizations. Thus in India we see a system where the rural residents drew, and still draw, power from the promises of political parties in order to contend with the governing state. In China, rural residents draw power from a strong central state to fight what are perceived as local state abuses.

Partha Chatterjee has used the term "political society" to refer to the domain where the state interacts with the majority of its citizen-subjects in postcolonial democracies such as India (Chatterjee 2004; 2008; 2011). These postcolonial democracies were not direct participants in the history of the evolution of the institutions of modern capitalist democracy (2004, 31). While "civil society" is the defender of citizenship in modern capitalist democracies, in countries such as India, participation in civil society is restricted to only those few people who are culturally equipped to negotiate it. Most of the people in such democracies, however, are denied rights as citizens and are subjects of state governance through welfare policies; they must operate in the "political society." For Chatterjee, the majority of these populations negotiate with their governments via the political society: "All this makes the claims of people in political society a matter of constant political negotiation, and the results are never secure or permanent. Their entitlements, even when recognized, never quite become rights" (Chatterjee 2011, 222).

Chatterjee rightly characterizes the popular politics in India as falling between regular institutional politics and wild, insurgent resistance. However, his portrayal of what people regard as their entitlements strikes me as faulty. Contrary to what he implies, rural dwellers in India (and China) do have a more or less certain conception of rights that are due to them, and they know how to use the divisions within the institutionalized domains of politics to put pressure on the state to concede those rights.

State and Rural Society in India

The Indian state faced a peculiar dilemma regarding development, after gaining political independence in 1947. Progress in the 20th century was possible only if societal organization could be altered in fundamental ways to advance economic growth. A classic problem involved changing rural societies in such a way as to ease the transfer of surplus food grain from the countryside to the urban population of industrial workers. The state, however, lacked resources to invest in the rural society, to create such a surplus. Many of its resources were oriented to the new urban industrial centers, just as in China, and just as in other postcolonial states of the moment. But, unlike in China, this postcolonial democracy inherited a rural population with universal suffrage. The state was dependent on the electoral support of the rural elites and the masses. It was difficult for the state to reshape the structures or squeeze the peasantry, as China was able to do. How did the Indian state respond, then, to this dilemma of having to modernize despite a limited state capacity to alter the countryside, coupled with a paucity of economic resources to invest and the need to consistently maintain electoral support? What was the nature of the state and rural society relations that emerged from the state's interventions in the countryside in this institutional context? In this section, I argue that while the Indian state experimented with many ways to manage the countryside—some of which failed and some of which succeeded, or succeeded only in part—it did succeed in creating a peasantry that depended on the state, and it was persistent in ensuring that the regional and national states intervened on the peasants' behalf against market forces, as well as other social forces. The peasants drew on a symbolic subjecthood that they had won within the development paradigms of the modern Indian state, to resist the rationality of the market and draw concessions from the governing state.

Jawaharlal Nehru, the first Indian prime minister and architect of Indian planning, said, "During the past two centuries [of colonial domination], we became static and fell away from the current of human progress" (Zaidi and Zaidi 1981, 155). The modernization program that followed the colonial period represented Nehru's attempts to make the Indian nation "work back into the trajectory of its 'normal' development" (Chatterjee 1986, 138). The government prioritized industrial development over agricultural development. However, an agrarian surplus was still needed, to feed the growing urban population. For a developing economy such as India, making a huge investment in agriculture to increase productivity was beyond its means. Instead, the government opted for a variety of institutional reforms and development programs to alter the Indian villages fundamentally and boost productivity. As Akhil Gupta points out:

> The idea that industrial growth would spur the demand for agricultural goods, combined with a belief that institutional changes in the rural areas would release forces that would boost productivity, led the planners to emphasize changes such as land reform, the rebuilding of institutions of village governance on democratic principles (the Panchayat system), and tenancy reform, instead of direct investment in agricultural infrastructure and input or output subsidies. (1998, 49)

Along with these institutional changes came developmental schemes like the Community Development Program (CDP), whose aim was to help the villagers modernize themselves and practice better agriculture. All these attempts, unfortunately, failed, some of them badly, because the state had limited capacity to implement them in the face of existing structures and cultures. However, I argue that they, coupled with electoral democracy, succeeded in creating a middle peasantry that could push the boundaries of rights and entitlements that rural residents could claim from the state.

LAND REFORMS AND THE RISE
OF THE MIDDLE PEASANTRY

One example of the state's attempt to effect institutional change was the land reform drive. A series of changes were made in land ownership through five-year plans. These included the abolition of *zamindari*, a revenue collection system employed under the British, as well as the institution of a limit on the ownership of land, and the provision of land to the landless. The land reform drive was not successful—many land reform promises were not delivered—due to the lack of political will at the implementation stage, when faced with the power and capabilities of the existing social structures. Since implementation of land reform was under the jurisdiction of the regional states, there were wide variations in the impact across the regions. Legislations in most states provided loopholes to help the dominant landowners to avoid land loss by distributing land to kin and relatives (Jodhka 2012). In Hyderabad, in anticipation of land reform legislation, many landowners resorted to subdivision and transfer of lands to avoid any losses on account of the ceiling provisions. The majority of tenants were evicted from their lands before the enforcement of the reform laws, or had submitted land voluntarily (Nair 1961, 58–68). However, the reforms heralded a new era where the landlords were forced to redistribute land among kith and kin, to sell "surplus" land to the peasants, and to manage the cultivation and supervision of their farms by employing hired labor and farm servants (Ghosh and Nagaraj 1978).

The reforms were relatively successful in redistributing land in states such as Kerala and West Bengal, where there had been earlier, strong peasant movements, and where communist parties came to power through elections (Herring 1983). However, even there, landless laborers were still without land (Ghosh and Nagaraj 1978; Radhakrishnan 1980; Radhakrishnan 1981). There is evidence of occupation by tenants of land in some cases. In Uttar Pradesh, tenants could own the land they leased if they paid a 10-year tax in advance to compensate the landowners. And surprisingly, some tenants did become owners through this new statute (Wiser and Wiser 2000). In a village in Rajasthan, though the abolition of existing land rights was far from satisfactory, it made for considerable changes in land ownership patterns; most of the land had moved to small and medium landowners, and incidence of tenancy declined considerably (Chakravarti 1975, 97–98, cited in Jodhka 2012). In Rajasthan, some tenants who cultivated land where the landlords were absent were successful in acquiring possession of land (Rosin 1981).

The land reform efforts thus created a large section of small and medium farmers, the "middle peasantry," who were eager to invest personally in production, to educate themselves, and be socially mobile.

EMBEDDING VILLAGES IN THE STATE THROUGH DEVELOPMENTAL SCHEMES

Along with these attempts at institutional change, the Indian state also tried to remold the villages through developmental schemes. The rationale behind these schemes was to make villagers responsible for their own development by closely following state directives and thus firmly embedding village society in state institutions and structures. Not surprisingly, the Indian planners wanted to implement developmental schemes inspired by their visits to China between 1952 and 1955 (Gupta 1998, 49–50). Though these schemes were not very successful, given the lack of the ability of the state to persuade the population to change their ways of life, they succeeded in making the Indian villages targets of development; they also turned rural residents into recipients of state welfare, and the development blocks became the conduit through which the state allocated resources.

The Indian state first implemented the Community Development Program (CDP) in 1952 as part of its First Five Year Plan.[3] They were further developed in 1964, and covered all regions in India. The state intervened in every aspect of village life: it introduced better agricultural practices to boost production and improve the economic well-being of peasants; it provided social education on health and sanitation; it organized entertainment and religious activities; and it demonstrated a better way of living, among other innovations (Dube 1958).[4] Under the CDP, a developmental project was implemented in a unit that was divided into three blocks of 100 villages each; each block was divided into developmental blocks of five villages, headed by a one village-level worker. Each project unit was assigned a project executive officer, a development officer at the district level, and a development committee headed by the chief ministers at the provincial level. The village-level workers gave field demonstrations on better farming and living. At the national level, the Planning Commission functioned as the central committee for the CDP (Sinha 2008, 75). Information about the program was spread through slogans, short films before movies, radio talks, and so on. For his study of the CDP, Saurabh Dube asked a village-level worker to write a journal documenting his life in a village in Uttar Pradesh. This worker spent his day doing field demonstrations, addressing superstitions, reporting to a project officer, recruiting midwives, organizing religious meetings to talk to villagers, and so forth (Dube 1956).[5]

Nevertheless, the CDP was a failure. There was no improvement in agricultural production, nor was there any other evidence of social change. Villagers participated out of fear of the state and the immediate state agents, and many villagers were coerced into voluntary work, which they resented (Dube 1958; Wiser and Wiser 2000);[6] they never really understood the rationale behind the schemes (Dube 1958; Karunaratne 1976; Mellor et al. 1968; Wiser and Wiser 2000). Dube pointed out that unlike in China, India did not use mass education on the same scale to create change in the rural society.

Charlotte Wiser, who studied the Uttar Pradesh village Karimpur for an extended period of time described how the "block" became part of the everyday vocabulary:

> The purpose [of the development blocks] is to provide every village with an opportunity to produce more, to learn more, to earn more, to consume more, and—as a result—to enjoy better living. The word "block" is now a part of the village vocabulary, heard chiefly among members of the village council. It is the service arm of the government and the officers within it are to render whatever advice or help is needed. (Wiser and Wiser 2000, 199)

The developmental block became the quintessential unit of development (Mitra 1992, 83), and eventually became the focal point of brokerage politics and clientelism, where upper-caste landowners and political party members determined the allocation of resources, most often to their own kind and to those who could satisfy their demands (Corbridge et al. 2005; Robinson 1988; Sinha 2008). The rural population had to bribe or enter the favor of these "middlemen," or rely on a kind or corrupt bureaucrat to meet their survival needs, such as the distribution of subsidized seeds, credit, pesticides, food grains, development schemes, and so forth.

GREEN REVOLUTION AND FARMERS' POLITICS

The Indian state introduced the Green Revolution in the 1960s, the idea behind which was to advance agricultural production in a selected few sites through the intensive use of technology (Frankel 1971). This move by the Planning Commission was influenced by food scarcity induced by crop failure and a decline in food aid from the United States. The Green Revolution was a United States–sponsored initiative and the Rockefeller and Ford Foundations collaborated with Indian universities to disseminate technical know-how and enhance the production and quality of seeds and fertilizers.

The selective implementation of the new technology took place in 114 of the around 325 districts in India. In these districts the state intervened to increase production through the use of high-yielding varieties of seed, chemical fertilizers, irrigation, agricultural credit, knowledge, and expertise, and by buying the harvested product at high prices. Unlike the land reform drive and the CDP, which sought to change and aimed to benefit the rich and poor alike in the countryside, the Green Revolution was "selective" in its goals. It was a success in raising food grain production in India. Whether it benefited all or a few is still contested, with different results from different regions in India. In this section, I will show that the Green Revolution first, marketized the Indian rural society; second, it established the state as the mediator of these market relations; and third, it laid the groundwork for a new politics of the farmers aimed at state intervention in the form of subsidies and concessions.

The Green Revolution embedded Indian rural society in the market and commodified the social relations that were previously embedded in reciprocity and caste and class hierarchies. The farmers produced for the market using new seeds, fertilizers, and machines. In Karimpur village in Uttar Pradesh, for example, the villagers obtained their seed from a seed store, and the seeds were not vulnerable to adverse weather conditions (Wiser and Wiser 2000). The state agricultural university at Pantnagar was, meanwhile, producing seeds in its own research projects, and in fairs in the nearby township new techniques were displayed. Supplies of fertilizer increased, as well as the number of private wells. Farmers started to engage in cash crop production, raising peanuts, potatoes, soybeans, and so on, and were selling much of their agricultural produce to the warehouse in the nearby town. While rich farmers used their existing resources to invest in the new technology, small farmers were dependent on credit. In Tamil Nadu, it was shown that farmers, both rich and poor, depended on cash advances from paddy traders (Harriss 1987) and that small farmers became increasingly indebted over time. The rich farmers who reaped most of the benefits started selling land and investing agricultural surplus in urban areas. Landless laborers found opportunities to work outside their villages, as well as wage labor within the village (Frankel 1971; Wiser and Wiser 2000).

This embeddedness in the market also equally embedded the farmers in the central state, since state intervention and subsidies were essential, especially for the small and middle farmers, for them to survive and make gains in a market-driven society. As John Harriss points out:

> A many-stranded relationship has developed; it involves electricity supplies and tariffs—so vital for the success of cultivation; state intervention in paddy and groundnut markets—another major political issue has been that of the level of product prices through so-called "cooperative" shops; latterly a scheme for supplying "nutritional noon meals" to all children of school going age; and credit supplied through rural development programs. (1987, 241)

This subsidized agrarian capitalism (Lutringer 2010) mobilized a new interest-based politics, on the part of farmers, who demanded policies and programs from the central state that favored the rural over the urban. In Uttar Pradesh, the middle and rich peasantry from the middle and backward castes that benefited from the Green Revolution became a formidable political force under the agrarian political party Bharatiya Kranti Dal (Indian Revolutionary Party, BKD) under the leadership of Charan Singh, and was the core support group of the Janata Party in its victory in the national elections in 1977. Charan Singh, in the course of time, became the second prime minister of India who had not come from the Congress (Brass 1995; Hasan 1989). Akhil Gupta (1998) narrates how on Singh's 76th birthday in 1978, a farmers' rally was conducted in Delhi in which one million farmers took part. The speeches at the rally portrayed Indian villages as colonies of the cities (ibid. 79). Singh, once he became a cabinet minister, "cut the duty on chemical fertilizers by half, reduced taxes on agricultural equipment, and increased government expenditure on rural electrification and dairy farms" (Byres 1988, 163, quoted in Gupta 1998, 79).

In the new wave of agrarian populism that swept the countryside, "India versus Bharat," a political phrase coined by farmer-politician Sharad Joshi, became a catchword for all farmer politicians to denote and differentiate the urban, developed, "modern," state-favored geographies of the nation from the rural, less developed, less-cared-about geographies, who demanded to be subjects of development (Brass 1995; Gupta 1998; Jaffrelot 2003; Varshney 1998). Strong farmers' movements emerged in the 1980s in states that benefited from the Green Revolution, among them the states of Maharashtra, Tamil Nadu, Karnataka, Punjab, Gujarat, and Uttar Pradesh (Brass 1994; Varshney 1998). Through the Bharatiya Kisan Union (BKU), middle farmers in Uttar Pradesh attempted to influence state regulation of agricultural markets, obtaining increased input subsidies and better procurement prices for their produce, and thus an increase in the rates of return and profitability of their farming activity (Lutringer 2010). The BKU was militant in its farmer activism: farmers refused to pay electricity charges and other fees, blocked roads and railway lines, blockaded villages from entry by outsiders, and held officials hostage (Lutringer 2010; Gupta 1998). Akhil Gupta narrates an incident when BKU members "rescued" arrested members from police custody, closed government wheat purchase centers if they considered the purchase price too low, stripped a police officer, and held a district official captive (Gupta 1998, 81). The BKU jointly agitated with farmers' organizations from other states such as the Karnataka Rajya Raitha Sangha (KRRS) in the 1980s and 1990s against the General Agreement on Tariffs and Trade (GATT), and multinational seed companies. The leader of the Shetkari Sanghatana (farmers' organization), Sharad Joshi, formed the Inter-State Co-ordination Committee of National Farmers composed of organizations from 14 states and led agitations for better prices of agricultural produce for the liquidation of rural debts, and against increases in electricity tariffs and state dumping of agricultural surpluses in domestic markets, which would lower prices. M. D. Nanjundaswamy, the leader of the KRRS, led agitations against the Monsanto seed company and a Kentucky Fried Chicken (KFC) outlet in Bangalore.

My account shows the emergence of a rural peasantry in India that demands that state, regional, and national administrations intervene on its behalf in the market, whether to reduce electricity charges, raise agricultural procurement prices, or continue giving subsidies. We see that while the land reforms resulted in the emergence of peasants with smaller holdings, the Community Development Program subjected these peasants to state development programs. Through the Green Revolution, these peasants became small agrarian capitalists subsidized by the state. Their resulting dependence on the state for better prices and better subsidies created the farmer politicians and farmers movements that fostered the ideology of agrarian populism and the interests of a capitalist movement. What we have now are farmers using organized means of dissent in the street to instill pressure on the state to concede demands that they perceive as just.

State and Rural Society in China

Examining the nature of peasant protests in contemporary China, Alvin So has argued that two decades of neoliberal programs have led to the formation of a split state, divided between a "benign" center and a "predatory" local apparatus (So 2007). Fiscal and administrative decentralization provided autonomy to local state agents such as the townships to make economic decisions, develop rural industries, and lure investment (Sinha 2005). This freedom, however, coupled with the state's inability to draw revenue directly from the villages after agricultural taxes were

abolished, is what gave rise to "the predatory state" (So 2009). Because
the abolition of agricultural taxes reduced the revenue of the townships
(Oi and Zhou 2007) they began to engage in corrupt practices such as
clandestine land dealings, bribery, and corruption to raise revenue (O'Brien
2009). If economic reform provided the means to develop the townships,
as well as providing incentives for corruption, it also gave the rural population some political freedom: decollectivization and the decentralization of political power in villages through the introduction of the organic
law village committees in 1987 gave Chinese rural residents right to govern their villages and hold free village elections (Perry and Goldman
2007). Quite naturally, the villagers, mounted protests, targeting the local state authorities and citing the central government regulations that
entitled them to rights that enabled them to challenge the local predatory state.

   This split between the central and the local apparatus is not however
the result only of neoliberal invention. Before these innovations, there had
been a symbiotic relation between Chinese peasants and the state,
which must have been at least partially behind the peasants' ability to
collectively mount protests. Even in the time of the emperors, ordinary
subjects were able to challenge power centers by questioning the "mandate of heaven," in the Mencian doctrine, and foment the popular uprisings that have characterized Chinese history (Perry 2001; 2008). Hung
(2011) argues that the contemporary forms of popular claim-making in
China have strong resemblances to historical forms of popular protests,
and he traces them to distinct trajectories of Chinese modernity. He
suggests that such repertoires have their origins in China's own early
modernity in the mid-Qing period, which embodied patterns of com-
mercialization, state centralization, and ideological developments that
were quite distinct from the Western trajectory (ibid.). Is the massive
popular protest against local authorities that we see happening in the
20th century simply the return of such traditional resistance to repression then? In this section, I argue to the contrary. I suggest that the split
between the local and central state, and the ability of the rural dwellers
to draw on rights granted by central state in their contentions, also has
strong roots in changes initiated by the communist state after the
1950s.

THE RURAL-URBAN DIVIDE

A review of state policies in China after the 1950s unmasks a familiar contradiction between accumulation and legitimacy: the Chinese state that was eager and impatient to industrialize had to squeeze the peasantry; it was an economic and, more important, an ideological imperative. However, there was also a political and practical imperative to maintain the legitimacy of a state that came to power through a peasant revolution. It could not neglect the peasant population entirely and had to provide for its welfare, while almost all the state's resources were diverted to urban industrial growth. Finally, there was the need of the time to "develop" and modernize peasant lives to befit the needs of material progress.

Though the communist state came into existence through peasant support and to champion the well-being of the peasants, the state in its modernization drive had to subordinate rural society to serve urban society. During the Communist Revolution in 1949, many peasants, tired of poverty, banditry, tax collectors' exactions, transgressions of the Kuomintang, and Japanese invaders, supported the communists (Chan, Madsen, and Unger 2009, 16). Even those peasants who were ardent supporters of the communists had little idea of the changes that were to follow after the establishment of the new communist state. They were, rather, passive recipients of the radical reforms in the countryside that were put in place without negotiations. The state made its presence felt immediately after the revolution through the introduction of land reforms. The communist state economic policy was aimed at pressuring the peasantry to create agricultural surpluses, and land redistribution had the instrumental objective of making reorganization of agricultural production possible. But these objectives came at a terrible cost. As Barrington Moore (1966) observed, "The peasants provided the 'dynamite' that smashed the old order. The tragedy of the peasant revolution is that it ushered in a supposedly inevitable phase of history—a ruthless terror in which the peasantry would cease to exist" (227). To quote Mobo Gao (1999), who was from a poor peasant family of a village in Jiangxi province—the name of which he bears as his surname—peasants in the Mao era had little free education or medical care, and had to pay taxes and sell grain to the state at a government-controlled price. Between 1952 and 1979, with agricultural taxes and the differential pricing of agricultural and industrial goods, the state extracted a total of 600 billion yuan from the peasantry. If we subtract government investment in agriculture, the total that the state extracted from the peasants was 434 billion yuan, or 24 percent of the total gross national product, solely from the agricultural sector in that period. In contrast, urban citizens enjoyed such benefits of the revolution as free education, free medical care, housing at a nominal rent, assured lifetime employment, and subsidized food supply. The *hukou*, the household registration system, determined the place of residence of a person according to the registration of her family, maintained the strict urban and rural residential divide, and ensured that the peasants were put in their place, which was the village in which they were born.

COLLECTIVIZATION AND ORIGINS
OF A VILLAGE COMMUNITY

Gregory Ruf (1998) has argued that it was the new style of management of rural China that was instituted after the revolution, by administrative villages, that brought about the contemporary village communities in China; they were rarely precommunist identities. Based on his anthropological research in Sichuan province, Ruf argues that families, dispersed across the countryside or hillsides, either alone or in clusters, perceived their communities in terms of exchange relations mediated through various agencies, whether earth gods, ancestral or religious associations, rotating credit societies, reciprocal labor groups, or marketing partners. Collectivization, household registration, and redistributive accounting created a new collectivity: the village as "a community of exchange, mediating between resident families and state authorities, between farmers and townspeople, between cadres and kin" (ibid. 71–72). In what follows, I examine the wave of collectivization that swept across China till the onslaught of the great famine between 1959 and 1961 and show that, through collectivization, a new identity was established for rural residents, in which they were producing directly for the state and were incorporated into governance as subjects of the state.

In China, to correct the small, inefficient size of peasant holdings and to uphold a socialist ideology, collectivization of farms started in 1952. Initially, the villages were organized into collectives on a cooperative basis. These small cooperatives were successful because the villagers could see the return for their input in terms of land, labor, and tools. Huaiyin Li (2009) has shown from the experience of his own village in Jiangsu province that since these village collectives were an extension of kinship and neighborhood ties, villagers trusted one another. In China overall, collectivization through cooperative efforts raised agricultural output by 27.8 percent, a result achieved without much peasant resistance (Lin 1990). However, the state became ambitious, and in its impulse to modernize quickly, it embarked on large-scale collectivization that had disastrous consequences in the countryside due to the speed and scale of the changes involved. In the urge to create huge grain surpluses while following the socialist ideal, large-scale communization of life and production began. The process of communization that started in Henan province in 1958, was completed in two months all over China and a total of 23,384 communes came into being, involving 112,174,651 households (Li 2009, 82). Villages metamorphosed into production teams, under bigger production brigades, which were part of even bigger production communes. Production brigades appointed production team leaders and accountants, enforced levies to raise funds for education and health, collected taxes, and implemented state policies (Gao 1999). Villagers were sent off to work in infrastructural projects to participate in the Great Leap Forward. To break the boundaries of localities and speed up work, the labor process was militarized and families were intentionally separated (Li 2009, 85).

The large-scale collectivization was a failure and was revoked after the famine that befell the country between 1959 and 1961. The weather conditions had been poor, and the production brigades and production teams overreported food grain production to the central state to save face. The massive collectivization scheme was poorly planned and hastily implemented, and disrupted the rhythms of village life so drastically that everyone resented it. Village China went back to small cooperatives. However, the drive demonstrates how the ordinary China peasant had been inescapably and coercively incorporated into the state-driven economic system.

RURAL TARGETS OF WELFARE

The rural residents of China were expected to participate in and contribute to state development through the Great Leap Forward, but they were also to modernize themselves, through the directives of the state-administrated welfare schemes. In that regard, the Chinese state and rural society relations closely follow the modality of political society that Partha Chatterjee (2004; 2011) describes as one where the state governs its subjects through welfare policies. In China, the welfare measures, more successful than in India due to greater state capacity to implement them, did help to keep the enormous mass of population under continuous discipline and surveillance. However, just as in India, these measures also made the state, in this case the central state, inarguably the primary caretaker of the rural people.

Philip Lee, then a professor of social medicine at the University of California in San Francisco, wrote glowingly in the *Western Journal of Medicine* about China's primary health care system after visiting the country in 1973 as part of a U.S. medical delegation (Lee 1974). He said that prior to the founding of the People's Republic of China in 1949, epidemics, infectious disease, and poor sanitation were widespread. He compared that with the then current conditions:

> The picture today is dramatically different. . . . [T]here has been a pronounced decline in the death rate, particularly infant mortality. Major epidemic diseases have been controlled[,] . . . nutritional status has been improved [and] massive campaigns of health education and environmental sanitation have been carried out. Large numbers of health workers have been trained, and a system has been developed that provides some health service for the great majority of the people.[7]

The state took serious care in the prevention and treatment of diseases. Gao (1999) describes the campaign to eradicate schistosomiasis, a debilitating disease that affected 10 million people in south China in the mid-1950s. A taskforce set up in 1956 by Mao to eliminate the disease was successful, and in 1958 it was eliminated from the worst affected county in south China. Gao states that during the 1960s and 1970s, to encourage the poor to participate in the treatment, every day spent by the patient in hospital was rewarded with the same amount of work points they would have earned working (ibid. 86). Up to 1978, 50 Gao villagers were treated for schistosomiasis, and a doctor that Gao knew had carried out 800 successful operations, all at the government's cost. It is said that Mao was so pleased to hear about the eradication of the disease that he spent a sleepless night writing a poem, the title of which was "Seeing off the God of Plague" (ibid. 85). In Gao's village, vaccination and immunization reduced child mortality from 40 percent in 1949–63 to 6 percent during 1963–78 (ibid. 75). Two doctors were sent to the village from the county at no cost to villagers. Before they retired, they had trained "barefoot doctors," local youths who were to walk barefoot like their fellow villagers, to provide treatment to the villagers, the cost of which was born by the production brigade.

Intensive literacy classes and primary education were extended to all villages, practices such as female foot binding were banned, and sanitation measures such as keeping chicken in coops rather than inside houses were advised. Earthquake shelters were organized in every household (Gao 1999; Li 2008). With the Cultural Revolution, Mao worship replaced religious worship, superstition was undermined, and in Chen village in the Pearl River delta, women publicly broke their jade bangles as a symbol of breaking from traditions (Chan et al. 2009).

Thus the Chinese state established a firm and inalterable presence in the lives of rural dwellers, not just as the enforcer of surpluses but also as the welfare provider. As a mother or father would do for their children, the central state had to pull people out of underdevelopment, and the conventions and traditions that bound them to their habitats had to be broken. Their superstitions needed to be corrected through an understanding of science. Their bodies and habitats had to be cleansed and sanitized and made free from diseases. They, especially the children, had to be fed nutritious food. Equally important was how they cooked food, what was cooked, how the food was served, and by whom. Population growth had to be curtailed using measures of fertility control, so that the benefits of welfare could be allocated more efficiently. Each birth had to be assisted by midwifery, and each midwife had to undergo training provided by the state. It came to be common sense to view the state as responsible for feeding, clothing, and "developing" the rural population.

THE SYMBOLIC POWER OF THE PEASANTS

These interventions and the people promoting them sometimes met with resistance. Huaiyin Li (2009) narrates the courage of the peasant representatives in criticizing the corrupt practices of the cadres, the grassroot public officials, and making them admit their wrongdoings in a meeting:

> It was reported that 75 percent of the 639 members who attended the Qingdong Commune's first meeting of *pingxiazhongnong* [lower and middle peasants] representatives in January 1965 actively criticized the cadres. Because of their criticism, 373 cadres confessed their involvement in the "four kinds of uncleanliness," by which they unlawfully obtained a total of 58,557.68 yuan of collective funds or illegal profits and 74,064 catties of grain in total. (ibid. 114)

This meeting was part of the socialist education campaign started in 1963 where cadres all over China were found to have these "four kinds of uncleanliness" (excessive eating and talking, embezzlement and theft, overdrawing and misappropriation, and speculation and profiteering). The *pingxiazhongnong* were given the responsibility of monitoring the cadres and making them admit their mistakes. Villagers also wrote "people's letters" to the county government and through their commune leaders, villagers could express their discontent at the local cadres (ibid. 121). Li argues that the state made the ordinary peasants regulate the cadres at the brigade and production team levels and ensured their conformity with government policies. This use of the peasants to regulate and enforce conformity among the cadres was especially far-reaching after the abandoning of the Great Leap Forward, when the state found the cadres unreliable. The peasants were provided the symbolic means to feel superior to the cadres through an ideology that peasants themselves produced and propagated, of their being the subjects of the state. These efforts continued into the Cultural Revolution and were used by the villagers to settle scores with their local intermediaries.

In fact this authority given to the villagers was the extension of the political and organizational rhetoric and strategy of "mass line" adopted by the Communist Party after 1949, whereby the party and the ordinary party and nonparty masses were always in touch with, and learned from, one another. The cadres were the intermediaries between the party and the people, and they needed to be educated by the masses. Local bureaucrats and the "sent-down youths" in the 1960s were to learn from the masses and reform their identities based on those experiences. After the Communist Revolution, during the land reform drive, a division was drawn between the poor peasants, who were the motor of the revolution and the new nation, and class enemies such as landowners; the former participated in denouncing the latter by shaming, excluding, and even annihilating them (Hu 2009). This new division, as Ruf (1998) argues, created a new social and political order by reordering the cosmos of the peasants, who assumed a new central role that they assigned to themselves in the processes under way in the village. At least, as Li argues, it provided them some discursive superiority in the countryside, where they were materially, utterly subordinated to the central state, although this aspect of their relationship was obscured. As a sentdown youth observed of another denouncement of cadres by villagers in a meeting in Chen village: "The idea was to instigate the peasants to 'speak bitterness' against the cadres just as during the land reform they'd spoken bitterness against the landlords" (Chan et al. 2009, 57).

In village China under Mao, rural residents were incorporated into the Chinese state in three ways. First, to support industrial growth, the state applied pressure to the peasantry in order to procure the necessary agricultural surplus. Through cooperative and collective farming and through using peasant labor for infrastructural projects, the state exploited the peasants. Second, the state entered the private worlds of the country dwellers by insisting on the correct ways of living. The state, in essence, assumed a parental role. This effort, however, proved insufficient to ensure the well-being of the peasants whom it was exploiting through the production system. Third, by making the rural residents the subject of the state through "mass line" rhetoric, the state made them take a high moral position that was "rightfully" given to them by the state, and to criticize and seek vengeance on the local cadres who collected and distributed resources to them.

Comparing India and China

In India and China, through the modernization drives following the 1950s, rural society was incorporated into the national state through the institutions and apparatuses of production, markets, welfare, and politics.

The village became the basic organizational unit through which the developmental institutions interacted with the rural society. New collective identities crystallized, based on these new village communities. Through economic programs, the rural residents produced for the market mediated by the national state. The welfare programs embedded the rural residents in the parental care of the state and molded their expectations of the latter. This multiplex embeddedness of rural people in the state also created a politics where the rural population expected certain rights and entitlements from the national state and often demanded these be given, and resisted when they were taken away. In other words, one can see the seeds of rightful resurgence emerging from such politics.

In India, the land reform efforts after the formation of the nation-state, though half-hearted in planning and implementation, created a growing section of small and middle-level farmers who were eager to invest in production and looked forward to being upwardly mobile. In China, the land reforms were radical, transferring land to the peasants and abolishing the land-owning class through condemnation by the peasants. Through the Community Development Program and other development programs in India, the state intervened to bring about better agricultural practices to boost production and improve the economic and social well-being of peasants. These programs embedded the Indian villages in the national state as targets of development. The Indian villages became the principal unit of resource allocation, and development blocks became the chief conduit through which welfare was delivered to the villages. In China, the villages that were hitherto split according to kinship and lineage loyalties were brought together by the collectivization programs. These programs, intended to boost agricultural production by pooling farmlands and resources, had the village collective as the basic organizational unit of collection and distribution of resources. In both China and India, the villages became the focus of development and welfare policies that further reorganized the everyday lives of the rural folk, which included agricultural inputs, sanitation, sterilization, vaccination, midwifery, and schooling.

In India, the U.S.-sponsored Green Revolution firmly incorporated the market in Indian rural society as well as the national state as the mediator of the new market relations. In China, through the collectivization drive, an ordinary peasant was inescapably incorporated into the state-driven economic system of production and market. Indian rural society, which had been embedded in reciprocal relations of class and caste hierarchies, became more or less integrated into the market. Large, medium, and small farmers started producing for the market, using new technology seeds and fertilizers, either investing their own capital or being dependent on credit, subsidies, and harvest purchases by the national state. The Chinese villagers worked in production teams, which were under production brigades, which were in turn under production communes, and the grain surplus was procured by the central state. Jean Oi (1991) has shown that even when the state did not procure the surplus, due to peasants' discontent, failed negotiations, or just the low level of state capacity, it still had other effective ways of maintaining the surplus from being redistributed back to the peasants.

In India, the middle peasantry, who enriched themselves through agrarian capitalism, organized as farmers' movements, and demanded that the national and regional state intervene in the market on its behalf. These farmer politicians agitated for better prices and better subsidies and against electricity bills and debts. These farmers, in other words, were using "rightful" resistance to pressure the state, quite different from the peasant revolts of the past that were based on "righteous" understandings of fairness and justice. In China, the high moral position given to peasants by the state through mass line politics and socialist education elevated the capacity of the peasants to criticize the local intermediaries among them and the state for wrongdoings and to appeal to the commune leaders and county officials to intervene on their behalf. I argue that the contemporary echoes of this politics are heard in the "rightful resistance" (O'Brien and Li 2006) that I spoke about at the start of the chapter, whereby villagers cite laws and regulations when they encounter malpractices of local government bodies, and when they withhold tax payments when they are not given fertilizer or fuel subsidies that the state is obliged to provide.

Conclusion

In this essay, I looked for the origins of rightful resistance in India and China. Kevin O'Brien and Lianjiang Li (2006) proposed the term "rightful resistance" to characterize popular resistance in the Chinese countryside. They found that this form of popular contention operated near the boundaries of authority, used the language of the official media, and exploited divisions within the state. They understood this "new" resistance as emerging from the raised awareness of citizen rights among the Chinese people after the neoliberal and democratic turn in China (2006, 10). I have tried to show in this essay that rightful resistance must have a longer history than they suggest, and might show more continuity with the Maoist past than they had imagined. Instead of locating the emergence of popular resistance in state and society relations in China's imperial past (Hung 2011; Perry 2001), I suggest that popular resistance may have emerged from the newly instituted state and society relations in postrevolutionary China, as part of its modernization and development drive. I propose a comparison with India, where similar popular resistance exists, and similar state programs have been instituted after political independence in 1947. I analyze state and rural society relations in India after the 1950s and show that rural society was incorporated into the national state through production, market, and welfare institutions and programs, and that as a result they developed a sense of rights and entitlements as rural subjects of the state, albeit not yet or ever as citizens. These have created a politics that is not that of citizens against the state in a social movement, nor of peasants against extractors in a moral economy, but nevertheless one legitimized by the state.

Notes

1. T. K. Rajalakshmi, "Farmer Power," *Frontline* 19, no. 12, June 8–21, 2002.
2. "Farmers Oppose Recovery Proceedings," *The Hindu*, February 28, 2015.
3. The CDP continued practices begun in the colonial era. Subir Sinha (2008) has shown how the colonial policies of rural welfare reflected colonial state interests in aligning village communities with state objectives. He explains. for instance, how the colonial state in Punjab granted community institutions, which were controlled by large landowners, the power to mobilize unpaid labor to clear the Shah Nahr canal system, thus reducing the state's own costs in financially tight times (Sinha 2008, quoting Gilmartin 1999).
4. Tania Li has examined the ways in which development strategies have been implemented in the Indonesian landscape to reform the rural subject (Li 2007). Li's iden-

tification of the key practices of these schemes as problematizing rural backwardness and using expert knowledge to alleviate it is a valuable insight to understand the CDP in India.

5. Dube's studies, done with the help of Cornell University, support points made by Gupta (1998) and Sinha (2008) that American soft power in the context of the Cold War was instrumental in putting community development schemes in place. However, rather than focusing on a transnational regime as Sinha does, I suggest that the national state was instrumental in imagining and putting into place these policies.

6. In the Wisers' account of Karimpur, there are accounts of how villagers were initiated into the use of cups and saucers, new ovens, and so on, which were then stowed away, never to be touched again (Wiser and Wiser 2000).

7. Lee's article (1974) was quoted in the news report "China's Village Doctors Take Great Strides," by Cui Weiyuan, in WHO bulletin 86, no. 12 (2008): 908–88.

References

Arnold, T. C. 2001. "Rethinking Moral Economy." *American Political Science Review* 95.1: 85–95.

Brass, Tom. 1994. "The Politics of Gender, Nature and Nation in the Discourse of the New Farmers' Movements." *Journal of Peasant Studies* 21.3–4: 27–71.

———, ed. 1995. *New Farmers' Movements in India*. Ilford, UK; Portland, OR: Frank Cass.

Byres, T. J. 1988. "Charan Singh, 1902–87: An Assessment." *Journal of Peasant Studies* 15.2: 139–89.

Chakravarti, A. 1975. *Contradiction and Change: Emerging Patterns of Authority in a Rajasthan Village*. Oxford: Oxford University Press.

Chan, Anita, Richard Madsen, and Jonathan Unger. 2009. *Chen Village: Revolution to Globalization*. 3rd ed. Berkeley: University of California Press.

Chatterjee, Partha. 1986. *Nationalist Thought and the Colonial World: The Derivative Discourse?* London: Zed Books.

———. 2004. *The Politics of the Governed: Reflections on Popular Politics in Most of the World*. New York: Columbia University Press.

———. 2008. "Democracy and Economic Transformation in India." *Economic and Political Weekly* 43.16: 53–62.

———. 2011. *Lineages of Political Society: Studies in Postcolonial Democracy*. New York: Columbia University Press.

Cheng, Tongshun. 1994. "Dangqian zhongguo nongmin de zhengzhi canyu" (Current political participation of Chinese peasants). Master's thesis, Nankai University, China.

Corbridge, Stuart, Glynn Williams, Manoj Srivastava, and René Véron. 2005. *Seeing the State: Governance and Governmentality in India*. Vol. 10. Cambridge: Cambridge University Press.

Dhanagare, D. N. 1973. "Peasant Movements in India, c. 1920–1950." Ph.D. diss., University of Sussex.

———. 1987. "Green Revolution and Social Inequalities in Rural India." *Economic and Political Weekly* 22.19–21: AN137–44.

Dube, S. C. 1956. "Some Problems of Communication in Rural Community Development." Report of February 9, 1956, Cornell University India program. Ithaca: Cornell University.

———. 1958. *India's Changing Villages*. Vol. 5. London: Routledge and Keagan Paul.

Frankel, Francine R. 1971. *India's Green Revolution: Economic Gains and Political Costs*. Princeton: Princeton University Press; London: Oxford University Press.

Gao, Mobo C. F. 1999. *Gao Village: Rural Life in Modern China*. Honolulu: University of Hawai'i Press.

Ghosh, Ratan, and K. Nagaraj. 1978. "Land Reforms in West Bengal." *Social Scientist* 6.6–7: 50–67.

Gilmartin, David. 1999. "The Irrigating Public: The State and Local Management in Colonial Irrigation." In *State, Society and the Environment in South Asia*, edited by Stig Toft Madsen, 236–65. Copenhagen: Nordic Institute of Asian Studies.

Gough, Kathleen. 1974. "Indian Peasant Uprisings." *Economic and Political Weekly* 9.32–34: 1391–412.

Gupta, Akhil. 1998. *Postcolonial Developments: Agriculture in the Making of Modern India*. Durham, NC: Duke University Press.

Harriss, John 1987. "Capitalism and Peasant Production: The Green Revolution in India." In *Peasants and Peasant Societies*, edited by Teodor Shanin, 227–46. London: Penguin.

Hasan, Z. 1989. "Power and Mobilization: Patterns of Resilience and Change in Uttar Pradesh Politics." In *Dominance and State Power in Modern India: Decline of a Social Order*, vol. 1, edited by Francine R. Frankel and M. S. A. Rao, 133–203. Oxford: Oxford University Press.

Herring, Ronald J. 1983. *Land to the Tiller: The Political Economy of Agrarian Reform in South Asia*. New Haven: Yale University Press.

Hu, Zongze. 2009. "Keeping Hope: Encountering and Imagining the National State in a North China Village." Ph.D. diss., Harvard University.

Hung, Ho-fung. 2011. *Protest with Chinese Characteristics: Demonstrations, Riots, and Petitions in the Mid-Qing Dynasty*. New York: Columbia University Press.

Jaffrelot, Christophe. 2003. *India's Silent Revolution: The Rise of the Lower Castes in North India*. New Delhi: Orient Blackswan.

Jodhka, Surinder S. 2012. *Village Society*. Hyderabad: Orient Blackswan.

Karunaratne, Garvin. 1976. "The Failure of the Community Development Programme in India." *Community Development Journal* 11.2: 95–118.

Lee, Philip R. 1974. "Medicine and Public Health in the People's Republic of China." *Western Journal of Medicine* 120 (5): 430–37.

Li, Huaiyin. 2009. *Village China under Socialism and Reform: A Micro History, 1948–2008*. Stanford: Stanford University Press.

Li, Tania Murray. 2007. *The Will to Improve: Governmentality, Development and the Practice of Politics*. Durham, NC: Duke University Press.

Lin, Justin Yifu. 1990. "Collectivization and China's Agricultural Crisis in 1959–1961." *Journal of Political Economy.* 19.6: 1228–52.

Lutringer, Christine. 2010. "A Movement of 'Subsidized Capitalists'? The Multi-Level Influence of the Bharatiya Kisan Union in India." *International Review of Sociology* 20.3: 513–31.

Mellor, John W., Thomas F. Weaver, Uma J. Lete, and Sheldon R. Simon. 1968. *Developing Rural India: Plan and Practice.* Ithaca: Cornell University Press.

Mitra, Subatra K. 1992. *Power, Protest, and Participation: Local Elites and the Politics of Development in India.* New York: Routledge.

Moore, Barrington, Jr. 1966. *Social Origins of Democracy and Dictatorship: Lord and Peasant in the Making of the Modern World.* Boston: Beacon.

Nair, Kusan. 1961. *Blossoms in the Dust.* London: Duckworth.

O'Brien, Kevin J. 2009. *Popular Protest in China.* Vol. 15. Cambridge, MA: Harvard University Press.

O'Brien, Kevin J., and Lianjiang Li. 2006. *Rightful Resistance in Rural China.* New York: Cambridge University Press.

Oi, Jean C. 1991. *State and Peasant in Contemporary China: The Political Economy of Village Government.* Vol. 30. Berkeley: University of California Press.

Oi, Jean C., and Shukai Zhou. 2007. "Fiscal Crisis in China's Townships: Causes and Consequences." In *Grassroots Political Reform in Contemporary China,* edited by Elizabeth J. Perry and Merle Goldman, 75–96. Cambridge, MA: Harvard University Press.

Perry, Elizabeth J. 2001. "Challenging the Mandate of Heaven: Popular Protest in Modern China." *Critical Asian Studies* 33.2: 163–80.

———. 2008. "Chinese Conceptions of 'Rights': From Mencius to Mao—and Now." *Perspectives on Politics* 6.1: 37–50.

Perry, Elizabeth J., and Merle Goldman. 2007. *Grassroots Political Reform in Contemporary China.* Vol. 14. Cambridge, MA: Harvard University Press.

Radhakrishnan, P. 1980. "Peasant Struggles and Land Reforms in Malabar." *Economic and Political Weekly* 15.50: 2095–102.

———. 1981. "Land Reforms in Theory and Practice: The Kerala Experience." *Economic and Political Weekly* 16.52: A129–37.

Robinson, Marguerite S. 1988. *Local Politics: The Law of the Fishes: Development through Political Change in Medak District, Andhra Pradesh (South India).* Delhi: Oxford University Press.

Rosin, Robert T. 1981. "Land reform in Rajasthan." *Current Anthropology* 22:, 75–76.

Ruf, Gregory A. 1998. *Cadres and Kin: Making a Socialist Village in West China, 1921–1991.* Stanford: Stanford University Press.

Scott, James C. 1976. *The Moral Economy of the Peasant: Subsistence and Rebellion in Southeast Asia.* New Haven: Yale University Press.

Sinha, Aseema. 2005. "Political Foundations of Market-Enhancing Federalism: Theoretical Lessons from India and China." *Comparative Politics* 37.3: 337–56.

Sinha, Subir. 2008. "Lineages of the Developmentalist State: Transnationality and Village India, 1900–1965." *Comparative Studies in Society and History* 50.1: 57–90.

So, Alvin Y. 2007. "Peasant Conflict and the Local Predatory State in the Chinese Countryside." *Journal of Peasant Studies* 34.3–4: 560–81.

Tilly, Charles. 2006. *Regimes and Repertoires*. Chicago: University of Chicago Press.

Thompson, E. P. 1971. "The Moral Economy of the English Crowd in the Eighteenth Century." *Past and Present* 50: 76–136.

Varshney, Ashutosh. 1998. *Democracy, Development, and the Countryside: Urban-Rural Struggles in India*. New York: Cambridge University Press.

Wiser, William H., and Charlotte V. Wiser, with Susan S. Wadley. 2000. *Behind Mud Walls: Seventy-Five Years in a North Indian Village*. Berkeley: University of California Press.

Zaidi, A. Moin, and Shaheda, Zaidi, eds. 1981. *The Encyclopaedia of the Indian National Congress*. Vol. 12. New Delhi: Sultan Chand.

PART III

Public Goods Provision

CHAPTER 5

Parallel Trajectories

The Development of the Welfare State in China and India

Nara Dillon

Communist China and democratic India have developed welfare states with lasting parallels not easily accounted for by their political regimes. Both countries began with a grand vision of social citizenship, establishing a broad array of social rights in their constitutions. Since then, neither country has had much success in fulfilling these rights on the ground. Although each government has adopted multiple welfare programs, most of them feature narrow population coverage and unequal benefits. The result is patchy social protection for the needy and another source of inequality in highly unequal societies.

Rather than from democratic elections or communist class struggle, these parallels in the Chinese and Indian welfare states stem from the outsize role that international influences and technocratic policy makers have played in their welfare politics. These forces led both countries to adopt similar welfare programs at similar points in time. Moreover, similar economic constraints have shaped implementation of these programs, posing obstacles that the advanced industrial countries never faced with their welfare states.

If the policies and constraints were similar, China and India's welfare reforms have been implemented in their own distinct ways, shaping different kinds of welfare states. Indian welfare programs have been administered in a highly bureaucratic manner shaped by a long-term, legalistic form of class struggle over redistribution. Ironically, Chinese programs have not featured such extensive class conflict, and they have relied on mobilization and improvisation as much as bureaucratic methods of administration. While these differences are related to regime type, they emerged out of political institutions and practices not usually considered to be central elements of political regimes: courts and campaigns. Simple models of welfare state development that focus on electoral politics or dictators' incentives fail to capture this more subtle, but significant variation between regimes. Veto points prove to be more important than majority coalitions.

More recently, neoliberalism has shaped another parallel trajectory of welfare state development in China and India. Market reforms have undermined some social protections in both countries, as in the welfare state retrenchment seen in other parts of the world. But the net impact of neoliberal welfare reforms in China and India has been the first significant expansion of their welfare states since the postwar period. So far, this new phase of state building has been more successful than in the postwar period, due to the combination of narrower, more pragmatic reform goals and significantly looser economic constraints after several decades of sustained economic growth. The expansion of social protection to groups previously excluded from the welfare state has contributed to much more significant poverty reduction than the postwar welfare reforms. But the legacy of the preexisting welfare state continues to limit the impact of these reforms on social citizenship in China and India, perpetuating many of the inequalities of their welfare states.

The postwar trajectory of welfare state development in China and India reveals the tensions between their nation-building and state-building temporalities. Rather than reinforcing each other as in the advanced industrial countries, the bold promise of equal social citizenship in a new sovereign nation was undermined by failures of state building in China and India. Given this legacy, neoliberalism has also had a distinctly different impact on China and India than it has on the advanced industrial countries, facilitating state building even as it erodes citizenship.

This chapter is organized into four parts. The first section details the key parallels in the development of the Chinese and Indian welfare states, while the second reviews previous research on welfare in both countries. The final two sections examine, first, the postwar welfare reforms of the 1950s and 1960s and then the recent rounds of reform in the 1990s and 2000s.

The Chinese and Indian Welfare States

To ground the comparison of the Chinese and Indian welfare states, this chapter focuses on similar programs: cash transfer programs for the elderly, such as social insurance, provident funds, social pensions, and social assistance. In the welfare states of advanced industrial countries these programs are the largest part of the welfare state, affecting more people and distributing more resources than any other welfare program. While old age pensions have also proven to be the largest component of China's welfare state, in India they have been overshadowed by the Public Distribution System (PDS), which provides subsidized food to the poor. China also provided food subsidies to urban consumers in the Mao era, but they were an integral part of the command economy rather than a separate program like India's PDS. Given these differences, focusing on similar programs within the larger context of the welfare state provides a baseline for comparison.

China and India established retirement programs for the elderly soon after gaining independence. China adopted a labor insurance program in 1951 and then transformed it into a broader social insurance program in the 1990s. Both of these Chinese programs have provided lifetime retirement pensions to workers 60 years or older who have contributed to the program for at least 15 years.[1] The comparable retirement program in India is the Employee Provident Fund, which was established in 1952 and provides workers with a large lump-sum payment upon retirement at age 58. In 1995, the Indian government added a small social insurance pension to the provident fund, providing modest monthly pensions in addition to the initial payout at retirement. In both China and India, payroll taxes on employers and workers finance these programs, and benefits are pegged to workers' income and the number of years they worked (ILO 2017, 324–28).

More recently, both India and China adopted new national social assistance programs to provide cash benefits to poor families whose incomes and assets fall below the poverty line. India adopted its first National Social Assistance Program in 1995. Similarly, China adopted its Urban Minimum Income Guarantee Program in 1999, followed by the Rural Minimum Income Guarantee Program in 2009. These means-tested programs are not restricted to the elderly, but older people make up a significant share of their caseloads in both countries. Both programs' benefits are pegged to the poverty line, which is set below the minimum wage to preserve work incentives. As a result, average benefits are significantly lower than those provided by the old age pension and provident fund programs (Rawat 2012, 32–34; Zhang 2012, 15–16).

Only a decade later, India and China adopted social pension programs in 2007 and 2009 respectively, seeking to significantly expand welfare coverage for the elderly. The Indian program is means-tested, providing pensions to all people over 60 years whose incomes falls below the poverty line. The Chinese program is universal, seeking to provide pensions to all rural citizens over 60 years, funded by a combination of individual contributions and government revenues (ibid.). In 2011, the Chinese government added a social pension program for urban residents without formal employment, which was then integrated into the rural social pension program in 2014 (Liu and Sun 2016, 20–21). Although the Indian government has not expanded its social pension program since 2007, it adopted the separate Social Security Act for Unorganised Workers in 2008 and the Food Security Act in 2013 (Kannan 2010, 341; Balani 2013, 1).

In sum, China and India established retirement programs in the 1950s, targeted social assistance programs in the 1990s, and broader social pension programs for the elderly in the 2000s. While Chinese retirement programs provide significantly better benefits than their Indian counterparts, benefit levels vary widely across programs and local jurisdictions in both countries. Within this framework of similar welfare programs adopted at similar times, China's welfare state has expanded further than India's. In terms of spending, China spent more than twice as much on its welfare and health programs in 2010 than India: 6.8 percent of GDP in China in comparison to 2.6 percent of GDP in India (or approximately 3.4 percent if the PDS program is included as well). Both countries, however, fall far behind the advanced industrial countries in welfare spending, and even lag behind other regions in the developing world such as Latin America. For example, in 2010 welfare spending in Western Europe averaged 26.7 percent of GDP, compared to 13.2 percent in Latin America (ILO 2014, 29799; Ziegler et al. 2011, 271; Balani 2013, 13).

Literature Review: Limits of the Welfare State

What explains these parallel welfare reforms? Few comparative studies of the welfare state include either China or India as cases, much less both of them. Furthermore, most comparative research focuses on explaining differences between their welfare states. Much of the quantitative research that includes China and India has focused on the relationship between regime type and the welfare state. Finding higher levels of welfare spending and better welfare outcomes in democracies, these scholars attribute the difference to the larger size of the electorate in democracies in comparison to the more elite "selectorates" involved in leadership selection in nondemocratic regimes. There is reason, however, to think that China and India are not simply outliers for their regime types. One limitation of many of these quantitative studies is that they exclude communist regimes as a rule, despite the fact that they are the nondemocratic regime type most closely associated with welfare (Haggard and Kaufman 2008; Huber and Stephens 2012; Williamson and Pampel 1993; Rudra and Haggard 2005).

One of the few large-scale comparative studies to focus on similarities between the Chinese and Indian welfare states is Ian Gough's effort to develop welfare regime typologies that can account for all developing countries. He classified both China and India as having "informal security regimes," in contrast to welfare state regimes in the advanced industrial countries and insecurity regimes in war-torn countries. This intermediate category features some state provision of welfare, but in a context where family and private welfare provision dominates. Within the broad category of informal security regimes, he ranks China as having an effective informal security regime, while India is considered less effective based on a variety of health, literacy, and poverty indicators (Gough 2004, 21, 43–44). To explain the emergence of these different regime types and their effectiveness, he points to the foundations for the welfare state lacking in many developing countries: strong states and well-developed capitalist labor and financial markets. Explaining why many developing countries lack these foundations, however, is left for future research.

In a qualitative comparison of China and India, Jean Dreze and Amartya Sen (1989) take the analysis a step further to trace differences in welfare outcomes in China and India to different kinds of state capacity fostered by their political regimes. On the one hand, they argue, democracy promotes state action in an emergency, when the free press and opposition parties mobilize popular pressure on the ruling party to respond. On the other hand, communist regimes are better at mobilizing consistent bureaucratic action to achieve policy goals, such as reducing illiteracy and hunger. In other words, they claim that democracies are more likely to develop the capacity necessary for episodic famine relief while communist regimes are more likely to develop the capacity necessary for ongoing welfare programs. Although this comparison helps to explain the variation in famine and malnutrition outcomes in the two countries, it does not account for the similarities in the development of their welfare states.

There have been more single-country case studies of the Indian and Chinese welfare states than comparative analyses. Like those of Sen and Dreze and Gough, these case studies also point to state capacity as a major constraint on welfare state development. Rather than regime, these studies identify weak, internally divided labor movements that fail to pressure political elites to develop state capacities that serve their interests. Research on both India and China points to skill as a source of division among workers (Rudra 2008; Perry 1993; Lu and Perry 1997). The Chinese case studies also identify patron-client ties in the workplace and institutional legacies of the prerevolutionary regime as additional sources of division, while the Indian case studies emphasize caste and subnational identities embedded in Indian federalism as complicating factors (Walder 1986; Frazier 2002; Jaffrelot 2003; Singh 2015). Finally, economic constraints have been identified as an obstacle to adopting welfare policies originally designed for industrialized economies (Dillon 2015).

While these similar constraints may help explain the limits of the Chinese and Indian welfare states, case studies also highlight the importance of international influences in their welfare politics at key points (Williamson and Pampel 1993; Walder 1986; Dillon 2015; Rudra 2008; Frazier 2010; Solinger 2009). The parallels in their welfare reforms over the last 60 years suggest that shared international influences must have been important all along. Put together, these case studies of China and India point to common international influences, limits in state capacity, and weak labor movements as variables shaping welfare state development. But beyond those commonalities, their domestic welfare politics are analyzed in distinctly different terms reflecting the profound differences in their political regimes.

The Founding of the Chinese and Indian Welfare States

To compare the parallels in the early years of the Chinese and Indian welfare states, this section first reviews their common international influences before focusing on their domestic welfare politics, first in India and then in China.

The close timing of the founding of the Chinese and Indian welfare states was shaped by decolonization in the wake of the Second World War. Welfare was an integral part of the modern state and citizenship that Indian and Chinese political leaders sought to establish in 1947 and 1949. Furthermore, the similar content of their welfare reforms was shaped by common international influences on both their welfare and economic development policies. These influences dated back to the interwar period. Both China and India were founding members of the International Labour Organization (ILO) in 1919. After the ILO endorsed social insurance as the international standard for welfare policy in 1932, the Chinese and Indian governments began to study how these policies could be adapted to local conditions (Dillon 2015, 45–53; Agarwala 1945, 6–11). Moreover, their delegates participated in the 1944 Philadelphia ILO conference, when the organization committed itself to the broader goal of achieving social security, or welfare as a social right, in the postwar period (ILO 1944).

Britain was another common source of influence on social policy during the Second World War, since China and India were both on the Allied side of the conflict. The 1942 Beveridge Report inspired interest and enthusiasm among Indian and Chinese policy makers alike with its vision of a universal, egalitarian welfare state for postwar Britain (Agarwala 1946, 575; Ma 2012, 337). The British Colonial Office also developed provident fund policies during the war for its colonies, seen as a more appropriate starting point for poor economies than the Beveridge Plan (Williamson and Pampel 1993, 147).

After the Second World War, both countries gained wider roles in new postwar international institutions even as Cold War divisions emerged. India hosted the first regional Asian ILO conference in 1947, when a large Chinese delegation contributed to the meeting's consensus around a plan for establishing welfare states: first creating comprehensive social insurance programs and then gradually expanding population coverage as their economies developed. Delegates from India and Nationalist China were also members of the United Nations drafting committee for the Universal Declaration of Human Rights in 1948. The delegates, Hansa Mehta and Zhang Pengjun, endorsed the social rights included in the charter, including the right to social security (Dillon 2015, 63–64; Jain 2005, 20).

The Chinese communists were cut off from the ILO and UN as the Chinese civil war heated up, but this legacy of shared influences help account for the similar range of social rights established in India's 1950 Constitution and China's 1954 Constitution. While the UN rights declaration framed the right to social security in broad terms, both the Indian and Chinese Constitutions specified a range of welfare rights, including a right to public assistance for the elderly.[2] While the Indian Constitution does not define the form this assistance might take, the Chinese Constitution lists social insurance, social assistance, and public health services.

These new social rights were not simply symbolic or aspirational—the new governments immediately put programs in place to fulfill them. As mentioned above, the Chinese communists adopted their Labor Insurance Program in 1951, several years before the constitution was in place. The official labor union drafted the new policy without ever considering any alternatives to social insurance, which the Soviet Union promoted as a socialist form of welfare. Chinese policy makers' one concession to the difficulties of enacting major welfare reforms in a period of war and economic recovery was to limit the initial scope of implementation to large employers with more than 100 workers (Dillon 2015, 69–75, 129–30).

The Indian policy process featured more consideration of alternatives. The legislative debate focused on the program designs introduced by the British: the question of whether to adopt a provident fund or a social insurance program. Provident funds were designed to be transitional programs that could gradually build up the administrative capacity for a full social insurance program, starting with more limited benefits and financial risk until the necessary data collection, financial resources, and bureaucratic structures could be developed. Seeking to avoid overburdening the economy, Indian policy makers chose the cheaper alternative as a first step toward the goal of social insurance (Williamson and Pampel 1993, 149). Furthermore, the scope of the provident fund was initially limited to large enterprises with more than 50 employees in the six largest sectors of the industrial economy, such as textiles and steel.

International influence continued to shape these programs after they were adopted, primarily through the technocrats in charge of economic development. China's development strategy was shaped in large part by the Soviet Union, which helped to establish China's new economic planning system and provided specific advice on welfare reform in the context of its First Five Year Plan (1953–57). Following Soviet and Eastern European models, Chinese planners put together an ambitious welfare reform agenda, including establishing transitional unemployment relief programs to cope with the disruptions of transitioning to a command economy at the beginning of the plan, followed by a major expansion of labor insurance into a social insurance program to cover the entire urban population at the end of the plan (Dillon 2015, 161–62).

Both Soviet and Chinese planners helped to shape the Indian economic planning system, although the powers of India's Planning Commission were significantly limited in comparison to its communist counterparts. Rather than restructuring and controlling the entire economy, the Indian Planning Commission was primarily an economic policy agency (Frankel 1998, 85–86, 125). Indian planners adopted a more modest welfare reform agenda than their Chinese counterparts, setting the goal of extending the provident fund to all large enterprises with more than 50 employees, regardless of economic sector, by the end of their First Five Year Plan (covering the fiscal years 1951–52 to 1955–56).[3]

Both the Chinese and Indian goals for economic development in their First Five Year Plans proved to be too ambitious. The gap between goals and reality was particularly wide in China, where economic planners had confidently predicted eliminating urban unemployment by the end of the First Five Year Plan, subsequently leading to the kind of labor shortages experienced in the Soviet Union and Eastern Europe during their First Five Year Plans (Dillon 2015, 170–71). Indian planners were only slightly less unrealistic, setting a goal of eliminating unemployment in 10 years. In fact, China's urban unemployment increased in the 1950s, while India made few gains in expanding the industrial workforce (Dillon 2015, 179–81; Frankel 1978, 118). With larger populations and significantly lower levels of employment than the Soviet Union during its First Five Year Plan, the impact of these economic development policies in China and India was far different.

As a result, the economic constraints on welfare reform were also much tighter than they had been for the Soviet Union 20 years earlier—or for that matter, much tighter than Western European countries in the 19th century, when welfare state programs such as social insurance were first invented. China and India's level of economic development in the 1950s was only 20–30 percent of the level of development achieved by Germany and Denmark 60 years earlier, when they pioneered these programs, much less when they began rapidly expanding these programs in the postwar era (Maddison 2001, 261, 304).

The policies and constraints may have been similar in China and India, but the failure of these reforms played out in very different ways, shaped by their political regimes. Theoretical models of regimes focused on coalition building and leadership selection do not capture this politics of implementation. Rather than in election campaigns and legislatures, India's welfare politics took place in the courts and the corporatist Central Provident Commission. China's welfare politics were shaped by the signature political practice of the Chinese communist regime: mass campaigns.

WELFARE REFORM IN INDIA

Disappointment with the results of India's First Five Year Plan led Nehru and the ruling Congress Party to expand the powers of the central planning commission in preparation for a more ambitious, socialist-influenced development strategy in the Second Five Year Plan (1956–61). Overcoming opposition from Indian businessmen, the new plan was built around an import substitution strategy and state-owned enterprises (Frankel 1978, 113–17, 128–31). Even though the goal of expanding coverage of the Employee Provident Fund to all industries had not been met in the First Five Year Plan, goals for social policy grew more ambitious in the Second Five Year Plan. The plan called for both expanding coverage to new industries and transforming the program into a social insurance program with lifetime benefits.[4]

Rather than through new legislation, these goals were accomplished through an administrative process established in the Central Provident Fund Commission, which was a tripartite corporatist institution with equal representation from business, labor and the state. With both state and labor representatives pressing for expansion of coverage, business opposition could not block the Provident Fund Commission's first decision: to expand to 11 new industrial sectors on top of the original six sectors in 1955 (EPFO 1955, 18–21).

Instead, business resisted expansion during implementation. Some employers did not cooperate with Provident Fund staff, refusing to turn over their employment records or denying them entry into their factories altogether. In a move even more effective than these kind of stalling tactics, other businesses sued the Provident Fund for overstepping its authority. Lawsuits over the fine print of the Employee Provident Fund statute and regulations questioned every word, including distinctions between industrial sectors, how to date the establishment of new factories, and whether factories could be split up to escape the 50-person size threshold for the program. The Provident Fund redirected staff from implementation to fighting this flurry of law suits (EPFO 1957, 16, 24).

Backdoor business opposition to the Employee Provident Fund did not subside over time. Even as the Provident Fund Commission settled into a routine of expanding coverage to several new industries every year, evasion and trivial law suits also became routine as well. By the 1960s, the EPF was facing thousands of court cases. To give an example of how far businesses were willing to take their resistance to the program, a steel company sued over the definition of "manufacturing" in the statute, arguing that their production was better described as "processing" and was therefore exempt from the program (EPFO 1966, 45). This persistent, large-scale resistance to welfare expansion through the courts prevented the provident fund program from reaching much further than the state-owned sector of the economy. The courts provided business with an expensive, but effective veto point on the implementation of the program.

WELFARE REFORM IN CHINA

The Chinese communists also failed to achieve their goals with welfare reform. The problem was not political opposition from employers; Chinese capitalists proved to be quite compliant in a revolutionary context. Instead, economic constraints and redistributive conflicts between workers and the urban poor complicated the Chinese Communist Party's (CCP) efforts to expand coverage.

China's welfare reforms were implemented through mass struggle campaigns rather than corporatist bureaucracies. From the beginning, these campaigns proved to be much more effective in overcoming political opposition to welfare than India's bureaucracies and courts. The initial implementation of labor insurance, for example, was accomplished by mobilizing workers against underground labor unions and labor racketeers, the CCP's chief rivals on the factory floor at that point. Even though capitalists were not the target of this campaign, employers offered little resistance to redistribution in this tense revolutionary atmosphere. In addition, the campaign helped to recruit workers into the new official labor union, and also helped to overcome the limits of state capacity at a point when the new regime was understaffed. Workers accomplished the biggest task in implementation themselves: determining each other's eligibility for labor insurance by reviewing each other's work and political history in small group meetings. As a result, the union was able to hand out the first pension checks on May Day, 1951, only a few months after implementation began, and well before the program's administration had even been established (Dillon 2015, 138–42).

Implementation of comprehensive unemployment relief began in 1953, at the beginning of the First Five Year Plan. Once again, the unemployed were mobilized to determine each others' eligibility for the program and to recruit them into the official labor union. Confident that labor shortages would develop quickly, the CCP's propaganda for unemployment relief promised a smooth transition to permanent jobs and labor insurance. But rather than a surge in new factory jobs, slow job growth and rapid rural-urban migration led to a surge in unemployment and protests by unemployed workers instead. Faced with this unexpected development, the CCP demobilized the unemployed in 1955. The official labor union ended their membership, shut down the unemployment relief program, and sent both rural migrants and unemployed workers to the countryside to support themselves by farming (Dillon 2015, 198–201). This pattern of mobilizing and then demobilizing welfare recipients within a few short years contributed to the instability of the period.

The next major campaign in the winter of 1955–56 was the urban revolution: the state takeover of private industry. The communist labor unions began organizing workers for the "mother" of all struggle campaigns. But capitalists had other ideas. When the campaign was announced, capitalists capitulated immediately, turning over their businesses to the state before the campaign even got under way. In the wake of this surprising political victory, the new communist managers of these state-owned enterprises found themselves in the unenviable position of imposing wage and benefit standardization on a workforce that had been mobilized for revolutionary redistribution. The result was a major strike wave in 1956–57, as workers sought to preserve the gains of the early 1950s. At the same time, unemployed workers also returned to the cities and took to the streets to protest for jobs and labor insurance. The redistributive conflict between workers and the unemployed was not direct, but their competition over scarce resources had the same end result. The implementation of the new social insurance regulations was quietly suspended in 1957 just before they were supposed to go into effect, sacrificing the expansion of labor insurance coverage to grandfather in the benefits and privileges of workers already protected by the program (Dillon 2015, 202–4, 211–20). The power to strike gave workers an effective veto point of their own.

Just as in India, the disappointments of the First Five Year Plan led to a more ambitious economic development strategy in the Second Five Year Plan—much more ambitious in the Chinese case. The Great Leap Forward mobilized people for economic development, seeking to jumpstart both grain and steel production. The new development strategy also layered new commune welfare programs on top of labor insurance. These new programs did not establish entitlements like labor insurance, but were instead designed to meet basic needs such as food, child care, and preventive health care from local resources. In the cities, these new programs were largely staffed by unemployed workers, giving them new jobs as well as new benefits (Dillon 2015, 233–35, 249–50).

In the chaos of the economic development campaign, policy makers in Beijing did not realize that these new welfare programs only contributed to the economic dislocations of the Great Leap Forward, exacerbating the famine that followed (Dillon 2015, 252–61). Economic collapse and the Great Leap famine forced them to pull back in 1962 and restore central planning. Commune welfare programs were shut down, state-owned enterprises laid off tens of millions of workers, and the unemployed were again sent to the countryside, with new restrictions in place to prevent them from returning to the city. Labor insurance, however, survived the crisis, protected from the deep budget cuts of the early 1960s.

Mass campaigns may have been powerful tools for implementing new policies and engineering social change, but they could also generate both political and economic instability. China's multiple different efforts to implement its ambitious welfare reforms in the 1950s and 1960s showed that political opposition to welfare expansion was not as significant a hurdle as economic constraints in the Chinese case. In addition, redistributive conflicts proved to be more complex than pitting capitalists against workers; conflicts among the workers and the urban poor over scarce resources continued long after capitalists had capitulated. In these conflicts, workers had key sources of power, such as the union and the power to strike, giving them an effective veto point in welfare reform that the unemployed did not have.

TECHNOCRATS' RESPONSE TO ECONOMIC CONSTRAINTS

India's slow growth and China's economic collapse in the 1960s led the technocrats in charge of economic policy in both countries to moderate their development goals. When China's central planning system was restored in the early 1960s, Chinese policy makers drew a basic lesson from their spectacular failures in the Great Leap Forward: that there is a trade-off between welfare and economic development. From that point forward, they accepted the limits of their narrow and unequal welfare state as a necessary compromise, delaying further welfare reform to some point in the indefinite future when the economy was more developed (Dillon 2015, 266).

Although India's failures were not nearly as severe, disappointment with the results of its development strategy also deepened in the 1960s. Economic planning was suspended for three years in 1966–68 while the central planning commission underwent reform (Frankel 1978, 307–11). Afterward, policy makers reduced the scope of their ambitions for India's welfare state. While the five year plans for the 1970s recognized that the needs of the elderly had not been met, they set no new goals for the Employee Provident Fund.[5] The proposal dating back to the second five-year plan to transform the provident fund into a social insurance program was delegated to the states, with no effort to reconcile how that would affect central programs such as the EPF. Moreover, a new proposal developed in the 1960s to create a social assistance program for the elderly was dropped (Bose 1988, 61). Food welfare programs, especially the Public Distribution System, were the only area of growth in the Indian welfare state in this period (Mooij 1998, 86). Rather than welfare, rural development programs became the central focus of India's antipoverty strategy (Saith and Harriss-White 2004, 309).

This turnaround in state policy, combined with continued resistance from business, led the Employee Provident Fund to steadily narrow the scope of its ambitions. By the 1970s, its annual review process for extending coverage to new industries was subdividing industrial sectors down to separate sectors for mining different ores, and even separate sectors for mining and processing the same ore (EPFO 1980, 21, 75–76). This routine seemed to show steady progress in expansion of the program to new sectors of the economy, but without any significant growth in the number of workers covered. The courts provided business with an effective veto point to halt the expansion of the EPF in implementation, long after losing the battle in the policy-making process in the legislature and the corporatist Central Provident Fund.

This comparison shows that both China and India saw their welfare reform agendas stall in the 1960s. After that point, population coverage in these retirement programs plateaued. By the end of the Cold War more than 20 years later, the Indian Employee Provident Fund reached only 11 percent of the labor force, while the Chinese Labor Insurance program covered 24 percent of the workforce (Palacios 1996, 31). With such narrow coverage targeted to industrial workers who had better pay and job security than most of the population, these welfare programs deepened inequalities in both countries. The goal of equal social citizenship and comprehensive social protection had been undermined by ongoing redistributive conflicts and limited state capacity to extend these programs for the elderly to the entire population. The way in which India's legal-bureaucratic failures and China's mobilizational failures played out may have been very different, but they had the same impact of limiting each country's nation-building project.

Welfare Reform Today

Why did China and India again adopt parallel welfare reforms in the 1990s and 2000s, after decades without major policy changes? For both countries, contemporary welfare politics have often been framed as a struggle between neoliberal globalization and growing popular resistance. But the Chinese and Indian welfare reforms of the 1990s and 2000s reveal a more complicated story in which international and domestic politics continue to be closely intertwined.

International events continue to shape the development of the Chinese and Indian welfare states. The demise of communism in Europe in 1989–91 had a major impact on both countries. India lost a major ally and trading partner with the collapse of the Soviet Union, while Chinese leaders worried that their regime might soon follow suit. Socialist economic development strategies, moreover, were discredited by these failures, giving strong impetus to the incipient market reforms both countries started in the 1980s.

In the wake of this crisis, both countries turned to the World Bank for advice on market reform, including welfare reform. The World Bank began to stake out a new role in international welfare policy in the debt crises of the 1980s as part of its structural adjustment policies. By the 1990s,

it had developed a comprehensive set of neoliberal welfare reforms to recommend to member countries. The larger goals of these policies included
eliminating budget deficits, minimizing market distortions, and preserv-
ing social safety nets for the poor. These reforms were packaged together
in a new "multipillar" model of the welfare state, with three separate pillars, or programs. The first, antipoverty pillar comprised a social assistance program targeted to the poor, while the second, retirement pillar
consisted of a privatized mandatory pension program, and the third, savings pillar consisted of voluntary private programs to promote long-term
savings and investments. Among these three different pillars, pension
privatization was by far the highest priority (World Bank 1994, 11–18, 26–29).
Efficiency replaced equity as the top priority in the neoliberal welfare
reform agenda.

The World Bank's leverage over Indian policy makers was direct, due
to a balance-of-payments crisis in 1991 that forced the Indian government to seek help from the IMF. A $500 million World Bank loan
helped the Indian government sustain some social spending through the
budget cuts of the early 1990s, and also helped to finance a new National
Renewal Fund to provide compensation and vocational training to
workers laid off during the restructuring of state-owned industry. The
World Bank used the loan to promote its welfare reform priorities, including more narrowly targeting welfare benefits to the poor and favor-
ing cash benefits over indirect subsidies and food distribution programs.
While the World Bank saw many of its reforms adopted in the loan
agreement, the Public Distribution System food welfare program ended
up being excluded because it was so sensitive politically (World Bank
1995, 2–4).

Over time, however, Indian economic planners and political leaders
embraced most of the World Bank's neoliberal welfare reform agenda.
For example, under a Congress-led government, India's Eighth Five Year
Plan (1992–97) quickly incorporated the World Bank policy of more narrowly targeting the poor for welfare, calling for "sharp" targeting of all
services and subsidies, including the Public Distribution System.[6] It took
a decade longer, but a coalition government led by the Bharatiya Janata
Party (BJP), widely seen as probusiness, endorsed pension privatization
in the Tenth Five Year Plan in 2002.[7] The subsequent Congress-led government also backed pension privatization, introducing its own pension

privatization bill in 2005 (Mehra 2007). By that point, India's techno-cratic economic policy makers and the two dominant parties had reached a consensus on neoliberal welfare reform.

China has successfully avoided any conditional IMF or World Bank loans, and so has never faced the same kind of pressure that Indian pol-icy makers experienced in the 1990s. But the Chinese government volun-tarily sought extensive advice from the World Bank on both its market and welfare reforms. In the 1990s, moreover, these two policy arenas were tightly linked. To facilitate the privatization of most small and medium state-owned enterprises, the Chinese government commissioned the World Bank to develop a series of detailed proposals for pension and social assistance reforms. The core of the proposal was to shift responsi-bility for administering labor insurance from the workplace to new state social insurance programs (Frazier 2010, 60). Although provincial and municipal governments were given considerable discretion over their pro-grams, the new reform was based on the multipillar model, with a new urban social assistance program, a mandatory social insurance program for formal sector works, and new privatized individual savings accounts.

The World Bank's continuing influence on Chinese and Indian pol-icy makers after this initial embrace of neoliberal welfare reform has been overlooked because of significant changes in the World Bank's welfare reform strategy in the 2000s that have not received as much attention as the controversial privatization reforms of the 1990s. These recent changes in the World Bank approach to welfare policy emerged in the wake of the East Asian financial crisis. The austerity programs imposed on these countries by the International Monetary Fund and the World Bank deep-ened poverty in the region, where safety-net welfare programs such as social assistance were rare (World Bank 1999, iii; Stiglitz 2003, 109–21). These failures prompted multiple efforts to rethink welfare reform. In 2001 the World Bank developed the concept of "social risk management," seeking to make societies more resilient in the face of external shocks, whether natural disasters or global financial crises. This new approach reconceptualized welfare programs as "social risk management instru-ments" and argued that "social protection interventions [are] *investments rather than costs*" (World Bank 2001, 9, 16). Welfare programs with broad coverage were now viewed more favorably for enhancing social resilience, rather than criticized for distorting labor markets. On the basis of these new ideas, the World Bank laid out ambitious agendas for welfare expansion for each subregion in Asia (ibid. 71–72).

The culmination of this evolving welfare reform agenda came in 2004 after a World Bank evaluation of the pension privatization reforms in Latin America revealed serious problems (Gill, Packard, and Yermo 2004, 5–11). As a result, the World Bank recommended placing a much higher priority on antipoverty programs with broad population coverage than on pension privatization in its multipillar model (ibid. 11; Holtzmann, Robalino, and Takayama 2009, 85–86). Even long-time critics of the World Bank have embraced the new welfare policy agenda, calling the new policies a fundamental turning point in the development of neoliberalism.[8]

The new World Bank conceptualization of welfare and economic development as complementary rather than trade-offs helped to overcome opposition from economic technocrats in China and India to expansion of the welfare state. For example, India's Eleventh Five Year Plan, adopted in 2007, incorporated the World Bank's new advice on welfare policy. The new Indian development strategy called for "simultaneous focus on a three-legged strategy—economic growth, income-poverty reduction through targeted programmes, and human capital formation—[that] will put India on a sustainable growth path."[9] The plan also argued that expanding social security coverage would boost the economy by promoting greater productivity and stimulating aggregate demand.[10] The contrast to India's previous five-year plan's rejection of any new government welfare spending is stark.

In China, the World Bank's influence was direct, since the government invited the international organization to participate in the policymaking process for China's Eleventh Five Year Plan (2006–10). The World Bank's 2003 World Development Report became required reading for the National Development and Reform Commission (NDRC), and in 2004 the World Bank sent a team of experts to provide more detailed advice to China's economic planners (Fan 2006, 718). The revised neoliberal approach to welfare was evident in the plan. The slogan "scientific development viewpoint" (*kexue fazhan guan*) is peppered throughout the document, which some economists argue is a translation of the World Bank's new ideas about human capabilities–centered economic growth

(Naughton 2005, 2). In contrast to the modest and vague goals for welfare reform in the 10th plan, the new plan set ambitious goals for the expansion of social protection that cadres would be required to meet by 2010, including expanding the coverage of pension programs to 35 percent of the urban population and health insurance to 80 percent of the rural population (Fan 2006, 711–12). These kinds of measurable goals for welfare implementation were unprecedented. In addition, the plan set more general goals of expanding rural pension coverage and "basically" completing the implementation of the social security system (State Council 2006, para. 4.1.3).

This new commitment to welfare expansion was explicitly endorsed by the top party leadership at the party's Sixth Plenum in October 2006, when the CCP announced a new goal of achieving universal coverage in China's social security programs by 2020 (CCP 2006). The impact on policy debates among academics, NGOs, and government officials in China was immediate. As recently as the spring of 2006, these debates had been couched in the familiar framework of the trade-offs between welfare and development. By the fall of 2006, Chinese policy experts shifted their focus from the question of whether to expand coverage to the question of how to expand it. For example, the official theme of the second annual China Social Security Forum in 2007 was "the construction of a social security system with both urban and rural coverage." Moreover, in his speech at the conference, Deputy Finance Minister Wang Jun overturned decades of Finance Ministry opposition to the expansion of rural pensions to discuss how the ministry could assist local governments in implementation (Zheng 2007).

Once economic policy makers eased the constraints on welfare reform in both countries in 2006, a surge of new social pension and other welfare programs with significantly broader population coverage quickly followed from 2007 to 2015.

How has implementation of this neoliberal welfare reform agenda of social assistance, pension privatization, and social pensions fared? Although Chinese policy goals continue to be more ambitious than India's, both of their contemporary reform agendas are more moderate in scope than the reforms of the 1950s, since they do not try to extend equal benefits to the entire labor force. Moreover, the economic constraints on welfare reform have eased considerably, especially in China. Indian per capita income tripled from independence to the close of the 20th century, while Chinese per capita income increased sevenfold over the same period. When we compare their level of economic development at that point to those in Europe during the postwar period of rapid welfare state expansion, both China and India have closed the gap considerably. China's per capita income was only 10 percent of the Western European average in 1950, but it reached 68 percent of that level by 2000. Moreover, China's level of employment had increased from 34 to 50 percent of the population over this period, exceeding Europe's average employment levels of 44 percent. India's gap with postwar Europe also closed from 13 to 38 percent over this 50-year period, although it also experienced a decline in employment levels from 45 to 39 percent of the population (Maddison 2001, 264, 350).

With a less ambitious welfare reform agenda and looser economic constraints, both countries have experienced more success in achieving their welfare reform goals. But once again, domestic welfare politics have reshaped implementation of these programs in fundamental ways.

WELFARE REFORM IN INDIA

Indian democracy deepened as elections grew more competitive and the BJP emerged as a major political party capable of challenging the Congress Party's hold on power (Kohli 2012; Heller 2000). By the 1990s, power began shifting back and forth between the two dominant parties in fragile multiparty coalitions that gave small parties more leverage as well. As a result, more opportunities for meaningful participation in the legislative policy process opened up to different social groups. Access to the courts was also democratized. After Indira Gandhi's temporary suspension of democratic rule in 1975–76, India's Supreme Court adopted a series of reforms to strengthen the judiciary. (See chapter 3 by Ruparelia in this volume.) One key change was to relax the rules regarding standing, allowing NGOs to pursue public interest litigation. Public interest lawsuits surged in the 1980s and 1990s, giving ordinary citizens and even the poor more access to the courts.

Business interests have probably gained the most from the new political competition. For example, a group of finance companies in Mumbai created the OASIS Foundation to advance the cause of pension privatization. In

2000, this foundation drew heavily on World Bank ideas to develop its own proposal for the privatization of India's provident fund (Project OASIS 2000, 14). This support helps explain why both the BJP and the Congress Party backed pension privatization in their bid to build alliances with different business associations (Kohli 2012, 41).

Despite these political gains for business, India's weak and divided labor movement has proven to be surprisingly adept in protecting its interests. Notably, the plans to privatize state-owned industry in the 1990s fizzled (Kohli 2012, 40). Similarly, when the BJP-led coalition government introduced its pension privatization bill in Parliament in 2003, its progress stalled in the face of opposition from trade unions and small leftist parties in the BJP government coalition. By reducing the scope of the initiative to privatizing only the government's own civil servant pension funds, the government pushed ahead with an executive order (Rudra 2008, 118; Alam 2006, 235–36). Two years later the Congress pension privatization bill met the same fate as its predecessor: small left-wing parties backed by organized labor threatened to withdraw from the ruling coalition in order to kill the bill (Mehra 2007). Coalition governments gave India's small labor movement veto power it never had before, counterbalancing the veto power that business had already gained in the courts. Even with the Indian Planning Commission and the two dominant political parties on board, they lacked the leverage to privatize the Employee Provident Fund.

In contrast to pension privatization, new social assistance programs for the poor have been the least controversial part of the targeting reforms. Business opposed new welfare commitments such as social assistance as too costly for government budgets (Project OASIS 2000, 14). But since funding for the new program came out of general tax revenues rather than dedicated taxes on business like the provident fund, opposition was not as fierce. Progressive activists did not lobby for social assistance programs because they saw food welfare programs as less vulnerable to speculators and inflation (Right to Food Campaign 2011, 21–22). But since India never had a national social assistance program before, they also did not resist this addition to the Indian welfare state. As a result, the new National Social Assistance Program to provide cash benefits to the poor was the first part of the neoliberal welfare reform agenda to be adopted in 1995. The new program expanded coverage and standardized minimum eligibility and benefit levels across state programs. But it did not go as far as making social assistance an entitlement. Instead, states were allowed to set a ceiling on the number of recipients in their programs.[11]

Reducing the scope of the Public Distribution System program to more narrowly target the poor has proven to be much more controversial, even though this reform was tightly linked with the social assistance reform in the World Bank proposal. As a result, the government waited until after the 1996 election to more narrowly target PDS benefits to the poor in 1997 (Mooij 1998, 92). The goal was to reduce government spending overall, while increasing the amount of subsidized food going to the poor in order to improve nutrition outcomes, especially child malnutrition and stunting. More narrowly targeting the poor, however, did not necessarily translate into lower welfare spending. Although PDS caseloads declined, spending nearly doubled (Ziegler et al. 2011, 271).

The targeting reforms quickly generated a backlash from activists pushing for a more egalitarian social democratic approach to welfare reform. India's Right to Food Campaign was launched in 2001 to try to establish a constitutional right to food. The People's Union for Civil Liberties (PUCL) filed a law suit with India's Supreme Court to force the government to ensure a constitutional right to food. The Supreme Court endorsed the NGO's case in 2002, mandating that eight different welfare programs, including the PDS and National Social Assistance Program, be treated as entitlements. But since the court was dependent on the legislature and bureaucracy to take action to fulfill these orders, it could do no more than place these reforms on the policy agenda, where they were largely ignored. Over the next decade, the Supreme Court issued another 66 interim orders to the central and state governments to fulfill their obligations, with little effect. The middle-class activists who spearheaded the court case may have had the skills and resources to win lawsuits, but they did not have the members or social networks to sustain mobilization of the poor people they sought to represent (Hertel 2014, 82–85).

It was only after India's economic policymakers adopted the complementary approach to welfare and development in 2006 that the government began responding to these court orders to enforce social rights. The Congress-led government used budget legislation to turn the national social assistance program into a social pension program in 2007, expanding coverage and reducing the age for eligibility to 60 years.[12] The renamed Indira Gandhi National Old Age Pension Scheme aimed to cover all households below the poverty line rather than capping program enrollment, helping to transform this cash transfer program into more of an entitlement.

Reforming the PDS continued to be highly controversial. It took another six years for the legislature to respond to the Supreme Court's mandate to enforce the right to food. The 2013 Food Security Act did not make subsidized food a universal right of citizenship, but it did expand coverage of the PDS from those below or near the poverty line to include 50 percent of the urban population and 75 percent of the rural population. This compromise was criticized from the right for the cost of the expansion and from the left for diluting the entitlements mandated by the courts (Hertel 2014, 87–88). But the law consolidated the PDS program, reversing the trend toward targeting its benefits more narrowly.

The limited ability of the poor or their advocates in civil society to enact their own welfare reforms is even more evident in the effort to extend retirement welfare programs to the majority of the Indian workforce. Seeking to mobilize electoral support, the Congress-led coalition government elected in 2004 campaigned on a platform of extending welfare protections to the informal sector (United Progressive Alliance 2004). To follow through on this promise, it established the National Commission for Enterprises in the Unorganised Sector, composed of academics, government officials, and a few labor union and business representatives. The commission's approach to welfare reform went far beyond the neoliberal reform agenda, calling for universal welfare coverage (NCEUS 2008, 343–44; Kannan 2010, 340–42).

But even if advocates for the poor won a convincing victory within this policy commission, they found little support in the legislature. The National Commission drafted a bill in 2006 to expand both provident fund and social pension coverage to ensure minimum pension benefits for all older Indians (NCEUS 2008, 211). India's labor unions endorsed the bill as long as it was a separate program with new sources of funding that would ensure that their members' retirement benefits would not be affected. To achieve that end, they proposed amendments to impose new employer contributions and dedicated government revenues to fund the program (ibid. 353–56). But by the time the Unorganised Workers' Social

Security Act was adopted in 2008, the Congress-led government stripped out all the provisions concerning old age pensions, enacting only minimal health and life insurance benefits for informal sector workers (Kannan 2010, 341). Despite the name of the legislation, the new program was nothing like a social security program.

This minor reform shows that popular forces still have limited leverage in welfare politics in India today. Labor unions were able to block pension privatization that would have affected their members' provident fund benefits. But this kind of veto power did not extend to mobilizing a majority coalition, especially for people outside the union. Moreover, the NGOs and other new organizations that sought to represent these workers did not have the same kind of membership, connections to political parties, or access to the policy making process enjoyed by organized labor.

These reform efforts show significant changes in India's welfare politics, with much more debate and wider participation in the policy process. Coalition governments gave labor new veto power in the policy process, but they cannot pass legislation without major party support. Similarly, the courts are much more effective at stopping government action than initiating it. The deepening of democracy has given popular forces more power relative to business and other elites in India, but their primary leverage in welfare politics has come through new veto points rather than mobilizing majority coalitions for redistribution.

WELFARE REFORM IN CHINA

Communism has not deepened in China with the move to a market economy and the revival of a new capitalist class in Chinese society. But the regime has evolved in important ways that have reshaped domestic welfare politics. Greater institutionalization of the regime has enhanced political stability and established a more regular policy-making process in the party-state bureaucracy. This policy process features multiple veto points, since a bureaucratic consensus has become necessary for major policy changes (Oksenberg and Lieberthal 1988). Another contribution to political stability has been the decline in the use of mass struggle campaigns. This gain in stability, however, also closed a major avenue for popular participation in policy implementation. Bureaucrats and party cadres now implement new welfare programs, rather than mobilizing welfare recipients to do it themselves. New avenues for political participation have opened up, however, including revival of the petition and court systems. Repression of street protests has also eased in the post-Mao era, and the number of protests have grown significantly over time. After the fall of communism in Europe in 1989–91, CCP leaders have grown increasingly responsive to economic protests in particular, going beyond tolerance to provide compensation or policy changes to bolster the regime's political support (Chen 2012; Perry 2001).

Even without mass campaigns to structure popular participation in program implementation, social groups use all of these avenues for formal and informal political participation to exert pressure on local officials, who have become key players in welfare politics. The pension reforms of the 1990s, for example, were haphazardly implemented until the late 1990s, when an informal alliance between business and local government officials came together out of shared interests in the privatization of state-owned industry. Privatizing the assets of state-owned enterprises and ending the flow of debt financing from state-owned banks created opportunities for both corruption and entrepreneurialism, while at the same time resolving fiscal and financial burden on local governments (Frazier 2010, 72). Even though the transition to the new government-run social insurance programs was completed relatively quickly in the late 1990s and early 2000s, the privatization reform of establishing a third pillar of individual retirement accounts was scuttled in the process. Under pressure to pay ongoing benefits for retirees, local officials used the funds in these individual accounts immediately, rather than investing them on behalf of workers (Frazier 2010, 47). This failure to implement private retirement accounts was in effect a veto of one of the most controversial elements of the pension reform regulations, showing that labor had some leverage in this process even if it could not stop the restructuring of state-owned industry.

The impact of labor protest on local officials is also evident in the surge of early retirements and benefit hikes in this period. The number of retirees increased 38 percent from 1995 to 2002, with the average age at retirement falling to 56 for men and 50 for women in many major cities. At the same time, average pension benefits skyrocketed over 400 percent over the 1990s, reaching 75 percent of average wages in the state-owned sector. In areas like the Northeast, where protests over corruption in privatization and welfare benefits were larger and more persistent than most other parts of the country, average benefits grew even higher. As a result, pension spending doubled from 1997 to 2002 (Frazier 2010, 58, 76–77, 86). The threat of strikes and protests in the late 1990s was a continuation of the veto power that labor first gained in the 1950s and 1960s, when workers were able to preserve their benefits at the expense of the unemployed.

Another sign that welfare politics in China have changed in a fundamental way is that the Communist Party now seems responsive to a much wider range of social classes than just organized labor. Peasant protests and the demands of unemployed workers now lead to compensation and policy changes rather than repression. But local government officials play the leading role in implementing the new social pension and social assistance programs, and in many rural areas the main axis of conflict over implementation lies between these officials and potential beneficiaries. Social pensions, for example, are funded from both government revenues and voluntary contributions by recipients. Since the agricultural tax was eliminated in 2006, rural governments are primarily reliant on revenues from higher levels of government. They not only face hard budget constraints, without the kind of social insurance reserves that urban governments can dip into, they also face funding shortfalls because they have so many unfunded mandates. By avoiding or delaying recruitment campaigns, local officials can save their share of the cost of the basic pension and matching funds in favor of directing their limited resources to higher priorities. Because of these pressures, coverage rates are higher in the provinces that receive full funding for the social pension program from the central government, regardless of their level of economic development or the size of their provincial budgets (Quan 2012, 24).

Even though the wide discretion granted to local officials in the Chinese communist regime has multiplied the number of effective veto points in implementation, the Chinese Communist Party has also developed an effective mechanism for overcoming them: top-down "managed campaigns." In the 2000s, CCP leader Hu Jintao revived and adapted campaign practices to implement his development and welfare reform agenda. But rather than mobilize the masses to implement reforms, Hu

Jintao's "managed campaigns" mobilized cadres across the bureaucratic divisions of the party-state to meet his policy goals, forcing the kind of bureaucratic consensus necessary for effective reform in China. For example, the New Socialist Countryside Campaign used these methods to accelerate economic development in the countryside (Perry 2011). Hu Jintao also incorporated the implementation of the new rural health insurance and social pensions programs, speeding the timeline to ensure that this key policy goal was achieved before he left office in 2012.

Xi Jinping has continued to support development of the social pension program since he took over leadership of the CCP. In addition, he declared a "War on Poverty" in 2015, setting a goal of eliminating absolute poverty in the countryside by 2020. Through the Precision Anti-Poverty Campaign, Xi mobilized government and party cadres into work teams charged with coordinating economic development and welfare programs in assigned villages, seeking to boost the incomes of all families below the poverty line (Zhao 2017). These top-down campaigns have not strengthened the official labor unions, much less mobilized the peasants and migrant workers who benefit from them. But the campaigns are effective in overcoming many of the veto points that local officials have gained in the policy process, enforcing the priorities of the central leadership long enough to implement new programs.

Comparing the politics of welfare reform in contemporary China and India shows that both countries adopted the social assistance and social pension reforms advocated by the World Bank, but rejected its top priority in welfare reform: pension privatization. Labor resistance to neoliberal reform was clearly important in both cases, but did not represent a new balance of power between business and popular social forces. Coalition governments in India and the threat of protest in China were powerful enough to veto reforms that threatened workers' benefits, but neither source of leverage was capable of building a wider coalition for more expansive welfare reforms that did not fit with the neoliberal reform agenda.

Even if the poor have not gained significant leverage from their large numbers at the ballot box or in street protests, political regime type has a major impact on the reach of the welfare state. The key difference is the number and of veto points in the policy process structured by these regimes. China's top-down mobilization of party cadres and government officials in managed campaigns has proven to be effective in overcoming bureaucratic veto points and implementing new programs. In contrast, the deepening of Indian democracy has created more veto points, including multiparty coalition governments and wider access to the courts, but no new mechanisms for overriding them.

This difference in their regimes is evident in the expansion of welfare coverage after these new rounds of reforms. Because of the new social pension programs, coverage in China's social insurance program has doubled to reach 49 percent of the work force, while India's Provident Fund expanded more modestly to 14 percent from 1990 to 2015. Combined with social pensions, this level of coverage translated into pensions for 71 percent of the population over age 60 in China and 24 percent of the same cohort in India in 2015 (ILO 2017, 350, 358, 363). These reforms have had a significant impact on poverty in both countries, since the new programs are targeted to the poor rather than industrial workers.

Expansion of the welfare state, however, has not had the same impact on reducing inequality. In India, for example, 10 percent of the elderly received provident fund benefits in 2015, and another 14 percent of this age cohort received social pensions worth 50 percent less on average (ILO 2017, 358; Rawat 2012, 32–34). Although the majority of elderly Indians received subsidized grain as well, their household quotas were insufficient to cover all their needs for food. While China now provides cash benefits to the majority of the older population, the level of inequality between its retirement programs is extreme: on average, social insurance benefits were 26 times as high as social pensions in 2010 (Zhang 2012, 15–16). The net result of these patterns of coverage and benefit levels is that the majority of Indian and Chinese senior citizens continue to work and rely on their children for support (Holzmann et al. 2009, 5). Even with significant expansion of the welfare state to provide cash benefits to the poorest elderly citizens, inequality continues to define the Chinese and Indian welfare states.

Conclusion

This comparison of more than 60 years of welfare state development shows that shared international influences and economic constraints have shaped China and India's parallel trajectories. While Indian democracy and Chinese communism have shaped welfare politics in both countries, their political regimes have a bigger impact on the implementation and administration of these programs than the timing and content of the policies that created them.

Simple models of political regimes that focus on the institutions for leadership selection and mobilizing political support fail to capture other aspects of China and India's political regimes that proved to be central to their welfare politics. Votes and union membership are not the only numbers that matter; the number of veto points help explain why welfare reform has proven to be more difficult in India than in China. In India's democracy, the courts have been as important to welfare politics as elections and political parties. Moreover, the courts provide groups with the resources to use them effective veto points to inhibit the implementation of policies they oppose. But courts are much less effective in forcing the adoption of new policies than stopping implementation of existing ones. Even after the Indian Supreme Court democratized access to the courts with its public interest litigation reform, court victories on behalf of the poor have not easily translated into new social rights, which require extensive cooperation from the legislative and executive branches. Thus an independent judiciary can undercut the electoral advantage of the poor in a democracy.

Similarly, political campaigns are not important in leadership selection in communist regimes, and no longer play much of a role in mobilizing political support in China today. But they are central to Chinese communist governance. Implementation of welfare reforms through political campaigns has proven to be more effective than the bureaucratic and legal processes employed in India, helping to explain why the Chinese have consistently outperformed their Indian counterparts in the implementation of new welfare programs. But campaigns can also foster instability and local variation that make it difficult to ensure equal treatment of all citizens to secure their social rights.

Simple models of welfare politics also fail to capture the complexity of redistributive conflicts in China and India. In addition to conflicts between workers and capitalists, conflicts between organized labor and other groups among the poor were also important. Early incorporation into the welfare state changed the interests of organized labor. Protecting their members' privileges put labor unions in conflict with other groups seeking welfare protection, making majority coalitions for redistribution more difficult to achieve. Labor unions in communist China protected their members' benefits at the expense of the unemployed, while labor unions in India made little effort to recruit members from the informal sector, much less to advance their interests in the policy process. In this context, simple models of electoral mobilization and measures of labor power fail to capture some of the most important dynamics of welfare politics.

The renewed push for a universal social security system in China and a universal right to food in India in the 21st century has sought to fulfill the vision of equal social citizenship laid out in their constitutions more than 60 years ago. This nation-building project has helped to fill in some of the gaps in the foundations of the Chinese and Indian welfare states. But the legacy of each country's failures in state building in the postwar period has also shaped the welfare reforms that have followed. By layering new welfare programs on top of existing ones, these new reforms perpetuate many of the inequalities in their welfare states. Combined with the new neoliberal emphasis on targeting and efficiency, the promise of more comprehensive social protection and more effective poverty reduction will probably not lead to greater equality among citizens.

Notes

1. Retirement ages for women and government officials are five to 10 years lower.
2. Constitution of India (1950), Article 41; Constitution of China (1954), Article 93.
3. Planning Commission 1952, chap. 34, paras. 54–55.
4. Planning Commission 1957 [*Second Five Year Plan*], chap. 27, para. 27.
5. Planning Commission 1971; Planning Commission 1978; EPFO 1980.
6. Planning Commission 1992, vol. I, paras. 2.2.10, 4.5.11.
7. Planning Commission 2002, vol. I, 67.
8. For example, James Ferguson sees the new welfare policies as a new development within neoliberalism, while Evelyne Huber and John Stephens argue that left-wing gov-

ernments in Latin America have forced the new policies onto the World Bank agenda. See Ferguson 2007; Huber and Stephens 2012, 177–78.

   9. Planning Commission 2008, vol. 3, 86.

  10. Planning Commission 2008, vol. 2, 152.

  11. *The Times of India*, July 30, 1995, 1; World Bank 2001b, 10.

  12. Planning Commission 2008, vol. 3, 98–99.

References

Agarwala, A.N. 1945. "Problems of Social Security for Industrial Workers in India." *International Labour Review* 51.1: 1–16.

———. 1946. "The Social Security Movement in India." *Economic Journal* 56.224: 568–82.

Alam, Moneer. 2006. *Ageing in India: Socio-Economic and Health Dimensions*. New Delhi: Academic Foundation.

Balani, Sakshi. 2013. "Functioning of the Public Distribution System: An Analytical Report." New Delhi: PRS Legislative Research.

Bose, A. B. 1988. "Policies and Programs for the Aging in India." *The Aging in India: Problems and Potentialities*, edited by A. B. Bose and K. D. Gangrade, 58–78. New Delhi: Abhinav Publications, 1988.

Chen, Xi. 2012. *Social Protest and Contentious Authoritarianism*. Cambridge: Cambridge University Press.

Chinese Communist Party (CCP). 2006. *Communique of the Sixth Plenum of the 16th CPC Central Committee* (October 12). http://www.china.org.cn/english/congress/226989.htm.

Dillon, Nara. 2015. *Radical Inequalities: The Revolutionary Chinese Welfare State in Comparative Perspective*. Cambridge, MA: Harvard Asia Center, Harvard University Press.

Dreze, Jean, and Amartya Sen. 1989. *Hunger and Public Action*. Oxford: Clarendon Press.

Employees' Provident Fund (EPF). 1955. *Annual Report for 1954–55*. New Delhi: Central Provident Fund Commissioner.

Employees' Provident Fund Organisation (EPFO). 1957. *Report on the Working of the Employees' Provident Fund Scheme 1955–56*. New Delhi: Central Provident Fund Commissioner.

———. 1958. *Report on the Working of the Employees' Provident Fund Scheme 1957–58*. New Delhi: New Delhi: Central Provident Fund Commissioner.

———. 1966. *Report on the Working of the Employees' Provident Fund Scheme 1964–65*. New Delhi: New Delhi: Central Provident Fund Commissioner.

———. 1976. *Report on the Working of the Employees' Provident Fund Scheme 1975–76*. New Delhi: New Delhi: Central Provident Fund Commissioner.

———. 1980. *Twenty-Seventh Annual Report, 1979–80*. New Delhi: Office of the Central Provident Fund Commisioner.

Fan, Cindy C. 2006. "China's Eleventh Five-Year Plan (2006–2010): From 'Getting Rich First' to 'Common Prosperity.'" *Eurasian Geography and Economics* 47.6: 708–32.

Ferguson, James. 2007. "Formalities of Poverty: Thinking about Social Assistance in Neoliberal South Africa." *African Studies Review* 50.2: 72–76.

Frankel, Francine R. 1978. *India's Political Economy, 1947–1977: The Gradual Revolution.* Princeton: Princeton University Press.

Frazier, Mark W. 2002. *The Making of the Chinese Industrial Workplace: State, Revolution, and Labor Management.* Cambridge: Cambridge University Press.

———. 2010. *Socialist Insecurity: Pensions and the Politics of Uneven Development in China.* Ithaca: Cornell University Press.

Gill, Indermit, Truman Packard, and Juan Yermo. 2004. *Keeping the Promise of Social Security in Latin America.* Stanford: Stanford University Press.

Gough, Ian. 2004. "Welfare Regimes in Development Contexts: A Global and Regional Analysis." In *Insecurity and Welfare Regimes in Asia, Africa and Latin America: Social Policy in Development Contexts,* edited by Ian Gough and Geof Wood, 15–48. Cambridge: Cambridge University Press,

Gough, Ian, and Geof Wood, eds. 2004. *Insecurity and Welfare Regimes in Asia, Africa and Latin America: Social Policy in Development Contexts.* Cambridge: Cambridge University Press.

Haggard, Stephan, and Robert R. Kaufman. 2008. *Development, Democracy, and Welfare States: Latin America, East Asia and Eastern Europe.* Princeton: Princeton University Press.

Heller, Patrick. 2000. "Degrees of Democracy: Some Comparative Lessons from India." *World Politics* 52.4: 484–519.

Hertel, Shareen. 2014. "Hungry for Justice: Social Mobilization on the Right to Food in India." *Development and Change* 46.1: 72–94.

Holtzmann, Robert, David A. Robalino, and Noriyuki Takayama, eds. 2009. *Closing the Coverage Gap: The Role of Social Pensions and other Retirement Income Transfers.* Washington, DC: World Bank.

Huber, Evelyne, and John D. Stephens. 2012. *Democracy and the Left: Social Policy and Inequality in Latin America.* Chicago: University of Chicago Press.

International Labour Organization (ILO). 1944. "The Twenty-Sixth Session of the International Labour Conference." *International Labour Review* 50.1.

———. 2014. *World Social Protection Report 2014/2015: Building Economic Recovery, Inclusive Development, and Social Justice.* Geneva: International Labour Office.

———. 2017. *World Social Protection Report 2017/2019: Universal Social Protection to Achieve the Sustainable Development Goals.* Geneva: International Labour Office.

Jaffrelot, Christophe. 2003. *India's Silent Revolution: The Rise of the Lower Castes in North India.* New York: Columbia University Press.

Jain, Devaki. 2005. *Women, Development, and the U.N.* Bloomington: Indiana University Press.

Kannan, Kappadath P. M. 2010. "Social Security for the Working Poor in India: Two National Initiatives." *Development* 53.3: 338–42.

Kohli, Atul. 2012. *Poverty amid Plenty in the New India.* New York: Cambridge University Press.

Liu, Tao, and Li Sun. 2016. "Pension Reform in China." *Journal of Aging and Social Policy* 28.1: 15–28.

Lu, Xiaobo, and Elizabeth J. Perry, eds. 1997. *Danwei: the Changing Chinese Workplace in Historical and Comparative Perspective.* Armonk, NY: M. E. Sharpe.

Ma, Tehyun. 2012. "A Chinese Beveridge Plan: The Discourse of Social Security and the Post-War Reconstruction of China." *European Journal of East Asian Studies* 11: 329–49.

Maddison, Angus. 2001. *The World Economy A Millennial Perspective.* Paris: OECD.

Mehra, Puja. 2007. "India: Left's Objections to Pension Reforms May Leave the Bulk of Workers Pensionless." *India Today*, February 10.

Mooij, Jos. 1998. "Food Policy and Politics: The Political Economy of the Public Distribution System in India." *Journal of Peasant Studies* 25.2: 77–101.

National Commission for Enterprises in the Unorganized Sector (NCEUS), Government of India. 2008. *Report on the Conditions of Work and Promotion of Livelihoods in the Unorganized Sector.* New Delhi: Academic Foundation.

Naughton, Barry. 2005. "The New Common Economic Program: China's Eleventh Five-Year Plan and What It Means." *China Leadership Monitor* 16: 1–10.

Oksenberg, Michel, and Kenneth Lieberthal. 1988. *Policy Making in China: Leaders, Structures, Processes.* Princeton: Princeton University Press.

Palacios, Robert. 1996. *Averting the Old Age Crisis: Technical Annex.* Washington, DC: World Bank.

Perry, Elizabeth J. 1993. *Shanghai on Strike: The Politics of Chinese Labor.* Stanford: Stanford University Press.

———. 2001. "Challenging the Mandate of Heaven: Popular Protest in Modern China." *Critical Asian Studies* 33.2: 163–80.

———. 2011."From Mass Campaigns to Managed Campaigns: Constructing a New Socialist Countryside." In *Mao's Invisible Hand: The Political Foundations of Adaptive Governance*, edited by Sebastian Heilmann and Elizabeth J. Perry. Cambridge, MA: Harvard University Asia Center.

Planning Commission, India. 1952. *First Five Year Plan.* New Delhi: Planning Commission. http://www.planningcommission.nic.in/plans/planrel/fiveyr/index1.html.

———. 1957. *Second Five Year Plan.* New Delhi: Planning Commission. http://www.planningcommission.nic.in/plans/planrel/fiveyr/index1.html

———. 1971. *Fourth Five Year Plan.* New Delhi: Planning Commission.

———. 1978. *Fifth Five Year Plan.* New Delhi: Planning Commission.

———. 2002. *Tenth Five Year Plan, 2002–2007.* Vol. 2. New Delhi: Oxford University Press.

———. 2008. *Eleventh Five Year Plan, 2007–2012.* Vol. 3. New Delhi: Oxford University Press.

Project OASIS Expert Committee. 2000. *The Project OASIS Report.* Mumbai: OASIS Foundation.

Quan, Lu. 2012. "Analyzing the Coverage Gap in China." London: HelpAge International.

Rawat, Bindlya. 2012. "India: Updating and Improving the Social Protection Index." Manila: Asian Development Bank.

Right to Food Campaign. 2011. "Right to Food" *Economic and Political Weekly* 46.33: 21–23.

Rudra, Nita. 2008. *Globalization and the Race to the Bottom in Developing Countries: Who Really Gets Hurt?* Cambridge: Cambridge University Press.

Rudra, Nita and Stephen Haggard. 2005. "Globalization, Democracy, and Effective Social Spending in the Developing World." *Comparative Political Studies* 38.9: 1–35.

Singh, Prerna. 2015. *How Solidarity Works for Welfare: Subnationalism and Social Development in India.* Cambridge: Cambridge University Press.

Solinger, Dorothy J. 2009. *State's Gains, Labor's Losses: China, France and Mexico Choose Global Liaisons.* Ithaca: Cornell University Press.

———. 2010. "The Urban *Dibao*: Guarantee for Minimum Livelihood or for Minimal Turmoil?" In *Marginalization In Urban China: Comparative Perspectives,* edited by Fulong Wu and Chris Webster, 253–77. Basingstoke, UK: Palgrave Macmillan

State Council, People's Republic of China. 2006. *Labor and Social Protection Development Program for the 11th Five Year Plan* (国务院,劳动和社会保障事业发展"十一五"规划纲要). http://www.gov.cn/zwgk/2006-11/08/content_436541.htm.

Stiglitz, Joseph E. 2003. *Globalization and Its Discontents.* New York: Norton.

United Progressive Alliance. 2004. "UPA Government to Adhere to Six Basic Principles of Governance." *Hindu Times,* May 28. http://www.thehindu.com/2004/05/28/stories/2004052807371200.htm.

Walder, Andrew G. 1986. *Communist Neo-Traditionalism: Work and Authority in Chinese Industry.* Berkeley: University of California Press.

Williamson, John B., and Fred C. Pampel. 1993. *Old-Age Security in Comparative Perspective.* Oxford: Oxford University Press.

World Bank. 1994. *Averting the Old Age Crisis: Policies to Protect the Old and Promote Growth.* New York: Oxford University Press.

———. 1995. *Implementation Completion Report: India Social Safety Net Sector Adjustment Program.* Washington, DC: World Bank.

———. 1999. *Towards an East Asian Protection Strategy.* Washington, DC: World Bank, Human Development Unit, East Asia and Pacific Region.

———. 2001. *Social Protection Sector Strategy: From Safety Net to Springboard.* Washington, DC: World Bank.

Zhang, Xiulan. 2012. *The People's Republic of China: Updating and Improving the Social Protection Index.* Manila: Asian Development Bank.

Zhao, Hanyu. 2017. "The Politics of Poverty Alleviation in Rural China: Xi Jinping's War on Poverty." M.A. thesis, Harvard University.

Zheng Xiaobo. 2007. 郑晓波, "逐步提高社保财政支出比重" 证券时报/2007 年/9 月/24 日/第A07 版 (Progressively increase social protection spending). *Securities Times,* September 24, A07.

Ziegler, Jean, Christophe Golay, Claire Mahon, and Sally-Anne Way, eds. 2011. *The Fight for the Right to Food: Lessons Learned.* New York: Palgrave Macmillan.

CHAPTER 6

Higher Education Reform in China and India

The Role of the State

Devesh Kapur and Elizabeth J. Perry

The quality of a country's system of higher education is a gauge of its current level of national development as well as a bellwether of future economic progress. It is therefore natural that the much ballyhooed "rise" of China and India should generate interest in the condition of their colleges and universities. A number of comparative questions merit investigation: Do these countries' long histories of higher education pose a benefit or a barrier to meeting global contemporary demands? Are their current systems of higher education suited to the "knowledge economy" of the 21st century, and able to drive innovation, economic growth, and national competitiveness? What roles do the Chinese and Indian states play in creating "world-class" universities capable of spurring and sustaining further intellectual and industrial development? Can these academic and economic goals be pursued without collateral damage to other valued goals of social equity and political stability?

The answers to these questions lie within broader and perhaps more fundamental questions about the role and purposes of higher education. How do universities reflect and remake conceptions of citizenship? Is the goal of higher education to create national elites or provide a ladder for social mobility? To influence and mold the minds of young people? To train people for a labor force or train a labor force that is in turn trainable by employers? To create a middle class—the accountants, doctors, engineers, lawyers, scientists, teachers—who will in turn build the institutions which are foundational to nation building? How does the allocation of resources across academic disciplines (among professional education, basic sciences, or liberal arts) affect the content of higher education and thereby the sensibilities of the burgeoning middle class to become either a conservative brake or a progressive force for social and political change? Does "massification" inevitably imply trade-offs between cost and quality, with elite universities simply reproducing existing social hierarchies?

Recent higher education reforms in China and India, backed by impressive increases in state spending (especially in the former) and expanded college enrollments, indicate that governments in both countries recognize the importance of tertiary education for promoting national development. In both cases, moreover, state development goals explicitly embrace a concern for social equity as well as economic growth. Despite such striking similarities in intent, the Chinese and Indian patterns of higher education reform have diverged markedly. "Communist" China, ironically enough, has shown a far greater willingness to sacrifice egalitarian ideals in the pursuit of globally competitive universities than has its democratic neighbor. Political factors account for much of the difference, but in ways that challenge conventional assumptions about the influence of regime type on education policy.

Historical Background

Both India and China are renowned for ancient traditions of higher education—heavily ethical in orientation—that were, however, as elitist as they were illustrious. In imperial China, higher learning (limited for the most part to males from affluent families) constituted a key pillar of state power, institutionalized through competitive Confucian examinations. Qiang Zha explains:

> Ever since the Han dynasty, formal institutions of scholarship had been a part of the structure of imperial rule, and a system of written examinations was gradually developed, which opened up an opportunity for young men to compete for positions in the imperial bureaucracy. Higher learning was thus a formalized part of the state system of rule, and those selected through these examinations were given positions of great responsibility on a meritocratic basis. (Zha 2011b, 21)

By socializing and selecting bright, ambitious young men for government service, higher education in imperial China constituted a cornerstone of political strength and stability that helped to sustain the system for centuries (Elman 2000; 2013). Although few poor families could actually afford the education required to succeed in the imperial examinations, the fact that examinees were not restricted by birth or class background endowed the system with an unusual degree of popular legitimacy. Chinese imperial rule was justified on the basis of what historian Joseph Levenson termed "culturalism," or a belief in the superiority and universality of Confucian values and practices imparted through a classical education. The promise of Confucian culturalism was not confined to the Sinic world; non-Chinese could also gain membership in this higher civilization so long as they learned to read literary Chinese and were properly educated in the Confucian classics (Levenson 1965). To be "cultured" (*you wenhua* 有文化) meant to be educated, to have been transformed (*hua* 化) through mastery of written Chinese (*wen* 文) and its Confucian ethos.

It is easy enough to point to similarities between past and present. The contemporary People's Republic of China, like imperial China, displays particular concern for higher education as both a pillar of state strength and a purveyor of social morality. Its officials are required to attain advanced academic degrees and to pass competitive civil service examinations. Its hundreds of Confucius Institutes around the world offer instruction in Chinese language and culture as an advertisement for the universal appeal of Chinese values. In short, higher education continues to function as an important element of statecraft. But contemporary state practices are far from an uninterrupted or organic outgrowth of traditional patterns; rather, they represent a deliberate effort (led by the Central Propaganda Department) to legitimize communist rule through cultural governance (Perry 2017). The gulf separating China's Confucian past from its communist present is, as Levenson argued, vast.

In the early 20th century, the introduction of alien ideas from abroad (through the founding of Christian schools by American and European missionaries, among other channels) undermined the authority of the ancien régime and encouraged revolutionary change (Lutz 1971; Yeh 1990; Bays and Widmer 2009). The early leaders of the Chinese Communist Party, including Mao Zedong, were intellectuals who had been radicalized in large part by their exposure to Western learning.[1] Their revolution, in turn, featured new forms of education—night schools for workers, part-time schools for peasants, party schools for cadres—designed to instill new "socialist" values in the course of literacy instruction.

In contrast, education in India had historically served a more ecclesiastical and exclusionary function. The historical weakness of the state in India meant that education was largely a private enterprise with limited state support. The learning traditions were oral, centered around the memorization of sacred texts. Women and lower castes were excluded. While evidence is fragmentary about education in ancient and medieval India, several of the large monasteries and temple schools became centers of higher education (what one might call universities today) with those at Taxila, Nalanda, and Vikramshila the most prominent (Scharfe 2002). Subsequently seven centuries of Islamic rule led to the demise of most centers of Brahmanical and Buddhist learning, especially across north India.

There is fragmentary evidence of diverse beliefs and practices rooted in India's rich and multiple religious traditions before the arrival of the British in India. But as with most matters associated with colonial rule, education in colonial India is a contentious subject in Indian historiography. By the mid-19th century a colonial higher education system began to emerge. It was designed to serve the colonial state and not foment any larger changes in society. It developed an examination system that created India's own mandarins, its elite civil service. But as the historian Bernard Kohn points out, "the conquest of India was a conquest of knowledge" and the result was the collapse of indigenous education systems symbolized in the shift in the language of instruction as English gradually replaced both classical and vernacular Indian languages (Kohn 1996, 16).

In China, after the victory of the revolution the communist authorities moved swiftly to revamp higher education so that it might once again serve to support rather than subvert political authority. Soon after the establishment of the PRC in 1949, the new government abolished all private colleges and universities (religious and secular alike) and implemented a Soviet-style system of specialized academies and institutes under tight Communist Party control. The only significant deviations from Soviet practice occurred when Mao Zedong personally intervened in educational policy, embracing initiatives intended to blur the distinction between "red" and "expert" and to reduce inequalities between city and country-side and among social classes (Munro 1977). On a well-publicized visit to Tianjin University in 1958, Mao called for a new model of higher educa-tion to underpin his Great Leap Forward that would combine firm party committee leadership with "mass line" practice and a blending of educa-tion and productive labor. Schools were to run factories and factories to run schools. This radical style of pedagogy was supposed to become uni-versal within 15 years; to accommodate increased enrollments, the num-ber of institutions of "higher education" jumped from 229 to 1,289 in the space of three years. In subsequent pronouncements before and during the Cultural Revolution (1966–76), Mao made clear that these institu-tions should focus on political education for worker-peasant students. Hands-on knowledge of "class struggle" was deemed more valuable than academic or professional training (Zhang 2009, 3–4). Most institutions of higher education ceased to function as such for much of the Cultural Revolution decade.

Only after Mao's death in 1976 did Deng Xiaoping and his colleagues show renewed interest in Western models of higher education as a source of alternative institutional and instructional forms that might better fa-cilitate their ambitious reform agenda. At the 12th National Party Con-gress in 1982, General Secretary Hu Yaobang pointed to the expansion and improvement of higher education (especially in science and technol-ogy) as essential to the country's strategy of economic modernization (ibid. 33). As had been the case before the communist revolution, Ameri-can and European universities were again regarded as a prototype for Chi-nese emulation.

In India, as in China, modern universities were a Western import.[2] The first modern Indian universities were established in 1857 in the Brit-ish "presidency" towns of Calcutta, Bombay, and Madras as the colonial government looked to educate a class of Indians who could staff the grow-ing bureaucracy. By 1882 India had four universities (with the addition of Punjab University in Lahore) and 67 colleges, which grew to five univer-sities and 145 colleges, with 18,000 students (almost all male) by the turn of the century. While initially the colleges were founded by missionaries, those funded and managed by Indians were the majority by the turn of the century. The system was decentralized, with much of the funding from private Indian sources. By 1922 there were 14 universities and 167 colleges, with 46,000 students under the control of elected provincial authorities, with little role for the national government. In 1947, when India became independent, 21 universities and 496 colleges were in operation.

In fact, India had a larger number of secondary and postsecondary students than several industrialized countries such as France, even though primary school enrollment rates were among the lowest in the world. By 1931, India's literacy rate was a mere 8.6 percent, although the small numbers of literates were highly educated. More than 10 percent of them could read and write in English, a second language, even as the vast majority of the people could not read or write in any language, starkly illustrating the unequal nature of the education system (Chaudhary 2010). India had the most Nobel Prizes in Asia prior to independence (and while Indians continued to garner Nobel Prizes in subsequent years, the latter-day Nobel laureates in the sciences were all based abroad).

India's higher education needs to be understood in the context of its education policies in general. At the heart is the paradox of the undoubted success of democracy in India—exceptional in many ways among poor countries—combined with its weak record in human development. The political economy literature argues that democratic governments are more likely to invest in universal education than authoritarian ones. Since broad-based education is fundamentally redistributive, elites will tend to block (or at least limit) access to education to narrow segments (Ansell 2010). And since autocracies are controlled by a narrower group of elites than democracies, the pressures to redistribute are less, and hence access to education is more limited. To put it simplistically, universal franchise should lead to (near) universal education, since the uneducated and poor have a voice. But India's record on basic education belies this prediction; authoritarian China has done far better at providing elementary education to its citizens. If India's "democratic exceptionalism" makes it an outlier, so does its record on primary education, which in turn has consequences for understanding higher education in India.

Two reasons have been advanced to explain this paradoxical Indian outcome. The first stems from the social coalition that made up the Congress, with upper castes linking up with the Scheduled castes and tribes and Muslims, the three largest marginalized communities in India.

Together they account for nearly 40 percent of the country's population. The hierarchies of the caste system had given the upper castes a monopoly on learning, and they were loath to extend it to those at the bottom of India's social hierarchies. Instead they offered "reservations" or affirmative action in higher education and government jobs, which effectively bought off elites among the lower castes. "By managing to direct educational investment away from the masses," the educated elites were "able to protect their scarcity rent" (Bardhan 1984, 52–53). A second reason lay in India's postindependence import substitution industrialization (ISI) development strategy. The resulting closed economy led to a focus on secondary and higher education that could provide the necessary skills for ISI production or to run the growing Indian bureaucracy to manage a planned economy. India's trade strategy, it is argued, affected the size and composition of education spending (Ansell 2010).

Meanwhile, thanks in part to Mao Zedong's personal promotion of rural education as a means of reducing social inequality and revolutionizing the countryside, the People's Republic of China provided basic schooling to the great majority of its citizens. Authoritarian politics proved to be no barrier to the massive extension of education (Gandhi 2008). In China, unlike India, the advancement of nation building and citizenship (Temporalities I and II; see introduction to this volume)—combined with an age-old thirst for education among the Chinese populace—had remarkable consequences. A country that in 1949 had been plagued by a worse illiteracy rate than India's, 30 years later could boast a nearly universal (albeit rudimentary) level of literacy (Peterson 1994).

India started out (in the First Five Year Plan in the early 1950s) with some emphasis on primary education, but this dropped steadily in the next two decades (until the mid-1970s). Between the early 1950s and early 1970s, the share of higher education spending in India increased from a quarter to a third of the education budget, while spending on primary education dropped—precisely in the period when China was putting in place universal primary education. Even as most Chinese universities closed their doors during the Cultural Revolution of the late 1960s and early 1970s, the expansion of primary education continued. In India, by contrast, by the early 1970s, as the economy languished, unemployment among university graduates grew and was one of the drivers of social unrest and political turmoil during this period. As a result, for the next quarter century higher education spending and growth in India stagnated, and the gross enrollment ratio barely grew by 2–3 percent as India's economy remained closed (figure 6.1a, figure 6.1b).

A simulation study in 2000 to predict the demand for education if India became as open to trade as China, found that such an opening would increase the demand for primary education by 12 percent, for higher secondary education by 32 percent, and for college education by 60 percent (Wood and Calandrino 2000, table 13). By this time India had begun to integrate itself into the global economy and this period also marked the onset of "massification" of its higher education.

In India, the share of total government spending on education earmarked for higher education stands today at 18 percent. In China, the comparable statistic is a little over 20 percent. Total government spending on education amounts to 4.2 percent of GDP in India; in China, the figure is 4.3 percent. In both countries, much of the recent increase in public spending has come from the central government, but local governments still account for the lion's share of total education spending.[3] However, in contrast to China the massification of Indian higher education has resulted primarily from the immense expansion of the private sector.

Patterns of "Massification"

The second half of the 20th century witnessed what has been called a "massification" of higher education across much of the globe, with the expansion of postsecondary school enrollments beyond elite circles to the population at large. The expansionary trend was pioneered in the United States (where 40 percent of the college-age cohort was enrolled in higher education in 1960), followed over the next two decades by Western Europe and Japan (Altbach 2011).[4] Fueled to some degree by a rising demand for higher education on the part of newly affluent middle classes, massification was also encouraged by national governments seeking to fuel economic growth.

By the end of the 20th century, state-led massification of higher education had become a common pattern, popularized in large measure by

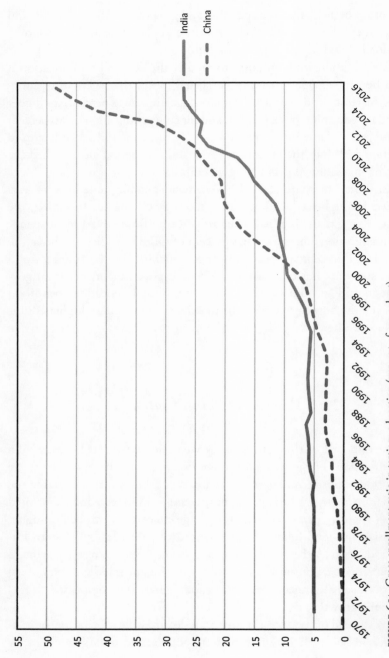

FIGURE 6.1A Gross enrollment ratio in tertiary education (percent of age cohort).
Source: UNESCO, Institute for Statistics

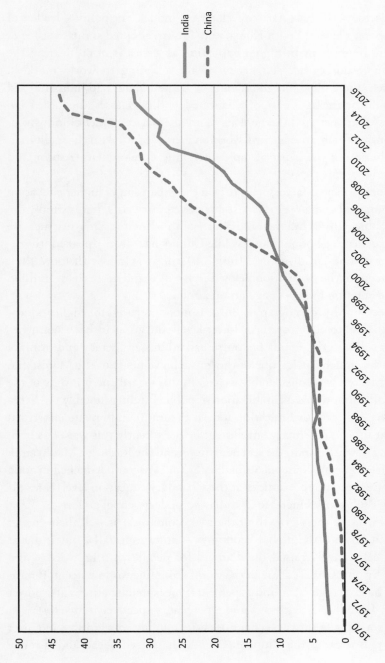

FIGURE 6.1B Enrollment in tertiary education (millions).
Source: UNESCO, Institute for Statistics

the success of the East Asian development model. The political leaders of Singapore, Taiwan, South Korea, and Taiwan adopted similar strategies of state investment in higher education as a means of cultivating the human resources deemed necessary for adapting to world markets. Whereas the United Kingdom and the United States had industrialized gradually on the basis of poorly educated working classes, the East Asian "tigers" demonstrated the benefits of an alternative model of industrialization in which an educated workforce enjoyed a relatively egalitarian distribution of the fruits of rapid economic development (Ashton and Green 1997, 7, 154–75).

Four principal factors have driven the expansion of higher education in China and India over the past quarter century. The first is simply demographic. China and then India have both witnessed a massive increase in the college age population. While China's has already peaked (the result of its one-child policy), India's is still growing, with more than 30 percent of the population below the age of 15 and more than 5 million people entering the 15–24 age group annually.

Second, this demographic bulge is more prepared for higher education thanks to the growth of lower-level education in both countries (figures 6.2a, 6.2b). China of course had addressed literacy and primary education much earlier, one of the key achievements of the Maoist era. India's record was considerably weaker in this regard and it is only in the new millennium that a combination of public funding (notably the Sarva Shiksha Abhiyan, or Education for All Program) and private efforts led to near universal primary enrollment. More recently this wave has been moving downstream to the secondary level and the Rashtriya Madhyamik Shiksha Abhiyan (National Secondary School Program) launched in 2009 to create greater opportunities at the secondary education level, is resulting in a substantial increase in India's secondary school cohort.

Third, the sheer growth of the two economies, as well their greater integration into the global economy—China especially, but India as well—has sharply raised the demand for people with knowledge and skills. By 2011 China's share in the world economy was 10 percent, if measured by exchange rates, and 15 percent if measured by purchasing power parity. In India's case it was 3 and 6 percent, respectively (table 6.1).

Around 1980 the two economies were roughly equal in size, but after three-plus decades the Chinese economy has raced ahead and is today

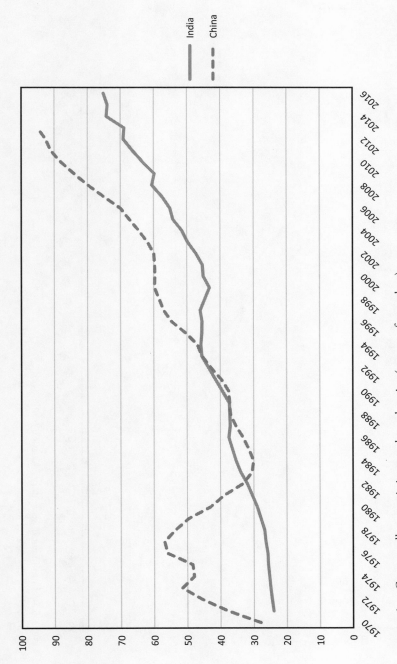

FIGURE 6.2A Gross enrollment ratio in secondary education (percent of age cohort).
Source: UNESCO, Institute for Statistics

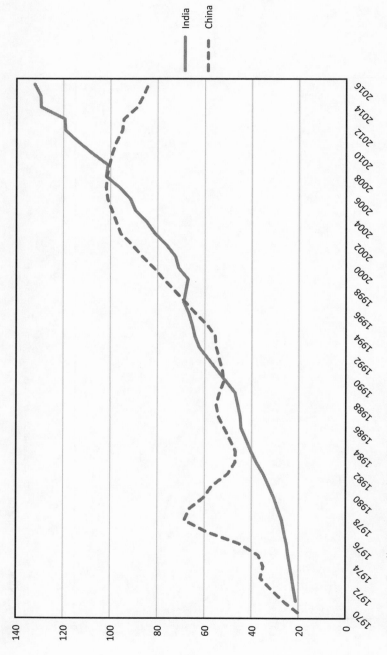

FIGURE 6.2B Enrollment in secondary education (millions).
Source: UNESCO, Institute for Statistics

Table 6.1

Purchasing power in China and India, 2014

		China	India
Expenditures (US$, billions)	Based on PPs	13,496	5,758
	Based on XRs	7,322	1,864
Expenditures per capita (US$)	Based on PPs	10,057	4,735
	Based on XRs	5,456	1,533
Price level index (World=100)		70	42
	Based on PPs	75	35
Expenditures per capita (World=100)	Based on XRs	52	15
	Based on PPs	20	10
Index (US=100)	Based on XRs	11	3
	Based on PPs	15	6
Share (World=100) Expenditures	Based on XRs	10	3
Population		20	18

SOURCE: World Bank, 2011 International Comparison Program (ICP), 2014.

NOTE: PP = purchasing power parity; XR = exchange rate

nearly three times the size of the Indian economy. The resource gap between their education sectors has widened into a gulf. While education has become a big business sector in both countries, value added in education services in China soared from $10.4 billion in 1990 to $257.6 billion in 2012, while in India it rose from $6.9 billion to $44.6 billion in the same period.[5]

Finally, demand for higher education is being driven by major changes in the aspirations of the Chinese and Indian populations as well as by state policy. Political leaders in both countries have endorsed a substantial increase in enrollments. In India, the stated goal is to move from a current enrollment of approximately 14 percent of its college-age population to 30 percent by 2020 (Kapur 2011, 89). In China, the proportion of the age cohort enrolled in higher education has already increased from a miniscule 1.2 percent in 1978 to some 30 percent today; by 2020 it is slated to reach 40 percent of the age cohort.[6] As the world's two most populous countries, this rapid increase in enrollments is particularly impressive; today China and India lead the world in terms of the absolute number of students enrolled in institutions of higher learning (figures 6.1a, 6.1b).

Despite a shared commitment to increased enrollments, patterns of expansion in the two countries are in fact quite different. In China, massification (*dazhonghua* 大众化) has been centered at public universities. As China abandoned the specialized Soviet model that had structured its higher education system during Mao's day to embrace an alternative Anglo-American model of the "comprehensive university" (*zonghe daxue* 综合大学), the Ministry of Education encouraged formerly separate institutes, colleges, and universities to amalgamate. Between 1992 and 2000, some 556 previously separate schools were combined into 232 amalgamated institutions (Liu 2003, 1). The mergers were accompanied by a major increase in the number of students, creating what were often only loosely integrated megauniversities (*juxing daxue* 巨型大学) with enrollments of tens of thousands of students and operations spread over multiple campuses. In 1999, Chinese higher education enrolled 8.8 million students (10.5 percent of the age cohort); by 2006 the enrollment figure had increased nearly threefold to 25 million students (22 percent of the age cohort) (Zhang 2009, 44). Although private schools also proliferated in this period, public institutions still accounted for more than 80 percent of enrollments in 2008 (table 6.2).[7]

In early 2014, China's State Council approved a policy to convert some 600 provincial and local public colleges and universities into institutions for vocational training. Concerned about rising unemployment among the glut of college graduates generated by the rapid massification of higher education, the central government hoped to reverse the worrisome trend by encouraging more applied and professional instruction tailored to market demand. As a result of this action, vocational schools are slated to increase as a proportion of higher education institutions from 55 percent to 70–80 percent.[8] For 2014, the Ministry of Education announced that of the 6.98 million students admitted to higher education through the unified university entrance examination, 3.63 million would pursue regular undergraduate degrees while the other 3.35 million would be enrolled in technical training programs.[9]

In contrast to China, most of the growth in enrollments in higher education in India has taken place through the establishment of new private colleges in the last decade, with the bulk of expansion in professional and technical education like engineering, business, pharmacy, and the

Table 6.2
Number of higher education institutions in China

	Institutions providing graduate programs (研究生培养机构)	Regular HEIs (普通高校)	Number of regular HEIs that are private (民办)	HEIs for adults (成人高等学校)	Other nonstate/ private HEIs (民办的其他高等教育机构)
2003	720	1552	173	558	1104
2004	769	1731	226	505	1187
2005	766	1792	250	481	1077
2006	767	1867	276	444	994
2007	795	1908	295	413	906
2008	796	2263	638	400	866
2009	796	2305	656	384	812
2010	797	2358	674	365	836
2011	755	2409	696	353	830
2012	811	2442	706	348	not listed

SOURCES: For 2003–10: 高等教育学校 (机构) 数 (Number of higher education institutions [HEIs]), in 中国教育统计年鉴 2003–2010. For 2011: Ministry of Education, 高等教育学校（机构）数 (Number of higher education institutions), www.moe.gov.cn/publicfiles/business/htmlfiles/moe/s7382/201305/152554.html (accessed April 3, 2014). For 2012: Ministry of Education, 高等教育学校（机构）数 (Number of higher education institutions), http://www.moe.gov.cn/publicfiles/business/htmlfiles/moe/s7567/201309/156873.html (accessed April 3, 2014).

like. Between 2000–2001 and 2014–15, the number of colleges in India increased from 12,806 to 40,760, which meant an average of more than five new colleges were established every day in this period and the number of students increased by 1.8 million *annually* (figure 6.3a).

By 2011 India had 659 universities (degree granting institutions)—152 central universities under the federal government, 316 state universities, and 191 private ones (figure 6.3b). The bulk of students were enrolled in undergraduate colleges affiliated to a university, of which 69 were central government–managed colleges, 13,024 were under various state governments, and 19,930 were private colleges (figure 6.3c). There were another 12,748 diploma-granting institutions, of which 9,541 were private and the remaining 3,207 under different state governments. By 2015–16, 28.5 million students were enrolled in 753 universities and 41,435 colleges (University Grants Commission 2016, 83, 123).

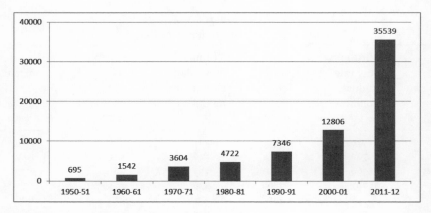

FIGURE 6.3A Number of colleges in India.
Source: National Mission on Higher Education

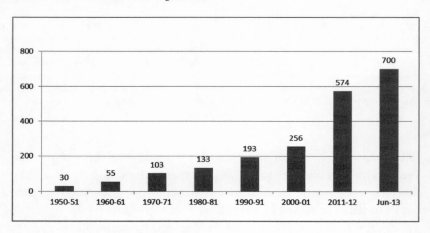

FIGURE 6.3B Number of universities in India.
Source: National Mission on Higher Education

The vast majority of Indian college students are enrolled in private and state institutions of poor quality, with no research facilities and a dearth of qualified faculty. Although private higher education institutions are de jure nonprofit, they are de facto commercial and profit-maximizing. Recently, however, there have been new private entrants of higher quality supported by philanthropists. Federal higher education institutions (the so-called central universities) continue to attract better students due

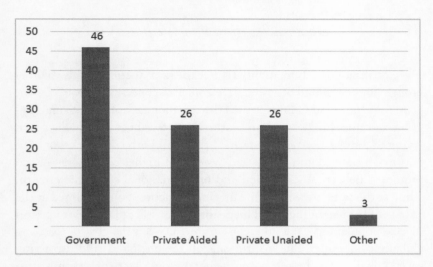

FIGURE 6.3C Percentage of different types of colleges in India.
Source: National Mission on Higher Education

to their better funding, greater autonomy from politics, selection criteria (competitive national exams), relatively modest fees (and scholarships and loans for needy students), and some commitment to research. After an initial burst in the 1950s and 1960s, there was a hiatus for nearly three decades before a new expansion of central universities in the 2000s. However, the vast majority of students in public universities are in state universities. Indian states differ considerably in their economic performance and the political parties that dominate them. However, apart from a handful of exceptions, virtually all state universities are poorly governed. They charge little and teach little, yet there is little political pressure or leadership to undertake painful reforms.

China's most prestigious universities are also centrally managed, but a number of provincial and municipal-level institutions have succeeded in attracting high-caliber faculty and students. Subnational variation is extreme. Wealthy cities and provinces—most notably Beijing and Shanghai—invest heavily in their institutions of higher education in order to satisfy the demands of their residents, as well as to stimulate local economic growth. Places with scant resources are another story, however.

Decentralization and Inequality

The globalization of Temporality III (see the introduction to this volume) brought another round of shared developmental concerns to the two Asian giants. As India and China pursued the common task of liberalizing sluggish economies in the late 20th century, they faced parallel challenges in trying to remake their ivory towers. Leaders in both countries sought to reform centralized and politicized systems of higher education so as to promote intellectual innovation and propel national economic growth, while at the same time retaining affirmative action policies aimed at the redress of long-standing social inequalities that still afflict their huge and diverse populations. The inherent tension between the goal of fostering globally competitive elite institutions, on the one hand, and furthering social equality, on the other, was heightened by the demographic pressures of unprecedentedly large younger generations entering the college-age years. These basic similarities notwithstanding, the ways in which China and India have gone about the process of reforming their systems of higher education turn out to be surprisingly different in many respects. Ironically, India, despite its democratic and federalist political system, has shown less appetite for relinquishing central control or diluting state-sponsored affirmative action programs than its communist counterpart.

To be sure, in both China and India the central state continues to play a major role in defining and directing higher education. Indian higher education has been dubbed "the last refuge of the License Raj" (Kapur 2010, 316), whereas in China college campuses are second only to military installations in terms of the degree of Communist Party penetration and control. Indeed, the rigorous military training and routinized political instruction to which Chinese college students are subject render the distinction between army camps and university campuses somewhat moot. Both states also express a commitment to reducing social inequities through affirmative action in admissions policies for underprivileged segments of their populations. In the case of India, the objective is to reduce discrimination based on caste and region; in the case of China, the aim is to level the playing field for its 55 officially designated "national minorities" as well as for impoverished Han Chinese. According to

Article 9 of the Higher Education Law of the People's Republic of China, "The State takes measures to enable students who come from ethnic groups and students who have financial difficulties to receive higher education."[10]

In China, the difficulty of achieving affirmative action goals is intensified by severe regional disparities in educational infrastructure, quality, cost, and access. Wealthy provinces and municipalities such as Zhejiang, Beijing, and Shanghai provide substantial local government assistance to fund their famous institutions of higher learning, but universities in less prosperous places are forced to take out sizable bank loans that translate into skyrocketing tuition fees. The result is a price tag even at some public universities that exceeds the means of many Chinese families. To be sure, regional differences are not a new feature of Chinese higher education. After the reorganization of the early 1950s, 85 of China's 201 remaining institutions of higher education were located in east China, with 43 (or one-fifth of the national total) in Shanghai alone (Zhang 2009, 9). The origins of today's elite universities can be found in that 1952 reorganization effort (although many of the institutions had important pre-1949 roots as well). Concentrated in the richer east China cities and provinces, the top universities today attract a disproportionate share of students from privileged backgrounds—a national survey of 50 institutions in 10 provinces found, for example, that students from families of government officials were 18 times as likely as those with unemployed or laid-off parents to gain admission to national elite universities. Students from impoverished backgrounds are heavily concentrated in local institutions and vocational colleges (Zha 2011b, 36). The unified national entrance examination for higher education (*gaodeng xuexiao zhaosheng quanguo tongyi kaoshi* 高等学校招生全国统一考试) is also stacked in favor of students in Beijing and Shanghai, whose municipal governments reserve extra slots at their renowned public universities for students with local household registration even when their examination scores are well below those of outside applicants.

Since the mid-1980s, Chinese institutions of higher education have been encouraged to further diversify their financial base by seeking non-government sources of support in the form of tuition fees, profits from school-sponsored enterprises and consultancies, and philanthropic giving. Before this period, colleges and universities were entirely dependent upon government funding and higher education was provided free of charge. Since the 1990s, however, nongovernment funds have accounted for a rapidly rising proportion of operating expenses: 30 percent in 1995, 44 percent in 2000, and 56 percent in 2007 (Zhu and Lou 2011, 79). With Chinese society shouldering a growing percentage of the cost of higher education, the content and quality of instruction is increasingly subject to market demand. Such a trend may be welcomed as a sign of reduced government control, but it comes at a steep price. Practical and applied knowledge tends to be preferred over liberal arts and basic research. Wealthy families are better able to secure high-quality education for their children. And the better schools are increasingly concentrated in the more economically developed urban areas (ibid. 97). A recent survey summarizes the outcome—in China "college is a rich, Han, urban male club" (Wang et al. 2013).

In India there are multiple axes of inequalities in higher education, across social (caste) and religious groups, across states, the rural-urban divide, and gender and income. Unlike China, however, these inequalities have been declining in recent years, with one exception—the gap between income groups appears to be widening. For instance the number of women enrolled in higher education per 100 men was a dismal 13 in 1950 and gradually rose to 28 in 1970 and 46 in 1990. It rose more rapidly in the next quarter century to 86 in 2014–15. In the case of other social and religious groups, while the gaps in higher education are large in the overall population (reflecting past inequalities), they decline considerably among those currently enrolled in college.

The unequal representation in Indian higher education is mainly due to inequalities at the lower rungs of the education ladder and only secondarily due to unequal access to tertiary education per se (Azam and Blom 2008). Completing higher secondary education is a necessary condition to enter the portals of higher education. In 1999 the higher secondary completion rates for India's low castes, tribals, upper castes, and Muslims were 4.93, 4.35, 21.99, and 7.12 percent, respectively. By 2009, these had climbed to 9.44, 7.98, 32.83, and 10.63 percent, respectively (Basant and Sen 2013). However, until recently Indian policies have focused much more on affirmative action in higher education instead of improving higher secondary completion rates for weaker social groups. Increasingly, the rapid expansion of private higher education has meant that access depends on the ability to pay, which means almost inevitably that, despite a massive expansion in bank loans for higher education from 3 billion rupees in 2000 to nearly 620 billion rupees (approximately $10 billion) in 2014, those with higher incomes will have greater access.

Politics and Political Leadership

Convergent comparison illuminates political as well as pedagogical differences. Indian prime ministers routinely bemoan the abysmal condition of Indian higher education, while nonetheless refraining from active intervention. In the PRC, by contrast, there is a continuing tradition of forceful intervention in education policy by central leaders. Strong political leaders, as part of their statecraft credentials, are expected to make dramatic pronouncements on education. Mao Zedong established the pattern with his famous "Talks on Education," delivered shortly before the outbreak of the Cultural Revolution (Schram 1974). Mao drew upon China's own experience of revolutionary education to criticize the Soviet "revisionist" model of specialized academies and institutes in favor of practical and highly politicized forms of mass education. The result was that most Chinese universities ceased to function for the better part of a decade. Deng Xiaoping's post-Mao educational reforms sought to repair the damage of the Cultural Revolution, resuscitating Chinese higher education to serve as a powerful engine of national economic modernization. Deng's dramatic restoration of the national college entrance examination in 1977 signaled a return to academic merit, in place of revolutionary fervor, as the key criterion for admission and advancement. The decision in 1999 to radically expand college enrollments was also made by the top leadership, who "ignored opposition from the Ministry of Education (MOE), overturned established policies, and assumed *de facto* control over MOE bureaucratic power" (Wang 2014, 132).

General Secretary Jiang Zemin and his colleagues ensured that the massification of Chinese higher education would be accompanied by an elitist pattern of strategic state investment. On the occasion of Peking

University's centennial celebration in May of 1998, a speech by Jiang Zemin launched what came to be known as Project 985 (for the year and month of Jiang's announcement), by which impressive infusions of central state funding were to be funneled to a small handful of universities deemed capable of becoming "world-class universities." Project 985 had been anticipated a few years earlier by Project 211, a Ministry of Education initiative that showered financial resources on China's supposedly top 100 universities, in hopes that at least a subset of them might reach "global standards" in the 21st century. But Project 985 was even more selective than its forerunner; at first limiting its support to a mere nine universities and then expanding to include an additional 34 institutions. The funding formula within Project 985 was also hierarchical—Peking University and Tsinghua University were given the privilege of being exclusively funded by the central government (with 1.8 billion RMB each for the first three years of Project 985), whereas other Project 985 recipients were forced to seek matching funds from various sources at lower levels of the political system (Zha 2011b, 31). The result of this targeted funding by the central government has been a further stratification of Chinese universities, with a small number of aspiring global players on top of the pyramid structure; a sizeable number of provincial universities, independent colleges, and degree-granting private universities in the middle; and a still larger number of vocational colleges bringing up the bottom tier (ibid. 32). China's current president, Xi Jinping, has already put his personal stamp on higher education policy by calling for "world-class universities with Chinese characteristics" in a May 2014 speech at Peking University. Rather than simply imitate famous foreign universities, Chinese educators were encouraged to develop an alternative (if unspecified) model. Xi explained, "The world can have only one Harvard . . . but China can have its own Peking, Tsinghua, Fudan, Nanjing and Zhejiang universities."[11] Two years later, at a two-day congress on ideological and political work in higher education, Xi made clear that "universities with Chinese characteristics" must adhere to Marxist principles under the firm leadership of the Chinese Communist Party.[12]

Whereas Indian politicians have been driving the proliferation of private colleges in that country, in China government officials are closely tied to the expansion and enrichment of public universities. At Chinese public universities, the nexus between academic administration and political position is formally recognized. Presidents and party secretaries at public universities are considered part of the party/state nomenklatura, with those at leading institutions holding a bureaucratic rank equivalent to that of a vice minister of a central ministry. By contrast, the recent growth of private universities in China is primarily propelled by entrepreneurs hoping to turn a profit.[13]

The university system in India is the collateral damage of Indian politics. The vast majority of government colleges in small towns offer dismal educational outcomes. For politicians, the benefits of the "License-control Raj" extend beyond old-fashioned "rent seeking" by manipulating contracts, appointments, admissions, and grades in government-run colleges and universities, to the use of higher education admissions for vote banks and partisan politics and a source of new entrepreneurial activities (in private higher education) (Kapur and Mehta 2008). India's governance weaknesses beset public services more generally, and the shortcomings of higher education are simply one more manifestation of this affliction.

Three key factors have shaped the political economy of India's higher education: the structure of inequality in India; the principal cleavages in Indian politics; and the nature of the Indian state. India's historic severe degree of educational inequality led to a populist redistributive backlash when hitherto marginalized social groups came to power. However, the specific redistributive mechanisms were conditioned by the principal cleavages in Indian politics and the nature of the Indian state. The growth of identity politics sharply enhanced political mobilization around two key cleavages in Indian society: caste and religion. Consequently, redistributive measures followed these two cleavages (especially caste) rather than other possibilities, such as income, region (urban-rural), gender, or parental education. Moreover, given the fiscal constraints of the Indian state and the shifting locus of rents, redistribution focused on much more "visible" forms, which explains why Indian politicians have obsessed over reservations in elite institutions of higher education rather than improve early childhood health (which affects cognitive abilities later in life), the quality of primary and secondary schooling, and the thousands of government colleges of abysmal quality.

Regulation and Governance

In China, the communist party-state's administrative and propaganda apparatus continues to play a key role in governing the country's universities. During the Mao period, institutions of higher education were typically managed by various central government ministries (with, for example, the Ministry of Coal operating institutes for mining technology, the Ministry of Machine Building running institutes of mechanical engineering, the Ministry of Public Health administering medical schools, and so on). Today, however, the Ministry of Education is the only central ministry encouraged to manage universities (with 72 institutions falling under its direct auspices); the great majority of the country's public institutions of higher education have been placed under the control of provincial and other local governments (Zhang 2009, 59).

Relative to their Indian counterparts, Chinese universities appear quite autonomous. Academic decisions (faculty hires and promotions, new teaching programs and research institutes, cooperative agreements with foreign universities, and so on) are for the most part decided within universities, albeit with review and ultimate approval vested in the Ministry of Education or other relevant government (and party) agencies. At the larger comprehensive universities, basic personnel and curricular and research operations are further devolved to the faculty or school level with only overall budget, construction, and major personnel decisions made by the university administration.

This apparent autonomy is, however, tempered by the central role of the Chinese Communist Party. Not only are leaders at major public universities part of the nomenklatura system of the communist party-state; the university's party committee exercises a veto option over all important university decisions. The basic system of party control was imported from the Soviet Union in the 1950s, but it operates even more forcefully in its Chinese version: "In universities and other key education institutions in the Soviet Union, the party secretary's job was to oversee party members. In China . . . the party secretary has the ability to control both party members and appointments and also oversee the curriculum, outranking the titular head of the institution, the president" (McGregor 2012,

79). Under Xi Jinping, party control over the universities has tightened. Even joint ventures with foreign partners are now required to have a party secretary, who will enjoy vice chancellor status, as well as a seat on the university's Board of Trustees.[14]

This campus governance structure is embedded within a larger framework of party supervision and direction. The Communist Party's central and provincial propaganda departments set the agenda, conduct the selection and evaluation process, and regulate the funding for major research projects in the humanities and social sciences. The recent surge of grants for projects on the "theoretical innovations of General-Secretary Xi Jinping's pronouncements" is illustrative of this situation.[15]

The continued influence (and interference) of the Communist Party in academic matters is often criticized as an impediment to the development of Chinese higher education on grounds that great universities cannot flourish in an illiberal political environment (Kirby 2014). At the same time, it must be acknowledged that the close connection between government and academia that prevails in the PRC affords the Chinese state a strategic advantage in targeting and leveraging the resources of higher education in service to its own national and local priorities. Few other countries (with the notable exception of Singapore) are as well positioned to advance and exploit university training and research for state-directed development.

Since the higher education reform of 1998, Chinese university administration has generally become more streamlined and efficiency-minded. For example, after the process of amalgamation, Harbin Industrial University saw its 42 administrative agencies reduced to 13. Whereas previously the university bureaucracy had included 25 party/government agencies, after 1998 the number stood at only three: one for university administration, one for student work, and one for discipline and surveillance. The nine party/mass association agencies that had operated on campus prior to 1998 were reduced to two: a political work department and a union office (Ying 2008, 414).

China's commitment to reduce the size of academic administration stands in stark contrast to higher education trends in other parts of the world. In the United States, the number of administrators and professional staff at universities and colleges has doubled in the past 25 years—a rate of increase more than twice that of student enrollments in the same period. The notable rise in the cost of higher education in the United States has been linked directly to the proliferation of highly paid administrators (Marcus 2014). While American higher education is succumbing to what—to adapt a phrase from Clifford Geertz—we might term "academic involution," China is running its megauniversities with an ever leaner staff.[16] This creates an onerous work burden for administrators, but it also reduces red tape and thereby renders Chinese universities readily responsive to party secretaries' directives.

In comparison to China—and indeed relative to its own preindependence past—Indian higher education is centralized, politicized, and paradoxically anti-intellectual. The prevailing political ideological climate in which elite institutions are seen as antidemocratic, finds its natural response in political control to influence admissions policies, internal organization, and the structure of courses and funding. The fact that the system nonetheless produces a noticeable number of high-quality students is due largely to Darwinian selection mechanisms rather than to pedagogic achievements.

Higher education in India suffers from political, administrative, and regulatory interference on virtually every aspect of higher education— be it admissions policies, internal organization, fees and salaries, or the structure of courses and funding, although the sheer size of the system is forcing some degree of loosening. Regulatory approvals are extremely rigid with regard to infrastructure requirements (in principle but not in practice) and an insistence on academic conformity to centrally mandated course outlines, degree structures, and admissions policies. The highly centralized regulatory process produces an adverse selection in the kind of entrepreneurs that invest, since the success of a project depends less upon the pedagogic design of the project than the ability to manipulate the regulatory system (Kapur and Mehta 2008). Severe governance weaknesses—of the regulatory system as well as within individual institutions—have resulted in Indian courts emerging as a significant actor shaping higher education policy, often not for the better. And a key stakeholder—faculty—is either absent (manifest in the acute shortage of qualified faculty) or at best poorly trained and rarely the flag bearers of professional norms and standards.

Internationalization and Innovation

In both China and India, the state's principal goal in espousing higher education reform is to facilitate the transition from a manufacturing economy to a "knowledge" economy propelled by technological innovation. In keeping with the logic of Temporality III, the Indian and Chinese central governments have both expressed support for a range of neoliberal policies intended to render their systems of higher education better equipped for international economic competition in the 21st century. In both cases, moreover, *globalization* has been embraced as a pillar of the reform agenda. Openness to international academic ideas, standards, and talent is explicitly endorsed. Attentiveness to world university rankings and attractiveness to foreign students, faculty, and curricula are underscored.

In light of these broad similarities, the differences between the two countries are especially intriguing. Despite the deep involvement of the Chinese Communist Party and its Central Propaganda Department, the PRC's system of higher education has shown a remarkable receptivity to outside initiative. To illustrate the contrast between the Asian giants, consider the following two recent and well-publicized developments in transnational philanthropy: the Indian government's grant of Rs 25 crore (US$5 million) to establish a new Indira Gandhi Centre for Sustainable Development at Oxford University; and the Chinese government's announcement of a US$300 million gift (principally from American businessman Stephen Schwarzman) to establish at Tsinghua University a new Schwarzman College intended to rival Oxford's legendary Rhodes Scholarship.[17] In the former case, a modest sum of government money flows out of Delhi to attach an official Indian name to one of the world's elite universities located in the United Kingdom; in the latter case, 60 times as much private money flows toward Beijing to attach an entrepreneurial American name to China's top engineering school in a bid to accelerate its ascent into the rarified ranks of the international elite. The latter strategy appears to be paying off handsomely; although the Schwarzman College did not officially open its doors until the fall of 2016, according to the 2015–16 *U.S. News and World Report* rankings of colleges and universities, Tsinghua University had already beat out MIT as the top engineering school in the world.[18] Not to be left behind, Peking University hastily announced plans for a new Yenching Academy—reportedly financed by Chinese businessmen—that welcomed its own variant of Rhodes Scholars from elite universities around the world (for an M.A. in Chinese studies taught in English) one year sooner than neighboring Tsinghua, in the fall of 2015.

While these particular examples may seem idiosyncratic or extreme, they are symptomatic of broader differences in the two countries' globalization strategies that have developed over time. Postindependent India had actively sought global collaborations as it set about creating the new Indian Institutes of Technology and Indian Institutes of Management that would become centers of excellence in higher education. Thus the Indian Institute of Technology, Kanpur, established in 1959, benefited in its first decade from the Kanpur Indo-American Programme, where a consortium of nine U.S. universities helped set up the research laboratories and academic programs. The Indian Institute of Management, Ahmedabad (established in 1961), collaborated with the Kellogg School, Wharton School, and Harvard Business School in its initial years, while the Indian Institute of Management, Calcutta, was developed in collaboration with MIT. Faculty training and program design were the key elements in these collaborations.

A less heralded, but equally successful international collaboration occurred in the development of Indian agriculture higher education institutions modeled on U.S. land grant universities. Nine new state agricultural universities were created (one per state) in collaboration with five U.S. universities, who supplied 300 professors on assignments of two or more years to these nine Indian universities. And more recently, given the deep crisis in public health in India, the Indian government has partnered with the Gates Foundation (as well as the World Bank, World Health Organization, and Wellcome Trust) in the creation of the Public Health Foundation of India (PHFI), an autonomous public-private partnership that is establishing new public health schools in India to address the country's India's poor record in this area.

In contrast with China, however, while foreign universities may collaborate with Indian partners through various mechanisms, they are not allowed directly to offer their own degree programs in India. Media reports cite a 2010 study by the Association of Indian Universities (AIU) that more than 600 foreign education providers were operating in India, largely through twinning programs (whereby students study partly in India and partly overseas) that either award a degree from the overseas partner or a dual degree (one from the local provider and one from the overseas partner) (Aggarwal 2013). Most such programs are in professional education (business-related degrees, engineering, and hotel management), with the providers mainly from the United Kingdom and United States. A new development stems from the Indian government's endeavor to set up community colleges for workforce development to fill major skills gaps in trades. Many of these are developing institution-to-institution tie-ups with U.S. community colleges (IIE 2013).

The Indian government's introduction of a Foreign Educational Institutions (Regulation of Entry and Operations) Bill in Parliament in 2010 proved contentious. To get around it, in late 2013 the apex regulator (UGC) crafted a set of administrative rules that would provide a legal framework for overseas institutions to establish and operate campuses in India as not-for-profit entities.[19] The rules lacked clarity on the degree of autonomy the foreign institutions would enjoy and how that would differ from the regimen to which private Indian institutions are subject. It became increasingly clear that the more these institutions were exempt from the plethora of regulations to which their Indian counterparts were subject, the more uneven the playing field vis-à-vis domestic institutions became; but if they enjoyed little autonomy, the less inclined they would be to enter India, rendering the entire effort moot. For now the effort appears to have been effectively put on a back-burner and instead in 2016 the Indian government announced that it would provide the regulatory architecture to 10 public and 10 private institutions that would enable them to emerge as world-class teaching and research institutions.

In the PRC, degree-granting programs by leading foreign universities were introduced over 30 years ago and today flourish in abundance, particularly at China's top public universities. Johns Hopkins University pioneered the Chinese pattern in 1986 with the establishment on the campus of Nanjing University of the Hopkins-Nanjing Center for Chinese and American Studies, which offers a master of arts degree in international studies awarded jointly by Johns Hopkins and Nanjing University that is accredited in both the United States and China. When China became a full-fledged member of the World Trade Organization in 2001, international educational cooperation was extended to all sectors of education except for military, political, and Communist Party training. By 2009, the Chinese government had approved more than a thousand joint Chinese-foreign educational programs and institutions in more than 20 provinces (Zhu and Lou 2011, 125–26). Several foreign universities have established new branch campuses or joint ventures in China that award only foreign degrees; among the most noteworthy are NYU Shanghai, the University of Nottingham Ningbo, and Duke Kunshan University. The PRC has also aggressively sought mutual recognition of academic credentials, diplomas, and degrees with other countries; by 2006 it had succeeded in signing academic reciprocity agreements with 19 countries (including Germany, France, the United Kingdom, Australia, and New Zealand) (Zhou 2006, 249–50).

The number of foreign students in China and India reflects a similar disparity. India reported just over 42,993 foreign students enrolled in its colleges and universities in 2014–15 (table 6.3a). China hosted 10 times that number—396,635 foreign students in 2015—a more than 5 percent increase over the previous year (table 6.3b).

This increase has been fueled in good part by state initiative, evident in the number of foreign students receiving Chinese government scholarships. The top five places of origin for in-bound international students in 2015 were South Korea, United States, Thailand, India, and Russia, with India recently emerging among the top five in students. Nonetheless, considering India's geographical proximity and gigantic population, its students are substantially underrepresented in Chinese colleges and universities and vice versa. An important reason why India has been unable to host foreign students is the severe shortage of quality institutions. However, this is changing as the number of decent private institutions that have a strong interest in attracting foreign students is growing.

With America currently enjoying the reputation of having the best higher education system in the world, it is only natural that American campuses would be a magnet for bright students from across the globe, especially from Asian countries where educational ambitions outstrip local opportunities. Not surprisingly, China and India, followed closely by South Korea, are the top countries of origin for foreign students in the United States, together contributing nearly half of all international stu-

Table 6.3a
Foreign students in India, top countries of origin (2014–2015)

Nepal	8,694
Afghanistan	3,717
Bhutan	2,697
Sudan	2,104
Nigeria	1,952
Malaysia	1,924
Sri Lanka	1,610
Iran	1,544
Iraq	1,386
United Arab Emirates	1,284
United States	979
Total	42,993

SOURCE: Government of India, Ministry of Human Resource Development, *Education Statistics at a Glance, 2016*, table 6F.

Table 6.3b
Number of foreign students in China by country, showing top 10 countries for each year

	2008	2011	2015
South Korea	66,806	62,442	66,675
United States	19,914	23,292	21,975
Japan	16,733	17,961	14,085
Thailand	8,476	14,145	19,976
Vietnam	10,396	13,549	—
Russia	8,939	13,340	16,197
Indonesia	7,084	10,957	12,694
India	8,145	9,370	16,694
Pakistan	5,199	8,516	15,654
Kazakhstan	5,666	8,287	13,198
Total	223,499	292,611	397,635

SOURCES: For 2011: Project Atlas report *International Students in China*, www.iie.org/Services/Project-Atlas/China/International-Students-In-China (accessed April 2, 2014). For 2015: Project Atlas report *International Students in China*, https://www.iie.org/Research-and-Insights/Project-Atlas/Explore-Data/China/Inbound-Mobility---Most-Recent (accessed April 22, 2017).

NOTE: France (with 10,436) replaced Vietnam as one of the top 10 countries in 2015.

Table 6.4a
Number of foreign students from China and India in the United States

Year	Chinese students	Indian students
1980–81	2,770	9,250
1985–86	13,980	16,070
1990–91	39,597	28,857
1995–96	39,613	31,743
2000–01	59,939	54,664
2005–06	62,582	76,503
2010–11	157,558	103,895
2015–16	328,547	165,918

SOURCE: Institute of International Education, "Academic Levels and Place of Origin," https://www.iie.org/Research-and-Insights/Open-Doors/Data/International-Students/Academic-Level-and-Place-of-Origin (accessed April 22, 2017).

Table 6.4b
Number of foreign students from China and India in the United Kingdom

Year	Students from China	Students from India
2008–9	47,035	34,065
2009–10	56,990	38,500
2010–11	67,325	39,090
2011–12	78,715	29,900
2012–13	83,790	22,385
2013–14	87,895	19,750
2015–16	91,215	16,745

SOURCES: Higher Education Statistics Agency (HESA), "Table 6—Top ten non-EU countries of domicile in 2012/13 for student enrolments on HE [higher education] courses by location of HE institution and country of domicile 2008/09 to 2012/13," www.hesa.ac.uk/content/view/1897/239/ (accessed April 9, 2014); "Table 9—Top ten non-European Union countries of domicile in 2013/14 for HE student enrolments by location of HE provider and country of domicile 2009/10 to 2013/14," https://www.hesa.ac.uk/sfr210 (accessed September 4, 2015); "Chart 8—Top ten non-European Union countries of domicile in 2015/16 for HE student enrolments 2011/12 and 2015/16," https://www.hesa.ac.uk/news/12-01-2017/sfr242-student-enrolments-and-qualifications (accessed April 22, 2017).

dents on American college and university campuses (table 6.4a). In the past academic year (2015–16), the 328,547 students from China comprised 31.5 percent of all international students studying in the United States. Although ranked second (with 165,918), India contributed just half of the number of students coming from China.[20] Despite India's historic connection to Great Britain, an even bigger discrepancy exists in British academe; in 2015–16 a total of 91,215 Chinese students were studying at universities in the United Kingdom, compared to a mere 16,745 Indians (table 6.4b).

The PRC government has made a major national investment, via its lavishly funded China Scholarship Council (CSC), in providing thousands of full scholarships each year to send advanced graduate students and younger faculty abroad. In some cases, CSC recipients enroll in multiyear foreign degree programs; in other cases, they simply spend a year of study and research at leading universities around the world. Many universities and local governments in China also offer substantial material incentives for overseas academic experience. Jilin University, for example, requires that all its assistant and associate professors spend at least one calendar year on a study or research program abroad in order to become eligible for promotion to the next rank. Similarly, the municipal government of Shanghai offers a generous financial bonus to faculty members at the city's various universities upon their return from a year abroad on an approved research program.

At both central and local levels, Chinese government strategies for promoting the globalization of higher education are self-consciously tailored to the criteria used in the major rankings of world universities (*Times Higher Education*, Shanghai Jiao Tong University Academic Rankings of World Universities, Quacquarelli Symonds, *US News and World Report*, and so on). Because articles published in English-language journals listed in the Science Citation Index (SCI) and Social Science Citation Index (SSCI) count heavily in these ranking schemes, Chinese universities (again with substantial state support) have established massive postdoctoral fellowship programs designed to recruit young researchers whose sole responsibility is to produce such articles. The postdoctoral fellows are generally hired on short-term contracts renewable upon fulfillment of the publication quota. Needless to say, their lack of teaching duties means that they contribute little if anything to the instructional life of the university. Regular faculty members are encouraged to produce such articles as well, and are rewarded with handsome bonuses (typically the equivalent of US$10,000 and more) if they succeed in doing so. With English considered the lingua franca of academia these days, the world rankings consider the percentage of courses taught in English to be an indicator of a university's degree of globalization. Again faculty members are offered sizable bonuses (US$5,000 or more per course) as an incentive for compliance; unfortunately, the English language competence of some of those who accept the extra remuneration for conducting their classes in "English" is questionable at best.

Although the Indian media and senior government officials have been wringing their hands over the lack of any Indian university in the top world rankings, they have taken only limited steps to address the issue. The disparity with China is clear. In the QS rankings of top Asian universities in 2014, for example, China had nine universities in the top 50 and 22 in the top 100, whereas India had just two and eight, respectively. Two factors weigh heavily in university rankings: publications and international students. We have already noted the large difference in attracting foreign students. The relentless publications drive so evident in Chinese universities is also much weaker in India, and the gap between them has been growing (figure 6.4).

One reason might be a more severe brain drain from India. For instance, a recently compiled dataset of the educational background of faculty in the top 50 computer science programs in American universities found that of the 20 most common undergraduate institutions, 15 are in the United States, four in India, and one in China.[21]

It is of course hard to judge how such disparities in rankings translate into actual educational value. For Chinese universities that aspire to become "world-class universities" (*shijie yiliu daxue* 世界一流大学), a term popularized by Jiang Zemin's May 1998 speech at Peking University and subsequently reinforced in statements by Xi Jinping, academic excellence is gauged less in terms of the quality of teaching and learning than in measurable prestige indicators. At Nanjing University, for example, significant resources were diverted to support the research of particularly promising members of the science faculty in hopes that someday one of them would become China's first Nobel laureate scientist (Li et al. 2011, 161). It came as a shock, therefore, when in 2015 the first Chinese scientist to receive a Nobel Prize, Tu Youyou, turned out to be an 84-year-old woman whose path-breaking research (on traditional Chinese medicinal herbs) had been conducted during the height of Mao's Cultural Revolution!

Much effort is expended to internationalize the faculty of Chinese universities by hiring foreign nationals as well as offering tempting terms

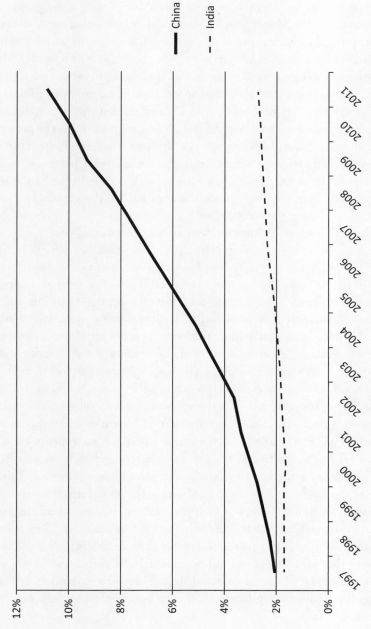

FIGURE 6.4 Publications of science and engineering articles from China and India in all fields, 1997–2011 (percent of world total).

for Chinese citizens who return home after completing their graduate studies abroad. The Ministry of Education has established a national center that provides a wide array of services for returned students, including applying for start-up research funds on their behalf (Zhou 2006, 257). The Changjiang Scholars Award Program has also served to attract outstanding talent from overseas, providing internationally competitive salaries and research funding for scholars with a global reputation (ibid. 258). One piece of suggestive evidence on the effect of such initiatives is the growth of research articles with international coauthors. For China internationally coauthored articles in science and engineering fields increased more than tenfold from 2,914 in 1995 to 31,081 in 2012, while for India the increase was considerably more modest (somewhat less than fivefold), from 1,583 to 7,332 during the same period.[22]

The only aspect of international education where India is edging out China is in cross-border delivery of education services (what is known as Mode 1 in the GATS, or General Agreement on Trade in Services, of the WTO). The emergence of MOOCs—"massive online open courses"—built on open-source teaching platforms, including video lessons and discussion forums and even virtual laboratories where students can carry out simulated experiments, is a potential game changer in higher education. A recent analysis of participants in such courses finds that the first movers are young, well-educated, and employed, with a bias toward young males more pronounced in non-OECD countries (Gayle et al. 2013). While a majority were from developed countries (and a third from the U.S. alone), the second largest country was India (Alcorn et al. 2015). This is one instance where China appears handicapped relative to India due both to its comparatively low level of English language competency and to the extensive internet "firewalls" that make accessing these courses more difficult for prospective students in the PRC. The actual efficacy of such courses remains, however, a matter of some debate (Kim 2015). Their value in professional and science and technology courses appears much greater than in the humanities, and of course they affect teaching and not research. In both countries, however, the absence of course material in local languages (and in India's case multiple Indian languages), further limits their use to a minority of their populations.

Conclusions

While it is clear there has been massive growth in higher education in both China and India in recent years, whether measured by the number of students enrolled or the amounts of public and private money expended, it is unclear just how meaningful this large growth is. There is for instance little knowledge of what is happening *within* universities and to the students who spend a considerable part of their prime years in these institutions. This reflects a larger lacuna in analytical work on higher education. In general researchers have found it exceedingly difficult to get a good grip on two critical outcome measures: (1) quality in higher education beyond research publications and postdegree earnings; and (2) the value added by higher education over and beyond the student's innate abilities. It is entirely possible that even in systems that are of good quality, the credentialing aspects of higher education benefit the few who have access to it and crowd out from labor markets others with similar ability but who lack access. Just as an arms race does not lead to greater security despite much greater spending, the upward spiral in education credentialing may not yield social or economic benefits commensurate to the expenditure (Wolf 2004).

The evolution of higher education and the debates surrounding higher education in China and India have focused primarily on its instrumental role, in particular training skilled labor for a growing economy and promoting higher education's role in advancing research and innovation. However, the normative role of higher education—for instance, does it make for better citizens or fairer and more resilient societies—is little debated, perhaps because these relationships are poorly understood to begin with. To be sure, Chinese propaganda departments at all levels devote considerable resources to the teaching of both "cultural literacy" (*wenhua sushi jiaoyu* 文化素质教育) and "ideology" (sixiang zhengzhi jiaoyu 思想政治教育), under the pretext that such courses help foster patriotic and politically reliable citizens. But students and faculty alike tend to regard such instruction as a tedious waste of time.

Rival conceptions of citizenship inevitably generate disagreements about which educational processes yield the desired ends. The very promise of higher education also makes this a politically contentious issue. Universities are inherently political because they influence the minds and life chances of young adults. And they are becoming even more so because of the growing awareness of the distributional implications of higher education. As private provision and international education grow, issues of equity and access will become even more contentious. Many of the underlying handicaps faced by students from lower socioeconomic groups appear to occur much earlier in the life cycle—at the primary and secondary school level—but policies to overcome these handicaps are deferred to higher education, often too little and too late. An important reason why Chinese higher education has galloped ahead of India, is that it strengthened its primary and secondary education systems first, which India is only now attempting to achieve. Consequently, Indian higher education became a victim of distributional politics which China appears so far to have by and large avoided. But recent protests by Chinese migrant workers (instigated by the now banned New Citizens' Movement) demanding open access to the university entrance examination indicate the potential volatility of these concerns in China as well.

Contrasts between the two Asian giants may also be traceable to deeper historical roots. China's obsession with competitive credentialing suggests a culturally specific conception of statecraft linking educational success to state power. In 2008, Chinese universities conferred more than 50,000 doctoral degrees, outpacing the United States to become the world's biggest producer of doctorates. However, in contrast to the United States, where doctoral degree holders typically go into teaching or research, in China more than half of the new doctoral degree recipients took jobs within the government bureaucracy at national or provincial levels. As Qiang Zha observes, the Chinese pattern "resulted from an explicit or implicit strategy of absorbing academic elites into the polity and bureaucracy in order to heighten the government's legitimacy" (Zha 2011a, 468). Chinese often remark that whereas the brightest Americans go into business or academia, relegating the least talented to government service, in China precisely the opposite pattern prevails.

The fierce competition among Chinese college students for admission into the Communist Party is another indication of the allure of official position to those with ambition and education. The *Economist* reports that "in 1997 just over 4% of undergraduates were party members. Within a decade the proportion had doubled. In some colleges more than 80% of upper-year students now apply for membership."[23] The explanation for this sudden surge of interest in party membership lies not in some newfound ideological zeal on the part of the younger generation, but in a more familiar pattern of intellectuals' attraction to bureaucratic employment. With the recent glut of graduates produced by expanded university enrollments, desirable jobs are in short supply and government posts—which offer security and benefits and for which party membership is a distinct advantage—are highly sought after.

Further evidence of the connection between education and statecraft can be seen in the Chinese government's aggressive efforts to extend its cultural influence beyond its own territorial borders. The hundreds of Confucius Institutes recently established across the globe serve as platforms to promote the teaching of Chinese language and to encourage the study of Chinese culture more broadly. As of August 2016, there were nearly 500 full-service Confucius Institutes (mostly located on university campuses) and 1,000 smaller Confucius classrooms (affiliated to secondary and primary schools) in more than 130 countries. Ten years ago, the University of Maryland was the first American university to welcome a Confucius Institute. Today, Confucius Institutes exist on dozens of American campuses, including those of such prestigious universities as Stanford, Columbia, and Michigan.[24] Although the University of Chicago and Pennsylvania State University declined to renew their Confucius Institutes when the initial contract expired, the overall trend—in the United States as elsewhere around the globe—is for expansion rather than contraction in this form of Chinese "soft power."

The designation of China as a major focus for educational efforts was recognized by President Obama during his visit to Beijing in 2009, when he promised to send 100,000 American students to China over the next four years. A State Department spokesman subsequently explained the presidential initiative by observing that "China will have a much more important voice in world affairs in the coming years, and we need more Americans who can speak the language, who understand China, and who can do business more effectively with the Chinese."[25] Secretary of State Hillary Clinton, First Lady Michelle Obama, and the former U.S. ambassador to China, Jon Huntsman, all spoke out in favor of the proposal. In contrast to the Chinese government, however, which puts impressive sums of money behind its global educational initiatives, the U.S. government provided no new funding to back up Obama's call. Instead, Secretary Clinton announced the establishment of an independent nonprofit foundation, named the 100 Thousand Strong Foundation, whose purpose is to encourage philanthropic and corporate donations in support of the initiative. The Ford Foundation contributed $1 million in seed money to kick off what proved to be a decidedly lackluster fundraising drive (with the Bank of China pledging more to the effort than American corporations). In the end, the PRC government earmarked 20,000 of its own China Scholarship Council fellowships to underwrite the Obama initiative.[26]

What accounts for the Chinese state's unusual support for higher education, especially when compared to India? In the late 1940s, the world's two largest polities—independent India and the PRC—came into being. Over the next three decades, as detailed in the introduction to this volume, the economic trajectories of the two countries were remarkably parallel. Indeed, by the early 1980s India could claim the more developed higher education system, in part because China's universities had been severely damaged by the ravages of the Cultural Revolution. However, there was one glaring difference between the two countries: in striving to meet the global challenges of nation building and the enlargement of (social) citizenship rights, Mao's China had generated a more egalitarian human capital base through universal primary education and better public health. India's record, measured in terms of literacy and longevity rates, was feeble by comparison.

Over the next few decades the economic trajectories of the two countries diverged strikingly, even as they both sought to accommodate to global markets. Although India's growth was impressive, for a large country China's growth was unprecedented in human history. As India struggled to deliver universal primary education, its deeply unequal social structures produced a distributive politics that undermined its higher education system. In China's case, the very political forces that drove its remarkable growth also underpinned the transformation of its higher education system. Whether this transformation will be sustained, or will fall prey to the inevitable slowdown of the Chinese economy, remains to be seen.

The differences in higher education reform between the two Asian giants can be traced in large measure to political factors; some are deeply rooted in political culture and others are a product of their contemporary political systems. The disparities belie simple-minded arguments about democratic regimes enjoying more progressive educational policies than autocracies, however. Indeed, to the extent that for democracies the primary basis for legitimacy is procedural, whereas authoritarian governments must demonstrate positive policy performance in order to retain public approval (especially as the legitimating halo of revolution fades), one might a priori expect authoritarian China to "deliver" better public goods outcomes than democratic India. If this reversal of conventional wisdom holds water, then the divergent outcomes in higher education in the two countries are not so surprising after all.

Notes

1. Mao Zedong described the impact of "new learning" on his political awakening in Snow 1972.

2. Philip G. Altbach (2004, 15) aptly observes that "no Asian university is truly Asian in origin—all are based on European academic models and traditions."

3. Ministry of Human Resource Development, "Analysis of Budgeted Expenditure on Education 2009–10 to 2011–12" (2013); UNESCO Institute for Statistics, "UIS Statistics in Brief: Education Profile–China 2012."

4. The seminal work on the phenomenon of massification is Trow 1973. Trow distinguishes among "elite" higher education, which enrolls under 15 percent of the eligible age cohort, "mass" education, which enrolls 15–50 percent, and "universal" education, which enrolls over 50 percent.

5. NSF, "Science and Engineering Indicators 2012," table 6-4, and "Science and Engineering Indicators 2014," table 6-5.

6. "China Education," http://www.chinaeducenter.com/en/cedu.php (accessed November 22, 2013); *Washington Post*, February 12, 2012.

7. See also *Washington Post*, February 12, 2012.

8. *Xinhua Internet News*, March 24, 2014. http://news.xinhuanet.com/2014-03/24/c _126305589.htm.

9. *Zhongguo qingnian* [China youth] (June 7, 2004), 1.

10. "China Education," http://www.chinaeducenter.com/en/cedu.php (accessed November 20, 2013).

11. Xi Jinping, "Don't Turn Peking University into a Second Harvard or Cambridge," http://politics.people.com.cn/n/2014/0506/c1001-24978632.html (accessed April 10, 2017). In Chinese.

12. *Xinhua Internet News*, December 9, 2016. http://news.xinhuanet.com/english/2016 -12/09/c_135891337.htm (accessed April 10, 2017).

13. Exceptions do exist, however. For example, Shanghai's private Jianqiao Xueyuan (Cambridge College) was founded by a wealthy Wenzhou businessman who at least claims that his motive is philanthropy (and filial piety in honoring his mother's Buddhist beliefs) rather than profit. The glitzy new private Shanghai Institute for the Visual Arts (SIVA), while bankrolled by six of the city's wealthiest entrepreneurs, is the brainchild of former vice mayor Gong Xueping, who is credited with building the new Shanghai Library, Shanghai Museum, and Shanghai Grand Theater during his tenure as vice mayor. According to Gong, the purpose of SIVA is to develop the city's "cultural production" so that Shanghai becomes known as a center of cultural creativity rather than simply an economic hub. (Author's interview with the president of Jianqiao Xueyuan, Shanghai, October 2012; interview with Gong Xueping, Shanghai, July 2010.)

14. More than 2,000 education joint ventures between Chinese and overseas universities have been established just since 2003. "Beijing Vies for Greater Control of Foreign Universities in China," *Financial Times* (November 17, 2017).

15. *South China Morning Post,* http://www.scmp.com/news/china/article/1609734/studies-xi-jinping-thought-or-ideology-grab-lions-share-funding-research (accessed April 11, 2017).

16. Clifford Geertz borrowed the term "involution" from the American anthropologist Alexander Goldenweiser to refer to the "overdriving of an established form in such a way that it becomes rigid through an inward overelaboration of detail." Rather than increased efficiency, there is a growth in "technical hairsplitting" to provide a niche for an ever increasing number of people (Geertz 1963, 80–90).

17. On the former, see Kapur 2012; on the latter, see "A Landmark Scholarship for the Defining Challenge of our Time," http://schwarzmanscholars.org/ (accessed December 8, 2013).

18. http://www.studyinchina.com.my/web/page/chinese-university-tops-mit-in-rankings/ (accessed November 15, 2017).

19. The foreign institutions intending to apply under the proposed rules must be not-for-profit legal entities that have been in existence for at least 20 years and registered by an accrediting agency of the country concerned or by an internationally accepted system of accreditation. Moreover, the order stipulates that the institution must be among the top 400 universities in the world (according to rankings published by the *Times Higher Education* (London), Quacquarelli Symonds, or Shanghai Jiao Tong University Academic Rankings of World Universities).

20. http://www.nytimes.com/2011/10/14/world/asia/squeezed-out-in-india-students-turn-to-united-states.html (accessed December 10, 2013). If we turn the equation around, we find that there are almost three times as many American college students in China compared to India. *Daily News and Analysis,* http://www.dnaindia.com/mumbai/report-number-of-indian-students-to-the-us-drops-by-3-5pct-1917036 (accessed December 8, 2013).

21. Alexandra Papoutsaki et al., "Dataset of 2200 Faculty in 50 Top US Computer Science Graduate Programs," http://cs.brown.edu/people/alexpap/faculty_dataset.html (accessed November 16, 2017).

22. National Science Board, Science and Engineering Indicator (2014), table 5-41.

23. "Students and the Party: Rushing to Join," *The Economist*, February 22, 2014. See also Guo 2005, 387–90.

24. https://confucianweekly.com/2016/08/19/the-increasing-demand-for-confucius -institutes-worldwide/ (accessed April 8, 2017).

25. *The Chronicle of Higher Education*, November 18, 2009.

26. "Thirty-Five Years of Student Exchange between the U.S. and China," http:// projectpengyou.org/press-release-35-years-of-student-exchange-between-the-u-s-and -china-celebrated-at-the-great-hall-of-the-people/ (accessed November 16, 2017).

References

Aggarwal, Megha. 2013. "Local Shores, Global Dreams." *The Hindu*, November 17. http://www.thehindu.com/features/education/college-and-university/local-shores -global-dreams/article5357872.ece.

Alcorn, Brandon, Gayle Christensen, and Devesh Kapur. 2015. "Higher Education and MOOCs in India and the Global South." *Change: The Magazine of Higher Learning* 47.3: 42–49.

Altbach, Philip. G. 2004. "The Past and Future of Asian Universities." In *Asian Universities: Historical Perspectives and Contemporary Challenges*, edited by Philip G. Altbach and Toru Umaboshi, 13–32. Baltimore: Johns Hopkins University Press.

———. 2011. "The Global Academic Revolution." *Journal of Educational Planning and Administration* 25.4: 302–13.

Ansell, Ben W. 2010. *From the Ballot to the Blackboard. The Redistributive Political Economy of Education*. Cambridge Studies in Comparative Politics. New York: Cambridge University Press.

Ashton, David, and Francis Green. 1997. *Education, Training and the Global Economy*. Northampton, MA: Edward Elgar.

Azam, Mehtabul, and Andreas Blom. 2008. *Progress in Participation in Tertiary Education in India from 1983 to 2004*. World Bank Policy Research Working Paper 4793, December 2008. Washington, DC: World Bank.

Bardhan, Pranab. 1984. *The Political Economy of Development in India*. Oxford: Oxford University Press.

Basant, Rakesh, and Gitanjali Sen. 2013. "Access to Higher Education in India: An Exploration of Its Antecedents." IIM Ahmedabad Working Paper no. 2013-05-011, May 2013. Ahmedabad, Gujarat: Indian Institute of Management,.

Bays, Daniel H., and Ellen Widmer, eds. 2009. *China's Christian Colleges: Cross-Cultural Connections, 1900–1950*. Stanford: Stanford University Press.

Chaudhary, Latika. 2010. "Land Revenues, Schools and Literacy: A Historical Examination of Public and Private Funding of Education." *Indian Economic and Social History Review* 47.2: 179–204.

Elman, Benjamin A. 2000. *A Cultural History of Civil Examinations in Late Imperial China*. Berkeley: University of California Press.

————. 2013. *Civil Examinations and Meritocracy in Late Imperial China*. Cambridge, MA: Harvard University Press.

Gandhi, Jennifer. 2008. *Political Institutions under Dictatorship*. Cambridge: Cambridge University Press.

Gayle, Christensen, Andrew Steinmetz, Brandon Alcorn, Amy Bennett, Deirdre Woods, and Ezekiel J. Emanuel. 2013. *The MOOC Phenomenon: Who Takes Massive Open Online Courses and Why?* http://papers.ssrn.com/sol3/papers.cfm?abstract_id=2350964.

Geertz, Clifford. 1963. *Agricultural Involution: The Processes of Ecological Change in Indonesia*. Berkeley: University of California Press.

Guo, Gang. 2005. "Party Recruitment of College Students in China." *Journal of Contemporary China* 14.43: 371–93.

Institute for International Economics (IIE). 2013. *The U.S. Community College Model: Potential for Applications in India*. New York: Institute for International Economics.

Kapur, Devesh, and Mehta, Pratap Bhanu. 2008. "Mortgaging the Future? Indian Higher Education." *Brookings-NCAER India Policy Forum* 4: 101–57.

————. 2010 "Indian Higher Education." In *American Universities in a Global Market*, edited by Charles Clotfelter, 305-334. NBER, University of Chicago Press.

————. 2011. "Addressing the Trilemma of Higher Education." *Seminar* 617: 87–92.

————. 2012."The Elite's Classrooms." *Business Standard*, November 12.

Kim, Paul. 2015. *Massive Open Online Courses: The MOOC Revolution*. New York: Routledge.

Kirby, William C. 2014. "The Chinese Century? Challenges of Higher Education." *Daedalus* 143.2: 145–56.

Kohn, Bernard. 1996. *Colonialism and Its Forms of Knowledge: The British in India*. Princeton: Princeton University Press.

Levenson, Joseph R. 1965. *Confucian China and Its Modern Fate*. Berkeley: University of California Press.

Li, Jun, and Jing Lin, with Gong Fang. 2011. "Nanjing University—Redeeming the Past by Academic Merit." In *Portraits of 21st Century Universities: In the Move to Mass Higher Education*, edited by Ruth Hayhoe, Jun Li, Jing Lin, and Qiang Zha, 131–61. Hong Kong: University of Hong Kong.

Liu, Jirong. 2003. "Gaodeng xuexiao hebing zuzhi de lilun yu shizheng yanjiu" (A study of the theory and practice of the amalgamation of higher education schools). Ph.D. diss., Zhejiang University, China.

Lutz, Jessie Gregory. 1971. *China and the Christian Colleges, 1850–1950*. Ithaca: Cornell University Press.

Marcus, Joe. 2014. "New Analysis Shows Problem Boom in Higher Education Administrators." *Huffington Post*, February 6.

McGregor, Richard. 2012. *The Party: The Secret Word of China's Communist Rulers*. New York: HarperCollins.

Munro, Donald J. 1977. *The Concept of Man in Contemporary China*. Ann Arbor: University of Michigan.

Perry, Elizabeth J. 2017. "Cultural Governance in Contemporary China: 'Re-Orienting' Party Propaganda." In *To Govern China*, edited by Vivienne Shue and Patricia Thornton, 29–55. Oxford: Oxford University Press.

Peterson, Glen. 1994. "State Literacy Ideologies and the Transformation of Rural China." *Australian Journal of Chinese Affairs* 32: 95–120.

Scharfe, Hartmut. 2002. *Education in Ancient India*. Leiden: Brill.

Schram, Stuart. 1974. *Chairman Mao Talks to the People: Talks and Letters, 1956–1971*. New York: Pantheon.

Snow, Edgar. 1972. *Red Star over China*. New York: Bantam Books.

Trow, Martin A. 1973. *Problems in the Transition from Elite to Mass Higher Education*. Berkeley, CA: Carnegie Commission on Higher Education.

University Grants Commission. 2016. *Annual Report 2015–16*, New Delhi.

Wang, Qinghua. 2014. "Crisis Management, Regime Survival and 'Guerrilla-Style' Policy-Making: The 1999 Decision to Radically Expand Higher Education in China." *China Journal* 71: 132–52.

Wang, Xiaobing, Chengfang Liu, Linxiu Zhang, Yaojiang Shi, and Scott Rozelle. 2013. "College Is a Rich, Han, Urban Male Club: Research Notes from a Census Survey of Four Tier One Colleges in China." *China Quarterly* 214: 456–70.

Wolf, Alison. 2004. "Education and Economic Performance: Simplistic Theories and Their Policy Consequences." *Oxford Review of Economic Policy* 20.2: 315–33.

Wood, Adrian, and Michele Calandrino. 2000. "When the Other Giant Awakens: Trade and Human Resources in India." *Economic and Political Weekly* 35.52–53: 4677–94.

Yeh, Wen-hsin. 1990. *The Alienated Academy: Culture and Politics in Republican China, 1919–1937*. Cambridge, MA: Harvard University Press, 1990.

Ying, Wangjiang, 2008. *Zhongguo gaodeng jiaoyu gaige yu fazhan 30nian* (30 years of Chinese higher education reform and development). Shanghai: Shanghai Finance University Press.

Zha, Qiang. 2011a. "Is There an Emerging Chinese Model of the University?" In *Portraits of 21st-Century Universities: In the Move to Mass Higher Education*, edited by Ruth Hayhoe, Jun Li, Jing Lin, and Qiang Zha, 451–71. Hong Kong: University of Hong Kong.

———. 2011b. "Understanding China's Move to Mass Higher Education from a Policy Perspective." In *Portraits of 21st-Century Universities: In the Move to Mass Higher Education*, edited by Ruth Hayhoe, Jun Li, Jing Lin, and Qiang Zha, 20–57. Hong Kong: University of Hong Kong.

Zhang, Yingqiang. 2009. *Jingying yu dazhong: Zhongguo gaodeng jiaoyu 60nian* (Elite and mass: 60 years of Chinese higher education). Hangzhou: Zhejiang University Press.

Zhou, Ji. 2006. *Higher Education in China*. Singapore: Thomson.

Zhu, Hong, and Shiyan Lou. 2011. *Development and Reform of Higher Education in China*. Oxford: Woodhead Publishing.

PART IV

Transnational Migration and Investment

CHAPTER 7

Rescaling State-Society Relations in China and India

KELLEE S. TSAI

"I made all my contacts with local government officials when they were visiting MIT. I was a graduate student at the time, and served as their translator. They never would have spoken to me in Shanghai, but things were different when we were all at MIT."
— CEO of an IT consulting firm, Shanghai, May 2014

"If not for you all, there wouldn't have been an IT revolution."
— Narendra Modi to 18,000 Indian Americans, Madison Square Garden, New York, September 2014

"Anywhere there's a market in the world with Chinese, you can find Wenzhou people."
— Private entrepreneur, Wenzhou, April 2014

China and India's economic ascendance in the 21st century has drawn attention to their national political economies, as well as the developmental experience of particular localities. The fact that China and India have the largest diasporic populations in the world—at 55 million and 25 million, respectively—has also attracted comparative studies on the economic contributions of their returnees and ethnic investors (Khanna 2008; Saxenian 2005; Ye 2014). Both national and local state policies have played a role in mediating diasporic relations. Yet within the study of comparative politics, "state-society relations" typically refers to the relationship between a Weberian nation-state and citizens residing within its administratively defined and coercively enforced territorial borders. This chapter departs from conventional usages of both "state" and "society" by focusing on the local state in combination with a less territorialized conception of society. In so doing, it also illustrates the insights that can be derived by shifting away from methodological nationalism, a theme echoed by other contributions to this volume.

The rationale for this "dual-definitional stretch"—both downward (local state) and outward (transnational society)—has an empirical basis. First, the local government represents the day-to-day point of contact with "the state" for most people. Government regulations, fees for service, and public goods are generally administered through local state channels even if they are mandated nationally. The local state represents the first point of accountability for most citizens, and noncitizens for that matter. Second, limiting the scope of "society" to populations currently residing within national borders unnecessarily excludes temporary migrants and diasporic communities who continue to identify with a locality. A more expansive notion of society recognizes the possibility of return migration, remittances from abroad, and the formation of translocal native place networks. Transnational migrants represent potential human, financial, and social resources for local, as well as national, development.

Theoretically, the chapter extends the economist Albert Hirschman's classic categorical troika of "exit, voice, and loyalty" (EVL) to the literature on new transnationalism (Hirschman 1970). EVL serves as a deceptively parsimonious heuristic for revealing the nonexclusive relationship among three types of strategies for dealing with one's immediate environment: exit (migration), voice (participation), and loyalty (support). Migration (exit) may not be permanent, but even when it is, remaining abroad does not preclude deep-rooted identity (local and/or national loyalty), or meaningful impact on homeland affairs (voice). For these reasons, the reflexive association of society with domestic groups is incomplete.

Empirically, the chapter demonstrates the logic of this dual-definitional stretch of state-society relations by examining different expressions of "cosmopolitan capitalism" in three paired localities in China and India: (1) Wenzhou, Zhejiang/Surat, Gujarat, which having strong commercial networks; (2) Zhongguancun, Beijing/Bangalore, which represent major information-technology hubs; and (3) Guangdong/Kerala, whose coastal location has facilitated outmigration. The first pair of localities (Wenzhou and Surat) are the home bases of transnational networks of merchants who have developed reliable forms of cross-border informal finance, and in special industries, have gained a market share disproportionate to their populations. The second pair (Zhongguancun and Bangalore) are the Silicon Valleys of China and India respectively. Both have earned global reputations in the IT sector in a remarkably short period of time, and have also been held up by their national governments as exemplars for return migration. The third pair of cases (Guangdong and Kerala) are long-standing exporters of labor, whose localities have been shaped—albeit unevenly—by remittances, diasporic investment, and internal migration. Each subnational paired case illustrates why the conventional state-society framework should be expanded to capture the nuances of (local) state and (transnational) society relations. Furthermore, the methodological rationale for this research design is consistent with the logic of "convergent comparison," as recommended by Prasenjit Duara and Elizabeth J. Perry, in their introduction to this volume, "to appreciate that particular developments within nations are conditioned as much by circulatory global forces *and* subnational currents as by purely national or internal processes."

The chapter proceeds as follows. The first section reviews existing literature that challenges the conventional definition of state-society relations by disaggregating the state, on the one hand, and deterritorializing the range of actors that constitute society, on the other. These insights are valuable for understanding the dynamics of transnational migration, as seen when juxtaposed with Hirschman's EVL framework. The second part compares three pairs of localities in China and India to demonstrate the empirical relevance of a more fluid approach to analyzing state-society relations. The third section concludes.

Challenges to the State-Society Dichotomy

LOWERING THE STATE

Since the statist revival among political scientists in the 1980s (Evans et al. 1985), multiple critiques of the Weberian conception of the state have emerged. Qualifications to the notion of the state (as a "set of institutions possessing monopoly over the legitimate use of force within territorial boundaries") have grown primarily from studies of developing, postcolonial, and newly established countries. In the latter contexts, the state is more likely to fall short of key components of Weber's definition. States may be "weak" because the political system is not well institutionalized compared to the authority of local social forces (Migdal 1988). States do not necessarily monopolize the use of violence or enforcement of national security (Mandel 2002; Volkov 2002). And the territorial boundaries of the state may be unsettled (Spruyt 2005; Young 1994). Many internationally recognized nation-states are characterized by these definitional deficiencies.

Another line of critique concerns the narrowness of focusing on the central state apparatus. Even before the resurgence in state-centric theorizing, various studies explored the role of local states in subnational governance (Sellers 2010, 130–31). Charles Tiebout noted the relationship between local provision of public goods and citizens who could "vote with their feet" by moving to other localities (1956, 416–24). Others detailed the importance of local leadership in mediating among diverse interests and urban redevelopment (Dahl 1961; Stone 1989). In the 1990s, the study of China's reform-era political economy highlighted the impact of fiscal decentralization in incentivizing localities to promote economic development (Oi 1992; 1999). Local states competed with one another in various industries in a manner dubbed "market-preserving federalism" (Montinola, Qian, and Weingast 1996) and engaged in "competitive liberalization" to attract foreign direct investment (Yang 1997; Zweig 2002).

Distinguishing between the central state writ large and subnational governments is an initial step in acknowledging the potential agency of local states. Regional distinctions can also be made among local states. In large decentralized countries, localities pursue varying political and economic strategies; and indeed, some local states are more predatory than developmental. In Russia, governmental performance varies provincially (Stoner-Weiss 2002). In Italy, the effectiveness of democratic institutions varies regionally (Putnam 1993). For comparable historical reasons, subnational differences in political dynamics were evident in Brazil's transition to democracy (Hagopian 1996). In both China and India, local governments vary in the treatment of private enterprises and foreign direct investment (Sinha 2005; Tsai 2007; Chen 2014).

In short, there are empirical, and therefore, methodological rationales for decentralizing analytic attention to the state (Snyder 2001). The local state merits attention not only as an administrative extension of the central state, but also as a semiautonomous agent that pursues contextually contingent political and economic strategies. Local states have different histories, preferences, governance capabilities, and developmental impact. Moreover, local state agents interact more directly with society than the national government.[1] The local state simultaneously represents the central state and instills a distinct imprint on state-society relations.

EXPANDING SOCIETY

Just as there are well-established reasons to focus on the state at a lower level of analysis, the case for enlarging the scope of "society" is equally compelling. Given the territorially bound foundation of the Weberian state, most discussions of state-society relations reflexively treat society as being contained within administratively enforced borders. Accounts of primordial attachment to territory reinforce this tendency (Grosby 1995). Yet a sizable multidisciplinary literature—in political science, anthropology, sociology, geography, and migration studies—exists on deterritorialized collective identity, and transnational networks and society. The empirical scope of such studies transcends national boundaries, while maintaining, perhaps ironically, territoriality as an organizing reference point.

For international migrants, sustained identity with the homeland or a particular locality may have implications for national politics. At one end, a political diaspora comprising revolutionaries, exiles, and dissidents constitute a territorially displaced extension of society, either mobilizing or waiting for an opportune moment to reenter territorial state and society (Adamson 2012). The Jewish/Zionist, Chinese Nationalist, Albanian, Armenian, and Greek Cypriot diasporas are well-known examples of this politically motivated category. First-generation migrants, whom Sidney Tarrow calls "rooted cosmopolitans," can be especially effective as transnational activists because they came of age in their homelands and continue to participate in domestic networks while abroad (Tarrow

2005; cf. Keck and Sikkink 1998). Other diasporic populations include longer-term, multigenerational communities that have sustained identity with the homeland, if not political aspirations (Sheffer 2003), though the extent of active identity may vary temporally (Chan 2015).

Beyond political science, anthropologists have explored this deterritorial dimension of society through various lenses. Arjun Appadurai coined the term "ethnoscape" to denote "the landscape of persons who constitute the shifting world in which we live: tourists, immigrants, refugees, exiles, guest workers, and other moving groups and persons [who] constitute an essential feature of the world, and appear to affect the politics of and between nations to a hitherto unprecedented degree" (Appadurai 1990, 297). In a kindred vein, the volume *Nations Unbound: Transnational Projects and the Deterritorialized Nation-State* defines transnationalism as "the process by which immigrants forge and sustain multi-stranded social relations that link together their societies of origin and settlement" (Basch, Schiller, and Blanc 1994, 7). The complex cultural logics of transnationalism in late capitalism is perhaps best articulated by Aihwa Ong's (1999) notion of "flexible citizenship," deriving from her ethnographic study of the China's diasporic elites.

Taken together, these studies focus on a deterritorialized, yet national conception of diasporic society. This stance should be distinguished from the literature on global citizenship and transnational civil society, which erases the nation-state as a mobilizing frame. The transnational human rights activists in Margaret Keck and Kathryn Sikkink's now-classic *Activists beyond Borders: Advocacy Networks in International Politics*, for example, appeal to universal moral values in campaigning for changes that "transcend a specific cultural or political context" (Keck and Sikkink 1998, 204). Their advocacy concerns truly *trans*national issues. Such activists are not the "long-distance nationalists," "flexible citizens," or sojourners who comprise the expanded definition of society (Anderson 1992; Basch, Schiller, and Fouron 2001; Ong 1999). The expanded definition is bounded by identity with imagined or actual territorial origins.

This chapter concerns migrant populations that retain some degree of native identity, however cosmopolitan in expression, and whose practices and movements may have implications for the homeland's political economy. The developmental impact of diasporas may take the form of financial remittances, return migration (social remittances), outmigration of elites opposed to popular enfranchisement, and influence on foreign policy (Kapur 2010). Diasporic communities may also contribute to economic development through foreign direct investment and "diaspora bonds" issued by national governments (Burgess and Pérez-Armendáriz 2013; Pellerin and Mullings 2013, 89–120; Leblang 2010, 584–600). In short, diasporic society may be smaller than domestic society, but the former's relevance for understanding state-society relations with greater empirical accuracy should be acknowledged. Society is mobile, and thus extends beyond coercively enforced territorial boundaries. This leaves room for shifting, layered, and contingent visions of the nation and community that may be reconstructed (rather than merely reproduced) over time (Duara 1995). This chapter, to borrow Prasenjit Duara's provocative phrasing, proposes to rescue society from the nation-state as a conceptual move to recognize the cosmopolitan possibilities for (local) development. The rescue effort entails a dual-definitional stretch—of ratcheting down the level of the state, while deterritorializing the scope of society (fig. 7.1). It intentionally transgresses the organizing principles of methodological nationalism.

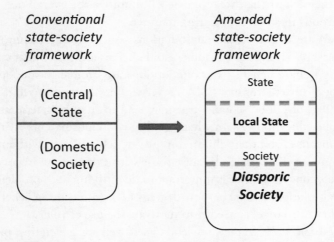

FIGURE 7.1 Dual-definitional stretch in state-society relations.

IMPLICATIONS OF MIGRATION
FOR STATE-SOCIETY RELATIONS

Empirically, this rescue effort is premised on possibility and practice of international migration. People move abroad. But why? What motivates outmigration compared with other options? Hirschman's apparently simplistic exit-voice-loyalty framework, combined with the dual-definitional stretch provides an analytic opportunity for understanding state-society relations in a more nuanced and dynamic manner.

Hirschman's theory starts from the premise that "under any economic, social, or political system, individuals, business firms, and organizations in general are subject to lapses from efficient, rational, law-abiding, virtuous, or otherwise functional behavior" (1970, 1). Three choices follow. Rational individual or organizational actors may choose to *exit* their current situation, *voice* concerns, or demonstrate *loyalty*. The framework is intuitive and elegant, holding particular appeal to neoclassical economists. When Hirschman's *Exit, Voice, and Loyalty* was published in 1970, economists at the University of Chicago applied the logic of exit to policy arenas not typically governed by markets, such as public housing.[2] In the public choice tradition of Tiebout, mentioned earlier, dissatisfied citizens will vote with their feet. And the normative implication is that exit or the threat of exit will improve the overall delivery of public goods in a market-clearing manner.

There are, of course, several limitations associated with assuming that exit is a viable choice for consumers and citizens alike, and that exit will motivate welfare benefits. For one, options are limited in monopolistic or oligopolistic environments. Moreover, as Hirschman himself noted in the context of public schools, exit may lead to further deterioration in the public education system when "quality-conscious parents" with economic means enroll their children in private schools. Exit without voice contributes to this decline, because those with exit options are less likely to express concerns. Voice is important for identifying both problems and potential solutions. As such, some degree of *loyalty*, meaning belief in the possibility of change, is needed to motivate the use of voice.

The basic EVL framework lends itself well for generating propositions regarding political participation, governmental performance, and outmigration. Its three-pronged foundation also invites further analysis. Indeed, Hirschman subsequently made refinements concerning international exit and domestic politics (1978, 90–107). In particular, small states experience the effects of outmigration more than large ones. Hirschman's original formulation expected that exit without voice would have adverse effects. Yet mass outmigration from small European states in the 19th and early 20th century alleviated political pressures as disaffected populations departed (on ships with "many actual or potential anarchists and socialists, reformers and revolutionaries") (Hirschman 1978, 102). The extension of suffrage and protection of civil rights occurred in those same countries by the early 20th century. Devesh Kapur observes a similar phenomenon in India, where there has been outmigration of elites who might otherwise obstruct mass political empowerment (Kapur 2010, 162–84). A broader implication is that the exit of disloyal elites can facilitate regime consolidation and political stability, regardless of regime type (Hoffmann 2005, 436–61).

As suggested above, insights from the literature on new transnationalism provide additional depth to the EVL framework and the present analysis of state-society relations. Above all, migration (exit) is not as starkly fixed as implied by the original EVL framework. Return migration is possible. Even when physical exit is long-term or becomes permanent, however, identity with the homeland and/or locality may endure, evolve, or even intensify. Yet such identity does not necessarily imply loyalty to the ruling regime, as evident in the cases of exiled populations with dissenting political agendas. Exit does not prohibit either loyalty or voice with meaningful impact on domestic politics.

This is not meant to imply that all international migrants are politically disaffected or motivated to affect domestic change. To the contrary, the preponderance of migrants are economic (rather than political) migrants seeking better opportunities for employment, commercial trade, production sites, investment, and overall material well-being (Massey 1988).[3] For economic migrants, "voice" may be expressed financially in the form of remittances and return investment. Financial flows from diasporic populations signal some degree of identity or commercial connection with the homeland. Remittances may be interpreted as loyalty, not necessarily to the central state, but more likely, to kin or to a particular locality. Other forms of return capital, such as charitable donations, bank deposits, foreign direct investment, real estate purchases, and portfolio investment may reflect a mixture of affinity, commercial expectations, and confidence in the homeland/native place. But to be sure, there are fully assimilated coethnic investors who have purely commercial motives.

The often ambiguous drivers of ethnic capital are captured by the notion of "cosmopolitan capitalism," a term used by Gary Hamilton (1999) in the context of Chinese diasporic networks. Others have described the apparently exceptional characteristics of Chinese commercial practices as "*guanxi* capitalism," "bamboo capitalism," and more simply, "Chinese capitalism." Although these labels are cast in essentializing cultural terms, the transnational subcontracting networks described in these accounts are not limited to the Chinese diaspora. The "informal governmentality of the "connections of *guanxi* capitalism" described by Aiwah Ong (1999, 116–17, cited in Callahan 2004, 11) extends to other diasporic communities, including, for example, Arab traders between the third and 16th century, Jewish Maghrebi merchants in the 11th and 12th centuries (Shatzmiller 2011, 132–84), and 13th-century Venetian traders.

In contexts characterized by legal uncertainty or weak enforcement of contracts (such as long-distance trading networks), kinship, ethnicity, and other forms of particularistic identity provide the basis for trust needed for engaging in exchange relations (Landa 1995). Yet the scope of trust is characterized by a distinctly cosmopolitan rather than nativist sensibility. Cosmopolitanism may be "understood as an activity connecting and entangling places and people for the exchange of goods and knowledge" (Gestrich and Beerbühl 2011, 9). The commercial agents of cosmopolitanism are cosmopolitan capitalists who develop at least a minimal degree of multicultural fluency to survive, if not thrive, in generating income abroad, and/or brokering capital flows across territorial boundaries. Unlike the multinational corporation, the cosmopolitan capitalist not only engages in cross-border economic transactions, but in so doing, engages in ongoing cross-cultural translation and demystification of "the other." In this sense, deterritorialized society constitutes the core of cosmopolitan capitalism, which is not captured by the conventional association of society with domestic groups.

Understanding the implications of diasporic capital for the homeland requires disaggregation of national indicators. Macro-level accounts elide the reality of uneven distribution and disparate forms of remittances and ethnic foreign direct investment within national borders (Ye 2014). India and China, for example, have been the leading recipients of international remittances since 2005; together, they account for one-third of the world's total remittance flows (World Bank various years). These aggregate figures reflect the countries' large diasporic populations. Yet remittances ultimately go to a particular region or locality, not the entire country. As such, examining the *local* manifestations of return capital provides greater insight into debates about the developmental impact of migration and remittances (Brown 2006; Maimo and Ratha 2005).

Three Faces of Cosmopolitan Capitalism

Three subnational patterns of cosmopolitan capitalism are illustrated here through the following cross-national pairs: (1) *transnational trading*: Wenzhou, Zhejiang/Surat, Gujarat; (2) *high-technology hubs*: Zhongguancun, Beijing/Bangalore; and (3) *coastal cosmopolitans*: Guangdong/Kerala. In terms of case selection, this study combines a "within-nation" and "between-nation" comparative research design based on the logic of Mill's Method of Agreement. Each of the paired localities is located in a different country with a different regime type and national economic structure. But the cross-national dyads share key similarities in the historical and contemporary demographics of migratory trends; local state activism in harnessing benefits from migratory circulation; and the impact of return (human and financial) capital on local development, which encompasses economic growth, market development, technological capacity, and human development indicators. These individual localities are sometimes presented in a manner that appears to represent developmental dynamics in China or India as a whole. By contrast, based on the principle of convergent comparison, this study highlights the reality of intranational variation through three expressions of cosmopolitan capitalism, while pointing to the contextual and historical factors that may contribute to cross-national local similarities.

TRANSNATIONAL TRADERS FROM WENZHOU, ZHEJIANG, AND SURAT, GUJARAT

The first pair of localities—Wenzhou in Zhejiang province and Surat in the state of Gujarat—are port cities whose cosmopolitan capitalists have established flourishing transnational commercial networks. Wenzhou locals often say, "Anywhere there's a market in the world with Chinese, you can find Wenzhou people." Guangdong and Fujian provinces also have a rich history of outmigration (populating Hong Kong, Taiwan, and portions of Southeast Asia). But during the reform era, Wenzhou stood out for its early development of the local private economy and reliance on a creative variety of informal financing mechanisms well before the central government sanctioned such experimentation (see citations in Tsai 2002, 120–65). Meanwhile, Wenzhou's private entrepreneurs are known for leaving the mountainous locality in search of income-generating opportunities in other parts of the country and beyond, including Europe and Africa.

Gujurati merchants have a comparable reputation, though with greater historical interaction with European powers.[4] As the Mughal Empire's central port city, Surat attracted investment from British, French, Portuguese, and Dutch textile producers. By the late 19th century, Gujarati traders were operating in most coastal cities in East Africa, and had established an extensive commercial presence, ranging from small retailers (*dukawalla*) to larger companies engaged in high volumes of transnational trade (Vahed 2005). During the rise of European colonialism on the African continent, Gujaratis followed the expansion of railways and roads into the interior, creating new communities as "East Asian Africans," which became the springboard for further migration to Britain following African independence (UK Government Web Archive 2013).

Despite historical differences in the timing and trajectory of outmigration, the commercial imprint of Wenzhou and Surat/Gujarati capitalists shares striking similarities, both nationally and transnationally. First, both have vibrant local economies that serve as the hub for global production and distribution of products in special industries. By the 1990s, various rural counties in Wenzhou had already established substantial global market shares in small commodity items, such as buttons, cigarette lighters, footwear, eyeglasses, and industrial components such as pumps and valves. During a visit this author made to Qiaotou in 1997, for example, it was apparent that the rural township in Yongjia county was supplying 80 percent of the buttons used in apparel manufactured in Asia, and 80 percent of the world's zippers. Prior to China's WTO accession in 2001, Wenzhou produced over 60 percent of the world's cigarette lighters (*Want China Times*, January 12, 2012). And to date, the Yiwu Small Commodities Market is the world's largest wholesale market with over 70,000 stalls, attracting buyers from 89 countries, especially those from the Middle East, Africa, South Asia, and Central Asia (field interviews in Yiwu and Wenzhou by author, April 2014).

Surat's global reach in the diamond industry is no less impressive, and quite lucrative with annual sales of $14 billion (Coggiola 2014). Known as the diamond hub of the world, Surat is home to nearly 10,000 cutting and polishing workshops, processes 90 of the world's small diamonds, and accounts for over 70 percent of India's diamond exports (Samuel 2013). The industry originated from Gujarati traders who brought diamonds from East Africa back to Surat in the early 20th century. When global demand for diamonds expanded in the 1970s and early 1980s, Surat's cutting and polishing capacity took off (Engelshoven 1999, 353–77). By the late 1990s, Surat was a global player in the small diamond industry (Kapur 2010, 100).

Besides diamonds, Surat has a thriving textile industry, which involves the majority of the local workforce and is geared toward the domestic apparel market. The "Silk City's" traditional cotton mills and expertise in silk brocade and gold embroidery (*jari*) have extended into manufacturing of man-made fiber. Surat now accounts for 60 percent of India's polyester production.[5] Textile trade sources indicate that local producers export nonapparel man-made fiber mainly to Pakistan and Central Asia, and seek to increase exports to the United States, which imports nearly 40 percent of its textiles and garments from China (Thomas 2014c).

Despite the somewhat hyperbolic nomenclature of the "World's Largest Supermarket for Small Commodities" and "Diamond Hub of the World," respectively, Wenzhou and Surat do in fact dominate key markets that are disproportionate to their local "permanent" populations (at 7 million and 6 million, respectively. The reasons for this dominance merit far more historical explanation than can be supplied here. But it is clear that their diasporas, both past and contemporary, are essential contributors to their commercial success.[6] They constitute networked economic resources beyond the borders of the nation-state. With access to lower-cost textiles from Wenzhou, for example, the clothing factories in Prato owned by Wenzhou people dominate manufacturing in the nondesigner brand segment of Italy's apparel industry (Fels and Hamilton 2013). With offices in Mumbai, Hong Kong, New York, London, Tel Aviv, and Antwerp (the former headquarters of De Beers), Surat's diamontaires have displaced Hasidic Jewish dealers in Antwerp (Kapur 2010, 100–104; Engelshoven 1999, 353–77), a change that has consolidated Surat as *the* global center for cutting and polishing small diamonds. The capital formation supporting the local concentration and transnational expansion of Wenzhou and Surti dominance in these sectors derives from highly exclusive, native-place (and caste-based) networks of informal finance.

There are undoubtedly multigenerational and more recent migrants from Wenzhou and Surat who are not involved in business (e.g., wage workers, professionals, students, and unemployed relatives) and who may be assimilated abroad. Nonetheless, substantial segments of Wenzhou and Surat's local economies are connected to the commercial diaspora, and therefore, may be viewed as a transnational extension of society.

The question, then, is how to analyze the impact of the commercial diaspora on state-society relations. Examining the activities of both government-organ and societal associations based on native place or industrial sector is a starting point.

In Wenzhou, the municipal government takes pride in the propensity of local merchants to trade abroad and has an office dedicated to overseas Wenzhou affairs, which receives international delegations and also visits Wenzhou associations in other countries.[7] The Overseas Chinese Association of Wenzhou (OCAW) maintains a website, the Wenzhou Overseas Network, *Wenzhou qiaowang*, which provides news about Wenzhou people living abroad, and links to Wenzhou overseas associations on all five continents.[8] Much of the web content highlights the contributions of overseas Wenzhou Chinese. For example, the OCAW reports that over 80 percent of Wenzhou's exports are brokered through its diasporic networks. External trade is important for Wenzhou's economy. Prior to the global financial crisis, trade reached a peak of 43 percent of the municipality's GDP, with exports accounting for 36 percent of local GDP.[9]

Apart from trade, the local government recognizes numerous other examples of overseas Wenzhou giving back to their native place, including individual remittances and charitable donations collected by associations from abroad, such as the Wenzhou Association of Overseas Businesspeople (field interviews in Wenzhou by author, April 2014).[10]

My field interviews indicate that Wenzhou's entrepreneurs are frustrated with local economic conditions, which include rising wages; declining asset values (local real estate prices have dropped by 40–50 percent since 2009); and various crises in informal financial markets (field interviews in Wenzhou, January 2016). Many are thus highly motivated to exit, as other Wenzhou entrepreneurs have done. Yet the impact of the present downturn should not be over-interpreted. The local state in Wenzhou is attuned to its diasporic society, and the attention is often reciprocated meaningfully.

Although India's (national) government has been less proactive than China in encouraging investment by nonresident Indians (NRIs) and persons of Indian origin (PIOs), the state of Gujarat recognized early on the value of encouraging Gujaratis to reinvest in the locality. This was motivated by the state's founding circumstances, as Gujarat was established in 1960 out of a portion of Bombay and the merger of Saurashtra and Kutch. Aseema Sinha observed that the loss of Bombay city to Maharashtra generated among Gujarat's new leaders, "an ideology of competitive developmentalism" with Bombay (Sinha 2005, 182). Gujarat thus pursued a variety of strategies such as tax breaks, subsidies, and low-cost labor to encourage investment from Gujaratis who had moved to Bombay city and elsewhere (Gorter 1996).

The local state's developmental orientation endures. The Gujarat Industrial Development Corporation is focused on attracting both domestic and international investment, and has approved 47 special economic zones.[11] One of the three such zones that are already operational is the Apparel Park in Surat, which is now the fourth fastest growing developing city in the world (Bhatt 2011). Competitive dynamics with Mumbai also continue, which entrepreneurs use to negotiate better business conditions in Surat. For example, in 2014 over large 50 diamond companies in Mumbai announced their intention to relocate to Surat where a new "world-class" diamond market would be constructed (Thomas 2014b). Shortly thereafter, the Surat Diamond Association announced intentions to lobby rigorously for an international airport in Surat; otherwise, the claim is that Mumbai would be a more attractive city for Surat's transnational diamantaires (ibid.).[12] In Belgium alone, there are 14,000 Gujaratis, mainly from Surat, of which 5,000 are engaged in the diamond trade (Thomas 2013). Notwithstanding the fact that India's prime minister Narendra Modi is from Gujarat, the Non-Resident Gujarati center in Surat and the Non-Resident Indian Division of the Gujarat Chamber of Commerce are institutional channels for having their voices heard (field interviews in Ahmedabad and Ghandinagar, January 2016).

HIGH-TECHNOLOGY HUBS: ASIA'S SILICON VALLEYS, ZHONGGUANCUN AND BANGALORE

In the span of less than two decades, the district of Zhongguancun in Beijing and Bangalore in Karnataka have developed into the information and communications technology (ICT) centers of China and India, respectively. Zhongguancun is home to Lenovo, Stone, and Baidu, and about half of the Chinese firms currently listed on NASDAQ are based in Zhongguancun. Bangalore is the "Outsourcing Capital of the World": 400 of the Fortune 500 companies outsource IT services from Bangalore, and Bangalore accounts for over 35 percent of India's software exports (Karnataka Information Communication Technology Group 2013). The economic transformation of these localities cannot be attributed solely to comparatively lower prices in factor endowments (land, labor, capital). Zhongguancun and Bangalore are both strategically selected beneficiaries of national industrial policy for ICT development, while their local governments have also provided a supportive environment. At the same time, their ICT sectors rely on blended domestic and diasporic networks of human, intellectual, social, and financial capital. Economic geographers who study regional innovation systems emphasize the importance of tacit knowledge shared by individuals and organizations who interact with one another on a regular basis (Storper and Venables 2004; Cooke 2001). Zhongguancun and Bangalore possess such local networks, but what distinguishes them as significant sites for global sourcing of technology are their diasporic ties and attractiveness as sites for returnees. Anne Saxenian (2005) refers to the return migration of well-trained technical professionals, managers, and venture capitalists as "brain circulation."

As with the Wenzhou/Surat pair, characterizing the nature of state-society relations in Zhongguancun and Bangalore involves dynamics that extend beyond administrative boundaries. Unlike the Wenzhou/Surat cases, however, central state policies have played a key role in Zhongguancun /Bangalore's IT development, and returnees in that sector are not necessarily natives to Beijing/Bangalore, though they may have attended schools in those localities.

The vision for Zhongguancun's development as "China's Silicon Valley" dates back to 1980 when a physicist from the Chinese Academy of Sciences, Chen Chunxian, returned from a government-sponsored trip to the United States (Zhou 2008). Professor Chen subsequently established China's first private (*minying*) technology service company in northwestern Beijing's Haidian district where Peking University, Tsinghua University, and dozens of other colleges and universities are concentrated. The area also includes over 200 scientific institutions such as the Chinese Academy of Sciences and the Chinese Academy of Engineering. By the time that Beijing designated Zhongguancun as an experimental high-technology zone in 1988, the main street in Zhongguancun was already known as "Electronics Avenue," with dozens of *minying* computer hardware and software businesses. Many of these firms, including Legend (now Lenovo), were established by academics from local universities who raised funds through informal sources, and were quietly sponsored by their state units (Segal 2002, 51–86).

Multinational corporations such as IBM, Microsoft, and Fujitsu, started establishing operations in Zhongguancun in the early 1990s, and were producing ICT for the domestic market by the end of the decade. By the 2000s, an increasing number of Chinese who were educated or had worked abroad (including the founders of Baidu, China's leading internet search engine) returned to pursue opportunities in the ICT industry (Wang et al. 2011). As of 2012, Zhongguancun had over 5,000 enterprises with 16,000 returnees, of which 12,000 had received graduate training abroad (Zhongguancun Index 2013, 8).[13] Zhongguancun now encompasses two dozen science and technology parks and 29 overseas students pioneer parks.

Zhongguancun's development as China's ICT center evolved out of a synergistic combination of central state policies, spatial concentration of China's best universities, entrepreneurialism, *and* "brain circulation."

Since 2003, state efforts to promote "indigenous innovation" have included funding facilities to encourage start-ups by overseas returnees (Zhou 2008, 45–62). These include access to "state-sponsored incubators, small start-up grants, basic guarantees for small loans, rent breaks, and other limited subsidies" (ibid. 138). But in general, the most attractive sources of funding are returnees themselves. Venture capitalists with overseas ICT experience understand the financing needs of the market better than employees of state banks, and are more interested in growth potential than risk management (field interviews in Beijing, June and December 2016).

Like Zhongguancun, Bangalore also started with a promising base of human capital. Shortly after independence, India's central government relocated important industries away from border regions to Bangalore, the capital of Karnataka state in southern India (Basant 2008, 147–94). Major public enterprises included Hindustan Machine Tools, Bharat Electronics Limited, Bharat Heavy Electrical, Hindustan Aeronautics Limited, and Indian Telephone Industries. Significant state investment in Bangalore's defense industry, combined with dozens of engineering colleges, research organizations, and the Indian Institute of Science, created a solid industrial infrastructure and supply of well-trained technical staff. By the late 1960s, Bangalore had become a center for scientific and defense-related research.

Well before economic liberalization and the authorization of Software Technology Parks in Bangalore in 1991, the Foreign Exchange Regulation Act of 1975 and limits on imports of computer hardware in the early 1980s had two notable impacts on subsequent developments in Bangalore and India's computer industry (ibid. 5–6). First, due to restrictions on foreign ownership of firms, IBM departed from India in 1978, leaving behind 1,200 unemployed software specialists. A number of former IBM employees established small computer companies in Bangalore, while many moved abroad for better IT employment opportunities (Heeks 1996, 70). Both groups contributed to the export-oriented development of ICT in Bangalore. Local software companies faced difficulties in entering a limited domestic market and thus turned to the external one for product development. Although they were not started by former IBM employees, Wipro and Infosys are successful examples of domestic firms that began operating in the early 1980s. Meanwhile, Bangalore's expatriates rose through the ranks of various multinational IT companies, and became a bridge for multinational corporations to outsource their services through Bangalore.

While the initial group of ICT firms in Beijing's ZGC were established by local scientists and engineers, the development of Bangalore's ICT industry was led more by multinational corporations that swiftly engaged local firms in outsourcing production for export markets (Wang, Cheng, and Ganapati 2012). The establishment of Texas Instruments in 1986 as India's first wholly foreign-owned software subsidiary paved the way for other major companies, including General Electric, Hewlett-Packard, Motorola, and Siemens, to set up operations in Bangalore. The introduction of software technology parks and dedicated satellite communications infrastructure provided an inviting environment during the 1990s, but the Indian diaspora also played a critical role in generating confidence about Bangalore among multinational corporations. For example, one study found that 71 out of the 75 corporations operating in Bangalore's software technology park were directed by Indians with previous work experience in the United States or other countries (Ghamawat 2000). As Devesh Kapur observes, "The Indian diaspora's success in Silicon Valley . . . has created a 'brand-name,'" wherein an "Indian software programmer sends an *ex ante* signal of quality" (2010, 91). In other words, earlier outmigration of well-educated scientists, engineers, and professionals became an asset for domestic ICT development. Rather than unidirectional exit or brain drain, migrants represent a potential societal resource. The state-level nonresident Indian Karnataka Forum recognizes and seeks to harness this resource.[14]

Over ten years ago, Yasheng Huang and Tarun Khanna (2003) observed in *Foreign Policy*, "With the help of its diaspora, China has won the race to be the world's factory. With the help of its diaspora, India could become the world's technology lab." Another group of researchers finds that Zhongguancun lags Bangalore in software services, but leads in ICT innovation (Wang, Cheng, and Ganapati 2012). But regardless of relative competitiveness from an industry perspective, noting the relevance of their respective diasporas is less controversial. Overall, China's ICT returnees have been particularly attuned to localizing multinational corporation technology and products for the domestic market, which contrasts from the Indian diaspora's role in building Bangalore's outsourcing capabilities (ibid.). Bangalore's most recent returnees are also becoming IT entrepreneurs by leveraging professional networks from former Silicon Valley employers (field interviews in Bangalore, January 2015 and January 2018). What distinguishes the technology hub pattern of cosmopolitan capitalism is that Beijing and Bangalore attract nonnative national returnees. The social impact of their privileged status merits further study.

COASTAL COSMOPOLITANS: THE MIGRANTS OF GUANGDONG AND KERALA

Based on economic indicators, the pairing of Guangdong province and the state of Kerala may seem puzzling at first glance. During the reform era, Guangdong developed into a major manufacturing center and was one of China's fastest growing provinces with a population of nearly 106 million. Even after the global financial crisis of 2008–9, Guangdong still ranks first among China's 31 provinces in terms of GDP. Kerala's economy, on the other hand, relies on services and agriculture, and had more modest rates of growth until the mid-2000s. Yet the "Kerala model" of development is renowned for its extensive provision of social services and maintaining the highest human development indicators in India (Heller 1999; Tsai 2006).[15]

Their internal politics also lie at opposite ends of the ideological spectrum. Guangdong people have traditionally been more liberal and market-oriented in orientation. In the political context of modern China, Guangdong has a "rightist" reputation.[16] As in Wenzhou, the local state in Guangdong was more permissive of private commerce years before it was legalized by Beijing. By contrast, Kerala's politics are unabashedly leftist. The Left Democratic Front coalition in Kerala, led by the Communist Party of India (Marxist) (CPM), enjoys widespread popular support with regular electoral success (alternating with the United Democratic Front coalition). Unlike the Chinese Communist Party, which has pragmatically adapted its official ideology to accommodate the effects of marketization, the CPM retains a more orthodox Marxist agenda. Furthermore, even though Kerala's industrial wages are higher than those in neighboring states, labor unrest is common.

Despite these differences in the two localities' contemporary political economy, they share cross-national similarities in geographic position and significance for national migration history. Both have long coastlines that for centuries, served as ports of exit for their respective populations. Both have also attracted internal migrants from other parts of the country. They are circuits for both domestic and external migration.

Guangdong is adjacent to Hong Kong, a gateway to the South China Sea. The various Chinatowns that emerged in North America, Britain, and Australia during the 19th century were also established by (mainly Cantonese-speaking) migrants from Guangdong province. Localities with high levels of outmigration developed networks with particular destinations. For example, migrant workers from Taishan settled in North America, and accounted for 60 percent of the Chinese population in the United States in the 19th century (Zhang 1998, 36). In the 1930s, one study found that remittances to Chaozhou and Shantou originated from Thailand, Malaya, Vietnam, and Indonesia (Wu 1937, cited in Hoe 2013, 28). Hakka people from Meixian (formerly Jiaying) became gold miners in Borneo and also settled in Taiwan (Zhang 1998, 39). Twentieth-century outmigration from Guangdong to Hong Kong reflected stressful periods in the China's political economy (e.g., Communist Revolution, Great Leap Forward, Cultural Revolution). Due to its locational advantages for attracting foreign direct investment, during the reform era, Guangdong was selected for three of the first four special economic zones (Shenzhen, Shantou, Zhuhai); and has since attracted over 20 million migrants from inland provinces. Meanwhile, although emigration to Hong Kong continued in the 1990s, the primary port of Chinese outmigration shifted to Chang Le, Fujian (Chin 1999; Keefe 2009, 33–44). Overall, Guangdong's migrants form a multigenerational mix of overseas Chinese populations. The earlier Chinatown settlements have evolved into a diverse diaspora that encompasses assimilated coethnics, people in Hong Kong with a distinct postcolonial identity, and transnational Cantonese in a variety of commercial sectors and noncommercial professions.

Kerala lies on India's southwestern coastal tip, flanking the Arabian Sea. Early 20th-century waves of migration from Kerala comprised semiskilled workers who went to Ceylon, Malaya, Burma, and large cities in south Asia such as Calcutta, Karachi, and Bombay. Following the establishment of new oil fields in the Middle East, and accompanying demand for labor in construction and infrastructural development, mass migration from India to the Gulf accelerated in the 1970s and 1980s. Workers from Kerala accounted for 80 percent of these migrants. Besides Gulf migration, professionals in the medical, engineering, IT, and academic sectors also migrated to North America and Europe. As in Guangdong, Kerala's migration patterns have been shaped by both local conditions and the cumulative effects of migration networks. Migration of manual labor, for example, is more prevalent from northern districts such as Malappuram and Kannur, while nurses migrate from Christian-dominant areas with more developed educational infrastructure.[17] In recent years, Kerala has also attracted about 2.5 million migrant laborers from other Indian states who seek better employment opportunities (Nair 2014). Meanwhile, outmigration continues, primarily to the United Arab Emirates and Saudi Arabia, but also to other parts of the world.

Notwithstanding Guangdong's neoliberalism and Kerala's populism, the fact that both have multigenerational as well as more recent diasporic populations has had complex developmental implications. Their local states are sensitive to these realities, and have adapted a proactive stance toward incorporating their transnational extensions of society. They value their diasporas. In this sense, local state identity is as much shaped by outmigration as native place retains some degree of identity for those who have left.

From the mid-19th century until the establishment of the People's Republic of China, remittances contributed significantly to certain localities in Guangdong, especially migrant-sending districts (*qiaoxiang*) along the Pearl River Delta, such as Taishan, Panyu, and Xinyi. For most households, remittances were used for daily, subsistence-level necessities. Contemporaneously, diasporic capital changed the nature of local production and consumerism (e.g., with the establishment of Gold Mountain banks, factories, and luxury markets); and contributed to building schools, orphanages, hospitals, ancestral halls, roads, bridges, and even the Xinning Railway (Nair 2014; Hoe 2013). During the Mao era, transfers from abroad were limited due to political campaigns attacking capitalist influences. But substantial inflows of remittances and charitable donations from Guangdong's diaspora resumed during the reform period. Foreign direct investment from Hong Kong and other overseas Chinese played a pivotal role in building Guangdong's manufacturing and commercial infrastructure. From 1979 to 1999, nearly 75 percent of the province's foreign direct investment arrived through Hong Kong—and of that amount, 97 percent was invested by ethnic Chinese residing in Hong Kong and Macau, with the remaining 3 percent coming from the Chinese diaspora in Southeast Asia (Hoe 2013, 35, table 2.6). Guangzhou, Dongguan, and Shenzhen developed most rapidly, but local governments in other parts of Guangdong also actively pursued overseas Chinese investment. Overseas Chinese Affairs offices courted "native sons" and "compatriots" (*tongbao*) residing abroad. Local governments offered "foreign" investors a host of preferential policies, including tax holidays and access to land. Indeed, the operating environment for foreign-invested enterprises was more favorable than that for domestic private enterprises, which incentivized local businesses to disguise themselves as foreign-invested enterprises.[18] Arguably, the relationship between the local state and transnational society in Guangdong has been more mutually supportive than (central) state-(domestic) society relations in recent decades (field interviews in Guangdong by author, April 2014 and December 2016).

Compared with Guangdong, remittances have been more central to Kerala's local development than foreign-invested enterprise. This reflects broader cross-national realities: India has been the world's leading recipient of remittances since 2005; China ranks second in terms of remittances, but has attracted far more foreign-invested enterprises than India (World Investment Report various years).[19] The reasons for this variation in remittances versus foreign-invested enterprise have been discussed elsewhere (Tsai 2010; Ye 2014). For the present analysis, the point is that remittances represent a major component of Kerala's economy. At the peak of the Gulf boom during 1980–81, remittances to localities with large numbers of migrants—known as "Gulf pockets"—reached 50 percent of local GDP (Kurien 1994, 765). More recent statistics indicate that workers' remittances from the Gulf continue to contribute a nontrivial proportion of local and national capital. In 2016, remittances to Kerala reached $9.8 billion, accounting for over one-third of India's total remittances (field interviews in Thiruvanathapuram, January 2017). That same year, remittances contributed to 36 percent of Kerala's net state domestic product and therefore, per capita GDP (ibid.). The impact of remittances compared with the state's fiscal resources is even more staggering: remittances exceed the state's revenues receipts by 160 percent; account for over 6.2 times of central transfers to Kerala; and represent more than double the amount of annual state expenditures (Mistry 2014, 4). The state's remarkable human development indicators (high literacy, low infant mortality, longer life expectancy, greater female education) have been financed in large part by the availability of remittances. As a result, the local state is acutely aware of trends in migration and remittances, and in 1996 established a Non-Resident Keralites Affairs Department to assist its expatriate population.[20] The department provides nonresident Keralites with a wide range of services, including grievance resolution, pension benefits, and resettlement of returnees. Kerala is a particularly salient case of how cosmopolitan laborers, if not capitalists, represent an integral component of society.

Yet Kerala is also a highly diverse state with 14 districts and a population of 33.4 million (as of 2011). There is variation in the geographic and religious demographics of migration, as well as in the volume of remittances and uses of diasporic capital (table 7.1). Muslims are more likely to migrate abroad than other religious groups; they account for 44.3 percent of migrants from Kerala, but only 26 percent of the population (Zachariah and Rajan 2013). Hindus represent 55 percent of Kerala's population, comprise 36.4 percent of Kerala's international migrants, and nearly two-thirds (64.6 percent) of the state's *domestic* migrants to other parts of India. The distribution of remittances received by households in different religious groups roughly mirrors their portion of Kerala's migrants (ibid.).[21]

An ethnographic study by Prema Ann Kurien in three "Gulf pockets" with different dominant religions offers a revealing glimpse into the variation in remittance-financed patterns of consumption, investment, and exchange (1994, 765). In a northern Mappilas (Keralite Muslim) village called Veni,[22] male migrants usually work in the informal sector in the Gulf. While abroad, enclave communities of Mappilas participate in rotating credit and savings associations (chitty groups) and remit larger sums of laundered "tube money" to their kin. Veni now has a central market area with gold jewelry shops, video libraries, and department stores. By contrast, the southern village of Cherur is dominated by Ezhavas (lower-caste Keralite Hindu), whose male migrants are employed in

Table 7.1
Migration and remittances among religious groups in Kerala

	Hindus	Muslims	Christians
Percent of Kerala's population	**56**	24	19
Percent of Kerala's international migrants	36.4	**44.3**	~18
Emigrants per 100 households	18	**59**	29
Percent of households with emigrants or return emigrants	19.6	**53.3**	21.3
Percent of Kerala's remittances	36.4	**46.5**	17.1

SOURCE: Zachariah and Rajan 2013.

NOTE: Boldface numbers represents the largest number/percentage in a particular category.

the Gulf on formal contracts as plumbers, electricians, drivers, mechanics, and masons. Rather than for local commercial development, remittances are used for lavish life-cycle ceremonies such as weddings and Hindu festivals, as well as school fees for English-medium schools. The third village of Cherur in central Kerala is dominated by Syrian Christians (upper-caste Keralite Christian). Cherur's migrants are well-educated and employed as nurses, clerical workers, and engineers in the Gulf. Unlike the first two villages, which send only men abroad, migration from Cherur is more likely to include immediate family members. Remittances in Cherur are concentrated in higher education, bank deposits, and real estate.

These sketches demonstrate the enduring loyalty of those who have exited and returned, as well as the locally contingent uses of remittances. The cases also highlight the complexity of characterizing the impact of Kerala's diaspora on local state-society relations. The state of Kerala understands the centrality of remittances for its developmental model. Yet remittances have created marked inequalities between migrant and nonmigrant households. The Kerala Migration Survey of 2011 found that only 17.1 percent of households received remittances, meaning that over 80 percent of households in Kerala do not benefit directly from additional income for consumption, private health providers, private schools, higher-quality houses, savings, or land purchases. Based on its 2004–5 survey, the National Sample Survey Organization reports that Kerala has the highest levels of rural and urban inequality among the 15 most populous Indian states (Bhagwati and Panagariya 2013, 69). But the fact that Kerala ranked first in the organization's expenditure survey for 2009–10 in terms of per capita expenditures is largely due to remittances—even if the expenditures are unevenly distributed.[23]

Table 7.2 summarizes the patterns of circulation and local state engagement in each of the three modes of cosmopolitan capitalism discussed above. The emphases of local state developmentalism reflect the financial and human resources presented by migratory trends. In *transnational trading* areas, the local state recognizes that the local economy is intimately tied with diasporic success in specialized industries and nurtures local-transnational networking. State policy in the *high-technology hubs* focuses on attracting highly skilled cosmopolitan returnees through dedicated technology zones. In the *coastal cosmopolitan* pattern, the local state prioritizes attracting foreign direct investment and remittances from coethnics. Notwithstanding rich historical, demographic, and political

Table 7.2
Local state-society patterns in cosmopolitan capitalism

Pattern	Migratory Trends	Local State Engagement
Transnational Trading Wenzhou/Surat	Permanent outmigration Circular migration	Favorable policy environment for global trade in specialized markets
		State-sponsored business associations and conferences for commercial diaspora
High-Technology Hubs Zhongguancun/ Bangalore	"Brain circulation" Nonnative return migration	Recruitment of highly skilled returnees in partnership with national policies
		Dedicated high-technology parks
Coastal Cosmopolitans Guangdong/Kerala	Permanent outmigration Temporary migration Internal and domestic migration	Dedicated offices for diaspora services & relations
		Encourages ethnic FDI and remittances

differences among the individual cases, what they have in common is active state engagement with mobile populations.

Conclusion

Examining state-society relations at different levels of analysis expands the scope of interactions that may be relevant for developmental processes. Local states represent the central state administratively, but their policy preferences and practices may exhibit relative autonomy from the center, even in authoritarian regimes. By the same token, limiting the scope of society to populations immediately contained within the borders of the nation-state myopically excludes transnational members of society. In the study of state-society relations, the argument has been made across different disciplines for *either* focusing on the local state, *or* recognizing that social identity and action transcends territorial borders. Rarely both. Engaging in the dual-definitional stretch of lowering the state and deterritorializing society reveals dynamics that are imprecisely captured by the Weberian definition of the state, and the accompanying assumption of domestic society.

A potential critique of this dual-definitional stretch is that it runs the risk of concept stretching, which the "democracy with adjectives" literature straddles delicately (Collier and Levitsky 1997, 430–51). Building on Hirschman's classic exit-voice-loyalty framework is intended to avoid such ad hoc dilution of conceptual discipline. In analyzing the impact of international migration on subnational development, the local state provides both juridical and territorial boundaries; and society (as defined by identity with native place or the broader nation) retains three options even if they are not mutually exclusive. The parameters of local state and transnational society are still contained. It is the dynamics engendered by their relationship that generate ambiguity when viewed from a conventional state-society perspective. Despite their distinct histories, by research design, the cases presented above share features that provide empirical illustrations of these claims.

All six cases involve economic migration (exit). The Wenzhou and Surat migrants are archetypal cosmopolitan capitalists whose commercial beginnings originated in their localities, supported by trust-based forms of informal finance, but now constitute a formidable transnational network of manufacturers, traders, and dealers in key industries. Their commercial success abroad has transformed not only the economic status of their families, but also that of their locality relative to others within the homeland. Some migrated due to dissatisfaction with local economic conditions. Others sought greater entrepreneurial opportunities. Regardless of their initial sense of loyalty, the collective impact of individual and networked decisions to move abroad has refracted a commercial reputation back to the locality. Voice can be articulated by example through transnational praxis and economic success. The local states of Wenzhou and Surat thus encourage and anticipate such expressions of economic loyalty.

Parallel dynamics can be seen in Guangdong and Kerala, though their much larger populations bring greater historical, ethnic, religious, socioeconomic, and occupational diversity into the analysis. The two areas alone could yield multiple pairs of research cases, particularly since they are also destinations for internal migrants. Yet it is precisely the reality of such domestic and diasporic diversity that guards the study from overgeneralizing from a single dyad, such as Wenzhou and Surat. Ethnic foreign direct investment and remittances have had mixed implications for Guangdong and Kerala. In both areas, they provided supplementary external sources of capital that enhanced the welfare of kin and contributed to local infrastructural development. These same funds financed higher-end consumerism and exacerbated local inequality. The aggregate effects of economic exit, voice, and loyalty are variegated. Nonetheless, the local states of Guangdong and Kerala tend to prioritize their relations with transnational economic society to ensure continuity of financial, if not physical loyalty in the form of return migration.

The local state is similarly attentive to transnational links in supporting Asia's Silicon Valleys, Zhongguancun and Bangalore. As national high technology hubs, their density of higher education institutions, preferential policies, and brain circulation are defining features of their rapid rise to prominence in the ICT sector. Enhancing competitiveness in ICT is consistent with state priorities at both the central and local levels. But in the early years, state policies did not explicitly promote educational migration and local entrepreneurialism. It was only after the value of transnational diasporic linkages to local ICT development became apparent that the state made a more concerted effort to incentivize return migration.

China has been active in this respect. At the end of 2009, it launched the "Thousand Talents Plan," which aims to attract 2,000 top-tier scientists, engineers, and professionals to China over five to 10 years (Zweig and Wang 2013).[24] Relatedly, the cadre evaluation system has recently shifted from attracting foreign direct investment to returnees. Besides Zhongguancun, other local governments have responded to the national Thousand Talents Plan by putting forth various programs to attract returnees (field interviews in Shanghai by author, May 2014).[25] In India, seven out of the 28 states have assorted government offices that promote nonresident Indian affairs, including the nonresident Indian division in Gujarat, Non-Resident Keralites Affairs Department in Kerala, and a Karnataka Diaspora Cell.[26] Most of these offices are geared toward developing a database of nonresident Indian and persons of Indian origin from particular localities and encouraging diasporic investment. The Non-Resident Keralites Affairs Department in Kerala provides more extensive services such as assistance in resolving nonpayment of salaries, addressing complaints against illegal overseas recruitment agencies, dealing with other state government departments, transporting the mortal remains of nonresident Keralites back to Kerala, and a social security network for nonresident Keralites. The division's charge is arguably more responsive to nonresident Keralites than most local governments are with their local citizens. Exit can coexist with voice and ongoing engagement with the local state. Loyalty may be reciprocated in local state-transnational society relations.

These observations do not discount the orthodox scope of state-society relations or the enduring appeal of Hirschman's exit-voice-loyalty framework for explaining certain types of questions. Distinguishing between citizens contained within national borders from those residing abroad remains relevant. Exit can occur without domestic voice or loyalty. Exit can be permanent, whether voluntary or involuntary. Moreover, this chapter has not examined political instances of mutual or asymmetric hostility between the local state and its diaspora, which merits attention in its own right. The foregoing focus on "most similar," generally positive, cases of local state-transnational society relations is only meant to remind us that theories of political economy may be incomplete when they reflexively exclude the local state and transnational society as potential developmental actors and resources. In the absence of local state agency, migratory circulation, and diasporic reinvestment, none of the six localities discussed would feature on the map of national leaders, social scientists, foreign investors, and journalists. The fact that they are known as cases of developmental success has everything to do with state-society relations, but not in the way conventionally understood. The dual-definitional stretch that I recommend captures empirical dynamics at alternative levels of analysis to provide a more complete account of local developmental processes.

Notes

1. Citizens residing in national capitals may not distinguish as much between municipal and national institutions and agents because the territories of these agencies overlap.

2. "Exit Albert Hirschman," *Economist*, December 22, 2012, https://www.economist .com/news/business/21568708-great-lateral-thinker-died-december-10th-exit-albert -hirschman.

3. Data are limited on the percentage of those who migrate primarily for political purposes or possess a political agenda. As of 2013, about 7 percent of international migrants were classified as refugees, which is only a small portion of those who might be regarded as "political migrants." UN Department of Economic and Social Affairs, Population Division, "The Number of International Migrants Reaches 232 Million," *Population Facts* no. 2013.2, September 2013, 4.

4. Although Wenzhou was opened to the foreign tea trade in the late 19th century, it was one of the few coastal cities that remained unoccupied by foreigners.

5. *CottonYarnMarket*, February 15, 2014.

6. It is not easy to find reliable statistics on the scale of diasporas from particular localities. Wenzhou government statistics indicate that as of 2011, 430,000 Wenzhou people were living abroad, including 300,000 in Europe. Wenzhou Municipal Government 2012, 242; Foreign Affairs Office of the Wenzhou City People's Government, http:// www.wzfao.gov.cn/en/index.jsp?ido=z1b6tuus&id1=z1b74u8b&sid=z1c49wfr (accessed May 2014). This may be an underestimate. Overseas Wenzhou association leaders estimate that 230,000 are residing in the United States, and that an estimated 130,000 reside in Europe. John T. Ma, "The Wenzhounese Community in New York City," October 2000, translation by Him Mark Lai (2004), http://www.thefreelibrary.com/ The+Wenzhouese+community+in+New+York+City.-a0113304619 (accessed May 2014).

7. The local government reports that there were over 260 Wenzhou native-place associations abroad as of 2011. Wenzhou Municipal Government 2012, 243.

8. These links include information about the association membership of Wenzhou people in individual countries. For example, the Southern Africa Wenzhou Association has over 200 members; the one in Gabon has over 300 members; and the one in Benin has 26 Wenzhou companies and 87 individual memberships. See *Wenzhou qiaowang*, http://www.wzqw.gov.cn/view.jsp?view.jsp?id0=z0gkrwmdof&id1=z0gkrwmdof&id2=z0gkrwmdof&id=z0glwocg90 (accessed May 2014).

9. Wenzhou Municipal Government 2008, part 6. In 2013 external trade was 32 percent of Wenzhou's GDP, and exports accounted for 28 percent of GDP. Wenzhou Municipal Government 2014, part 6.

10. Local business associations also mobilize charitable donations from private entrepreneurs, but such contributions are viewed by private entrepreneurs as mandatory rather than voluntary. Perhaps ironically, private entrepreneurs based in Wenzhou view local trade associations as being less helpful than those in other countries. When local entrepreneurs have a concern, they are more likely to go directly to local officials with whom they have good relations (*guanxi*) than through associational channels. Interviews by author in Wenzhou, April 2014.

11. These are detailed at the Gujarat Industrial Development Corporation website at http://gidc.gujarat.gov.in/GIDC_At_A_Glance_Key_Indicators.html (accessed December 21, 2017).

12. By way of comparison, note that Yiwu has its own international airport, which used to be an airfield devoted to the People's Liberation Army for military training until the 1990s.

13. Zhongguancun Science Park Administrative Committee, *Zhongguancun Index 2013*, 8. http://www.zgc.gov.cn.

14. Non-Resident Indian Forum Karnataka, Government of India, http://www.nriforumkarnataka.org/ (accessed December 21, 2017).

15. Heller (1999) has described Kerala as a "democratic developmental state."

16. The first revolt of the Taiping rebellion occurred in Guangdong. The birthplace of Sun Yat-sen, Guangdong became a base for Guomindang Nationalist preparations for the Northern Expedition during the Civil War.

17. Interviews by author, Thiruvananthapuram and Kochi, Kerala, January 2017.

18. Registering as a "fake foreign-invested enterprise" (*jia waizi qiye*) is accomplished by registering a shell company and a bank account in Hong Kong or off-shore islands and transferring funds from abroad in the guise of foreign direct investment.

19. From 1992 to 2004, China attracted about 16 times more foreign direct investment than India ($312.4 billion in China vs. $19.9 billion in India). See UNCTAD, *World Investment Report*, 1994 through 2004.

20. A description of the Non-Resident Keralites Affairs Department is available at the Government of Kerala site at https://www.kerala.gov.in/.

21. It is beyond the scope of this chapter to consider the potential political implications of this relative imbalance in outmigration among Muslims, Hindus, and Christians. Note that in Lebanon, outmigration has served to redistribute domestic resources available for political competition (Pearlman 2013).

22. The three villages described in Kurien's study are referred to by pseudonyms.

23. "Cracking the Kerala Myth," *Times of India*, January 2, 2012.

24. For additional details, see Recruitment Program of Global Talents at http://www.1000plan.org/en/ (accessed December 21, 2017).

25. Interviews by author in Shanghai, May 2014. Nanjing, for example, recently launched a "321 Program," which aims to attract 3,000 leading technological entrepreneurs, nurture 200 technological entrepreneurs, and recruit 100 entrepreneurs to be included in the Thousand Talents program.

26. These government entities are summarized on the Government of India website under "Opportunities for Overseas Indians" at https://business.gov.in/overseas/organisational_set_up_state.php.

References

Adamson, F. B. 2012. "Constructing the Diaspora: Diaspora Identity Politics and Transnational Social Movements." In *Politics from Afar: Transnational Diasporas and Networks*, edited by Terrence Lyons and Peter Mandaville, 25–42. London: C. Hurst.

Anderson, B. 1992. *Long-Distance Nationalism: World Capitalism and the Rise of Identity Politics*. Amsterdam: University of Amsterdam Center for Asian Studies.

Appadurai, A. 1990. "Disjuncture and Difference in the Global Cultural Economy." *Theory, Culture, and Society* 7: 295–310.

Basant, R. 2008. "Bangalore Cluster: Evolution, Growth, and Challenges." In *Growing Industrial Clusters in Asia: Serendipity and Science*, edited by Shahid Yusuf, Kaoru Nabeshima, and Shoichi Yamashita, 147–93. Washington, DC: IBRD/ World Bank.

Basch, L., N. G. Schiller, and C. S. Blanc, eds. 1994. *Nations Unbound: Transnational Projects and the Deterritorialized Nation State*. London: Routledge.

Basch, L., G. Schiller, and G. E. Fouron. 2001. *Georges Woke Up Laughing: Long Distance Nationalism and the Search for Home*. Durham, NC: Duke University Press.

Bhagwati, J., and A. Panagariya. 2013. *Why Growth Matters: How Economic Growth in India Reduced Poverty and the Lessons for Other Developing Countries*. New York: Public Affairs.

Bhatt, H. 2011. "Surat Fourth Fastest Growing City in World." *Times of India*, July 23.

Brown, S. S. 2006. "Can Remittances Spur Development? A Critical Survey." *International Studies Review* 8: 55–75.

Burgess, K., and C. Pérez-Armendáriz. 2013. "Explaining the Mixed Record of Diaspora Bonds." Paper presented at the American Political Science Association conference, Chicago, IL, August 28–September 1.

Callahan, W. 2004. *Contingent States: Greater China and Transnational Relations*. Minneapolis: University of Minnesota Press.

Chan, S. 2015. "The Case for Diaspora: A Temporal Approach to the Chinese Experience." *Journal of Asian Studies* 74.1 (February): 107–28.

Chen, L. 2014. "Varieties of Global Capital and the Paradox of Local Upgrading in China." *Politics & Society* 42.2: 223–52.

Chin, Ko-Lin. 1999. *Smuggled Chinese: Clandestine Immigration to the United States*. Philadelphia: Temple University Press.

Coggiola, M. G. 2014. "How a Freewheeling India Market Became the Hub of the Global Diamond Trade." *Worldcrunch*, April 9. http://www.worldcrunch.com/business -finance/how-a-freewheeling-indian-market-became-the-hub-of-the-global -diamond-trade/diamonds-surat-gujarat-business-wealth/c2s11337/#.U231Zq2SyyM.

Collier, D., and S. Levitsky. 1997. "Democracy with Adjectives: Conceptual Innovation in Comparative Research." *World Politics* 49: 430–51.

Cooke, P. 2001. "Regional Innovation Systems, Clusters and the Knowledge Economy." *Industrial and Corporate Change* 10.4: 945–74.

Dahl, R. 1961. *Who Governs?* New Haven: Yale University Press.

Duara, P. 1995. *Rescuing History from the Nation: Questioning Narratives of Modern China*. Chicago: University of Chicago Press.

Engelshoven, M. 1999. "Diamond and Patels: A Report on the Diamond Industry of Surat," *Contributions to Indian Sociology* 33.1–2: 353–77.

Evans, P., D. Reuschemeyer, and T. Skocpol, eds. 1985. *Bringing the State Back In*. New York: Cambridge University Press.

Fels, D., and G. Hamilton. 2013. "The Social Sources of Migration and Enterprise: Italian Peasants and Chinese Migrants in Prato." CARIM-East Research Report 2013/46. http://www.carim-east.eu/media/CARIM-East%20RR-2013-46.pdf.

Gestrich, A., and M. S. Beerbühl, eds. 2011. "Introduction." *Cosmopolitan Networks in Commerce and Society, 1660–1914*. London: German Historical Institute.

Ghamawat, P. 2000. *The Indian Software Industry at the Millennium*. Harvard Business Case, no. 9-700-036. Cambridge, MA: Harvard Business School.

Gorter, P. 1996. *Small Industrialists, Big Ambitions: Economic and Political Networks on a Large Industrial Estate in West India*. Delhi: Oxford University Press.

Grosby, S. 1995. "Territoriality: The Transcendental, Primordial Feature of Modern Societies." *Nations and Nationalism* 1.2: 143–62.

Hagopian, F. 1996. *Traditional Politics and Regime Change in Brazil*. New York: Cambridge University Press.

Hamilton, G., ed. 1999. *Cosmopolitan Capitalists: Hong Kong and the Chinese Diaspora at the End of the 20th Century*. Seattle: University of Washington Press.

Heeks, R. 1996. *India's Software Industry: State Policy, Liberalization and Industrial Development*. New Delhi: Sage Publications.

Heller, P. 1999. *The Labor of Development: Workers and the Transformation of Capitalism in Kerala, India*. Ithaca: Cornell University Press.

Hirschman, A. O. 1970. *Exit, Voice, and Loyalty: Responses to Decline in Firms, Organization, and States*. New York: Cambridge University Press.

———. 1978. "Exit, Voice, and the State." *World Politics* 31.1 (October): 90–107.

Hoe, Y. C. 2013. *Guangdong and Chinese Diaspora: The Changing Landscape of Qiaoxiang*. London: Routledge.

Hoffmann, B. 2005. "Emigration and Regime Stability: Explaining the Persistence of Cuban Socialism." *Journal of Communist Studies and Transition Politics* 21.4: 436–61.

Huang, Y., and T. Kanna. 2003. "Can India Overtake China?" *Foreign Policy* 137: 74–81.

Karnataka Information Communication Technology Group. 2013. "KIG 2020 Final Report." Bangalore, January. https://www.scribd.com/document/343991330/KIG-2020 -final-report-pdf. Accessed December 20, 2017.

Kapur, D. 2010. *Diaspora Development and Democracy: The Domestic Impact of International Migration from India*. Princeton: Princeton University Press.

Keck, M. E., and K. Sikkink. 1998. *Activists beyond Borders: Advocacy Networks in International Politics*. Ithaca: Cornell University Press.

Keefe, P. R. 2009. "Snakeheads and Smuggling: The Dynamics of Illegal Chinese Immigration." *World Policy Journal* 26: 33–44.

Khanna, T. 2008. *Billions of Entrepreneurs: How China and India Are Reshaping Their Futures and Yours*. Cambridge, MA: Harvard Business Review Press.

Kurien, P. A. 1994. "Non-Economic Bases of Human Behavior: The Consumption, Investment Exchange Patterns of Three Emigrant Communities in Kerala, India." *Development and Change* 25.4: 757–83.

Landa, J. T. 1995. *Trust, Ethnicity, and Identity: Beyond the New Institutional Economics of Ethnic Trading Networks, Contract Law, and Gift Exchange*. Ann Arbor: University of Michigan Press.

Leblang, D. 2010. "Familiarity Breeds Investment: Diaspora Networks and International Investment." *American Political Science Review* 104.3: 584–600.

Maimo, S. M. and D. Ratha, eds. 2005. *Remittances: Development Impact and Future Prospects*. Washington, DC: IBRD/World Bank.

Mandel, R. 2002. *Armies without States: The Privatization of Security*. London: Lynne Rienner Publishers.

Massey, D. S. 1988. "Economic Development and International Migration in Comparative Perspective." *Population and Development Review* 14.3: 383–413.

Migdal, J. S. 1988. *Strong Societies and Weak States: State-Society Relations and State Capabilities in the Third World*. Princeton: Princeton University Press.

Mistry, M. B. 2014. "Kerala Muslims—Impact of Gulf Remittances." *Islamic Voice*. http://islamicvoice.com/kerala-muslims-impact-of-gulf-remittances/. Accessed December 21, 2017.

Montinola, G. Y. Qian, and B. R. Weingast. 1996. "Federalism, Chinese Style: The Political Basis for Economic Success." *World Politics* 48.1: 50–81.

Nair, J. G. 2014. "Migrants' Impact on Kerala's Economy." *Manoramaonline.com*, May 19. http://www.english.manoramaonline.com. Accessed December 21, 2017.

Oi, J. C. 1992. "Fiscal Reform and the Economic Foundations of Local State Corporatism in China." *World Politics* 45: 99–126.

———. 1999. *Rural China Takes Off: Institutional Foundations of Economic Reform*. Berkeley: University of California Press.

Ong, A. 1999. *Flexible Citizenship: The Cultural Logics of Transnationality*. Durham, NC: Duke University Press.

Pearlman, W. 2013. "Emigration and Power: A Study of Sects in Lebanon, 1860–2010." *Politics and Society* 4: 103–33.

Pellerin, H., and B. Mullings. 2013. "The 'Diaspora Option': Migration and the Changing Political Economy of Development." *Review of International Political Economy* 20.1: 89–120.

Putnam, R. 1993. *Making Democracy Work: Civil Traditions in Modern Italy.* Princeton: Princeton University Press.

Samuel, L. 2013. "Robust Exports: Gujarat Takes Markets to Storm." *Narendra Modi* website, October 24. http://www.narendramodi.in/robust-exports-gujarat-takes -markets-to-storm/. Accessed May 2014.

Saxenian, A. 2005. "From Brain Drain to Brain Circulation: Transnational Communities and Regional Upgrading in India and China." *Studies in Comparative International Development* 40.2: 35–61.

Segal, A. 2002. *Digital Dragon: High Technology Enterprises in China.* Chap. 3. Ithaca: Cornell University Press.

Sellers, J. M. 2010. "State-Society Relations Beyond the Weberian State." In *Handbook of Governance*, edited by Mark Bevir, 130–31, London: Sage Publications.

Shatzmiller, M. 2011. "Economic Performance and Economic Growth in the Early Islamic World." *Journal of the Economic and Social History of the Orient* 54: 132–84.

Sheffer, G. 2003. *Diaspora Politics: At Home Abroad.* New York: Cambridge University Press.

Sinha, A. 2005. *The Regional Roots of Developmental Politics in India: A Divided Leviathan.* Bloomington: Indiana University Press.

Snyder R. 2001. "Scaling Down: The Subnational Comparative Method." *Studies of Comparative International Development* 36.1: 93–110.

Spruyt, H. 2005. *Ending Empire: Contested Sovereignty and Territorial Partition.* Ithaca: Cornell University Press.

Stone, C. N. 1989. *Regime Politics: Governing Atlanta, 1946–1988.* Lawrence: University Press of Kansas.

Stoner-Weiss, K. 2002. *Local Heroes: The Political Economy of Russian Regional Governance.* Princeton: Princeton University Press.

Storper, M., and A. J. Venables. 2001. "Buzz: Face-to-Face Contact and the Urban Economy." *Journal of Economic Geography* 4.4: 351–70.

Tarrow, S. 2005. *The New Transnational Activism.* New York: Cambridge University Press.

Thomas, M. R. 2013. "Anti-Kidnap Programme for Antwerp Diamond Dealers." *Times of India*, 23 June.

———. 2014a. "Diamantaires to Push for International Airport." *Times of India*, May 9.

———. 2014b. "Mumbai May Lose Its Diamond Crown to Surat." *Times of India*, April 27.

———. 2014c. "Surat's Textile Exporters Eyeing US Market." *Times of India*, February 15.

Tiebout, C. 1956. "A Pure Theory of Local Expenditure." *Journal of Political Economy* 64: 416–24.

Tsai, K. S. 2002. *Back-Alley Banking: Private Entrepreneurs in China*. Ithaca: Cornell University Press.

———. 2007. *Capitalism without Democracy: The Private Sector in Contemporary China*. Ithaca: Cornell University Press.

———. 2010. "Friends, Family or Foreigners? The Political Economy of Diasporic FDI and Remittances in China and India." *China Report* 46.4: 387–429.

———. 2006. "Debating Decentralized Development: A Reconsideration of the Wenzhou and Kerala Models." *Indian Journal of Economics and Business*. Special issue, *India and China*: 47–67.

United Nations Conference on Trade and Development (UNCTAD). Various years. *World Investment Report*. Geneva: UNCTAD.

United Kingdom Government Web Archive. "The Roots of Emigration from Gujarat." *Moving Here Migration Histories*. http://webarchive.nationalarchives.gov.uk/+ /http://www.movinghere.org.uk//galleries/histories/asian/origins/local3.htm.

Vahed, G. 2005. "Passengers, Partnerships, and Promissory Notes: Gujarati Traders in Colonial Natal, 1870–1920." *International Journal of African Historical Studies* 38.3: 449–79.

Volkov, V. 2002. *Violent Entrepreneurs: The Use of Force in the Making of Russian Capitalism*. Ithaca: Cornell University Press.

Wang, H., D. Zweig, and X. Lin. 2011. "Returnee Entrepreneurs: Impact on China's Globalization Process." *Journal of Contemporary China* 20.70: 413–31.

Wang, J., S. Cheng, and S. Ganapati. 2012. "Path Dependence in Regional ICT Innovation: Differential Evolution of Zhongguancun and Bangalore." *Regional Science Policy and Practice* 4.3: 231–45.

Wenzhou Municipal Government. 2008. *Wenzhou Statistical Bulletin 2008*. Wenzhou, ZJ: Wenzhou Statistical Publishing.

———. 2012. *Wenzhou Yearbook 2012*. Wenzhou, ZJ: Wenzhou Statistical Publishing.

———. 2014. *Wenzhou Yearbook 2014*. Wenzhou, ZJ: Wenzhou Statistical Publishing.

World Bank. Various years. *Remittances: Impacts and Prospects*. Washington, DC: World Bank.

Wu, Chengxi. 1937. "Shantou de huaqiao huikuan" (Overseas remittances in Shantou). *Huaqiao banyuekan* 99–100 (Nanjing): 13–14.

Wu, Gungwu. 2000. *The Chinese Overseas: From Earthbound China to the Quest for Autonomy*. Cambridge, MA: Harvard University Press.

Yang, D. 1997. *Beyond Beijing: Liberalization and the Regions in China*. London: Routledge.

Ye, Min. 2014. *Diasporas and Foreign Direct Investment in China and India*. New York: Cambridge University Press.

Young, Oran R. 1994. *International Governance: Protecting the Environment in a Stateless Society*. Ithaca: Cornell University Press.

Zachariah, K. C., and I. S. Rajan. 2013. *Inflexion in Kerala's Gulf Connection: Report on Kerala Migration Survey 2011*. CDS Working Papers 450. Trivandrum: Center for Development Studies.

Zhang, Dehua. 1998. "Emigrant Communities in Guangdong: Taishan." In *The Encyclopedia of the Chinese Overseas*, edited by Lynn Pan, 36. Singapore: Chinese Heritage Centre.

Zhou, Y. 2008. *The Inside Story of China's High-Tech Industry: Making Silicon Valley in Beijing*. Plymouth, UK: Rowman and Littlefield.

Zweig, D. 2002. *Internationalizing China: Domestic Interests and Global Linkages*. Ithaca: Cornell University Press.

Zweig, D., and Huiyao Wang. 2013. "Can China Bring Back the Best? The Communist Party Organizes China's Search for Talent." *China Quarterly* 215 (September): 590–615.

CHAPTER 8

Foreign Direct Investment in China and India

History, Economics, and Politics

MIN YE

In 2003, Yasheng Huang of MIT's Sloan School and Tarun Khanna of Harvard Business School published a widely cited article, "Can India Overtake China?" Their answer was a resounding yes (Huang and Khanna 2003). The answer was also controversial. In 2003, China was the world's most successful country in terms of globalization, racking up the fastest growth rates for the longest time frame among major economies. It had just earned the popular title "The World's Factory." India was not doing badly, but growth rates, exports, and other indicators were far behind China's. Huang and Khanna's assessment, however, was not based on these indicators but on one argument, that is, that India's limited exposure to foreign direct investment (FDI) compared with China's high dependence on FDI would allow Indian indigenous business to rise and outdo their Chinese counterparts in the near future. Interestingly, the article had more followers in China than in India, particularly among Chinese officials who were eager to rein in foreign capital.

The polemic between foreign and domestic capital has a long tradition in international political economy. Robert Gilpin (1987) cautioned that FDI results in a struggle between two competing ideologies—nationalism and globalism. Successful earlier developers such as Japan, South Korea, and Taiwan in East Asia had shunned FDI during their high-growth era, the 1950s to the 1970s. Other developing economies such as Brazil, Argentina, and Mexico, at one point or another, had attempted to reduce the role of foreign capital in their economies. The late

1970s, indeed, was a period of "dislodging multinationals" in the developing world; Brazil and India were two salient cases in this trend (Encarnation 1989). Mary Gallagher (2005) was concerned that whereas FDI had helped the regime in China achieve rapid growth, it might generate a nationalist backlash that could destabilize the political system. Yasheng Huang (2003) went so far as to call Chinese government's pro-FDI policy "selling China."

Contrary to these concerns about FDI, economists and globalists have celebrated FDI and globalization in general. Influential international organizations and their chief economists have long operated to reduce restrictions toward FDI in the developing world, as summarized in a set of recommendations in what is popularly called the "Washington Consensus." Thomas Friedman (1999), for example, calls globalization "a golden jacket" that developing countries can "wear" to succeed. As the globalizing country becomes more prosperous, he notes, its politics, institutions, and society are bound to change. Friedman has openly praised China's embrace of FDI during reform. In *The World Is Flat* (2005), he used China as an example of globalization and argued for the unique roles that FDI plays in the economic takeoff of developing countries.

The chapter does not intend to settle the debate on FDI in the developing countries. There are merits on both sides of the issue. Rather, my main task is, first, to situate China and India's divergent FDI policies during reform in their postindependence development and to find political and historical roots for such divergence. My second task is to desegregate FDI, to explore different kinds of FDI and their different economic effects. The third is to synthesize policy and political lessons in China and India and, in the course of this discussion, to comment on India's current administration and future FDI.

FDI and Comparative History

PREREFORM POLITICAL ECONOMY: MAOISM VERSUS NEHRUISM

Since the 19th century, the histories of China and India have been remarkably similar. India became independent in 1947; the People's Republic of

China was founded in 1949. India was a colony of the British Empire for almost a hundred years; China suffered from a hundred years of exploitation by multiple Western powers, which ended in the invasion and occupation by Japan in the 1930s. When the two new regimes were founded, their grievances against the West were deep. They looked upon the Soviet Union, their main ally, for economic models. Nehru and Mao set up socialist systems in their respective countries.

There were many similarities between the two systems. First, there was a strong emphasis on building state-owned enterprises (SOEs), thus making the state the main force in the economy. Second, there was a clear preference for heavy industries, compared to light industries, channeling finance toward capital-intensive sectors. Third, there was a clear distrust of foreign capital and international trade. Both countries implemented an import-substituting industrialization strategy. But there were also marked differences. Most important, the Chinese system was radically socialist and violently antimarket. Only SOEs and rural collectives were allowed to operate. Private entrepreneurs were eliminated. In India, existing private businesses were allowed to continue but operated under stricter government controls. New entrants and expansion were discouraged.

CHINA'S MAOIST SOCIALISM

Before 1949, traditional China had what Barry Naughton (2007) described as a "household-based, bottom-heavy" economy that was efficient and suitable for China at the time. Socialist China turned its back on this tradition and ignored China's labor advantage. New leaders set out to develop a massive socialist industrial complex through direct government control. Instead of investing in labor-intensive sectors, they poured resources into capital-intensive factories producing metals, machinery, and chemicals—this socialist industrialization strategy was expensive. Between 1949 and 1956, the government established a "command economy," under which it eliminated market mechanisms and allocated resources directly. The system had the following characteristics:

- The government owned all large factories and transportation and communication enterprises. In the countryside, agricultural collectives took over ownership of the land and management of the farm economy.

- Planners issued commands that assigned production targets to firms and directly allocated resources and goods among different producers.
- Finances were used to audit and monitor performance, not to drive investment decisions. The government controlled the price system and set relative prices to channel resources into government hands and into the socialist industrialization.
- The government and Communist Party reinforced their control of the economy through a hierarchical personnel system, in which the Communist Party controlled managerial career paths.

The command system was a very effective way to subordinate individual economic decision making to the overall national development strategy. With planners pouring resources into industry, rapid industrial growth was not surprising. Between 1952 and 1978, industrial output grew at an average annual rate of 11.5 percent. Moreover, industry's share of total GDP climbed steadily over the same period from 18 to 44 percent, while agriculture's share declined from 51 to 28 percent. New industries were created, such as those producing electricity generating equipment, chemical fertilizers, and motor vehicles.

The socialist period was also highly unstable. According to Naughton (2007, 56), "Economic instability and a pattern of policy oscillation marked the years through 1978." Among the instabilities, the Great Leap Forward (1958–61) stands out as "the most peculiar, and the most terrible" (ibid. 56), of all these episodes, overshadowing even the Cultural Revolution (1966–76), which purged scholars, officials, and even members of the military. As the central state was engulfed in recurrent political crises, the central policy control was much weaker than the command economy intended. Yet because of the elimination of private business before 1956, Chinese economic decision making occured predominantly in the middle. "There was less decision-making authority at the top (central government) and bottom (enterprises) of the Chinese industrial economy. Those in the middle, typically local government officials could exercise more authority," observed Naughton (ibid. 58).

To summarize, there were three legacies from the socialist period that were critical to the reform era's FDI policies in China. First, the command economy wiped out private entrepreneurship and market mechanisms; remaining economic actors were predominantly state-owned enterprises and collectives in the countryside. Second, the self-inflicted political movements, often led by the revolutionary impulses of Chairman Mao, including the Great Leap Forward and the Cultural Revolution, weakened economic planners within the command system. The central government's role in decision making at the local level was limited. For decades before the economic reform, local governments had already shouldered much decision-making responsibility in the development and economic activities of their localities. Third, the command economy used distorted pricing and financing to channel resources into SOEs in heavy industries and imposed strict production targets and controls over SOEs. SOEs were both inefficient and deeply dependent on the state. In short, when China embarked on economic reform at the end of the 1970s, economic actors (private entrepreneurs and SOEs) were either nonexistent or too weak to either help the state grow the economy or challenge state policies.

INDIA'S SOCIALISM: COMMANDING HEIGHTS
AND THE MIXED ECONOMY

After independence, the Nehru administration set out to build the Indian version of socialism (Virmani 2010). It aimed to introduce and enhance the import substitution industrialization strategy; to reduce and eliminate market mechanism and private economic agents; and to extend the government into more and wider economic activities.

The extension of government roles was outlined in several core documents. The Industrial Policy Resolution of 1948 (IPR1948) laid out the basic industrial system, separating industries into four categories: state monopolies in defense, atomic energy, and railways; a mixed sector comprising aircraft, ship building, telecom equipment, mineral oil, coal, and iron; government control over 18 industries; and private enterprises. The Industries Act of 1952 gave the state legal power to implement this approach. In addition, the 1955 Import Control Order increased the government's roles and reduced India's exchange with external markets.

The 1956 Industrial Policy Resolution consolidated the socialist system in India. It reduced the four industrial categories to three. One was the State Monopoly (Schedule A) over 17 industries, among which four were exclusive to government (defense, atomic energy, railway, air transport) and where in 13 all new units were to be set up by the government but existing private units could continue to operate; another new category, Mixed Sector (Schedule B), had 12 industries, where the state would increasingly establish new units and increase participation but the private sector could also set up new units. The third category comprised private enterprises. The state's roles were further expanded with nationalization of industries and financial institutions, reservation of sectors for government investment, and legislative measures to control and direct private activity.

India's socialism differed from China's in important ways. Private entrepreneurs were preserved in India, while they were eliminated in China; and wealthy Indian families continued to grow and exploited the system quite well to their own advantage, creating what Asim Chaudhuri called "tycoon capitalism" (Chaudhuri 1980). The Indian government limited new entrants into the economy, and public units grew and monopolized new sectors; these public units were protected and became a hotbed of socialist ideas and interests—their voices were influential in government policymaking. In addition, India's national planning system was continuous and gradually penetrated into development at the local government level. However, because of the expansive roles of the Indian federal states and vibrant business actors at the private level, the local governments who were the middle actors did not gain experience or capacity to run local development, unlike in China.

Both China and India implemented socialist import substitution industrialization after their independence. The government's roles in economy were expanded, market mechanisms were reduced, and global exchange was minimized. But their distinct socialist experiences resulted in different legacies for their capitalist reforms: India saw the rise of powerful business families, whereas China had no such private businesses; India had limited market mechanisms, and China had none; in India, the national government dominated economic functions; whereas in China it was powerful local officials; finally, India had limited but continued exchange with Western capital, and China had none.

EARLY REFORM: DENG XIAOPING VERSUS INDIRA GANDHI

The Indian and Chinese leaders during the reform period had similar traits. And their paths to power were not always smooth. In China, Deng

Xiaoping spent two years after Mao's death consolidating power in late 1978, while Indira Gandhi returned to prime ministership in India in 1980. Both leaders had extensive experience in governing their respective countries. Deng had led the communist revolution in the 1920s and occupied key political positions by the 1970s. Thrice demoted from the central leadership, Deng, however, stayed active and gained local experiences that helped him understand the workings at the local level (Vogel 2011). Indira Gandhi was the daughter of Nehru, but had acquired her own experience in ruling India since 1966. In the 1971 national elections, Gandhi ran on her own name, the Congress Party-I, and won a major victory. She was voted out of office in 1977, and while she was sidelined, had three years to rethink India's economic direction. In short, when both leaders regained power in 1979 and 1980 respectively, they were ready to shift their national economies away from socialism to more market-oriented systems.

From the economic perspective, the two leaders faced remarkably similar circumstances regarding FDI in the 1970s. As table 8.1 shows, China and India were comparable in terms of both land and population, the two important factors of their countries' economic endowment. In export and import, China was ahead of India, but not much so. India's FDI was negligible, but it was more than China's. Consumption was low, and comparable. If Deng and Gandhi were economists, any reform policies they adopted would have been similar.

For better or for worse, Deng and Gandhi were both seasoned politicians who were clearly pro-growth. The social and political actors surrounding them influenced the elements of their reform programs. The result was a critical divergence in their respective reform policies, which sought to increase FDI in China and promote private industry in India.

FDI ZONES IN CHINA

Deng, at the age of 75, was eager to develop China in 1979. He made friends with leading businessmen from Hong Kong and Macao, such as Y. K. Pao, Gordon Wu, Lee Kashing, and Stanley Ho. He invited them to Beijing and asked for their contributions and advice on developing China. These overseas Chinese businessmen had mostly been born on the mainland, migrated during their youth, and made their fortunes during

Table 8.1

Pre-reform economic indicators for China and India

	Consumption (US$billion)	Exports (US$billion)	Imports (US$billion)	FDI stock (US$million)	FDI/GDCF[c] (%)	Land (million km²)	Population (million)
China	588	8.30	7.90	670[a]	0.08	9.60	943.40
India	466	7.60	7.00	1177[b]	0.10	2.95	642.10

SOURCES: The macroeconomic indicators are for 1977, database Penn World Table 7.0, library.princeton.edu (accessed January 15, 2005). For FDI stock and FDI/GDCF, United Nations Conference on Trade and Investment 1993.

NOTES

[a] Data for 1981

[b] Data for 1980

[c] Data for 1976–80 averages

FDI = foreign direct investment; GDCF = gross domestic capital formation the East Asian high-growth era. When they returned to visit their home-land in 1979, their sentiments were profound. They were struck by the poverty and underdevelopment in China and responded to Deng's request. In Y. K. Pao's own words, "I will do whatever it takes to help my motherland to develop."[1]

With the leader's encouragement, local governments, whose economic capacity was enhanced during the socialist period, became critical to China's reforms in the 1980s. In Guangdong and Fujian, the two southern provinces, local officials were eager to tap their connections to Hong Kong and Macao, where capital, technology, and global markets were abundantly available. In late 1978, the Hong Kong Merchants' Group collaborated with the Guangdong government and the minister of communications to build an export-processing zone in Shekou, a small island in today's Shenzhen. In their bid to the central government for approval, they pledged to use no government funding and to develop the zone entirely with investments from Hong Kong. Once the Shekou zone had been approved, the larger Shenzhen special economic zone was also approved by the central government.

Ezra Vogel (1989) has pointed out that the special zones cost the government practically nothing and were able to generate remarkable development. Shenzhen, previously consisting of fishing villages, emerged as one of the most modern cities in China in 1984. More than 85 percent of investment in its infrastructure came from FDI, whereas domestic funds, including national and local government allocations and bank loans, amounted to less than 15 percent. Furthermore, FDI in Shenzhen and Shekou predominantly came from diaspora regions. More than 90 percent of FDI in Shenzhen from 1979 to 1983 was from Hong Kong. In Shekou, in 1984 alone, Hong Kong and Thailand contributed more than 60 percent FDI.[2]

The special zones encountered ideological resistance launched by leftist planners in Beijing,[3] although they did not face backlash from economic actors. On the one hand, state-owned enterprises were relatively inconsequential in southern China, where the state had not invested much during the socialist period. Further, the state-owned enterprises were largely shielded from direct competition with FDI. In both Shekou and Shenzhen, industries were not present before 1978. Foreign capital came to build the infrastructure and industries that hired people, and manufactured products in the zones were oriented toward exports. Private entrepreneurs, moreover, had been absent during the socialist period. And in the 1980s, rural entrepreneurs newly emerged and grew, by building on connections with Hong Kong. As new economic actors, they joined, rather than resisted, the FDI-led development in South China.

Most important, Shenzhen's rapid and remarkable success led local governments elsewhere to copy the measures adopted there, including the use of FDI and the mechanisms of the market. Shanghai is a good example. Mayor Zhu Rongji successfully lobbied the central government in 1988 to approve the development of Pudong, a vast rural area east of old Shanghai, precisely to draw FDI. The Shanghai government was keenly aware of the roles of overseas Chinese and sought out business people in Hong Kong, Macao, Taiwan, and Southeast Asia. The slogan of the local officials was to develop Pudong into "a little Hong Kong." Under the drive to emulate capitalism, diaspora FDI was strongly welcomed.

DOMESTIC DEREGULATION IN INDIA

Several changes had taken place in India before Indira Gandhi's return to power in 1980. During the 1970s, Indian elites gradually recognized the limitations of the socialist economy. New business elites, with connections with traditional business families, began to emerge. Among them was Gandhi's second son, Sanjay Gandhi. In 1971, Sanjay Gandhi founded the state automaker, Maruti Udyog; the company, however, failed to advance beyond the development phase and ran at a loss. He consulted business leaders such as K. K. Birla and took their advice to diversify Maruti into a wide range of different operations, including business consultancies and private companies.

With these business ventures, Sanjay Gandhi's views on socialism reversed. He developed a strong dislike for bureaucracy, the public sector, and government control and regulation of the economy. As a highly vocal critic of socialist controls, he acquired a reputation as the "voice of big business." In 1975, he went as far as to pronounce that the public sector should be allowed to die "a natural death" in a highly publicized interview.

When Indira Gandhi was voted out of power in 1977, the leftists and socialists abandoned her, and she was persecuted, along with her family, by the ruling Janata Party for the two years of emergency rule that she had imposed before her ouster. Her son's business friends, meanwhile, supported Indira Gandhi's campaign to return to power. When she won the elections in 1980, there were clear signals of a "changed priority" for the government and for the new prime minister. A 1981 *Times of India* editorial read, "A change of considerable significance is taking place in India . . . [T]he emphasis has shifted from distributive justice to growth."[4] Her economic advisers declared, "Mrs Gandhi was determined to get the firm foundation of economic reform" (Sengupta 2001, 55). Indira Gandhi promoted new political and economic advisers with ample experience in private business and global organizations, among them L. K. Jha, P. C. Alexander, and Arjun Sengupta.

Drawing on India's *Union Budgets and Economic Surveys*, Gandhi favored domestic business. No external liberalization was seriously considered. The new initiatives fell into four categories: the first was to deregulate private business by decontrolling steel and cement prices, manufactured imports, entry and expansion by national firms, delicensing 20 industries, and diluting the antimonopoly act; the second, to support private industries by offering incentives, credits, and tax reliefs to big business; the third, to suppress labor by discouraging labor activism; and the fourth, to limit the public sector by cutting subsidies and investment in public units.

In 1984, Gandhi was assassinated and her elder son, Rajiv Gandhi, came to power. Son of one prime minister and grandson of another, he had grown up in the center of wealth and power. He had childhood friends in the business world and was fascinated with technology and sciences in the West. He was therefore eager to support domestic entrepreneurs in growing these new technology sectors and inviting foreign players from the United States. Rajiv Gandhi's new budget in 1985 reduced taxes, cut duties, and eliminated licensing restrictions in 25 industries; it also sought to reduce investment in the public sectors.

The support for private business was warmly welcomed; the cuts in public sectors were, predictably, opposed by thinkers, politicians, and managers on the left. Rajiv Gandhi wanted more Western investors to promote technology and industry in India, but despite his openness to such investment, government support for it was nonexistent. Established domestic producers feared competition from foreign products or foreign producers and thus pressured the government to limit the access of foreigners in India. As the *Economic Times* later observed, "The pace of domestic liberalization has not been slackened. . . . [E]xternal liberalization was not really an objective of the policy."[5]

Unlike China, 1980s India had plenty of business interest in government policy making. In addition to a few dozen business families, three national-level business associations were highly effective in shaping the policy debates and in rallying support or opposition to specific policies. These associations included the Federation of Indian Chambers of Commerce and Industry (FICCI), founded in 1927 by the Calcutta industrialist B. M. Birla; the Associated Chambers of Commerce and Industry of India (ASSOCHAM), reorganized to represent private business members in the 1980s; and the Confederation of Indian Industry (CII), which represented technology-related new industries and rose to prominence under Rajiv Gandhi, under the name Confederation of Engineering India. Across the board, the industries' common call to the government was to "build Indian private business" before opening to foreign competitors.

CHINA AND INDIA'S FDI SINCE THE 1990S

The trend to globalization accelerated in the 1990s. China became a major beneficiary of FDI, and in 1993 it emerged as the largest recipient of FDI in the developing world. India also implemented aggressive liberalization in the early 1990s, in the wake of a balance of payments crisis. In 1993, it appeared that the two Asian giants were converging with regard to their *policies of FDI*. But in fact, the *politics of FDI* in each country continued to diverge from the 1980s to the end of the 1990s.

The politics of FDI played out in three ways. First, domestic business in China was relatively weak, and new businesses did not mount an effective opposition to FDI. By contrast in India, domestic entrepreneurs were connected and powerful; they welcomed FDI insofar as it benefited themselves. Second, local governments in China were on-the-ground policy makers and implementers; they were convinced of the value of FDI to the local economy and embraced FDI by giving it preferential treatment. In India, local officials were generally not used to economic planning; technocrats in the federal government were the main policy makers, and they were, in turn, subject to influence by business elites.

Third, overseas Chinese were the main investors in China and concentrated their investments in manufacturing and exports; relationships between coethnic foreign investors and local actors were relatively stable. In India, investors came, but were mostly non-Indian Western companies that aimed at India's domestic markets; the joint ventures between Westerners and domestic players often suffered from friction.

CHINA'S ZONE FEVER

In an economy where internal capitalists are lacking and local governments are active agents for growth, we can expect those agents to seek out foreign capitalists if possible. In situations where local officials share social, linguistic, and ethnicity with foreign capitalists, it would be fairly easy for the two sets of actors to collaborate to produce unprecedented opportunities for each other. That was precisely how FDI liberalization took place in China in the 1990s, urged on by a top-down, growth-promoting central government.

China's economy had a good run at the local level in the 1980s, but the 1989 Tiananmen crisis abruptly broke the trend. After seeing what market reform could do, local governments were eager to reignite the "engine of reform." Deng's 1992 Southern Tour allowed them to do just that, channeling local governments' enthusiasm for market-oriented change and economic growth and ushering in a period of zone fever: everywhere, local governments established preferential zones to lure and host foreign investors. The early and dominant arrivers in these zones were overseas Chinese investors from Hong Kong, Macao, and Taiwan. Many of the Taiwanese investors came to China from their subsidiaries in Hong Kong, thus inflating the share of Hong Kong FDI on the mainland. Table 8.2 presents the sources of FDI in the four selected zones in four Chinese regions in 1993—Shenzhen, Shanghai, Wuhan, and Changchun. Overseas Chinese overwhelmingly dominated investors from Japan and America, the two top investors in the world in general.

Shanghai offers a good example of the process. It received the national government's authorization to develop Pudong in 1988, only to see its construction severely disrupted by the Tiananmen crisis. Even so, the local government made plans for more far-reaching reforms in the city

Table 8.2
Foreign direct investment in China, by region and source, 1993 (percent)

Sources	Shenzhen (South)	Shanghai, Pudong (East)	Wuhan (Central)	Changchun (Northern)
Hong Kong and Macao	65	65	82	65
Taiwan	3	12	8	7
Japan	15	8	1	2
U.S.	10	14	19	11

SOURCES: He 1994, 364–65; *Wuhan City Statistical Bureau* 1996, 359–60; Huang 1995, 139; Changchun City Statistical Bureau 1994, 283.

NOTE: Japanese and U.S. companies' investments in China via their Hong Kong subsidiaries are counted as Japanese and American foreign direct investment, respectively.

once the national open policy resumed. Active local governments played critical roles in attracting diaspora capitalists. In order to attract Tang Xiangqian, the textile king in Hong Kong, who had been born in Shanghai and whose father had stayed on the mainland, the Shanghai government appointed Tang's father vice chairman of Shanghai's Chinese People's Political Consultative Conference (CPPCC), a prestigious body representing luminaries who worked with the ruling party. Tang Xiangqian thus became the first foreign investor in Shanghai, by establishing a textile factory in the city in 1980. In 1991, in order to attract the return of Tang Junnian, the chairman of Taiwan's Thompson Group, who had been born in Pudong, Shanghai's senior officials traveled to Beijing to meet with Tang and persuaded the business tycoon to tour his birthplace. Thompson later invested billions of U.S. dollars in Pudong and broader Shanghai. Throughout the 1990s, the Thompson group was the largest investor in Pudong and helped to attract other diaspora investors to the district.

Another example of proactive local government was Kunshan, a township-level city in Jiangsu, not far from Shanghai. In the 1990s, the Kunshan government looked at model export-processing zones in Taiwan and invited Taiwanese businessmen to visit their city. In 1992–93, among the 14 major FDI projects in Kunshan, 12 were by overseas Chinese from Hong Kong and Taiwan. In 2000, Kunshan's export processing zone was approved by its superior Jiangsu government. More than 760 Taiwanese firms were already operating there. By 2005, the small city had attracted one-tenth of Taiwanese investment in all China, making Kunshan the hub of components manufacturing and exports for companies such as Apple, Sony, Compaq, and Hewlett-Packard.

INDIA'S CRISIS, FDI, AND THE
BUSINESS BACKLASH

The 1991 crisis was a watershed event in India's economic reform. It ushered in a sustained period of FDI liberalization, though politics curtailed that process later in the decade. The crisis unfolded as a major balance of payments crisis was imminent; without quick and substantial external assistance, India would be forced to declare a national default. In June 1991, the Congress Party returned to power. Narasimha Rao was elected prime minister, and he appointed Manmohan Singh as finance minister. The former finance secretary Bimal Jalan reflected that the 1990–91 period was "among the cruelest in India's post-independence economic history" (Jalan 1991, 1).

The June 1991 Union Budget laid out the basic elements of an integrated strategy for trade, tax, and foreign exchange reforms. This was followed by the July 1991 Industrial Policy, which detailed measures to reduce the public sectors, promote private industry, and encourage external trade and foreign investment. In the following two years, liberalization continued and deepened. The government eliminated import licenses for most capital goods, raw materials, and other intermediates and reduced the maximum tariff from 400 percent to 85 percent. Automatic approval was permitted for FDI up to 40 percent in many sectors. Nonresident Indians could invest up to 100 percent equity, via the preferential nonresident Indian scheme. The government passed policies of export-oriented units and foreign investors in those units could hold up to 100 equity shares.

The liberalization process from 1991 to 1994 led to a rapid rise in foreign capital in India. FDI grew from $129 million in 1991 to $315 million in 1993 and further increased to $1,314 million in 1994. Portfolio investment had been almost nonexistent in 1991, but increased to $244 million in 1992. By 1994, it had reached $5 billion.

The arrival of foreign investors, however, met with a backlash from domestic producers in India. The politics that prevented opening to FDI in the 1980s continued to shape FDI policy in this decade. In 1991, K. K. Birla publicly announced that FDI was not in the best interest of the country or its industry; he and other businessmen succeeded in persuading the government to cap foreign equity in joint ventures at 40 percent in the new industrial policy. In the mid-1990s, a powerful anti-FDI business movement known as the Bombay Club surged to challenge India's FDI policy. Rahul Bajaj, owner of Bajaj Motors, which had overwhelming shares in India's two-wheeler and three-wheeler markets, acted as a dynamic chairman of the Bombay Club, and played an influential role in rallying domestic resistance to FDI. Further, anti-FDI groups redefined India's liberalization experiment in the later 1990s, with policies to constrain foreign investors and to enhance the gains for indigenous companies.

With implementation of the 1991 new industrial policy, foreign products and competitors put pressure on Indian domestic producers. A leading industrialist confessed in 1993, "I am afraid many of us did not understand the full ramifications [of FDI]."[6] L. M. Thapar, chairman of the Ballaupur Group, admitted, "We did not realize how quickly we would need funds to face the competition that was around the corner."[7] Ravi Ruia, Essar Gujarat's managing director also acknowledged in 1993, "I think the true implications of liberalization are only now gripping people, and they are realizing the problems."[8]

In mid-1996, joint ventures between Indian partners and foreign multinational corporations also turned sour, as frictions rose among the new partners. Statements from disillusioned Indian business representatives were quite hostile to foreign capital. EID Parry's managing director, M. V. Subbiah, complained, "The multinationals have a stronger financial power. They are gradually killing us." Another important industrialist, S. K. Birla of the VXL Group, affirmed, "If the multinationals are allowed to hold a majority stake in the Indian joint ventures in an unfettered way, Indians will be second-class citizens in their own country."[9]

The three industrial associations, FICCI, ASSOCHAM, and CII, aligned to ask the government to implement protectionist measures, which they argued would be critical for pushing back against the threats from foreign goods and investments. The government clearly was influenced by domestic business's concerns. Murli Manohar Joshi, minister of human resources development, said, "I am favorable to US investment, which helps to make a decent living for my people, but if there is a negative effect on small-scale industries, then no." Joshi pointed out, "India will negotiate from case to case, industry to industry."[10] On May 2, 1998, Prime Minister A. B. Vajpayee officially adopted a "carefully calibrated approach" to globalization. In December 1998, the new Bharatiya Janata Party government required that foreign firms wishing to set up a new Indian operation obtain a "no-objection" certificate from all Indian partners. Changes after 1998 will be examined later in this chapter.

THE TRANSITIONS FROM SOCIALISM
TO CAPITALISM

At this point, it would be useful to summarize the economic history in China and India from independence to 2000, when they entered the World Trade Organization, signaling more or less the completion of their transition from socialism to capitalism. The socialist period, to be sure, had very different economic policies from the reform era, in both China and India. Yet different socialist constructions left varied legacies that shaped the capitalist transitions in the two countries. And during the transitions (1980 to 2000), there was remarkable continuity in their respective policy changes toward FDI.

First, Chinese socialism eliminated private entrepreneurs, while in India private entrepreneurship not only continued but grew. Second, China's party control made its socialist construction more thorough, but state-owned enterprises, albeit arms of the ruling party, were relatively weak in their power to influence the state. All managerial jobs, resources, and output were, meanwhile, subject to the party's commands. India's public sectors were built up and protected, but enjoyed relative autonomy from the state, and thus emerged as influential political actors that nurtured socialist ideas and enjoyed leftist support. The third major difference concerned the roles of private business. Entrepreneurial Chinese migrated to nearby Asia, mostly Hong Kong, and became influential manufacturers, financiers, and developers in Pacific Asia. Their return coincided with China's opening in the 1980s. Indian private business stayed in the country, with some operating in the United Kingdom. They did not emerge as an important economic force in the world's economy.

Their different socialist legacies resulted in different politics of FDI during the period of reform in each country. In China, which lacked internal business forces, top leaders and local government embraced the returned Chinese investors and developed FDI-reliant industrialization and globalization. In India, domestic business became immediate allies of capitalist reform, while opposing opening to foreign capital. Even when the country was forced open by a major crisis, domestic business managed to persuade the government to limit and delay the entry of FDI once the effects of crisis wore off.

Thus from a historical point of view, the Chinese and Indian FDI policies were hostages of their respective states and society makeups, forged during their socialist periods. Reform-era governments in both countries proactively attempted to reform their socialist systems and to install more market-oriented mechanisms in order to achieve economic growth. Due to their large land mass, potential market, and cheap labor, each country drew the attention of global investors, but they met with different responses. China's lack of domestic capital permitted the government to open its arms to returning Chinese investors, whereas India's strong domestic business prevented more wholehearted opening.

Comparative Statistics on FDI

MARKET SEEKING VERSUS EXPORTING

Most studies of FDI examine its flows and trends but seldom examine FDI types and their resultant effects in the investment-receiving nations. In general, there are three kinds of FDI, each of which has different political and economic impacts on the host nation: resource-seeking FDI, market-seeking FDI, and efficiency-seeking FDI (that is, FDI that is export oriented). China and India, as the world's largest populations, have correspondingly huge market potential. It is natural that foreign producers would want to invest in these countries in order to sell their products to these potential buyers. In India, that is precisely what happened in the country's opening to FDI. A study by Saon Ray, Smita Miglani, and Neha Malik (2015), showed that FDI in India continued to come from market-seeking producers under Prime Minister Modi's Make in India campaign.

Market-seeking FDI has had positive economic effects in India, bringing in more tax revenue, employment, and advanced technology. The limitations of this kind of FDI are also clear: they create pressure on domestic producers and services providers and domestic capitalists are thus likely to rally public opinion and lobby against FDI; and they are more likely to import than export, thus contributing to persistent trade deficits in the country. Indeed, according to India's Finance Ministry annual reports (table 8.3), India's trade deficit has been substantial in recent years. In 2006, it had a surplus of $4.3 billion. Just one year later, it had a deficit of $5.8 billion, which grew to a deficit of $19.6 billion in 2012. The deficit was reduced somewhat to $11.3 billion in 2014, due to an overall reduction of trade in the country.

FDI in China comes largely from exports (that is, it is FDI of the efficiency-seeking type). (I cover the Chinese policy intervention that contributed to this pattern in the next section.) Table 8.4 presents the "export density" of FDI in China, compared with domestic producers (state-owned enterprises included). Export density is calculated by dividing a company's total industrial output by its exported output to arrive at their relative proportion. In 1998, the export density of Chinese FDIs was 40 percent; it increased to 44.2 percent in 2002. The export density of domestic producers was, by comparison, 16.7 percent in 1998 and 16.5 percent in 2002. According to a JETRO survey (2003), in 2002, 61.6 percent of Japanese affiliated companies in China exported

Table 8.3
Trade balances in India, 2006–2015 (in US$billion)

	2006–7	2007–8	2011–12	2012–13	2013–14	2014–15
Exports	9.1	11. 1	15.8	30.7	23.5	24.6
Imports	13.4	16.9	24.8	50.2	35.2	35.8
Trade balance	4.3	–5.8	–9.0	–19.6	–11.7	–11.3

SOURCES: Raw data are from Indian Ministry of Finance, annual reports, 2006–15.

Table 8.4
Export density of foreign direct investment in China (percent)

	1998	1999	2000	2001	2002
FDI	40	38.8	42.2	40.6	44.2
Domestic producers	16.7	16.4	17.3	16.2	16.5

SOURCES: Raw data are from *China Statistical Abstract*, 2003; *China Customs Statistics*, various years. For a more systematic discussion of FDI's export performance, see Long 2004.

more than 70 percent of their products, and an even higher percentage (82.5 percent) of Japanese investors in south China exported more than 70 percent of their products. Both ratios were much higher than that for Japanese investors in Asia on average (50 percent).

Throughout the 1990s, FDI inflows in India were much smaller than in China. In 1991, for example, while India attracted US$75 million in FDI, China took in $4.4 billion; in 1998, India attracted $2.6 billion, while China had $45.5 billion; in 2003, India had $5.8 billion, and China, $60.6 billion. More important, the difference in their performance in exports widened and FDI's contributions to the countries' respective exports were staggeringly different. In table 8.5 we see that, from 1991 to 2000, China's exports grew from $66 billion to $280 billion, a quadruple growth. India's meanwhile grew from $32 billion to $62 billion, less than double, during the same period. In terms of its contribution to exports in 1991, FDI in China contributed 18 percent, and in India only 3 percent. In 2000, FDI contributed 43 percent to China's exports, and only 3.5 percent in India.

MANUFACTURING VERSUS SERVICES

FDI in China focused predominantly on manufacturing industries. This was the case in the special zones in the 1980s, and it became more apparent in the 1990s. In 1999, 69 percent of FDI was in China's industry, of which 56 percent was in manufacturing and 9 percent in electrical power. The share of FDI in services was 26.9 percent, mostly in real estate. As of 2011, 57 percent of FDI was invested in manufacturing and 21 percent in real estate; investment in business services accounted for 7 percent. FDI

Table 8.5
Exports of China and India, 1991 and 2000

		1991	2000
Total exports	China	65,898	279,561
(US$ million)	India	32,387	61,887
Percent by foreign	China	18	43
direct investment	India	3	3.5

SOURCE: Raw data are from United Nations Conference on Trade and Investment 1996.

contributed extensively to China's manufacturing output in China throughout the reform era. In 1999, FDI's share in electronics, garments, and leather goods in China were 65 percent, 53 percent, and 52 percent, respectively. All these industries were critical to China's exports and employed abundant low-skilled labor.

In India before liberalization, FDI was heavily concentrated in manufacturing, and in the 1990s, manufacturing FDI grew slowly. After 2000, the bulk of FDI flows went to the service sector, including financial and information services. From 2004 to 2012, the sectors that received the largest U.S. investment were financial services, and the food and beverage industry, followed by manufacturing and construction. The United States was the top source of FDI in India, thus representing the overall sectoral pattern of FDI in India.

The reasons behind the lackluster performance of FDIs in Indian manufacturing are multifold, as noted in Anwarul Hoda and Durgesh K. Rai (2015); they include the absence of world-class infrastructure, a complex system of internal taxation, an unpredictable taxation environment, and regulations relating to land and labor. The effects of services versus manufacturing FDI, however, are more than economic.

FDI's small share in Indian manufacturing, or the lag in India's industry in general, has resulted in lopsided growth that has failed to utilize India's abundant labor force. (The services-led growth since 1998 has in fact been criticized as "jobless growth.") The lack of manufacturing FDI has also prevented India from being integrated into regional markets in Asia. Meenu Tewari, C. Veeramani, and Manjeeta Singh (2015, ii) asked, "At a time when regional production networks have been resurgent, especially in Asia, why has India's integration in regional markets not been deeper?" Indeed, India's 1991–93 liberalization had addressed both manufacturing and software services with schemes like those introduced elsewhere. But business resistance to FDI in the 1990s, on top of other hurdles, has limited the manufacturing sector FDI, while FDI in the services sector was less affected.

DIASPORA VERSUS NONETHNIC FDI

In an earlier study (2014), I argued that diasporas tend to be early entrants to recently opened economies. Once they enter, they are likely to build stronger ties with local actors, via their shared language, ethnicity, and social norms. This contention is supported by the evidence of diaspora investment in China. India's case is, however, more complicated. Diasporas in India had a higher share in FDI when the country opened to FDI in 1991–93. But their share declined sharply after the mid-1990s, the period when the anti-FDI backlash was strong. Table 8.6 contrasts the diasporas' shares in China and India from 1990 to 2010.

Overseas Chinese contributed to 70 percent of FDI in China in 1991, and 70 percent in 1995. In India, nonresident Indians contributed 29 percent in 1991, and 24 percent in 1995. In 1999 and 2000, diaspora investments accounted for 56 and 52 percent, respectively, in China, but stayed at only 3 percent in India. The shares declined to 2 and 1 percent after 2003 in India, and remained more or less stable during the same period in China.

The gap between diaspora FDI shares in China and India in the early 1990s was due to their different diaspora entrepreneurs. Overseas Chinese in Hong Kong, Macao, Taiwan, and Southeast Asia were major manufacturers, traders, developers, and financiers during the high-growth era in Asia Pacific. China's FDI-reliant industrialization during the reform era was directly related to the relocation of these diaspora capitalists to the mainland. The sharp decline in India's diaspora investments after 1998 was stunning, however. Indeed, when the government implemented more favorable policies for diaspora investment from 1991 to 1993, in many sectors nonresident Indian investment could have reached 100 percent; nonresident Indian investments accounted for almost one-third of total FDI in India. However, in the mid-1990s, the government

Table 8.6
Share of diaspora investment in China and India (percent)

	1991	1995	1999	2000	2003	2007	2010
China	70	70	56	52	46	45	66
India	29	24	3	3	2	1	1

SOURCE: Raw data on China are from China National Statistical Bureau, various years; on India, from online database IndiaStat. From library.harvard.edu (accessed October 15, 2010).

made a close alliance with indigenous companies (Kohli 2012). As a result, India's FDI liberalization shifted direction and took the route of a "globalization" in which leading Indian businesses formed partnerships with Western multinational corporations who promised portfolio fund, technology, and global connections in exchange for shares in the Indian market.

India's interaction with diaspora communities is telling, too. In 1991–93, Manmohan Singh visited countries such as Thailand and Singapore, where small diaspora entrepreneurs were available. He listened attentively to these nonresident Indians, who explained how easy it was to set up factories in other countries and what India should do to encourage more FDI. Upon his return to India, Singh would adopt measures to address their concerns (Kapur 2010). But in 2003, when Prime Minister Vajpayee spoke at the first Pravasi Bharatiya Divas, a conference cosponsored by the government and business associations FICCI and CII, the message was: "We do not want your investment; we want your ideas. We do not want your riches; we want the richness of your experience."[11] Between 1993 and 2003, no concrete incentives were put in place to attract diaspora investment, despite the fact that political rights had been offered to diaspora professionals living abroad.

As in China, diaspora investment in India has high export density, suggesting that diaspora entrepreneurs are more likely than foreigners and indigenous producers to export. Table 8.7 compares the export density of diaspora and other FDIs in India, based on data published in 2000. In a wide range of sectors, including food, textile, metals, jewelry, and services, diaspora-invested companies exported significantly more than those invested in by foreigners. These companies also exported more than domestic companies, indicating that diaspora entrepreneurs were exploiting their comparative advantage in the domestic and global markets.

Table 8.7
Export density of diaspora and other foreign direct investments
in India (percent)

Industry	FDI	Diaspora FDI	Difference	All Companies
Leather	8.86	84.15	75.29	33.05
Jewelry	20.75	94.00	73.25	62.68
Metals	24.82	51.43	26.61	8.21
Food	12.50	36.09	23.59	11.57
Medical and photographic equipment	2.63	21.47	18.84	8.35
Rubber, plastic, petroleum	3.08	12.42	9.34	3.13
Textiles	14.73	23.93	9.2	19.89
Services	44.19	52.58	8.39	5.2
Nonmetals	3.36	7.69	4.33	5.49
Machinery	8.94	12.42	3.48	6.95
Paper	0.03	2.77	2.74	2.86
Chemicals	8.82	11.53	2.71	10.15
Automobiles	6.66	7.83	1.17	7.03
Software and computer systems	27.85	3.85	-24	31.20

SOURCE: Raw data from Guha and Ray 2000.

Only in software and computer systems, were diaspora investors much more internally oriented than other investors.

In short, in the early 1990s, India's FDI policy favored nonresident Indians, and via software and hardware electronic parks it also promoted exports. Diaspora investments were key, with their high propensity to export. Recent studies such as that by Ray, Migaln, and Malik (2015) show that after 2000, Americans emerged as the top investors in India. American FDI is primarily market-seeking and concentrated in places where production/distribution opportunities for domestic markets are available.

Domestic market-seeking FDI has created tension in India in recent years: Walmart's efforts to enter and capture the growing Indian middle-class market, for example, backfired and resulted in resistance to FDI as a whole. Warranted or not, the fear was that Walmart's operation would replace thousands of small retailers in India. Western insurance providers also face resistance from small insurance distributors in India. The Western media's interest in expanding into India led to major opposition by Indians in the news and print industry. In other words, the Western brand names and their proclaimed ambition to capture India's rising new markets have resulted in domestic resistance to FDI as a whole.

Policy and Politics of FDI

The debates on globalization and the roles of FDI have produced arguments pro and con: whether FDI is good or bad, or whether a country is pro- or anti-FDI. Depending on their economic values and beliefs, scholars and policy makers tend to praise either China or India. FDI types and the government's role in shaping incoming FDI types and effects are insufficiently explored in policy studies. Indeed, the Chinese FDI policy cannot be simply called pro-FDI; the government has "intervened" considerably in the various types of FDI to shape FDI's effects in the country. There are lessons in China that can be learned. In India, the government was proactive in its openness to FDI in the early 1990s, but electoral outcomes after this date led to political and policy adjustments that were not conducive to development in the nation. New administrative moves in 2014, however, show some promising signs for renewed growth in this area.

CHINA'S LESSONS FOR INDUSTRIALIZATION AND EXPORTS

There are two general types of industrialization strategies—import substitution industrialization (ISI) and export-promoting industrialization (EPI). After World War II, most developing countries adopted import-substituting industrialization, limiting the imports of industrial products and promoting indigenous industry. South Korea, India, Brazil, and China all adopted ISI soon after independence. South Korea implemented ISI for a little over a decade. In the 1960s, however, South Korea normalized its relationship with Japan and switched to EPI. Under the EPI strategy, the South Korean government still promoted indigenous capital, but it imposed export requirements on domestic producers. EPI was implemented with an eye to improving business performance, and to do so, the government "disciplined" domestic business while providing it with support (Amsden 1989). In South Korea, however, FDI was strictly avoided: domestic capitalists grew and competed in the world market.

Brazil and India did not switch from ISI to EPI. Although the ISI strategy had been substantially diluted since the 1980s, the governments did not implement EPI in any systematic fashion. The reasons for not implementing EPI in Brazil and India are both economic and political. One the one hand, as latecomers in development, it is hard for the two countries to move from domestic production to competitive exports. Technology and capital are generally lacking, and earlier producers tend to predominate in export networks and global connections. On the other hand, domestic producers, if they have choices, mobilize to oppose pressures to export. In Brazil, India, and similar countries with influential domestic capitalists, EPI is rarely implemented for these reasons.

China's route to EPI was remarkable. Before reform, it implemented a radical, socialist ISI, and this resulted in pervasive yet ineffective state producers with no private entrepreneurs. In 1978, the country seemed very unlikely to implement EPI. From 1980 to 2000, however, China imposed export conditions on incoming FDI and used FDI to pursue an EPI strategy. A close look at the preferential policies in the special zones reveals that beneficial policies were available mainly to exporters. In Shenzhen and Shekou, all the products made in the zones were for export. In 1986, such strict and onerous conditions were removed, but the exports orientation continued in all new zones in China. In Kunshan, the FDI projects on which the local government applied highly favorable conditions had high export ratios. Most of the projects exported more than 50 percent of their products, and many exported 100 percent.[12]

The WTO rule forbids mandatory exports conditions on foreign investors. Upon its entry into the organization, therefore, China implemented voluntary and liberalization-plus incentives to exporting FDI. For example, if an investor exports more than 70 percent of its product, the corporate tax would be halved, in addition to enjoying discounted land use and utilities. Raw materials and components imported to make exported products were duty free. Materials and equipment for making semifinished products that were to be used in exporting goods were also duty free.

As China became the world's largest trade surplus nation, global pressure on its export-led model has grown. From 2005 to 2008, the government did away with many of the incentives to FDI in exports. In 2005, the 11th FDI five-year plan prohibited FDI that was export-only. In 2008, however, due to a pressure to increase employment, the prohibition was removed. Low-tech, employment-generating FDI was supported again in the 2009 FDI policy.[13]

The export orientation was important for China to attract investors who specialized in exporting and to develop industries that fit China's endowments. China had abundant labor, and FDI was concentrated in labor-intensive sectors. Ensuring this outcome, however, was not automatic or easy. In the 1980s and the 1990s, the formal labor regime in China was rigid and distorted. In the urban areas, workers preferred to work for state-owned enterprises, which were not only their employers but also made up their social and political lives. Foreign investors had a slim chance of hiring cheap labor in the urban areas. But with the help of local governments, they established factories in special zones and hired migrant workers from afar. Migrant workers were typically from the countryside, which did not have formal employment opportunities or employment with benefits. Primary education under socialism was instrumental in preparing workers for the foreign investors, because rural youth were adequately trained to operate simple machines, follow managerial orders, and work in a garment factory, for example.

Exporting industries also need factories, roads, and ports. The Chinese government thus made infrastructure construction the priority of its investment and areas for FDI. Foreign investors were welcomed to help build such infrastructure. The first four special economic zones were all in south China, near a port. The 14 "open cities" of 1984 were again port cities in the coastal areas, and in 1988 openness was expanded to key transport cities along the Yangtze River. Towns and cities near these ports became viable sites for manufacturing and exporting FDI.

Local experimentation was another key to the diffusion of FDI. China's FDI policy was not made or implemented according to a blueprint, but through experiments in various localities. Associated with China's economic reform were two ideas: practice is the only criterion of truth; and that one crosses the river by feeling the stone. In the 1980s, the government decentralized economic power and incentives to the local governments. To decentralize power, the central government offered local officials freedom to pursue measures that could bring rapid economic growth. To create incentives, the central government allowed local officials to keep gains from growth locally.

Local governments in China were implementers of the socialist construction, particularly in the rural areas, and had experienced independent policy making, particularly when Beijing policy makers were busy purging each other. Upon reform, local governments were pragmatic and relatively experienced in development. They were eager to increase local revenue, provide local jobs, and improve living conditions in the localities. Lacking domestic capitalists, local governments in south China first embraced FDI from Hong Kong and achieved remarkable economic success. Other localities in the coastal region wanted to emulate this success by attracting FDI as well. These early successes propelled FDI into a de facto "shortcut" to industry and jobs that were very attractive to growth-minded local governments. Local governments in more areas adopted pro-FDI policy with more preferential measures. The results were impressive. In Kunshan in 1999, FDI contributed to the local economy more than 50 percent of the city's revenue, more than 60 percent of the taxes, more than 70 percent of industrial sales, more than 80 percent of investment in fixed assets, and more than 90 percent of exports.[14]

China's successful opening to FDI was due to "good timing and location," which eased the global relocation of production networks from other Asian countries to mainland China. Yet market forces alone would not have been sufficient; policy and government were important to such FDI's success. At the national level, policy makers prioritized exporting industries that provided jobs and helped to earn foreign exchange. While this export orientation deterred some market-seeking investors, it clearly facilitated the entry and supported the operation of exports-oriented FDI by offering "domestic plus" preferential treatment to FDI. To be sure, as I noted earlier, with exports as the condition for this preferential treatment, the national government also imposed "discipline" on the supported FDI. On the other hand, local governments were important to China's early experience of FDI and the rapid diffusion of FDI policy across the country. Growth-minded local officials, eager to bring revenue and jobs to their locality by means of export-creating investments, helped to create the conditions for FDI's success in China and China's success in the world.

ELECTIONS AND FDI IN INDIA

Politics are important to a country's efforts at economic globalization. In India, the political system is reactive to elections, and development tends to suffer when politicians draw risk-averse lessons from electoral results. In the early 1990s, after the 1991 crisis, Manmohan Singh, as the finance minister under Prime Minister Narasimha Rao, pressed ahead with new industrial policies that opened the country to FDI, invited nonresident Indians to invest in the country, and passed policies to build export-oriented units. Economic results were impressive, but the political consequences were more uncertain. Domestic business began to face competition from foreign goods and foreign investors before their own exporting industries could take off. Domestic capitalists, the industrial associations, and their controlled media rallied against FDI in the country.

Despite a growing economy, the Congress Party lost its majority in the 1996 national elections, entered into two years of hung parliament, and lost altogether to the Bharatiya Janata Party (BJP) opposition party in 1998. When BJP came to power, it passed FDI-restricting measures, including Press Note 18, which required foreign investors to receive a "no objection" letter from all their Indian partners before they launch any new operation.

Leading Indian companies, however, were not really antiglobalization. They in fact became quite successful in globalization. Tata, a multi-industry conglomerate, for example, achieved a renaissance in the 2000s, by relying on global financing, acquisition, and expansion. Infosys, the largest services provider in India, drew almost all of its revenues from abroad; its revenue from domestic sales accounted for less than 2 percent in 2007. Birla, a leader in the cable industry, relied on venture capitalists in the United States to orchestrate its expansion and achieved its dominance in India's rapidly rising cellular market. These companies became the face of India in the world. The BJP government was instrumental to these companies' globalization. It emphasized economic ties with the United States, embraced professional Indians outside the country, and often consulted the stances of big businesses in its dealings abroad.

Facing the national elections in 2004, the BJP government appeared strong and secure. With lots of support from the business world, it campaigned under the banner "India Shining"—highlighting the new and globalized image of Indian business. This image, however, did not strike a chord with the vast group of poor voters in rural India, and BJP suffered a surprising defeat in the elections in 2004. The causes were manifold, among which, for example, was the failure of urban workers, the key constituents of BJP, to show up for voting, while the poor, rural voters had higher turnout rates. More fundamentally, as Kohli (2012) points out, inequality was rising, social welfare was declining relatively, and the poor were not benefiting from the new economic growth under BJP. It was a mandate against the economic direction that India was taking. Election results also demonstrated a rapid resurgence of regional parties, which received the second largest number of votes in contested states. The rise of regional parties indicates that voters in rural India were distanced from the national government, whether led by BJP or the Congress Party, and suggests that local governments and local parties perhaps were not included in the India Shining policy that dominated from 1998 to 2004.

Two elections (1996, 2004) voted out two parties that had been reasonably successful in promoting economic growth. When the Congress Party came to power, it appointed Manmohan Singh, the former finance minister in 1991–96, as prime minister, and he led India from 2004 to 2014. Although he had shown a reformist resolve in 1991, Singh took a back seat in India's economic development during his 10 years in office. While domestic business-led globalization continued and services-led growth expanded, no major policy interventions were adopted under Singh's rule. In order to win elections, the Congress Party, on the one hand, groomed the legacy of Nehru and, on the other hand, applied symbolic social programs to attract poor voters, such as a guaranteed 100 days per year employment to the poor. These gestures did not meet the rising aspirations of the Indian population, and in the national elections of 2014 the Congress Party suffered a major defeat; instead, the BJP candidate Narendra Modi won handily.

Modi, the former governor of the state of Gujarat, is a controversial figure in India. He is a strong backer of Hindu nationalism and is credited for his strong leadership of Gujarat. His victory was a manifestation of the Indian voters' call for an "effective leader" who would redirect industrialization and development so they worked for all the people. If China can be of any lesson to India at this point, the poor and rural populations are not against globalization; they want to be part of globalization and industrialization. India's elections in 1996, 2004, and 2014 were, in a way, not truly anti-incumbent but, rather, were calls for government intervention that could include them in the new and globalized India.

Early indications are that Modi is serious about more inclusive development. "We are creating a stable economic environment. Railway is the thread that binds India, it will now be a fast track for India's transformation," the prime minister said at the Hannover Messe Fair, the world's biggest industrial fair, on April 13, 2015. In the 2015–16 *Union Budget*, he publicized his vision to make India the manufacturing hub of the world through the Skill India and Make in India programs. Recent moves include the national investment and manufacturing zones being set up across India, the single-window approval mechanism for investments, the fast-tracking of critical infrastructure projects, efforts to tackle the emotive issue of land, and the establishment of a cabinet committee on investments, chaired by the prime minister.[15]

Modi's moves suggest that he has taken in the lessons from his predecessors and from China. Instead of being anti-FDI or pro-FDI, he tries to promote manufacturing FDI that would enhance India's exports. He has shown greater appreciation for investments from East Asia, where exports and manufacturing are more salient. In September 2014, Modi spent five days in Japan and urged Japanese companies to consider India a "competitive low-cost manufacturing hub."[16] When the Chinese leader Xi Jinping visited India in the same month, he announced that China would invest $20 billion in India over five years to help with infrastructure and manufacturing. India, for its part, agreed to build industrial parks for Chinese investors, which would reduce India's imports from China.[17] Modi, during his visit to China, attended the China-India Business Forum and met top CEOs of Chinese companies in Shanghai. En route to South Korea, he met the business leaders of Korean chaebols, including Hyundai, the steel maker Pohang Iron and Steel Company (POSCO), and Samsung.[18]

India has jumped in its ranking as a FDI destination, thanks to Modi's Make in India push. The concentration of FDI in the Internet, financial, and services sectors has not altered, however, a fact that implies that attracting manufacturing and exports-oriented FDI is still hard in India. The challenges include India's bloated bureaucracy, rigid labor markets, and poor infrastructure, to name a few. If China is any lesson to India, the task of reforming infrastructure, labor, and bureaucracies is doable, but Modi or India's national government cannot do it alone. Local governments and regional parties need to be brought in. Regional parties are already very successful in national elections. If they were given the incentives and capacity to implement development programs in their localities, Modi's Make in India would have a much greater chance of success. But how to mobilize local actors, how to train local officials, and how to educate manufacturing labor are daunting tasks for the Indian government.

Conclusion

Most comparisons of China and India tend to make judgments about which country is doing better than the other. This chapter has tried to avoid such judgments and instead to focus on providing as much historical, economic, and political comparison as possible on FDI in China and India. The first conclusion we could reach, based on this comparison, is that the divergence we see at present in FDI in these countries is rooted in their development histories since independence. During the socialist period, the more radical programs of China eliminated capitalists, and in India, its more gradual socialism kept private businesses active while building up state-owned enterprises. In China, purges and political campaigns undermined the roles of central bureaucracies and left local governments as de facto policy makers and implementers in China. In India, local governments were politicized and many depended on central transfers for local development; few have become development agents. When China's reform-era leaders shifted toward economic growth, the country oriented toward FDI relatively quickly, with local governments as chief actors to facilitate FDI. India's reformist leaders, on the other hand, had to confront a strong domestic business lobby against FDI at the national level. At the local level, development results were unimpressive during India's reform, further dampening popular support for FDI in general.

The chapter also disaggregates FDI by orientation, sectors, and sources. China's FDI is quite different from India's in that overseas Chinese led the country's exporting and manufacturing FDI. Such FDI was relatively easy to operate in China and incorporated Chinese labor and local governments. India's FDI, instead, is mostly in services, aimed at domestic markets and made by Western companies. Its impact on and competition with local actors tends to be contentious. More important, such FDI cannot utilize the vast demographic advantages that India possesses.

Another conclusion that emerges from the comparison made in this chapter regards the different performance of national governments in their respective countries. While China's FDI was helped by its socialist legacy and abundant diaspora capital, government intervention through exports promotion and decentralization to local governments has enhanced FDI's performance in China and made China such a development success in globalization. In India, on the contrary, the governments since the 1990s became politically risk-averse and economically inactive and allowed India's globalization and development to be skewed toward urban and business elites. In a democracy, that means election losses for the ruling party. India's current leader, Narendra Modi, appears to have learned the right economic lessons and is trying to build broad-based growth. Can he do it on his own? Can he do it in a democracy? The answers to those questions are still moot today.

Notes

1. Quoted in Yu 2000.
2. China Special Economic Zones Yearbook Compilation Office 1985, 231, 202.

3. The campaigns against spiritual pollution and bourgeois practices, in 1982 and 1984 respectively, were targeted at special zones in south China.

4. *Times of India*, February 22, 1981.

5. *Economic Times*, February 24, 1986.

6. *The Statesman*, October 11, 1993.

7. *Business India,* November 22–December 5, 1993, 54.

8. *Business World*, October 20–November 2, 1993, 24.

9. *Economic Times*, March 24 and April 18, 1996.

10. Interview, quoted in Frankel 2005.

11. A. B. Vajpayee, speech at the First Pravasi Bharatiya Divas in 2003.

12. See Kunshan City Compilation Office 1994.

13. http://www.chinalawblog.com/2009/01/the_latest_on_foreign_direct_i.html.

14. "Kunshan chengwei taishang touzi redian qu" (Kunshan became a hot area for Taiwanese investment), in Kunshan City Compilation Office 2001, 108.

15. "Neighbors Woo India," *New Straits Times*, October 9, 2014.

16. Ibid.

17. Ibid.

18. Each photo was separately posted on Modi's Google+ account.

References

Amsden, Alice. 1989. *Asia's Next Giant: South Korea and Late Industrialization*. New York: Oxford University Press.

Changchun Statistical Bureau. 1994. *Changchun tongji nianjian, 1994*. Beijing: China Statistical Publishing.

Chauduri, Asim. 1980. "Conglomerate Big Business Groups in India: Some Traits of Tycoon Capitalism." *Social Scientist* 8.7: 38–51.

China National Statistical Bureau, various years. *China Statistical Yearbooks*. Beijing: China Statistical Publishing.

China Special Economic Zones Yearbook Compilation Office. 1985. *Yearbook of China's Special Economic Zones, 1984*. Hong Kong: China SEZ Yearbook Publisher.

Encarnation, Dennis. 1989. *Dislodging Multinationals: India's Strategy in Comparative Perspective*. Ithaca: Cornell University Press.

Frankel, Francine. 2005. *India's Political Economy, 1947–2004: The Gradual Revolution*. New Delhi: Oxford University Press.

Friedman, Thomas.1999. *The Lexus and the Olive Tree: Understanding Globalization*. New York: Farrar, Straus and Giroux.

———. 2005. *The World Is Flat: A Brief History of the Twenty-First Century*. New York: Farrar, Straus and Giroux.

Gallagher, Mary. 2005. *Contagious Capitalism: Globalization and the Politics of Labor in China*. Princeton: Princeton University Press.

Gilpin, Robert. 1987. *The Political Economy of International Relations*. Princeton: Princeton University Press.

Guha, Ashok, and Amit Ray. 2000. *Multinational versus Expatriate FDI: A Comparative Analysis of the Chinese and Indian Experience*. Working Paper no. 58. New Delhi: Indian Council for Research on International Economic Relations,

Hoda, Anwarul, and Durgesh K. Rai. 2015. *Labor Regulations and Growth of Manufacturing and Employment in India: Balancing Protection and Flexibility*. Working Paper no. 298, New Delhi: Indian Council for Research on International Economic Relations.

Hu, Ping, ed.1994. *Zhongguo jingji tequ yu yanhai jingji jishu kaifaqu nianjian 1993*. Beijing: Reform Publisher.

Huang, Qifang, ed. 1994. *Pudong xinqu tongji nianjian, 1994*. Beijing: China Statistical Publishing.

Huang, Yasheng. 2003. *Selling China: Foreign Direct Investment during the Reform Era*. New York: Cambridge University Press.

Huang, Yasheng, and Tarun Khanna. 2003. "Can India Overtake China?" *Foreign Policy*, July 1. http://foreignpolicy.com/2003/07/01/can-india-overtake-china/.

Jalan, Bimal. 1991. *India's Economic Crisis: The Way Ahead*. Delhi: Oxford University Press.

Japan External Trade Organization (JETRO). 2003. "Japanese-Affiliated Manufacturers in Asia, Survey, 2002 Summary." www.jetro.go.jp/ec/e/stat/surveys/manufacturers _asia.pdf.

Kapur, Devesh. 2010. *Diasporas, Democracy, and Development in India*. Princeton: Princeton University Press.

Kohli, Atul. 2012. *Poverty amid Plenty: Political Economy of the New India*. Cambridge: Cambridge University Press.

Kunshan City Compilation Office. 1994. *Kunshan nianjian, 1988–1993*. China: Shanghai kexue jishu chubanshe.

———. 2001. *Kunshan nianjian 2000*. China: Shanghai kexue jishu chubanshe.

Long, Guoqiang. 2004. "China's Policies on FDI: Review and Evaluation." In *Does Foreign Direct Investment Promote Development?*, edited by Theodore H. Moran, Edward M. Graham, and Magnus Blomström, 315–36. Washington, DC: Center for Global Development.

Naughton, Barry. 2007. *The Chinese Economy: Transition and Growth*. Cambridge, MA: MIT Press.

Ray, Saon, Smita Migalni, and Neha Malik. 2015. *Impact of American Investment in India*. Working Paper no. 296. New Delhi: Indian Council for Research on International Economic Relations.

Sengupta, Arjun. 2001. *Reforms, Equity, and the IMF: An Economist's World*. New Delhi: Har Anand Publications.

Tewari, Meenu, C. Veeramani, and Manjeeta Singh. 2015. *The Potential for Involving India in Regional Production Networks: Analyzing Vertically Specialized Trade Patterns between India and ASEAN*. Working Paper no. 292. New Delhi: Indian Council for Research on International Economic Relations.

United Nations Conference on Trade and Investment. 1993. *World Investment Report 1993*. Geneva: United Nations Publications.

———. 1996. *World Investment Report 1996*. Geneva: United Nations Publications.

———. 2006. *World Investment Report 2006*. Geneva: United Nations Publications.

Virmani, Arvind. 2010. *Policy Regimes, Growth and Poverty in India: Lessons of Government Failure and Entrepreneurial Failure and Entrepreneurial Success!* Working Paper no. 170. New Delhi: Indian Council for Research on International Economic Relations.

Vogel, Ezra. 1989. *One Step ahead in China: Guangdong under Reform*. Cambridge, MA: Harvard University Press.

———. 2011. *Deng Xiaoping and the Transformation of China*. Cambridge, MA: Belknap Press of Harvard University Press.

Wuhan City Statistical Bureau. 1996. *Wuhan tongji nianjian 1996*. Beijing: China Statistical Publishing.

Ye, Min. 2014. *Diasporas and Foreign Direct Investment in China and India*. New York: Cambridge University Press.

Yu, X. 2000. *Deng Xiaoping yu Bao Yugang* (Deng Xiaoping and Y. K. Pao). Beijing: Chinese Cultural Publisher.

APPENDIX

India-China Timeline, 1947–2016

Year	Events in China	Events in India
1947–1949	1949 – Chinese Communists win the Chinese Civil War, Jiang Jieshi and the Nationalists flee to Taiwan, and Mao Zedong proclaims the founding of the People's Republic of China. 1949 – The communists, now in control of most of China, continue to encourage violence against landlords, pursue land reform, and encourage gradual collectivization.	1947 – British India achieves independence but is partitioned into India and Pakistan. Jawaharlal Nehru becomes prime minister of India. 1947 – Nehru commits to socialism and import substitution, declaring that the state will occupy the "commanding heights" of the economy, especially heavy industry. 1947–1948 – Nehru and Sardar Vallabhbhai Patel convince hundreds of sovereign "Princely States," which had been granted protectorate status by the British, to join India. Roughly 30,000 Indian troops invade the richest and largest state, Hyderabad, in Operation Polo. 1947–1948 – Communal violence between Hindus and Muslims leads to the deaths of hundreds of thousands.

(continued)

Year	Events in China	Events in India
1947–1949		1947–1948 – India and Pakistan go to war over the status of Kashmir, two-thirds of which is ultimately held by India, and one-third of which is held by Pakistan.
		1948 – Mahatma Gandhi is assassinated by Nathuram Godse, a Hindu nationalist.
1950–1952	1950 – China and the Soviet Union sign the Treaty of Mutual Friendship and Cooperation and form a 30-year alliance following Mao's visit to Moscow.	1951 – India's First Five Year Plan, modeled after the Soviet Union
	1950 – Chinese troops cross the Yalu River and enter the Korean War in support of North Korea and against South Korean and UN forces.	
	1950 – Campaign to Suppress Counterrevolutionaries begins.	
	1950 – New Marriage Law is promulgated.	
	1950–1951 – Chinese troops invade Tibet, bringing it under Chinese control.	
	1951–1952 – Three Antis and Five Antis Campaign against Corruption and "enemies of the people is conducted.	
1953–1955	1953 – Gao Gang affair occurs, marking the first high-level leadership purge of the PRC.	1954 – Nehru gives a speech in Colombo that helps launch the Non-Aligned Movement to avoid affiliation with the two superpowers.
	1953 – First Five Year Plan, following a Soviet-style model of industrial growth, begins.	Apr. 1954 – India and China sign a treaty of friendship, the Five Principles of Peaceful Coexistence, known India as the Panchsheel Treaty, and India recognizes Chinese rule over Tibet.
	1954 – Chinese artillery shell offshore islands held by Taiwan, launching the First Taiwan Strait Crisis.	
	1955 – Sufan purge of "hidden counterrevolutionaries" begins.	

Year	Events in China	Events in India
1956–1958	**1956** – Nikita Khrushchev reveals his "secret speech" in which he criticizes Stalin, whom Mao had praised and whose policies he had invoked to justify his own, setting in motion an eventual Sino-Soviet split.	**1955** – The Indian government commits to a socialist society.
	1956–1957 – Mao Zedong launches the Hundred Flowers Campaign encouraging free expression, even in political speech, and then launches the Anti-Rightist Campaign that arrested and punished dissenters.	**1956** – States Reorganisation Commission redraws the Indian states along linguistic lines.
	1958 – China abolishes private land ownership, accelerates the establishment of agricultural communes, and begins the Great Leap Forward, which in turn leads to widespread rural famine and the deaths of tens of millions of Chinese peasants.	**1956** – India's Second Five Year Plan is designed for rapid industrialization with steel, coal, shipbuilding, nuclear, and aerospace reserved to state enterprises.
	1958 – Chinese artillery again shell offshore islands held by Taiwan, initiating the Second Taiwan Strait Crisis.	**1956**—Nehru fosters a neutral stance between communism and capitalism and founds the Non-Aligned Movement.
1959–1961	**1959** – Tibetans revolt against Chinese rule, the Dalai Lama and thousands of others flee to India, and China violently suppresses the rebellion.	**1959** – Major steel plants built with Western and Soviet technology in Rourkela, Durgapur, and Bhilai begin operations.
	1960 – The Soviet Union recalls all its technical specialists and experts, who had been assisting in Chinese industrialization, as ties with China worsen.	**1961** – Indian troops seize Goa, Daman, and Diu from Portugal by force.

(continued)

Year	Events in China	Events in India
1962–1964	**1962** – China defeats India in a border war, asserts control over Aksai Chin, and then unilaterally announces a ceasefire.	**1962** – China defeats India in a border war, asserts control over Aksai Chin, and then unilaterally announces a ceasefire.
	1962 – China ends the Great Leap Forward, and Mao faces party criticism for his role in its formulation and promotion. He begins to leave policy matters to Deng Xiaoping and Liu Shaoqi.	**1962** – The Green Revolution is initiated in Indian agriculture leading to high yields in wheat-growing regions of the north.
	1963 – The Socialist Education Campaign is initiated to clean up the bureaucracy.	**1964** – Prime Minister Jawaharlal Nehru dies and Lal Bahadur Shastri becomes prime minister.
	1964 – China successfully detonates a nuclear device.	
1965–1967	**1966** – China carries out its first successful test of a nuclear ballistic missile.	**1965** – India and Pakistan again go to war over Kashmir.
	1966 – Mao Zedong launches the Great Proletarian Cultural Revolution in concert with his wife, Jiang Qing, and allies such as Lin Biao. The Cultural Revolution brings a Maoist personality cult, violent attacks by young Red Guards against authority figures and cultural relics, crackdown on markets, and purges of government officials including Deng Xiaoping and Liu Shaoqi.	**1966** – Prime Minister Lal Bahadur Shastri dies in Tashkent, and Indira Gandhi, Nehru's daughter, becomes prime minister. **Mar. 1967** – Maoists (Naxalites) begin armed insurrections in West Bengal and South India.
1968–1970	**1969** – China and the Soviet Union engage in an armed clash over Zhenbao Island in the Ussuri River, which signals a full split in Sino-Soviet ties.	

Year	Events in China	Events in India
1971–1973	1971 – Lin Biao, his wife, and son die mysteriously in a plane crash over the Soviet Union. 1971 – China joins the United Nations and assumes the Republic of Taiwan's seat on the UN Security Council. 1972 – President Richard Nixon visits China. The two countries sign the Shanghai Communique, in which the United States acknowledges the "One China" policy, and both sides promise to work toward normalization.	1971 – The Indian military intervenes in East Pakistan and supports Bengali nationalists in the creation of the new state of Bangladesh. 1971 – India and the Soviet Union sign a 20-year treaty of friendship, effectively ending India's nonaligned status.
1974–1976	1976 – Mao dies in September and the Gang of Four, including Jiang Qing and Shanghai radicals, is arrested in October, bringing the Cultural Revolution decade to an end. 1976 – Deng Xiaoping becomes the dominant Chinese political figure.	1974 – India conducts an underground test of a nuclear weapon. Jun. 1974 – Jayaprakash Narayan leads the students of Bihar on a march for "total revolution." 1975–1977 – Indira Gandhi declares a state of emergency, arrests thousands of political opponents, and introduces compulsory birth control.
1977–1979	1978 – Deng announces a period of "reform and opening up," which begins with decollectivizing agriculture, inviting foreign investment, and encouraging entrepreneurship. 1978–1979 – Democracy Wall Movement, which called for political liberalization 1979 – The United States and China normalize diplomatic relations following the signing of a joint communique. The United States ends diplomatic recognition of Taiwan.	1977 – Indira Gandhi and the Congress Party are routed in general elections that see all opposition parties unite to form a coalition government. 1978 – The "Electronic City" is founded in Bangalore, India.

(continued)

Year	Events in China	Events in India
1977–1979	**1979** – China and Vietnam fight a border war. **1979** – China introduces the One-Child Policy.	
1980–1982	**1980** – Hu Yaobang and Zhao Ziyang emerge as Deng Xiaoping's top lieutenants and are charged with implementing his economic reforms. Hu becomes the general secretary of the Communist Party and Zhao becomes premier, though both effectively remain subordinate to Deng Xiaoping.	**1980** – Indira Gandhi returns to power following victory in the 1980 general elections.
1983–1985	**1983–1984** – Antispiritual Pollution Campaign is launched to counter intellectual liberalization.	**1984** – Prime Minister Indira Gandhi orders the Indian military to storm the Golden Temple, the holiest Sikh site, which had been occupied by Sikh militants. **1984** – Indira Gandhi is assassinated by two of her Sikh bodyguards. Her son, Rajiv Gandhi, becomes prime minister. **1984** – Thousands die after a gas leak at a Union Carbide pesticide plant in Bhopal, India. **1985–1986** – The Indian Supreme Court rules in favor of Shah Bano, a Muslim woman who sought alimony from her husband, despite the fact Muslim personal law did not require it. To appeal to outraged Muslims, the Congress Party passes legislation effectively stripping Muslim women of the right to alimony under common law.

Year	Events in China	Events in India
1986–1988	1987 – Hu Yaobang is dismissed following student protests. Zhao Ziyang becomes general secretary.	1987 – India deploys troops to Sri Lanka to disarm militants in the Sri Lanka Civil War.
		1987–1990 – A violent insurgency in Kashmir begins and obtains Pakistani support following accusations that the central government interfered to support Farooq Abdullah, a pro-Indian candidate, in Kashmiri elections. The insurgency continues to the present day.
1989–1991	1989 – Chinese demonstrations break out following the death of Hu Yaobang and eventually become prodemocracy protests. Chinese troops open fire on demonstrators in Tiananmen Square. Zhao Ziyang is placed under house arrest.	1989 – Congress is forced from power after the 1989 general elections after a diverse coalition of opposition parties unite to form a minority government.
	1989 – Jiang Zemin emerges as the paramount leader with support from Deng Xiaoping, Li Xiannian, and Chen Yun.	1991 – Rajiv Gandhi is assassinated by a suicide bomber sympathetic to the Sri Lankan Liberation Tigers of Tamil Eelam.
	1991 – Patriotic Education Campaign is launched to prevent future student protests.	1991 – Congress forms a coalition led by Prime Minister Narasimha Rao, who tasks the minister of finance, Manmohan Singh, with beginning a program of free-market economic reforms.
		1991 – The Indian government sets up the Software Technology Parks of India (STPI) to promote software exports and opens the first park in the Electronics City of Bangalore.
1992–1994	1992 – Deng Xiaoping makes a tour of southern China and succeeds in restoring momentum to his economic reforms, which had stalled following the Tiananmen Square massacre.	1992 – Hindu extremists trigger religious violence after destroying the Babri Masjid, a mosque built atop an area purported to have been the birthplace of Rama, a seminal Indian religious figure.

(continued)

Year	Events in China	Events in India
1995–1997	**1995–1996** – China fires missiles into the Taiwan Strait in response to the visit of the Taiwanese president, Lee Teng-hui, to the United States and in advance of upcoming Taiwanese elections. The United States dispatches two carrier groups to the Taiwan Strait in response. **1997** – Deng Xiaoping dies. **1997** – China gains control over Hong Kong.	**1996** – The Bharitya Janata Party (BJP) emerges as the largest single party, and Congress endures its worst ever electoral defeat.
1998–2000	**1998** – Premier Zhu Rongji implements reforms following the Asian Financial Crisis that restructure state-owned enterprises, slim the public bureaucracy, curtail "iron rice bowl" cradle-to-grave benefits for millions of public employees, and impose tuition for higher education. **1998** – China installs major components of the Great Firewall, which allows the government to limit access to foreign websites and politically objectionable content. **1999** – 10,000 Falungong protesters gather in front of the Zhongnanhai leadership compound, precipitating a crackdown against the "heterodox cult." **1999** – NATO accidently bombs the Chinese embassy in Belgrade, leading to widespread nationalist protests in China.	**1998** – Atal Bihari Vajpayee becomes prime minister of India. **1998** – India carries out nuclear tests and faces international condemnation and U.S. sanctions. **1999** – India and Pakistan fight a brief war over Kargil. **2000** – President Bill Clinton makes a historic visit to India in a successful bid to improve ties, laying the foundation for closer cooperation between the United States and India.

Year	Events in China	Events in India
2001–2003	**2001** – A Chinese fighter and an American reconnaissance aircraft collide, forcing the American plane to land in Hainan. The American crew is held and interrogated for ten days before being released. **2001** – China joins the World Trade Organization. **2002** – Hu Jintao becomes China's paramount leader. **2003** – The SARS virus spreads through Hong Kong and other parts of China. **2003** – China launches its first manned spacecraft.	**2001** – The Indian Space Research Organization achieves the ability to independently launch geosynchronous satellites. **2001** – The United States lifts sanctions imposed on India after the 1998 nuclear tests. **2001** – Suicide gunmen affiliated with Lashkar-e-Taiba and Jaish-e Mohammed attack the Indian Parliament in New Delhi. India sanctions Pakistan for its support of those groups. **2002** – India and Pakistan mass troops along their shared border as both sides prepare for war. **2002** – India launches a successful test of a nuclear-capable ballistic missile. **2002** – Communal violence breaks out in Gujarat after dozens of Hindu pilgrims are killed in a train fire believed at the time to have been set by Muslims. Hundreds of Muslims are killed in retaliation. Gujarat chief minister, Narendra Modi, is criticized for failing to stop the violence. **2003** – Bangalore in India has more software engineers than Silicon Valley (working mostly for U.S. companies).

(continued)

Year	Events in China	Events in India
2004–2006	**2005** – Nationalist protests erupt throughout China in response to Japan's pursuit of a seat on the UN Security Council and accusations that its textbooks gloss over its Second World War conduct. **2006** – The Three Gorges Dam is completed.	**2004** – Congress defeats the BJP. Manmohan Singh, architect of Indian economic reforms, becomes prime minister while Sonia Gandhi, widow of former prime minister Rajiv Gandhi, wields power behind the scenes. **2004** – The Asian tsunami strikes India's Andaman and Nicobar Islands and coastal communities in South India. **2006** – Prime Minister Manmohan Singh launches the National Rural Employment Guarantee Act, which guarantees 100 days of paid labor to adults who are willing to perform unskilled manual labor. Regarded as among the largest workfare projects in the world. **2006** – The United States and India sign a landmark civilian nuclear deal that cements closer ties between the two countries.
2007–2009	**2008** – Wenchuan earthquake takes a massive toll, sparking a major upsurge in domestic NGO activity. **2008** – China hosts the 2008 Olympics. **2008** – More than 50,000 children fall ill after drinking tainted milk. **2008** – A "stability maintenance" policy is adopted, with increased surveillance and suppression of popular protest in aftermath of unrest in both Tibet and Xinjiang.	**2008** – Ten suicide gunmen from Pakistan attacked several locations in downtown Mumbai, killing nearly 200 people.

Year	Events in China	Events in India
2010–2012	**2010** – China passes Japan to become world's second largest economy.	**2011** – Anna Hazare launches a 12-day hunger strike to protest corruption that draws widespread media attention.
	2012 – Former Chongqing party secretary Bo Xilai is arrested after his police chief, Wang Lijun, seeks asylum at a U.S. consulate.	**2012** – The brutal gang rape of an Indian woman on a New Delhi bus leads to nationwide protests against sexual violence and police indifference.
	2012 – Xi Jinping becomes China's paramount leader.	
	2012 – Xi Jinping launches an anticorruption campaign implemented by the Discipline Inspection Commission led by Wang Qishan, which eventually targets several high-level officials, including former Politburo Standing Committee member Zhou Yongkang and former Central Military Commission vice chairman Xu Caihou.	
2013–2015	**2015** – China officially ends the One-Child Policy and allows all families to have two children.	**2014** – India becomes the world's third-largest economy by purchasing power, according to IMF data.
		2014 – The BJP wins an outright majority and Narendra Modi becomes prime minister.
2016	**2016** – The IMF declares that China has overtaken the United States to become the world's largest economy by purchasing power.	**2016** – As part of an effort to crack down on corruption and tax invasion, Prime Minister Modi launches a policy of "demonetization" that replaces 86% of the money stock with new notes. Those with large cash holdings must prove their income is legitimate to receive new notes at banks.
		2016 – Prime Minister Modi succeeds in amending the constitution to enable a national goods-and-services tax, a long-sought reformist goal. The national tax replaces a cumbersome patchwork of more than 17 state and federal taxes and makes it significantly easier to do business in India.